5TH EDITION

Corporate Financial Analysis

In a Global Environment

DIANA R. HARRINGTON

Distinguished Professor, Finance

Babson College

S O U T H - W E S T E R N College Publishing

An International Thomson Publishing Company

Publisher/Team Director: Jack W. Calhoun
Managing Editor: Andrea Shaw
Production Editor: Peggy Buskey
Marketing Manager: Lisa L. Lysne
Production House: Cover to Cover Publishing
Cover Design: Rick Moore
Internal Design: Joe Devine

Library of Congress Cataloging-in-Publication Data

Harrington, Diana R., 1940-
    Corporate financial analysis in a global environment / Diana R.
    Harrington. -- 5th ed.
        p.   cm.
    Includes bibliographical references and index.
    ISBN 0-538-86939-9
    1. Corporations--Finance.   I. Title.
    HG4026.H34   1997
    658. 15--dc21   97-6561
                                                                        CIP

    4 5 6 7 8 D 1 4 3 2 1 0 9 8

Printed in the United States of America

I(T)P®
International Thomson Publishing
South-Western College Publishing is an ITP Company.
The ITP trademark is used under license.

P R E F A C E

Corporate Financial Analysis was written with the objective of discussing financial analysis as it relates to managerial decision making. The goal of the manager is to enhance the value of the company. Managers can create value through the financial decisions they make, and good financial analysis can assist the manager in making better decisions—decisions that enhance the value of the firm. Value creation, and the role that good analysis can play in helping the manager to make value-enhancing decisions, is the topic of this book.

This book takes a practical orientation toward value. Thus, it does not present abstract financial theory or rigorous mathematical proofs; rather, it explains how the tools, concepts, and theories of finance can be used to improve decision making. Current examples of actual business situations are used throughout the book to illustrate the application of modern financial theories and techniques. In acknowledgment of our shrinking world and the multinational character of the financial arena students will enter, this fourth edition also contains explanations of common concepts in international finance.

USING THIS BOOK

The book was written for three different groups of readers. First, the book is intended to be used by students studying finance. Although written as a companion reference for students taking finance case courses, the book also has been and will continue to be useful for students who want a basic supplement to a more advanced textbook, or for instructors who wish to discuss the applications or concepts presented in more theoretical finance courses.

Second, the book is useful for executive management education in courses where basic techniques of financial analysis are needed or used. Experience in teaching executives suggests that a straightforward, pragmatic approach is required in such courses, and this book was written and revised with this requirement in mind.

Third, the book can serve as a useful reference for the practicing manager who wants a review of financial concepts and techniques. Thus, the book can be used effectively as a stand-alone reference.

Since managers and students of management can best develop the ability to apply techniques and concepts of financial decision making through practice, problems are included at the end of each chapter. The reader is encouraged to work through these problems and refer to the solutions in Appendix C at the end of the book.

The use of computer-based financial modeling can significantly enhance the ability of a manager to analyze financial problems and decisions, and the book includes explanations of how this can be done. Appendix A is an overview of financial modeling techniques; Appendix B is a primer for using one of the most popular spreadsheet programs, Microsoft's Excel©. Managers or students wanting to enhance their modeling skills can do so by modeling the problems at the end of each chapter and comparing their models to the Excel background solutions contained in Appendix C.

ACKNOWLEDGMENTS

The book is a compilation of ideas and materials developed during the past few years at Babson College; the Darden Graduate School of Business at the University of Virginia; the Kellogg School of Management at Northwestern University; and by my previous author, Brent Wilson at Brigham Young University; and the Telesis Partnership. The material has benefited from the responses of students in undergraduate and MBA classes as well as colleagues, and has been refined through the comments of executives attending executive management courses.

Many people have directly or indirectly contributed to the quality of the material in this book. Brent Wilson co-authored the first three editions. Colleagues, students, and business executives not only encouraged the writing of each edition, but have made helpful suggestions for improving the presentation of the concepts and ideas. For this edition, James Parrino of the Telesis Partnership and Babson College contributed directly in international accounting.

Diana R. Harrington

The author would like to dedicate this book to her daughter Maya Anna Maria del Carmen Harrington and her Papa.

C O N T E N T S

Analyzing Corporate Performance

Over the past decade, our world has changed more profoundly and more rapidly than we could ever have believed. Not only have political systems been challenged and changed, but many of the basic notions on which we have based personal and corporate financial decisions have been contested. Companies now have to compete with others from all over the world for customers and for suppliers of labor, goods, and capital. The markets for goods and capital have become increasingly integrated, and even managers' control of the daily activities of our companies has come under attack.[1]

These changes have profoundly affected all our lives, and it is important for corporate managers, shareholders, lenders, customers, and suppliers to understand the performance of the corporations on which they rely. All who depend on a corporation for products, services, or a job must be informed about their company's ability to meet their demands over time and in this changing world. This chapter's purpose is to provide the basic tools that any individual can use to begin an analysis of corporate performance and strength. These tools are simple to calculate, but they require some experience to use well. One's skill in their use increases with experience.

I. WHO NEEDS TO ANALYZE CORPORATE PERFORMANCE?

All kinds of people need insight into corporate performance:

Customers: The company's customers are concerned with the company's viability as a vendor of goods or services. Qualified vendors are able to fulfill both their contractual obligations and the customers' needs, and will be able to provide future service for their products.

Suppliers: Suppliers provide all types of the resources that a company uses:

---

[1] In fact, we are seeing the formation of economic cartels. The first of these was in the European Common Market, where much more complete economic integration culminated in Europe 1992 and currency integration in 1999. Economic unions, such as NAFTA and MERCOSUR, have been or are forming in South and North America and Asia.

Goods and services: Individuals and companies that provide goods and/or services to a company are concerned with whether the company can pay its obligations on time and whether it will continue to be a customer. These suppliers also include those who work for the company, supplying labor.[2]

Capital: Money is a good that is provided to corporations by lenders and by shareholders. *Lenders* are concerned with the corporation's ability to pay the interest, repay the loan, and abide by the loan covenants during the time the loan is outstanding. *Shareholders*, the company's owners and potential owners, are interested in evaluating the skill of the company's management and in determining the financial strength of a company as an element in determining the company's future and its value.[3]

Employees: Employees need to better understand the forces affecting their company. The future of their company, the industry, and their jobs depend upon them understanding the company's potential and contributing to its innovation.

The topic of this chapter is how to evaluate and interpret historical financial performance. We will show you how to calculate and interpret ratios created from information contained in the company's financial statements. In addition, we will use three simple ratios to relate corporate financial performance to the shareholders' response to past and anticipated performance. The chapter uses information from actual companies operating in the United States, and the appendix to this chapter shows you how to extend this analysis to companies operating in different countries.[4]

Remember, the past performance of a company, as shown in its financial statements, may help predict future performance, but while past performance is interesting, many managers and analysts are more interested in what will happen in the future. Therefore, how historical statements and analysis of those statements can be used to help forecast the future will be the subject of Chapter 2. First, let's look at the various financial statements that most companies provide to their internal and external analysts.

---

[2] In the 1980s, a significant number of the largest U.S. companies with publicly traded stock changed ownership. Many of these ownership changes also resulted in serious reductions in their companies' work forces.

[3] The value of a company is determined by many things: its earning power, the sustainability of its earnings, the riskiness of the business it is in, and how management conducts the business. Each of these topics will be explored in this book.

[4] We use companies operating in the United States because many of our readers are based in the United States, or deal with U.S.-based companies, and thus are most familiar with U.S. accounting principles. A truly useful and comprehensive analysis of a company should, however, include the performance of its worldwide components and competitors. For that, a knowledge of other countries' accounting standards is needed. A brief discussion of this topic appears in the appendix to this chapter.

II. FINANCIAL STATEMENTS

The types of financial information published in financial statements vary among countries, each of which has different requirements for disclosure of information. Regulations in the United States, the United Kingdom, other Commonwealth countries, and the European Common Market require the most complete disclosure. However, most industrialized countries require that financial statements disclose sufficient data to allow a meaningful analysis of performance. The growing trend of major international companies to raise funds in foreign capital markets necessitates that these multinational companies provide the minimum level of financial information expected by investors in the countries where they are raising capital.

In all countries, public disclosure requirements apply only to publicly owned companies. Privately owned corporations may not be required to disclose publicly any financial information. However, some groups, such as banks, may have access to financial statements from privately owned companies.

In the United States, publicly owned companies are required to prepare four financial statements: statements of earnings, of financial position, of cash flows, and of changes in shareholders' equity. Typically, such statements are prepared quarterly.

1. Statement of Earnings

The statement of earnings, also known as the income statement or profit and loss statement, shows the total revenues earned and the total expenses incurred to generate these revenues by a company during a specific period of time. The difference between revenues and expenses is termed net income (also known as earnings or profit) or net loss for the period.[5]

This statement summarizes all revenue or expense transactions during a specified period of time, the reporting period. A quarterly report includes only the transactions made during a three-month reporting period. An annual report includes all income and expense items for a year. Exhibit 1-1 is an example of an annual statement of earnings.[6] It is the 1995 statement for Hannaford Bros. Co., a U.S. supermarket chain. The company is involved in the distribution and retail sale of food, prescription drugs, and related products through supermarkets and combination stores. Hannaford is a multi-regional food retailer, with 134 supermarkets located throughout Maine and New Hampshire, and in parts of Vermont, Massachusetts, New York, Virginia, North Carolina, and South Carolina, primarily under the names Shop'n Save, Hannaford, and Wilson's. Over the past twelve years the company also opened

---

[5] Note that the Hannaford financial statements used in this chapter's examples use the term consolidated. This means that subsidiaries owned by Hannaford are operated and treated as if they were fully integrated into the company's activities.

[6] Note that expenses, or negative numbers, are identified by parentheses.

EXHIBIT 1-1 Hannaford Bros. Co.

STATEMENT OF CONSOLIDATED EARNINGS
FOR THE YEAR ENDED DECEMBER 31 (in thousands)

	1995
Net sales	$ 2,568,061
Cost of sales	(1,951,248)
Gross profit	616,813
Selling and general expenses	(481,017)
Earnings before interest and taxes	135,796
Interest income	2,510
Interest expense	(21,878)
Operating profit	116,428
Income taxes	(46,227)
Net income	$ 70,201
Weighted-average common and common equivalent shares (in thousands)	42,092
Net income per share	$1.67

or acquired 71 combination stores that incorporate a traditional all-department supermarket, bakery, and video rental center, as well as expanded lines of general merchandise. The company also operates 74 pharmacies within its supermarkets and combination stores.

2. Statement of Financial Position

The statement of financial position is also referred to as the **balance sheet**. This statement reports the corporation's assets, liabilities, and owners' equity at a particular date in time, which is usually the end of the reporting period. The corporation's assets must balance with the funds used to purchase the assets (hence the term balance sheet). Funds provided by lenders are recorded on the balance sheet as liabilities; funds provided by shareholders are recorded as owners' equity. For publicly held corporations it is called shareholders' equity.[7]

The statement of financial position, the balance sheet, differs from the statement of earnings in that it reports the firm's status at a point in time, the end of the reporting period. While the earnings statement reports on the flow of transactions or funds, the statement of financial position reports on the resulting financial status. Thus, a quarterly report specifies the status of the assets, liabilities, and owners' equity at the end of a quarter; an annual report indicates

---

[7] Publicly held companies are those whose equity (common stock) is traded in the capital markets.

status at the conclusion of the reporting year. The Hannaford statement of financial position, or balance sheet, for the end of 1995 is presented in Exhibit 1-2. Note that Hannaford Bros. Co.'s fiscal year is the same as the calendar year.

3. Statement of Cash Flows

Previously known as the **statement of changes in financial position** or **funds flow statement,** the **cash flow statement** reports the amounts of cash generated by the company during the period, as well as the disposition of cash. The difference between the sum of the sources of cash and the sum of its uses is typically reported as a change in cash or net working capital.[8]

Another way to analyze changes that occur over the period is to create a **statement of sources and uses.** To do this the analyst simply compares the current statement of financial position with that of the previous reporting period. This analysis can highlight the changes that have occurred in the company's

EXHIBIT 1-2   Hannaford Bros. Co.

STATEMENT OF CONSOLIDATED FINANCIAL POSITION
AS OF DECEMBER 31 (in thousands)

Assets	1995	1994
Current Assets:		
Cash and cash equivalents	$ 7,017	$ 40,955
Accounts receivable	15,556	14,240
Inventories	157,968	132,423
Prepaid expenses	7,217	6,210
Deferred income taxes	6,584	7,519
Total current assets	194,342	201,347
Property, plant, and equipment:		
Land and improvements	90,430	81,667
Buildings	228,858	203,645
Furniture, fixtures, and equipment	333,492	294,792
Leasehold interests and improvements	188,730	169,178
Construction in progress	16,179	6,193
Total gross property, plant, and equipment	857,689	755,475
Less allowance for depreciation	280,563	251,534
Total net property, plant, and equipment	577,126	503,941
Leased property under capital leases	56,691	58,821
Other assets	133,671	113,496
Total assets	$ 961,830	$ 877,605

----

[8]   Net working capital is current assets minus current liabilities.

EXHIBIT 1-2 *(continued)*

Liabilities and Shareholders' Equity	1995	1994
Current Liabilities:		
Current maturities of long-term debt	$ 11,246	$ 14,409
Obligations under capital leases	1,467	1,382
Accounts payable	113,846	89,927
Accrued expenses	44,271	48,755
Income taxes payable	0	4,167
Total current liabilities	170,830	158,640
Long-term debt	150,648	153,687
Obligations under capital leases	69,747	69,552
Deferred income tax liabilities	23,229	21,886
Other long-term liabilities	28,699	19,365
Shareholders' equity:		
Common stock, $0.75 par value:		
Authorized: 110,000,000 shares		
Issued: 42,298,230 shares		
at December 31, 1995 and 41,779,342		
shares at December 31,1994	31,724	31,335
Additional paid-in capital	121,974	110,669
Preferred stock purchase rights	423	418
Retained earnings	364,556	312,053
Total shareholders' equity	518,677	454,475
Total liabilities and stockholders' equity	$ 961,830	$ 877,605

financial position and can be especially useful when no cash flow statement is readily available.

A company generates new financial resources in several ways: by borrowing additional funds, increasing owners' equity, retaining the period's earnings, and/or decreasing assets (for instance, selling excess equipment). The resources thus generated can be used to increase assets by purchasing new equipment, decrease liabilities by paying off loans, or decrease owners' equity by paying a dividend or repurchasing outstanding shares.

The cash flow statement from the 1995 Hannaford Bros. Co. Annual Report is shown in Exhibit 1-3.

4. Statement of Changes in Shareholders' Equity

This report is called the **statement of changes in shareholders' equity** or the **statement of retained earnings**. It provides additional detail on the composition of the owners' equity accounts for the company. Its purpose is to highlight

EXHIBIT 1-3 Hannaford Bros. Co.

STATEMENT OF CONSOLIDATED CASH FLOWS
AS OF DECEMBER 31 (in thousands)

	1995	1994
Operating Activities:		
Net income	$ 70,201	$ 62,288
Adjustments to reconcile net income to net cash provided by operating activities:		
Depreciation and amortization	69,016	62,756
Decrease (increase) in inventories	(25,545)	6,372
Decrease (increase) in receivables and prepaids	(1,196)	6,903
Increase (decrease) in accounts payable and accrued expenses	27,821	4,988
Increase (decrease) in income taxes payable	(5,409)	2,274
Increase (decrease) in deferred taxes	2,279	(1,466)
Other operating activities	1,059	(178)
Net cash provided by operating activities	138,226	143,937
Cash flows from investing activities:[9]		
Acquisition of Wilson's Supermarkets	0	(110,201)
Acquisition of property, plant, and equipment	(133,587)	(83,969)
Sale of property, plant, and equipment	2,607	9,641
Increase in other assets	(26,729)	(4,984)
Decrease (increase) in short-term investments	—	19,855
Net cash used in investing activities	(157,709)	(169,658)
Cash flows from financing activities:[10]		
Principal payments under capital lease obligations	(1,404)	(1,359)
Proceeds from issuance of long-term debt	11,400	25,500
Payments of long-term debt	(18,452)	(26,550)
Issuance of common stock	11,694	9,348
Dividends paid	(17,693)	(15,876)
Redemption of preferred stock	0	(1,883)
Net cash used in financing activities	(14,455)	(10,820)
Net decrease in cash and cash equivalents	(33,938)	(36,541)
Cash and equivalents at beginning of year	40,955	77,496
Cash and equivalents at end of year	$ 7,017	$ 40,955

changes in owners' equity or retained earnings that have occurred during the reporting period. This statement is similar to the cash flow statement; however, it focuses specifically on changes within the owners' equity segment of the balance sheet. Exhibit 1-4 shows the statement of changes in shareholders' equity for Hannaford from its 1995 Annual Report.

....

[9] Activities around managing resources.
[10] Activities around funding assets.

EXHIBIT 1-4　Hannaford Bros. Co.

CHANGES IN SHAREHOLDERS' EQUITY (in thousands)

	Common Stock		Additional Paid-in Capital	Preferred Stock Purchase Rights	Retained Earnings
	Shares	Amount			
Balance, January 2, 1993	40,776	$30,582	$ 91,673	$408	$ 223,133
Net earnings					56,705
Cash dividends:					
Redeemable preferred stock					(220)
Common stock					(13,967)
Preferred stock purchase rights				4	(4)
Shares issued to certain shareholders per agreement	127	95	2,660		
Shares issued under employee benefit plans	268	201	4,548		
Shares issued through redemption of preferred stock	40	30	867		
Balance, January 1, 1994	41,211	30,908	99,748	412	265,647
Net earnings					62,288
Cash dividends:					
Redeemable preferred stock					(74)
Common stock					(15,802)
Preferred stock purchase rights				6	(6)
Shares issued to certain shareholders per agreement	143	108	3,152		
Shares issued under employee benefit plans	332	249	5,839		
Shares issued in the acquisition of Wilson's Supermarkets	93	70	1,930		
Balance, December 31, 1994	41,779	31,335	110,669	418	312,053
Net earnings					70,201
Cash dividends:					
Common stock					(17,693)
Preferred stock purchase rights				5	(5)
Shares issued to certain shareholders per agreement	132	99	3,376		
Shares issued under employee benefit plans	387	290	7,929		
Balance, December 30, 1995	42,298	$31,724	$121,974	$423	$ 364,556

5. Financial Statement Footnotes

In addition to the data contained in these financial statements, companies also include significant financial information in notes to the statements. These footnotes typically contain information about taxes, contingent liabilities, and non-consolidated subsidiaries, as well as depreciation schedules for property, plant, and equipment and details about debt.

Because specific accounting policies can have a significant impact on the performance reported in financial statements, companies usually include in the notes an explanation of major accounting procedures used in preparing the statements. For instance, recent changes in accounting policies require that U.S. companies, beginning after December 15, 1992, report the present value of the cost of providing non-pension related post-retirement benefits, such as health care. Previously, U.S. companies reported the costs of these benefits as they were paid or when the employee retired, not as they were earned during the employee's career. This accounting change had a significant impact on the earnings of many U.S. companies at the time.

Included in the notes to the financial statements of all companies in countries that abide by international accounting standards is information about their accounting standards and policies. For purposes of brevity, the notes to the Hannaford Bros. Co. annual report have not been reproduced here.

III. ANALYSIS OF FINANCIAL STATEMENTS

When analyzing financial statements, one must keep in mind the purpose of the analysis. Since different analysts are interested in different aspects of a corporation's performance, no single type of analysis is appropriate for all situations. However, there are several general factors the analyst should bear in mind when reviewing data on financial statements.

First, all financial statement data are historical. Although one may make projections based on such data, the accuracy of these projections depends both on the forecaster's ability and the continued pertinence of the historical relationships to current or future operations and to industry and economic conditions.

Second, historical data are collected and reported on the basis of particular accounting principles. These accounting principles and rules vary from country to country. Even within a country, several approaches to specific issues may be allowed at one time, and these approaches may change over time. Although in many countries notes to financial statements summarize some of the significant accounting principles, the analyst should be aware of the impact that accounting methods and changes in them can have on the reported performance of a company. Because obtaining information on the differences that exist in accounting principles between countries can be difficult, we have included an appendix to this chapter, "Cross-Border Ratio Analysis," to aid the reader.

Third, because of the variability of seasonal funds flows and requirements in some businesses, the analyst should be aware of the timing of the reporting. For some companies in highly seasonal or cyclical industries, comparisons of results from different reporting periods should be approached cautiously.

Despite these concerns, an analyst can develop an insightful examination of a corporation's financial performance. The most common method of analyzing financial statements is the use of ratios. These ratios are simple mathematical relationships between various items on financial statements. In this chapter we describe the most commonly used ratios. To examine specific companies or industries, specialized ratios may be used or developed by the analyst. The analytical skill lies not in computing ratios but in determining which ratios to use in each case and interpreting the results. The ratios, by themselves, are relatively meaningless. Only by comparing ratios over time and between companies—and by determining the underlying causes of the differences among them—does ratio analysis help the owner, analyst, or manager gain insight into corporate performance.

The key ratios used for analyzing the internal performance of a company can be categorized into three groups: (1) profitability ratios, (2) asset utilization or efficiency ratios, and (3) capitalization or leverage ratios. The key ratios can be combined to determine the rate of return for a company and its owners and the rate at which the company can grow—the sustainable rate of growth. By adding data about the company's stock market performance, the analyst can gain insight into how the company's owners view the company's performance.

1. Profitability Ratios

Analysts use a number of methods to determine the relative profitability of a company. The key ratio is called the **return on sales** (ROS), which relates a company's net earnings or income to its sales.[11] This ratio is also referred to as **net profit ratio** or **profit margin**. Using data from the Hannaford Bros. Co.'s annual financial statements, this ratio is calculated as follows.[12] Note that because the financial statements report performance in thousands of dollars, all the calculations in this chapter are done in thousands; thus, Hannaford's net income was $70,201 thousand, or $70 million, in 1995.

$$\text{Return on sales} = \frac{\text{Net income}}{\text{Net sales}}$$

$$= \frac{\$70,201}{\$2,568,061}$$

$$= 0.0273 \text{ or } 2.73\%$$

---

[11] Net sales are generally net of discounts, returns, and allowances to customers. If no net sales figure is reported, analysts resort to using sales or revenues.
[12] The 1995 Hannaford Bros. financial data will be used in the remainder of the chapter to illustrate calculation of ratios.

Exhibit 1-5 shows the ROS ratios for a number of industries in the United States for 1995. As you can see, there is a wide range of profit margins among industries operating in one country. The profitability of companies differs among industry groups and depends on their competitive situations. For example, grocery stores operate with very low profit margins because competition in this industry tends to be based on low prices. To cover all costs, and make a profit for shareholders, high volume is typical in this industry. On the other hand, profit margins in industries with highly differentiated products, such as cosmetics, are generally much higher, and the volume of sales of each item much lower. The differences among returns for companies in one industry, but headquartered in different countries, shows the same range of outcomes, even when adjusted for the accounting problems described in the chapter's appendix.

In addition to the differences in ROS among industries, profitability can change for any company or industry over time. Cyclical companies usually have much lower returns on sales at the bottom of a business cycle: costs tend to be high, but prices have been kept low in an effort to lure the few buyers that exist. At the top of a cycle, companies are able to raise or maintain their prices and, since they are operating close to capacity, fixed costs per unit tend to be low. The automobile industry is an example of a cyclical industry. Exhibit 1-6 shows the profits of one of its major participants, General Motors, over ten years. The impact of the business cycle on the profitability of this company is clear. Obviously, it is important for the analyst to know and understand the nature of a company's business to properly interpret ratios.

The return on sales is the key profitability ratio. This ratio tells the analyst what proportion of the revenues remain after all expenses are met. However,

EXHIBIT 1-5   1995 Return on Sales (Various U.S. Industries)

Industry	Return on Sales
Advertising	5.33%
Book publishing	7.38
Catalog and mail-order houses	2.19
Chemical and allied products	3.52
Computer peripheral equipment	2.29
Electronic components	(0.02)
Electric housewares	7.65
Furniture and fixtures	7.66
Malt beverages	6.94
Motors and generators	5.24
Paper and paper products	0.93
Supermarkets	1.09
Tires and rubber goods	5.48

SOURCE: Data calculated from CompuStat.

EXHIBIT 1-6 General Motors' Return on Sales (1985-1995)

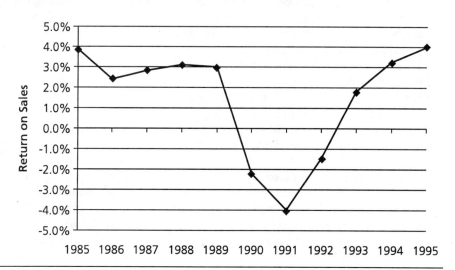

when the analyst sees significant changes in the ROS over time or relative to other companies, more information is needed: the analyst needs to examine what contributes to the return on sales. This can be done by looking at the expenses.

Companies make and sell products in many ways. Companies with low profit margins may have high costs of production; high marketing, selling, or research expenses; or a combination of these factors. Changes in profitability may reflect changes in these costs. Thus, as a first in understanding the sources of profitability, many analysts look at the profit a company earns after direct costs of production. This ratio is called the **gross margin**.

$$\text{Gross margin} \quad = \quad \frac{\text{Gross profit}^{13}}{\text{Net sales}}$$

$$= \quad \frac{\$616,813}{\$2,568,061}$$

$$= \quad 0.240 \text{ or } 24.0\%$$

For Hannaford, the gross margin was 24.0 percent. Another way to think of this is that 76.0 percent of every dollar of revenue Hannaford earned was used to cover the direct costs of producing or obtaining the products it sells. Because

---

[13] Gross margin is net revenues minus cost of goods sold.

the net profit margin was 2.7 percent, the rest of the company's profits, 21.3 percent, went to cover all other expenses.

In addition to production costs, companies must sell their products and pay the general costs of administration, including interest on debt and research and development. To determine the relative profitability of a company after all costs except taxes, analysts use the **operating margin**.

$$\text{Operating margin} = \frac{\text{Operating profit}^{14}}{\text{Net sales}}$$

$$= \frac{\$116,428}{\$2,568,061}$$

$$= 0.0453 \text{ or } 4.53\%$$

Hannaford's gross margin was 24.0 percent; the operating margin, 4.5 percent. The difference between the two, 19.5 percent, is the portion of the net sales that Hannaford spent on nonproduction-related expenses. This portion can vary substantially over time and among companies. It depends, among other things, on the importance of new product development and the efficiency of corporate headquarters.

Analysts who want to know how profitably a company produces and markets its goods, not how inexpensively it finances itself, may calculate yet another ratio, **EBIT/Sales**. EBIT stands for earnings before interest and taxes, and Hannaford's was 5.3 percent.

$$\text{EBIT/Sales} = \frac{\text{Earnings before interest and taxes}}{\text{Net sales}}$$

$$= \frac{\$135,796}{\$2,568,061}$$

$$= 0.0529 \text{ or } 5.29\%$$

The final profitability ratio that is in widespread use, particularly among stock analysts, is **EBITDA**. Actually the ratio is EBITDA/Sales, with EBITDA standing for earnings before interest, taxes, depreciation, and amortization. Using this ratio the analyst attempts to eliminate all the outside influences and timing effects on the profitability figure. Thus financing costs, interest, depreciation, timing of the capital expenses dictated by tax authorities, and taxes are ignored in calculating EBITDA. For Hannaford, gross profit was $616,813, but this included depreciation expenses of $69,016. The EBIT figure comes from the income statement in Exhibit 1-1, but, since Hannaford does not report depreciation on this statement as a separate item, the depreciation amount comes from the consolidated cash flow statement (Exhibit 1-3).

....

[14] Operating margin is gross profit minus operating expenses such as selling, general, and administrative expenses.

$$\text{EBITDA/Sales} \quad = \quad \frac{\text{EBITDA}}{\text{Sales}}$$

$$= \quad \frac{\$685,829}{\$2,568,061}$$

$$= \quad 0.267 \text{ or } 26.7\%$$

The EBITDA ratio is one that has gained widespread acceptance among financial analysts as they attempt to find a ratio that represents real cash earnings.[15] It is also believed that this ratio is more comparable for companies operating under different accounting systems.

There is yet another way in which analysts often examine the statement of earnings or income statement, the statement from which all these profitability ratios were derived. That analysis is called a **component percentage analysis**. These statements are also called **common-sized statements**. To calculate component percentages, the analyst simply relates each item on the income statement to revenues or sales. This form of ratio analysis is used to examine the composition of various items on financial statements. A percentage breakdown of the statement of earnings is frequently used and facilitates a comparison of trends over time. The 1995 component percentage analysis for Hannaford, Exhibit 1-7, shows in detail the cost-revenue relationships for the company.

2. Asset Utilization Ratios

A company typically acquires assets for use in producing sales revenues and, ultimately, profits. The ratios that indicate the effectiveness of asset utilization

---

EXHIBIT 1-7　　Hannaford Bros. Co.

PERCENTAGE COMPONENTS FOR STATEMENT OF EARNINGS
YEAR ENDED DECEMBER 31, 1995 (in thousands)

	Dollars	Percentage
Net sales	$2,568,061	100.00%
Cost of sales	1,951,248	75.98
Gross profit	616,813	24.02
Selling and general expenses	481,017	18.73
Earnings before interest and taxes	135,796	5.29
Interest income	2,510	0.09
Interest expense	(21,878)	-0.85
Operating profit	116,428	4.53
Income taxes	46,227	1.80
Net income	$ 70,201	2.73%

---

[15] This ratio attempts to find a proxy for free cash flow, a figure we discuss extensively in Chapter 4.

are often called **efficiency** or **turnover ratios**. The information needed to calculate these ratios is taken from both the statement of earnings and the statement of financial position.

The first ratio an analyst turns to in evaluating the efficiency of any company is **total asset turnover** (TATO).

$$\text{Total asset turnover} = \frac{\text{Net sales}}{\text{Assets}}$$

$$= \frac{\$2,568,061}{\$961,830}$$

$$= 2.67 \text{ or } 267\%^{16}$$

Note that average assets is a more representative figure than total assets if a company has had a large increase or decrease in assets during the prior year. This is true when comparing the size of an asset base with income or with revenue, because revenues and profits are earned over a year while asset accounts are measured at a point in time, in Hannaford's case, the end of the year. In practice, the analyst must determine whether significant changes in the accounts did occur over the period and, if so, how to adapt the ratios. Note, special care must be taken to be certain that the ratios are calculated in a similar fashion when comparing data provided by others. Using average assets for Hannaford, the ratio would be 279 percent. It is important to be consistent throughout an analysis. While to avoid distortions average assets is preferable, most reported data is based on the year-end asset figure.

As you can see, Hannaford's sales were more than twice as large as its year-end 1995 assets. The nature of the company's business dictates a high utilization of assets. Exhibit 1-8 shows the 1995 asset efficiency for the same U.S. industries shown in Exhibit 1-5. Differences in asset utilization, that is, capital intensity, are dramatic, but upon further thought, not surprising.[17] For example, you might have suspected that manufacturing companies would need considerable assets to produce their products. The most asset-intensive industry, paper and paper products, because of low profit margins and low operational efficiency (asset utilization ratio), has the lowest positive return on assets (ROA) of the companies on the list. The supermarket industry's ROA was more than double its ROS.

Once again, the ratio alone does not lead the analyst to any easy conclusions about a company. However, when the information is joined with information about the nature of the business, the industry, and economic conditions, the

---

[16] We report this and all ratios, except the price/earnings ratio, as a percentage. Some analysts and reporting services report some ratios, this one is an example, as a multiple. For instance, you might see 2.67X or 2.67 reported for the asset turnover ratio. When using data from another source, be certain you know the reporting method.

[17] Capital intensity is the degree to which capital goods—property, plant, and equipment—are used to produce products, rather than labor. If products are produced with a high level of labor and little capital investment, the production process is called labor-intensive.

EXHIBIT 1-8   1995 Return on Assets—Various U.S. Industries

Industry	Return on Sales	Total Asset Turnover	ROA
Advertising	5.33%	76.17%	4.06%
Book publishing	7.38	83.60	6.17
Catalog and mail-order houses	2.19	189.95	4.16
Chemical and allied products	3.52	163.92	5.77
Computer peripheral equipment	2.29	140.61	3.22
Electronic components	(0.02)	150.00	(0.03)
Electric housewares	7.65	114.25	8.74
Furniture and fixtures	7.66	72.06	5.52
Malt beverages	6.94	81.12	5.63
Motors and generators	5.24	149.81	7.80
Paper and paper products	0.93	232.26	2.16
Supermarkets	1.09	336.00	3.67
Tires and rubber goods	5.48	136.50	7.48

SOURCE: Data calculated from CompuStat.

skilled analyst can gain insight. Later in this chapter we will compare Hannaford's financial performance across time and with others in its industry.

TATO has another very useful property. By multiplying TATO by return on sales, one calculates the return on assets (ROA).

$$\text{Return on assets} = \text{Return on sales} \times \text{Total asset turnover}$$

$$= \frac{\text{Net income}}{\text{Net sales}} \times \frac{\text{Net sales}}{\text{Assets}}$$

$$= \frac{\text{Net income}}{\text{Assets}}$$

Using this relationship for Hannaford, the ROA is calculated as follows:

$$
\begin{aligned}
\text{ROA} &= \text{ROS} \times \text{TATO} \\
&= 0.0273 \times 2.67 \\
&= 0.073 \text{ or } 7.3\%
\end{aligned}
$$

One can, of course, calculate the ROA directly:

$$
\begin{aligned}
\text{ROA} &= \frac{\text{Net income}}{\text{Assets}} \\
&= \frac{\$70,201}{\$961,830} \\
&= 0.073 \text{ or } 7.3\%
\end{aligned}
$$

By understanding this relationship, you can easily see why capital-intensive companies have lower returns on assets, all other things being equal, than do service companies with fewer assets.

After examining the overall asset efficiency of a company, the analyst may want to delve into the way the company uses some or all of its assets. This is particularly true if the analyst finds the asset efficiency to be different from what was expected. Since inventory is a very large asset for many companies, the analyst may want to know how efficiently the company has used its inventory. To estimate that, the analyst could calculate the **inventory turnover** ratio.

$$\text{Inventory turnover} = \frac{\text{Cost of sales}}{\text{Inventory}}$$

$$= \frac{\$1,951,248}{\$157,968}$$

$$= 12.35 \text{ or } 1,235\%$$

This ratio indicates the percentage of Hannaford's inventory that was sold and replaced during the reporting period, in this case one year. Note two things: first, if inventory grew substantially during the year, average inventory might be a more useful denominator than inventory; second, the numerator is the cost of sales, not net sales. The reason for using cost of sales is to factor out the profit portion of sales, leaving only the production costs contained in cost of sales. If the net sales figure were used and the company had high prices relative to costs, the ratio would be higher than the actual inventory turnover. It is also important to remember that the quality of the information contained in this ratio depends on how the company values its inventory. A knowledgeable analyst will want to determine the method used for inventory valuation. The appendix to this chapter contains a discussion of inventory valuation methods.

A high inventory turnover ratio indicates that the company is using its financial resources efficiently by maintaining low inventories. Hannaford's inventory turnover is relatively quick. The nature of some companies' production processes—for instance, aircraft manufacturers—makes achieving a high inventory turnover ratio impossible, while others, like grocery stores, deal in more perishable items and thus would be expected to have a rapid turnover of inventory.[18]

Because Hannaford has a TATO ratio that is lower than its inventory turnover ratio, the analyst will no doubt wonder how efficiently other assets are being utilized by the company. For instance, the analyst might look at the accounts receivable, the quantity of the company's sales for which it has not received payment. The ratio of **accounts receivable to net sales** indicates the

---

[18] We could also calculate the days of inventory on hand by multiplying Inventory/Cost of sales by 365 days. Hannaford has inventory that will last for 29.4 days.

relative proportion of the company's sales made on credit and still outstanding at the end of the reporting period.

$$\text{Accounts receivable/Sales} = \frac{\text{Accounts receivable}}{\text{Net sales}}$$

$$= \frac{\$15,556}{\$2,568,061}$$

$$= 0.0061 \text{ or } 0.61\%$$

As you can see, of the sales made by Hannaford in 1995, approximately 0.6 percent remained unpaid at the end of 1995. This is certainly what we would have expected from a grocery store chain where virtually all sales are made for cash or paid for with credit or debit cards.[19]

We can also use this ratio to determine the **days' sales outstanding** or the **receivables collection period**. Companies that sell their products on credit, such as furniture manufacturers, will have long collection periods.

$$\text{Days' sales outstanding} = \frac{\text{Accounts receivable}}{\text{Net sales}} \times 365$$

$$= \frac{\$15,556}{\$2,568,061} \times 365$$

$$= 2.2 \text{ days}$$

Hannaford's customers paid their bills in an average of 2.2 days. Given the nature of the supermarket industry, the company's extremely small days' sales outstanding is not surprising. For other industries, such as computer peripheral equipment, credit terms of net 30 are more common (that is, payment is due within 30 days after the goods are received).

Other analysts might want to look at the efficiency with which the company manages its short-term liabilities. For instance, the company's suppliers might wonder how much the company owes to suppliers in relation to what it purchased from them. To determine this, the ratio of **accounts payable to purchases** would be analyzed. However, most external analysts do not have the purchases figure, so the ratio of **accounts payable to cost of sales** is typically substituted.

$$\text{Accounts payable/Cost of sales} = \frac{\text{Accounts payable}}{\text{Cost of sales}}$$

$$= \frac{\$113,846}{\$1,951,248}$$

$$= 0.0583 \text{ or } 5.83\%$$

---

[19]   Had we wanted to know the average accounts receivable outstanding over the year, we could have used average accounts receivable in the ratio.

Another way to see how promptly the company is paying its obligations is to measure the **payables payment period**.

$$\text{Payables payment period} = \frac{\text{Accounts payable}}{\text{Cost of sales}} \times 365$$

$$= \frac{\$113,846}{\$1,951,248} \times 365$$

$$= 21.3 \text{ days}$$

Hannaford pays its suppliers much more slowly than its customers pay Hannaford. Companies that use their suppliers as a major source of funding, such as Hannaford, will have longer payables payment periods.

For companies with seasonal sales, care must be taken in calculating this ratio as well as in calculating days' sales outstanding and inventory turnover. Using the annual cost of sales may inflate or deflate the ratios, and provide an unrealistic look at the actual patterns experienced by the company. In such situations some analysts calculate monthly ratios based on the cost of sales for that month, or an average for several months during the same season, rather than using annual cost of sales.

In addition to, or in place of, these ratios, the analyst may perform a **component percentage analysis** of the company's balance sheet. In this analysis, also known as a **common-size statement**, each asset, liability, and equity account balance is compared with the total asset figure. This analysis is especially useful for comparing changes over time. Such a component analysis is shown in Exhibit 1-9.

After the analyst has fully investigated the profitability, return on sales, and asset efficiency of the company, the next step is to see how the company has been financed. Earlier we could have deduced from the income statement's low interest expense that Hannaford either had little debt or had debt that was inexpensive. Let's see which is the case.

3. Capitalization Ratios

Capitalization or **financial leverage ratios** provide information about the sources the company has used to finance its investment in assets. The term **financial leverage** is used to indicate the impact debt financing has on the returns of the company to its owners; if the income generated by investment in assets is greater than the cost of debt, the equity holders will benefit from financing an increased amount of assets through borrowing. The term **gearing** is also used in referring to this concept. Later we will see how financial leverage or gearing affects the return on equity.

Leverage ratios are based on information from a company's balance sheet. Of primary interest to a company's owners is the **assets to equity ratio**. This ratio measures the proportion of the assets that are financed by its owners.

EXHIBIT 1-9   Hannaford Bros. Co.

COMPONENT ANALYSIS OF BALANCE-SHEET ITEMS
AS OF DECEMBER 31, 1995 (dollars in thousands)

Assets	Dollars	Percentage
Current assets:		
Cash and cash equivalents	$ 7,017	0.73%
Accounts receivable	15,556	1.62
Inventories	157,968	16.42
Prepaid expenses	7,217	0.75
Deferred income taxes	6,584	0.69
Total current assets	194,342	20.21%
Property, plant, and equipment:		
Land and improvements	90,430	9.40%
Buildings	228,858	23.79
Furniture, fixtures, and equipment	333,492	34.67
Leasehold interests and improvements	188,730	19.62
Construction in progress	16,179	1.68
Total gross property, plant, and equipment	857,689	89.17%
Less allowance for depreciation	280,563	29.17
Total net property, plant, and equipment	577,126	60.00%
Leased property under capital leases	56,691	5.89
Other assets	133,671	13.90
Total assets	$961,830	100.00%

Liabilities and Shareholders' Equity		
Current liabilities:		
Accounts payable	$113,846	11.84%
Accrued expenses	44,271	4.60
Income taxes payable	0	0.00
Total current liabilities	158,117	16.44%
Long-term debt and capital leases	233,108	24.24
Deferred income tax liabilities	23,229	2.42
Other long-term liabilities	28,699	2.98
Shareholders' equity:		
Common stock, $0.75 par value:		
Authorized: 110,000,000 shares		
Issued: 42,298,230 shares at December 31, 1995		
and 41,779,342 shares at December 31,1994	31,724	3.30
Additional paid-in capital	121,974	12.68
Preferred stock purchase rights	423	0.04
Retained earnings	364,556	37.90
Total shareholders' equity	518,677	53.93%
Total liabilities and shareholders' equity	$961,830	100.00%

NOTE: Some subtotals do not sum due to rounding.

Because we want to know the company's position at the end of the year, we do not use averages of the accounts over the year. Instead, we use the balance at the end of the year. For Hannaford, this ratio is calculated as follows:

$$\text{Assets to equity} = \frac{\text{Assets}}{\text{Shareholders' equity}}$$

$$= \frac{\$961,830}{\$518,677}$$

$$= 1.854 \text{ or } 185.4\%$$

If the ratio of assets to equity were 100 percent, the company would be totally financed by its owners. A company with a higher ratio finances a large proportion of its assets with debt, or is said to be more highly leveraged. Since Hannaford's ratio is 185 percent, it has significant debt. To determine whether this level of leverage is high, we will need other ratios. We will look at others after we see what else we can do with a leverage ratio.

The assets to equity ratio shows the proportion of the firm financed by its owners. When it is combined with ROA, we can find the return that shareholders earned on the book value of their investment in the company, the **return on equity** (ROE).[20]

$$\text{Return on equity} = \text{ROS} \times \text{TATO} \times \text{Leverage}$$

$$= \frac{\text{Net income}}{\text{Net sales}} \times \frac{\text{Net sales}}{\text{Assets}} \times \frac{\text{Assets}}{\text{Equity}}$$

$$= \text{ROA} \times \text{Leverage}$$

$$= \frac{\text{Net income}}{\text{Assets}} \times \frac{\text{Assets}}{\text{Equity}}$$

$$= \frac{\text{Net income}}{\text{Equity}}$$

For Hannaford, the return on equity is calculated as follows:

$$\text{ROE} = \text{ROS} \times \text{TATO} \times \text{Leverage}$$

$$= 0.0273 \times 2.67 \times 1.854$$

$$= 0.135 \text{ or } 13.5\%$$

Looking at this relationship, you can see that debt financing has a minimal effect on the return that shareholders in Hannaford have earned. If the company had been financed with more debt—for instance, an assets to equity ratio

---

[20] The book value is the per share value of the total equity reported on the statement of financial position, the balance sheet.

of 300 percent—the ROE would have been 21.9 percent.[21] If it had been financed by shareholders alone, the return on equity would have been 7.3 percent, exactly the same as the return the company earned on its assets. If, in addition, the total asset turnover (TATO) were 100 percent, the ROS, ROA, and ROE would be the same. The fewer assets a company uses to generate sales, and the more debt it uses to finance those assets, the higher the return shareholders earn.

The impact of leverage can be seen by looking at Exhibit 1-10. Financial leverage can increase returns to shareholders: the supermarket industry had a 1.09 percent return on sales, but a return on equity of 13.3 percent because of the combined impacts of high operational leverage, the proportion of assets used to generate sales; and the financial leverage, the proportion of equity used in financing the company. In contrast, lower operational and financial leverage turned higher ROS into modest ROE for the book publishing and malt beverages industries.

Constituents other than shareholders are interested in the way a company finances itself. Lenders, who may provide a large portion of the company's capital resources, are especially interested in the way the company is capitalized. While they could certainly deduce their position from the ratio of assets to equity, they have developed ratios that show their position directly.[22] Two lender-perspective ratios are commonly used: **long-term debt to equity** and

EXHIBIT 1-10   Industry Average Financial Leverage and Return on Equity, 1995

Industry	Return on Sales	Total Asset Turnover	ROA	Assets/ Equity	ROE
Advertising	5.33%	76.17%	4.06%	402.96%	16.36%
Book publishing	7.38	83.60	6.17	293.19	18.09
Catalog and mail-order houses	2.19	189.95	4.16	235.82	9.81
Chemical and allied products	3.52	163.92	5.77	196.36	11.33
Computer peripheral equipment	2.29	140.61	3.22	180.43	5.81
Electronic components	(0.02)	150.00	(0.03)	200.00	(0.06)
Electric housewares	7.65	114.25	8.74	161.67	14.13
Furniture and fixtures	7.66	72.06	5.52	295.65	16.32
Malt beverages	6.94	81.12	5.63	213.32	12.01
Motors and generators	5.24	149.81	7.85	295.80	23.22
Paper and paper products	0.93	232.26	2.16	286.57	6.19
Supermarkets	1.09	336.00	3.67	362.00	13.30
Tires and rubber goods	5.48	136.50	7.48	284.63	21.29

SOURCE: Data from CompuStat

[21]   This is determined by multiplying the ROS of 2.73 percent by the TATO of 267 percent by an assets to equity ratio of 300 percent.
[22]   Assets/Debt is simply [1 - (Assets/Equity)].

long-term debt to total assets. For our Hannaford example, the first is calculated as follows:

$$\text{Long-term debt to equity} = \frac{\text{Long-term debt}}{\text{Equity}}$$

$$= \frac{\$233,108}{\$518,677}$$

$$= 0.449 \text{ or } 44.9\%$$

And the second is calculated as shown below.

$$\text{Long-term debt to assets} = \frac{\text{Long-term debt}}{\text{Assets}}$$

$$= \frac{\$233,108}{\$961,830}$$

$$= 0.242 \text{ or } 24.2\%$$

Note that in both these ratios we used the total long-term debt ($150,648) and the capital leases ($69,747), including the current maturities of the debt ($11,246) and the current capital lease obligations ($1,467). Capital leases are included since they constitute a long-term, contractual obligation that has many of the same features and obligations of debt.

One more ratio that analysts find useful in measuring a company's use of debt is debt to total capital. Total capital is the sum of the long-term debt and equity used to finance the business plus the total equity. This ratio is sometimes confused with the debt to total assets ratio. The ratio for Hannaford is calculated as follows:

$$\text{Long-term debt to total capital} = \frac{\text{Long-term debt}}{\text{Long-term debt } + \text{ Equity}}$$

$$= \frac{\$233,108}{\$233,108 \, + \, \$518,677}$$

$$= 0.310 \text{ or } 31.0\%$$

In determining the long-term debt of a company, analysts often disagree about the items to include. If the decision is made to include deferred taxes, long-term contingent liabilities, or other long-term liabilities, these items should be included consistently throughout any analysis.

The appropriate size of a capitalization ratio depends on the perspective of the analyst, the nature of the company, and its situation. Lenders such as bondholders and bankers typically prefer low debt ratios, which provide greater security for their loans. Since equity investors' returns are improved by more leverage, shareholders generally prefer more leverage. This leverage provides a higher return on equity if the company is profitable.[23] Issues involved in determining the appropriate amount of debt—the appropriate capital structure—are discussed in Chapter 7.

Lenders and other sources of short-term capital—for instance, suppliers—also want to know how the company will meet its obligations in the short run. Since some companies use significant amounts of short-term debt to finance their operations, three ratios have been found to be useful for examining the situation: **total liabilities to assets**, the **current ratio**, and the **acid-test ratio**. For Hannaford, the first of these is as follows:

$$\text{Total liabilities to assets} = \frac{\text{Total liabilities}}{\text{Total assets}}$$

$$= \frac{\$443,153}{\$961,830}$$

$$= 0.461 \text{ or } 46.1\%$$

Over 46 percent of Hannaford 's assets have been financed by lenders, including trade creditors, rather than by shareholders. By any ratio we choose, Hannaford is a somewhat leveraged, or geared, company.

The current and acid-test ratios measure the company's ability to pay its current liabilities alone. These ratios, also called **liquidity ratios**, reflect the size of short-term obligations. Hannaford 's current ratio is calculated as follows:

$$\text{Current ratio} = \frac{\text{Current assets}}{\text{Current liabilities}}$$

$$= \frac{\$194,342}{\$170,830}$$

$$= 1.138 \text{ or } 113.8\%$$

Companies with high liquidity ratios are considered more liquid than those with low ratios: their short-term assets are greater than their short-term liabilities. Being more liquid generally means that a company is better able to pay off its short-term obligations than is its less liquid peers. There is one catch, however. Some current assets may not be easy to turn into the cash needed to pay current liabilities. The current asset that is often hardest to turn into cash (at least, quickly) is inventory. By deducting inventory from current assets, the analyst can determine whether the company would be able to pay its current liabilities without resorting to selling inventory. Hannaford's **acid-test** or **quick ratio** is calculated as follows:

----

[23]   High degrees of financial leverage also, in times of decreased revenues and profits, result in low or negative returns on equity.

$$\text{Acid-test ratio} = \frac{\text{Cash} + \text{Short-term investments} + \text{Accounts receivable}}{\text{Current liabilities}}$$

$$= \frac{\$22,573}{\$170,830}$$

$$= 0.132 \text{ or } 13.2\%$$

Short-term investments can be investments in such things as marketable securities. Some analysts call these "near cash" since they are usually easily converted into cash in a very short period of time. Note, prepaid expenses and deferred income taxes have also been excluded. Both would be unavailable to cover current liabilities.

You can see that Hannaford is less liquid when inventory is removed from current assets. But is this a problem? Determining what constitutes a good or bad level of liquidity depends on who is analyzing the current or acid-test ratio. A banker who has made a short-term loan would like both ratios to be high, because the banker believes they indicate that the company has sufficient current assets to pay all current liabilities, including the bank's loan. On the other hand, the company's manager might prefer lower ratios, in the belief that they show the company has minimized funds invested in current assets that may yield low returns. Companies with rapid turnovers of receivables and inventories generally need a smaller liquidity cushion, and thus can have lower current and acid-test ratios than those with slower turnovers.

All these capitalization ratios show the relative ability of a company to repay the principal of its short- and long-term debt obligations. However, the ability to repay principal is only one of the concerns lenders have. In fact, it may be the lesser of two concerns: whether the company can repay the principal and whether the company can pay the interest on the debt. Because the lender's product is debt, and to make a profit the product must be sold, lenders are concerned less with actual repayment of the principal than with the company's ability to repay it if requested. Companies that have the ability to repay the debt make good candidates for loans, if they can pay the interest on the debt.

Lenders have developed several ratios to test the borrower's ability to pay interest. These are called **coverage ratios**. They test the company's ability to pay interest; interest and principal; or interest, principal, and other contractual obligations. They are also called **debt-service ratios**.

Over the long term, interest must be paid out of funds generated by company operations. Because earnings are usually the primary source of funds to service debt obligations, a frequently calculated coverage ratio is **EBIT coverage**.

$$\text{EBIT coverage} = \frac{\text{Earnings before interest and taxes}}{\text{Interest expense}}$$

$$= \frac{\$135,796}{\$21,878}$$

$$= 6.207 \text{ or } 620.7\%$$

Note that we used Hannaford's EBIT, not net income, in calculating this ratio, since both interest and its tax effect are deducted in calculating net income. Thus, EBIT is available to cover interest expense. With a ratio of 620.7 percent, Hannaford appears able to pay its interest easily.

Analysts use a number of other coverage ratios to determine the ability of a company to meet its interest obligations. For instance, an analyst might add depreciation to EBIT in estimating the coverage ratio. Cash is important because debt payments must be made with cash, not with earnings. To calculate the **cash flow coverage ratio**, we add to EBIT the depreciation from Exhibit 1-3.

$$\text{Cash flow coverage} \quad = \quad \frac{\text{EBIT} + \text{Depreciation}}{\text{Interest expense}}$$

$$= \quad \frac{\$135,796 + 69,016}{\$21,878}$$

$$= \quad 9.362 \text{ or } 936.2\%$$

If a company has depreciation, the ratio for cash flow coverage will always be larger than that for EBIT coverage. Other cash flows might be added or subtracted from the EBIT to determine the cash available to pay interest expenses.

While interest coverage is of primary concern, lenders also require principal payments, and thus they must be taken into account in an analysis. Principal payments are sometimes called **sinking fund payments**. These payments are not deductible for tax purposes, so they must be paid with after-tax funds. To determine the ability of the company to meet both interest and principal payments, the ratio of **debt-service coverage** is used. In this ratio, principal repayments are adjusted to a before-tax basis to compensate for their lack of tax deductibility. The principal obligations and marginal tax rates for a company can be found in the notes to financial statements.

$$\text{Debt-service coverage} \quad = \quad \frac{\text{Earnings before interest and taxes}}{\text{Interest} + [\text{Principal payments}/(1 - \text{Tax rate})]}$$

$$= \quad \frac{\$135,796}{\$21,878 + [(\$1,404 + \$18,452)/(1 - 0.38)]}$$

$$= \quad 2.520 \text{ or } 252\%$$

Note that for Hannaford, both the interest and debt-service coverage ratios are well above their minimums, 100 percent. In fact, even when principal payments are included, the company can cover its obligations, at least its debt obligations, more than two times.

These two basic ratios, interest coverage and debt-service coverage, can be adapted for other contractual or noncontractual obligations such as lease payments and dividends, or EBIT or cash flow can be used in the numerator. Each variation of these two basic ratios gives a somewhat different view of the company's ability to meet its contractual and perceived obligations. It is up to the analyst to determine which ratio gives a better view.

Lenders and lessors like coverage ratios to be high. Shareholders, seeking higher returns, prefer the ratios to be low. The best level for each of the ratios depends on the nature of the business, the economic situation, and the willingness of the owners or managers to take risk.

4. Sustainable Growth Rate

By combining return on sales, total asset turnover, and leverage, we determined shareholders' return on equity. However, while shareholders may earn that return on equity, they may not receive all the returns immediately. As illustrated in Exhibit 1-11, some of the returns may be provided to the shareholders in the form of cash dividends, while the rest are retained by the company to fund future growth.

One measure of the proportion of the earnings paid out to shareholders is the **dividend payout ratio** (DPO). Hannaford's payment of cash dividends for 1995 is shown in Exhibit 1-3.

$$\text{Dividend payout} = \frac{\text{Dividends paid}}{\text{Net income}}$$
$$= \frac{\$17{,}693}{\$70{,}201}$$
$$= 0.252 \text{ or } 25.2\%$$

The proportion of earnings retained for use by the firm, the **earnings retention ratio**, is simply the opposite of the payout ratio:

$$\text{Earnings retention} = 1 - \text{Dividend payout ratio}$$
$$= 1 - 0.252$$
$$= 0.748 \text{ or } 74.8\%$$

EXHIBIT 1-11   Disposition of Net Income to Shareholders

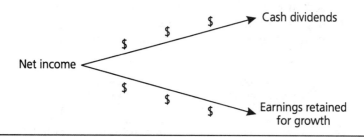

This ratio yields a useful result when combined with the ROS, TATO, and leverage ratios.[24] By multiplying them, we can determine the maximum rate at which the company can grow using internally generated funds, which is called the **sustainable growth rate** (SGR). Note that this analysis assumes that the ratios all stay the same; that is, as earnings are retained, they are matched with enough new debt to keep the ratio of assets to equity the same, and neither the TATO nor the ROS ratio changes. An example of the SGR is calculated as follows:

$$
\begin{aligned}
\text{SGR} &= \text{ROS} \times \text{TATO} \times \text{Leverage} \times \text{Retention Ratio} \\
&= \frac{\text{Net income}}{\text{Sales}} \times \frac{\text{Sales}}{\text{Assets}} \times \frac{\text{Assets}}{\text{Equity}} \times \frac{\text{Earnings retained}}{\text{Net income}} \\
&= \frac{\$70,201}{\$2,568,061} \times \frac{\$2,568,061}{\$961,830} \times \frac{\$961,830}{\$518,677} \times \frac{\$52,508}{\$70,201} \\
&= 0.0273 \times 2.670 \times 1.854 \times 0.748 \\
&= 0.101 \text{ or } 10.1\%
\end{aligned}
$$

This ratio may also be calculated using the following shortcut:

$$
\begin{aligned}
\text{SGR} &= \text{ROE} \times (1 - \text{DPO}) \\
&= 0.135 \times (1 - 0.252) \\
&= 0.101 \text{ or } 10.1\%
\end{aligned}
$$

The segmentation of the sustainable growth rate into the four sources of growth—profit, asset efficiency, leverage, and profit retention—allows the analyst to examine the individual factors that affect the growth rate. This approach provides for a clear diagnosis of past financial performance. In addition, understanding of this concept and an analysis of the SGR components can allow an analyst or manager to determine what would have happened if the company had followed a different strategy for any component. And if the sustainable growth rate turns out to be lower than expected or desired, management can review the various components to determine in which areas the company is underperforming. Exhibit 1-12 shows the components and sustainable growth rates for several different industries. There is a wide range of sustainable growth rates.

Hannaford, based only on its 1995 sustainable growth rate, could grow at a rate of approximately 10 percent per year. If Hannaford management wants the company to grow at a faster rate, it must change something. The most

---

[24] Most companies do not pay out more in dividends than they earn during a year. Hannaford, however, had a long-standing policy of never cutting dividends. Thus, in the face of a year with depressed earnings, management could either change the dividend policy or pay out more in dividends than the company had earned. To pay out more in dividends than its current year's earnings, a company can do one of three things: borrow, sell assets, or sell new common stock.

EXHIBIT 1-12 Industry Average Retention Ratios and Sustainable Growth Rates, 1995

Industry	Return on Sales	Total Asset Turnover	ROA	Assets/ Equity	ROE	Retention Ratio	Sustainable Growth Rate
Advertising	5.33%	76.17%	4.06%	402.96%	16.36%	100.00%	16.36%
Book publishing	7.38	83.60	6.17	293.19	18.09	41.46	7.50
Catalog and mail-order houses	2.19	189.95	4.16	235.82	9.81	79.88	7.84
Chemical and allied products	3.52	163.92	5.77	196.36	11.33	80.67	9.14
Computer peripheral equipment	2.29	140.61	3.22	180.43	5.81	86.81	5.04
Electronic components	(0.02)	150.00	(0.03)	200.00	(0.06)	100.00	(0.06)
Electric housewares	7.65	114.25	8.74	161.67	14.13	89.23	12.61
Furniture and fixtures	7.66	72.06	5.52	295.65	16.32	68.61	11.20
Malt beverages	6.94	81.12	5.63	213.32	12.01	61.74	7.41
Motors and generators	5.24	149.81	7.85	295.80	23.22	75.68	17.57
Paper and paper products	0.93	232.26	2.16	286.57	6.19	22.89	1.42
Supermarkets	1.09	336.00	3.67	362.00	13.30	73.95	9.80
Tires and rubber goods	5.48	136.50	7.48	284.63	21.29	80.85	17.21

SOURCE: Data from CompuStat.

obvious candidate to cut is the dividend. If Hannaford had cut its entire dividend in 1995, its sustainable growth rate would have been 13.5 percent.[25] Management could also target other ratios for change. However, changing the profit margin, asset efficiency, or even leverage often takes considerable time and effort.

All the ratios we have looked at thus far concern the health of the company. What we have not done is determine how Hannaford's shareholders are faring: What has happened to their share price and returns?

5. Market Ratios

In addition to ratios that are calculated using only data from the company's financial statements, analysts often calculate ratios using information from the market for publicly owned companies' stock. These ratios facilitate analyzing the company's financial market performance because the company's internal performance should and will be reflected in the capital market's evaluation. Since the return on investment for an equity owner may come primarily from changes in the market price of the equity, these ratios are of particular interest to the shareholders of a company. Because equity investors purchase shares of common stock in the company, most market ratios are calculated on a per-share basis. A typical starting point for market analysis is **earnings per share** (EPS). The figure for Hannaford shown in Exhibit 1-1 is $1.67.

$$\text{Earnings per share} = \frac{\text{Net income}}{\text{Number of common shares outstanding}}$$

$$= \frac{\$70,201}{42,092}$$

$$= \$1.67$$

Other ratios are based on the market price for a share of common stock. In January 1996, the share price for Hannaford was $25.375. Using this price, several useful ratios can be calculated. The first is the **price/earnings** or **P/E ratio**.

$$\text{Price/Earnings} = \frac{\text{Market price per share}}{\text{Earnings per share}}$$

$$= \frac{\$25.375}{\$1.67}$$

$$= 15.2 \text{ times or } 152\%$$

---

[25] Cutting the dividend is an action taken with extreme reluctance by directors and management. The reason is that they believe that it signals the marketplace, the current and potential security holders, that the company is in some difficulty. Thus, it believes that stock and bond prices will react negatively.

Note that the P/E ratio normally is not cited as a percentage but as a multiple: Hannaford's price was over 15 times its earnings. This ratio can be used to evaluate the relative financial performance of the stock. Most analysts believe that it gives an indication of how much investors are willing to pay for a dollar of the company's earnings, and it provides a scaled measure that allows market value comparisons of companies with different earnings levels.

Another ratio is used as a rough measure of whether management has created and is expected to create value for its shareholders. This ratio relates the market value per share of common stock to the book value or net worth per share. A ratio of **market-to-book value** greater than 100 percent indicates that shareholders are willing to pay a premium over the book value of the stock. The book value per share of a company is calculated by dividing shareholders' equity on the statement of financial position or balance sheet by the number of shares outstanding.

$$\text{Market-to-book value} = \frac{\text{Market value per share}}{\text{Book value per share}}$$

$$= \frac{\$25.375}{\$518,667/42,092}$$

$$= \frac{\$25.375}{\$12.32}$$

$$= 2.06 \text{ or } 206\%$$

The analyst should keep in mind that book values result from specific accounting conventions that require the use of historical values for assets. When historical values do not reflect the underlying economic value or earning potential of these assets, the use of replacement cost or inflation-adjusted valuations may result in a more meaningful ratio of market-to-book value. Market-to-book values, price/earnings ratios, and sustainable rates of growth for a number of industries are shown in Exhibit 1-13.

Typically, investors expect companies with high P/E ratios to grow to have more rapid increases in dividends in the future than companies with low P/E ratios because earnings retained now will feed the company's growth. Additionally, companies with higher sustainable growth rates are expected to have higher P/E ratios. Looking at Exhibit 1-13, you can see for yourself whether there is a relationship.

There is another ratio that is gaining widespread use. It is called the **spread**. This ratio is designed to give the analyst a measure of how well the company is doing, without the distortions of accounting conventions, and taking capital providers into account. While there are differences in the ways that this ratio is calculated, in general it is calculated as follows:

$$\text{Spread} = \text{Return on equity - Required return on equity}$$

EXHIBIT 1-13 Industry Average Market-to-Book Values, Price/Earnings Ratios, and Sustainable Growth Rates, 1995

Industry	Sustainable Growth Rate	Market Price to Book Value	Market Price to Earnings	ROE	Required Return	Spread
Advertising	16.36%	344.00%	23.50%	16.36%	10.80%	5.50%
Book publishing	7.50	323.00	22.50	18.09	11.90	6.20
Catalog and mail-order houses	7.84	495.00	23.40	9.81	11.00	(1.20)
Chemical and allied products	9.14	255.00	20.00	11.33	12.50	(1.20)
Computer peripheral equipment	5.04	364.00	23.10	5.81	13.60	(7.80)
Electronic components	(0.06)	251.00	43.10	(0.06)	10.80	(11.40)
Electric housewares	12.61	151.00	13.90	14.13	11.90	2.20
Furniture and fixtures	11.20	147.00	17.90	16.32	10.80	5.50
Malt beverages	7.41	125.00	62.10	12.01	11.90	0.10
Motors and generators	17.57	269.00	12.10	23.22	12.50	10.70
Paper and paper products	1.42	200.00	12.10	6.19	11.40	(5.20)
Supermarkets	9.80	220.00	17.70	13.30	11.90	1.40
Tires and rubber goods	17.21	250.00	14.90	21.29	11.90	9.40

SOURCE: Data from CompuStat.

For comparison, the analyst must have an estimate of the investors' expected or required ROE. We discuss how to calculate this in Chapter 6. For Hannaford, the required ROE is 10.8 percent. For a company like Hannaford, the spread would be 2.7 percent.

$$
\begin{aligned}
\text{Spread} \quad &= \quad 13.5\% - 10.8\% \\
&= \quad 2.7\%
\end{aligned}
$$

Many analysts adapt this measure. For instance, some use an adjusted return on equity, adjusting the earnings for transactions that affect accrual accounting earnings, such as depreciation, accounting adjustments, and investments. We discuss how such adjustments are made in Chapter 4. For Hannaford, the analyst would add back to the net income of $70,201, the depreciation of $69,016. It changes in such things as accounts receivable, inventories, accounts payable, and property, plant, and equipment of $109,219. The total adjusted earnings would be $100,199. The adjusted ROE would be 19.3 percent, and the resulting spread 8.5 percent.

EVA®, a similar ratio, is a proprietary version of the adjusted spread analysis.[26]

To determine whether this ratio is useful, analysts often compare the spread to the market-to-book value. This comparison suggests that investors can see beyond accrual accounting to the real value being created by the company, and reflect this value in the stock price. Since Hannaford's management, at least in 1995, had a very positive spread, we would expect investors to be pleased. The market-to-book value is 206.9%. This shows that investors have recognized the value that Hannaford has created. The average spreads for a variety of industries are shown in Exhibit 1-13. In Exhibit 1-14, you can see the relationship between the value created by the company, as measured by the spread, and the value recognized by shareholders, as represented by the market-to-book value either over time or for a number of companies. You will note that this ratio is for one year at a time, and reflects, in the main, investors' optimism or pessimism about the future. For some of the industries portrayed, for instance computer peripheral equipment, in spite of the 1995 return on equity, investors were very optimistic about the future.

Another ratio, **dividend yield**, indicates the return on a stock investment provided by the current dividend payment.

---

[26] A variation on the spread is called **economic value added**, or EVA®, as it is practiced by one consulting company. Here the adjusted earnings are before interest charges and are adjusted for noncash charges—charges that have no impact on the economic, real earnings of the company in that period. Adjustments would be made for such things as the present value of employees' benefits and goodwill that comes from an acquisition. The required return on capital is the return that capital providers require the company to earn. Required return on capital is discussed in Appendix B of Chapter 7.

EXHIBIT 1-14   The Spread and Market/Book Value for a Variety of Industries and Hannaford—1995

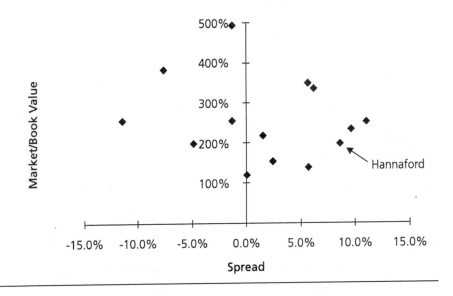

$$\text{Dividend yield} = \frac{\text{Dividends per share}}{\text{Market price per share}}$$

$$= \frac{\$0.42}{\$25.375}$$

$$= 0.017 \text{ or } 1.7\%$$

Hannaford's shareholders received a 1.7 percent dividend yield.

Of course, dividends are only part of the return investors expect from their investment in common stock; the remainder comes from the potential growth in future dividends that results from wise investment of the profits retained by the company. Usually companies with higher dividend yields are expected to have lower growth in future dividends. Since they are paying more of their earnings out in the form of current dividends, these companies typically have lower sustainable growth rates. Companies with lower current dividends usually are retaining more of their profits for future growth. This was reflected in their sustainable growth rates as shown in Exhibit 1-13.

This discussion of ratios is not intended to be all-inclusive. Rather, it is intended only to illustrate the types of ratios that may be calculated to provide the analyst or manager with insights into the performance of the corporation. Any number of ratios can be computed; the important consideration is to determine what information is relevant to the problem at hand, and then to undertake the appropriate analysis.

IV. COMPARATIVE RATIO ANALYSIS

Calculating the ratios or percentages is relatively simple. The critical ingredient in a useful analysis is the analyst's interpretation of these figures. To interpret the ratios, analysts generally compare a company's performance to that (1) from various time periods, (2) of one or more companies in the same industry, and (3) of the average performance of the industry. To ensure comparability of the results, and to be able to explain the differences in performance among various time periods or companies, the analyst must thoroughly understand the company, its products, marketing techniques, organization, the industry, and the way the ratios were calculated. Furthermore, the financial statements used to prepare the various ratios must be based on comparable accounting procedures or properly adjusted statements.

Using the Hannaford Bros. Co. financial statements as an example, we can see how much more we can discover about the company's performance by making such comparisons.

1. Historical Comparisons

The easiest first step in making historical comparisons is to do a full analysis of the components in the company's sustainable growth rate over time. This analysis, showing the five relevant ratios for Hannaford from 1991 to 1995, is given in Exhibit 1-15.

As you might have expected, Hannaford's 1991 performance was its worst in the past five years. The recession in the United States, with the decline in consumer spending, had an effect on the company. Particularly affected was the company's return on sales. However, given that people have to eat, the cyclical effects are not as dramatic as they would be for a consumer nondurable goods company such as a General Motors. What happened? An analysis of the component percentages of Hannaford's financial statements can help us determine the source of the change.

Exhibit 1-16 makes just such a comparison for the income statement. This comparison shows that cost of sales was the largest component of the company's expenses and that it increased at the end of the period. However, Hannaford had decreases in selling, general, and administrative costs, and

EXHIBIT 1-15 Hannaford Bros. Co.—Sustainable Growth Rate Component Analysis

	1991	1992	1993	1994	1995
Return on sales	2.16%	2.38%	2.66%	2.72%	2.73%
Total asset turnover	284.61	268.80	258.36	261.14	267.00
Assets to equity	236.91	222.27	200.49	193.10	185.44
Earnings retention	75.38	74.70	73.47	74.51	74.80
Sustainable growth rate	10.97	10.63	10.11	10.21	10.11

EXHIBIT 1-16 Hannaford Bros. Co.—Component Percentages for Consolidated Income Statements

	1991	1992	1993	1994	1995
Net sales	100.0%	100.0%	100.0%	100.0%	100.0%
Cost of sales	75.4	75.1	75.1	75.4	76.0
Selling and general expenses	20.0	19.9	19.4	19.1	18.7
Interest income	0.1	0.1	0.2	0.1	0.1
Interest expense	-1.1	-1.1	-1.1	-1.0	-0.9
Income taxes	1.5	1.6	1.8	1.8	1.8
Net income	2.2%	2.4%	2.7%	2.7%	2.7%

interest expense remained relatively flat. The combination of these changes improved the return on sales from a low of 2.16 percent in 1991 to 1995's high of 2.73 percent.

If you look further into these numbers, you will see that Hannaford acquired Wilson's Supermarkets in 1994, and opened more than 20 new stores over the course of 1994 and 1995. Moreover, over the past four years, Hannaford increased its net selling square footage by more than 75 percent. A key driver behind this growth was an increase in the number of combination stores operated by Hannaford. Combination stores, similar to so-called super-centers, offer expanded lines of general merchandise, videos, and other services in addition to the traditional all-department supermarket. The company views the key benefit to combination stores as being a higher revenue per square foot than basic supermarkets.[27] These increases in sales and profits were accomplished despite intense supermarket and expanding supercenter competition from Sam's Club, BJ's Wholesale, and Price/CostCo.

In addition to component analysis, the analyst can examine the growth in various accounts over the same periods. **Percentage change analysis** can be used to determine the relative change in an item (expense, income, asset, or liability) over time, since the magnitude of raw data can mask the changes. The analyst can then compare these percentage changes with the changes in related items over the same time period. Exhibit 1-17 shows this analysis for Hannaford. As you can see, this analysis gives you the change in each account each year.

2. Comparisons With Other Companies

Another type of analysis that is useful for analyzing a particular company's performance is to contrast two or more companies. Because financial require-

---

[27] Revenue per square foot is one of those industry-specific ratios we discussed earlier.

EXHIBIT 1-17   Hannaford Bros. Co.—Year-To-Year Statement
of Earnings Percentage Change

	1992	1993	1994	1995
Net sales	2.89%	-0.54%	11.53%	12.06%
Cost of sales	2.58	-0.53	11.95	12.89
Selling and general expenses	2.50	-2.93	9.54	9.93
Interest income	-0.15	74.40	-42.03	19.87
Interest expense	-0.15	0.73	2.20	-6.72
Income taxes	10.89	15.71	11.93	9.91
Net income	13.48%	11.00%	14.07%	12.70%

ments and uses of funds differ among industries, it is important that companies chosen for comparison first be limited to those within the same industry. Such an analysis is shown in Exhibit 1-18. Data for Winn-Dixie, another company in the supermarket industry, are compared with data for Hannaford.

The differences between the two companies lie in return on sales and total asset turnover. While Hannaford only recently embarked on an expansion, Winn-Dixie has actively engaged in expansion through new stores and acquisitions over ten years. In addition, Hannaford has maintained a policy of retaining more earnings to fuel growth while Winn-Dixie has sought to pay out more earnings to shareholders. However, Winn-Dixie has done a better job of utilizing its assets: its asset turnover is nearly twice that of Hannaford. As a result of this analysis, the analyst would determine that the higher TATO generated by Winn-Dixie is the principal factor leading to the difference between the two companies' returns on equity.

3. Comparisons With the Industry

Comparisons can include several companies or all of those in the relevant industry. Typically, industrywide comparisons are based on industry averages.

EXHIBIT 1-18   Comparison of Hannaford Bros. Co.
With Winn-Dixie Stores, Inc., 1995

	Hannaford	Winn-Dixie
Return on sales	2.73%	2.00%
Total asset turnover	267.00	474.75
Return on assets	7.30	9.35
Assets to equity	185.44	200.08
Dividend payout	25.20	49.68
Sustainable growth rate	10.11	9.56

These averages are available from several sources that collect and publish the data. Exhibit 1-19 compares the 1995 Hannaford data with 1995 industry averages.[28] Because of financial differences in companies of differing sizes, analysts commonly select from the industry a sample of companies that correspond in size with the target company. Such a selection was made in preparing Exhibit 1-19.

An analysis of the data indicates that Hannaford's performance compares favorably with that of the industry. It's cost of goods sold was lower than the industry average, giving Hannaford a higher after-tax profit margin of 2.73 percent as compared with 1.09 percent for the industry.

An analyst should assess a number of other things in looking at a company. If the performance being analyzed occurred over a period during which there was a significant change in industry or economic conditions (for instance, inflation), the analyst might want to look at the company's relative performance. For instance, factoring out inflation-driven growth might give the analyst quite a different view of a company's real growth over a period. How extensive the analysis is depends, in part, on how the analyst will use the results.

V. SUMMARY

Using the major external sources of financial information, the financial statements, an analyst can learn a great deal about the financial performance of a company through comparative ratio analysis. Calculating a ratio is not a difficult skill. It is in the choice of ratios and the interpretation of the results where skill is required.

Proper interpretation requires an understanding of the company as well as of the environment. Critical issues that need to be considered are general economic conditions, the competitive situation, and the business and financial

EXHIBIT 1-19   Comparison Of Hannaford Bros. Co. Ratios
With Those of the Industry, 1995

	Hannaford	Supermarket Industry Average
Return on sales	2.73%	1.09%
Total asset turnover	267.00	336.00
Return on assets	7.30	3.67
Assets to equity	185.44	362.00
Dividend payout	25.20	26.05
Sustainable growth rate	10.11	9.80

[28] These are the most recent data available. Because of the delay in collecting and compiling the data, industry data often lag behind individual companies' reported financial information.

strategies of the company. All of these factors, individually and in combination, affect the financial results for the company and the value that will be earned by the company's owners, its shareholders.

SELECTED REFERENCES

Sources of industry data and financial ratios are found in current issues of:

Dun & Bradstreet, *Industry Norms and Key Business Ratios.*

Robert Morris Associates, *Annual Statement Studies.*

Troy, Leo. *Almanac of Business and Industrial Financial Ratios.* Englewood Cliffs, N.J.: Prentice Hall.

The concept of sustainable growth is discussed in:

Copeland, Tom, Tim Koller, and Jack Murring. *Valuation: Measuring and Managing the Value of Companies.* New York: John Wiley & Sons, 1990.

Higgins, Robert C. "How Much Growth Can a Firm Afford?" *Financial Management,* Fall 1977, pp. 7-16.

Rappaport, Alfred, *Creating Shareholder Value.* New York: The Free Press, 1986.

Shapiro, Alan C. *Modern Corporate Finance.* 2nd ed. New York: Macmillan, 1994, chaps. 11 and 24.

Van Horne, James C. "Sustainable Growth Modeling." *Journal of Corporate Finance,* Winter 1987, pp. 19-25.

For discussion of the impact of inflation on ratio analysis, see:

Brigham, Eugene F., and Louis C. Gapenski. *Financial Management.* 7th ed. Fort Worth, Texas: The Dryden Press, 1994, chap. 2.

Fraser, Lyn M. *Understanding Financial Statements: Through the Maze of a Corporate Annual Report.* Reston, Va.: Reston Publishing, 1985.

Shapiro, Alan C. *Modern Corporate Finance.* 2nd ed. New York: Macmillan, 1994, chap. 22.

For information about spread and EVA® analysis, see:

Stern, Joel M., G. Bennett Stewart III, and Donald H. Chew, Jr. "The EVA® Financial Management System," *Journal of Applied Corporate Finance,* Summer 1995, pp. 32-47.

For further information on ratio analysis, see:

Brealey, Richard A., and Alan Marcus. *Fundamentals of Corporate Finance.* New York: McGraw-Hill, 1995, chap. 2.

Brealey, Richard A., and Stewart C. Myers. *Principles of Corporate Finance.* 4th ed. New York: McGraw-Hill, 1991, chap. 27.

Brigham, Eugene F., and Louis C. Gapenski. *Financial Management.* 7th ed. Fort Worth, Texas: The Dryden Press, 1994, chap. 2.

Gitman, Lawrence J. *Principles of Managerial Finance.* New York: Harper Collins, chaps. 3 and 4.

Gordon, Gus. *Understanding Financial Statements.* Cincinnati, OH: South-Western Publishing Co.

Pinches, George E. *Financial Management.* New York: Harper Collins, 1994, chap. 24.

Ross, Steven A., Randolph W. Westerfield, and Jeffrey F. Jaffe. *Corporate Finance.* 3rd ed. Homewood, Ill.: Richard D. Irwin, 1993, chap. 2.

Ross, Steven A., Randolph W. Westerfield, and Bradford D. Jordon. *Fundamentals of Corporate Finance.* 3rd ed. Homewood, Ill.: Richard D. Irwin, 1995, chaps. 2 and 3.

Shapiro, Alan C. *Modern Corporate Finance.* 2nd ed. New York: Macmillan, 1994, chaps. 22 and 23.

Weston, J. Fred, and Eugene F. Brigham. *Essentials of Managerial Finance.* 10th ed. Hinsdale, Ill.: Dryden Press, 1993, chap. 2.

STUDY QUESTIONS

1. Melissa Hampton was reviewing the recent performance of the EASY Chair Company, a company with a reputation for producing high-quality home furniture. Over the years, the name EASY had become synonymous with a kind of chair called a recliner. By 1996, the company was producing a variety of home furnishings, including reclining sofas, sleep sofas, living room cabinets, upholstered furniture, and solid-wood dining room furniture. In the past decade, the company had also entered the office furniture business by producing office systems and patient seating for clinics and hospitals. To determine the impact that diversification and expansion had on EASY, Ms. Hampton collected the following data for the company:

EASY CHAIR COMPANY
FINANCIAL DATA
(dollars in millions)

	1992	1993	1994	1995	1996
Sales	$341.7	$420.0	$486.8	$553.2	$592.3
Net income	$23.0	$24.7	$26.5	$27.5	$28.3
Dividends per share	$0.4	$0.4	$0.4	$0.5	$0.5
Number of shares	18.3	18.4	18.3	17.9	17.9
Total assets	$233.0	$269.9	$336.6	$349.0	$361.9
Total equity	$147.0	$165.3	$178.8	$194.3	$214.6

a. How has EASY's sustainable growth rate changed over time? What caused the changes?
b. The home furniture industry has the following ratios over the same time. How did EASY compare with the industry?

HOME FURNITURE INDUSTRY RATIOS

	1993	1994	1995	1996
Return on equity	15.74%	15.31%	15.54%	15.12%
Retention rate	72.00	71.00	71.00	71.00
Sustainable growth rate	11.33	10.87	11.03	10.73

2. Perplexed by the declining rate of growth of EASY's net income, Melissa Hampton pressed the company management for more detailed information. The management asks you, one of EASY's financial analysts, to compute component and percentage changes for the following statements and determine if there were any positive or negative trends.

EASY CHAIR COMPANY
INCOME STATEMENT
(in millions)

	1993	1994	1995	1996
Net sales	$ 420.0	$ 486.8	$ 553.2	$ 592.3
Cost of sales	(289.8)	(352.1)	(397.8)	(430.4)
Gross profit	130.2	134.7	155.4	161.9
Selling, general, and administrative expense	(85.5)	(91.4)	(106.9)	(111.6)
Income from operations	44.7	43.3	48.5	50.3
Interest expense	(1.9)	(4.0)	(7.6)	(7.2)
Other income	2.1	2.7	3.1	2.5
Income before taxes	44.9	42.0	44.0	45.6
Taxes	(20.3)	(15.5)	(16.5)	(17.3)
Net income	$ 24.6	$ 26.5	$ 27.5	$ 28.3

3. Ms. Hampton is not satisfied with EASY's performance. She believes that the company can achieve the following ratios:

EASY CHAIR COMPANY
MS. HAMPTON'S TARGET RATIOS

Dividend payout	45.0%
Market price	$15.00
Dividend yield	5.2%
Number of shares outstanding	18,000
Return on equity	13.7%
Long-term debt/equity	27.3
Current ratio	551.0
Acid-test ratio	407.3
Profit margin	5.1%
Gross margin	27.6
Return on assets	9.4
Inventory turnover	733.3
Operating profit	8.7%
Accounts receivable collection period	92.5 days
Accounts payable payment period	20.8 days
Tax rate	34.0%

Using Ms. Hampton's target ratios for EASY, complete the following financial statements:

EASY CHAIR COMPANY
MS. HAMPTON'S REVISED FINANCIAL STATEMENTS

Income Statement
Sales	_____
Cost of sales	_____
Gross profit	_____
Selling, general, and administrative expense	_____
Operating profit	_____
Interest	_____
Earnings before taxes	_____
Taxes	_____
Net income	_____

Balance Sheet
Cash	_____
Accounts receivable	_____
Inventory	_____
Total current assets	_____
Net property, plant, and equipment	_____
Total assets	_____
Accounts payable	_____
Other current liabilities	_____
Total current liabilities	_____
Long-term debt	_____
Total liabilities	_____
Owners' equity	_____
Total liabilities and owners' equity	_____
Dividends per share	_____

4. As the new financial analyst for Peterson's Chemicals, you have been asked to analyze the profitability problems encountered during the last two years. Current financial statements and selected industry averages are as follows:

PETERSON'S CHEMICALS
FINANCIAL STATEMENTS
(in millions)

Income Statement

	1995	1996
Sales	$ 1,435	$ 1,478
Cost of goods sold	(1,076)	(1,182)
Gross profit	359	296
Selling and administrative expenses	(445)	(443)
Operating profit	(86)	(147)
Interest expense	(29)	(27)
Net income	$ (115)	$ (174)

Balance Sheet

	1995	1996
Cash and equivalent	$ 76	$ 120
Accounts receivable, net	437	432
Inventory	284	324
Other current assets	38	37
Total current assets	835	913
Plant, property, and equipment	375	300
Total assets	$ 1,210	$ 1,213
Accounts payable	$ 412	$ 500
Other current liabilities	98	309
Total current liabilities	510	809
Long-term debt	300	178
Total liabilities	810	987
Owners' equity	400	226
Total liabilities and owners' equity	$ 1,210	$ 1,213

Using the financial statements, how does Peterson's compare to the following industry averages for 1995 and 1996?

CHEMICAL INDUSTRY AVERAGES

	Industry Ratios
Current ratio	150%
Acid-test ratio	90%
Receivables collection period	65 days
Payables payment period	60 days
Debt/equity	110%
Return on assets	7%
Return on equity	19%

5. Peterson's management has decided to reexamine the company's short-term credit policies. The chief financial officer estimates that reducing the receivables collection period to 78 days would result in a sales decrease of 3 percent. The purchasing department reports that by reducing the payables period to 68.5 days, discounts would be available that would reduce the cost of goods by 9 percent. Initially the cash required to finance these changes would come from additional long-term debt, resulting in a debt to equity ratio of 100 percent. As an analyst:

a. determine whether Peterson's Chemicals would have been profitable if management had made these changes at the beginning of 1996.

b. determine how the ROE and ROA would have been affected.

c. prepare new financial statements to reflect these changes.

Cross-Border Ratio Analysis[1]

One problem that can arise in ratio analysis is the problem of comparability: ratios cannot be used to compare two companies or industries if the accounting principles used by one firm differ from the principles used by the other firm. This is true whether the accounting affects the value of an asset, a liability, income, or an expense. Thus, it is important to understand the accounting principles that are being used, and to take those differences into account in making an analysis.

Understanding the general accounting principles U.S. firms use can be difficult; once the accounting rules are learned and understood, the task of comparing companies is relatively straightforward. While U.S. accounting rules allow some discretion about how some items are valued (e.g., inventory), the methods of accounting must be described in the footnotes to the financial statements. Thus, differences between the rules used by different companies can be noted and taken into account.

When comparing the financial statements of companies from different countries, the analyst has a much harder job. Accounting standards vary widely from country to country and, until recently, companies in many countries were not required to disclose the accounting principles on which their financial reports were created.[2]

In making industry comparisons, analysts choose to deal with this problem in two ways. First, many analysts simply ignore companies that operate using accounting principles from another country. This, however, is a dangerous approach. As world commerce becomes increasingly global, the analyst might ignore a major competitor, a significant industry participant, or a potentially interesting investment opportunity.

Other analysts take a different approach: they examine the worldwide industry but ignore differences in the methods of accounting. This approach purports to give the analyst a view of the global industry, but as you will see,

---

[1] This appendix was prepared with James Parrino, Telesis Consulting Group, Holliston, MA, and with assistance from Gary S. Schieneman, Smith New Court, New York.

[2] Various accounting groups around the world have attempted to harmonize the disparate accounting rules and principles. The result of these efforts is the *International Accounting Standards*, published by the International Accounting Standards Committee. These standards are being followed in most countries and have resulted in disclosure of the accounting principles on which the statements are prepared, but they have not resulted in a single set of accounting principles.

it can be very distorted. The error in this approach is amply demonstrated by Exhibit 1A-1, which shows data from non-U.S. companies that have been adjusted to meet U.S. generally accepted accounting principles (GAAP).[3] In this exhibit you can see how big an impact on reported performance a change in accounting principles can have. It is important to note that we do not suggest that one accounting system is superior to another, even though it may be. The point of this appendix is that different systems result in different reported performance, and the analyst must take these differences into account. This exhibit is not intended as a criticism of any accounting system, only a demonstration of the dangers that await the unwary.

If you are just becoming familiar with the accounting rules of one country, then how significant these accounting principle-based differences can be might not have been obvious to you. As an example of how distortions can occur, let's look at two ways of accounting for money spent on research and development.

Some accounting systems treat money spent on research and development as an expense, and thus deduct the cost from income in the year it was spent. Other accounting systems consider research and development an investment made in the company's future, and therefore treat it as an investment. As with any investment, it is capitalized by adding the cost to the balance in the long-term asset account and amortizing it over time. These two methods of dealing with research and development (R&D) reflect different philosophies regarding R&D. The philosophical difference is reflected in the resulting financial statements. The difference can be clearly seen in Exhibit 1A-2.

The companies shown in this exhibit are identical, except that one expenses its $20,000 in R&D and the other capitalizes it.[4] You will note that every major ratio calculated from the two sets of financial statements is affected by this accounting principle difference. In fact, the impact is even felt in the sustainable growth rates: the company that expenses R&D has a negative SGR, while the capitalizing company's SGR is positive. Remember, these companies are identical in every way, except the accounting for R&D: they earned and spent the same amount of money during the year.[5]

Obviously the difference between these two methods of accounting for R&D is timing—when the money spent is reported on the income statement. For the company that expenses R&D, it impacts the income statement in the year it is spent. The capitalizing company spreads out the impact over time. This difference in timing is at the root of most of the differences in accounting principles, and thus it is a useful thing to keep in mind.

---

[3]   Generally accepted accounting principles means accepted by the accounting organization operating in that jurisdiction, not that any particular set of principles is really generally accepted around the world.

[4]   We have used a dollar sign ($) to denote currency. This is for a matter of convenience only.

[5]   The question of whether they are identical or not actually depends on the tax code which impacts the amount of taxes that each would pay.

EXHIBIT 1A-1 Telecommunications Equipment Producers, 1986:
Financial Statement Changes To Adjust To U.S. Generally Accepted Accounting Principles

Company	Change in		Return on Assets		Return on Equity	
	Net Income	*Equity*	*Reported*	*Adjusted*	*Reported*	*Adjusted*
Mitel, Canada	7.4%	(20.1)%	(10.0)%	(9.4)%	(22.6)%	(21.1)%
Bell, Canada	(15.3)	(6.9)	4.9	4.2	14.0	12.6
Sumitomo Electric	(5.9)	(2.3)	2.6	2.4	8.7	8.4
Siemens	40.1	30.7	2.8	4.0	11.1	12.3
Philips	(11.0)	(12.4)	1.9	1.8	6.3	6.2
Ericsson	16.2	17.9	1.5	-1.8	8.2	8.1
British Telecom	14.9	(32.5)	9.0	10.0	20.7	40.0
GEC	(1.0)	2.0	8.4	8.3	16.6	16.2
Racal	(19.6)	50.4	3.6	2.6	10.5	6.6
Standard Telephone & Cables	(27.1)	60.1	8.4	4.8	22.0	9.4
NEC, U.S.	N.A.	N.A.	0.6	0.6	3.0	3.0

N.A. = Not applicable, because accounting is already by U.S. GAAP.

SOURCE: Speech given by Gary S. Schieneman, Smith New Court, to Association for Investment Management and Research and the European Federation of Financial Analysts Societies, November 1991, London, England.

EXHIBIT 1A-2 Impact of Expensing or Capitalizing
Research and Development Expenses

	Expensing Research and Development	Capitalizing Research and Development
Income Statement		
Revenues, net	$ 100,000	$ 100,000
Cost of sales	(45,000)	(45,000)
Other	0	0
Gross margin	55,000	55,000
Other costs and expenses:		
General and administrative	(20,000)	(20,000)
Depreciation and amortization	(7,500)	(7,500)
Research and development	(20,000)	0
Total costs and expenses	47,500	27,500
Earnings before interest and taxes	7,500	27,500
Net interest	(1,000)	(1,000)
Earnings before taxes	6,500	26,500
Income taxes	(2,145)	(8,745)
Net income from continuing operations	4,355	8,745
Net income	$ 4,355	$ 17,755
Balance Sheet		
Assets		
Cash and equivalents	$ 10,000	$ 10,000
Receivables, net	45,000	45,000
Inventories	35,000	35,000
Total current assets	90,000	90,000
Gross property, plant, and equipment	400,000	420,000
Accumulated depreciation	(150,000)	(150,000)
Net property, plant, and equipment	250,000	270,000
Total long-term assets	250,000	270,000
Total assets	$ 340,000	$ 360,000
Liabilities and Net Worth		
Accounts payable	$ 75,000	$ 75,000
Income taxes payable	10,000	10,000
Accruals	3,000	3,000
Total current liabilities	88,000	88,000
Long-term debt	125,000	125,000
Total long-term debt	125,000	125,000
Total long-term liabilities	125,000	125,000
Total liabilities	213,000	213,000
Common equity	127,000	147,000
Total net worth	127,000	147,000
Total liabilities and net worth	$ 340,000	$ 360,000

EXHIBIT 1A-2   *(continued)*

	Expensing Research and Development	Capitalizing Research and Development
Ratio Analysis		
Leverage Ratios		
Quick	62.50%	62.50%
Current	102.27	102.27
Assets/net worth	267.72	244.90
Long-term debt/total assets	36.76	34.72
Long-term debt/total capital	49.60	45.96
Noncurrent assets/net worth	196.85	183.67
Activity Ratios		
Sales/receivables	222.22%	222.22%
Average collection period	164 days	164 days
Sales/payables	133.33%	133.33%
Average payables period (cost of goods sold)	608 days	608 days
Inventory turnover	128.57%	128.57%
Fixed charge coverage	750.00%	2750.00%
Fixed asset turnover	40.00%	37.04%
Total asset turnover	29.41%	27.78%
Sustainable Growth Analysis		
(1) Earnings/revenue	4.36%	17.76%
(2) Revenue/assets	29.41	27.78
(3) Earnings/assets (3) = (1) × (2)	1.28	4.93
(4) Assets/net worth	267.72	244.90
(5) Return on equity (5) = (3) × (4)	3.43	12.07
(6) Dividend payout ratio	312.28	76.60
(7) Sustainable growth rate	(7.28)	2.83

The R&D example also shows how big an impact on financial performance different accounting methods can have. To understand the relative performance of two companies operating under different accounting principles, we must adjust the statements to a common standard.

In our increasingly global world, where a company of interest might be operated from a country other than the analyst's, it is important to know the accounting rules for that country. Accountants in a country know the accounting rules and usually do a good job of keeping track of changes in them, while analysts unfamiliar with the accounting rules must understand in detail the accounting rules that govern the company they are analyzing. Sometimes the differences in accounting rules between countries can be difficult to discover. For the analyst who wants to analyze the performance of an industry, memorizing the rules for each of several countries is a difficult task. For the novice, nonaccountant analyst, the task is impossible.

This is not to suggest that there is nothing to be done. There are some basic choices that must be made in creating an accounting system, and understanding those differences will help the analyst begin the task of analysis. In general, the main differences are in standards for valuing assets and liabilities and recording revenues and expenses. This appendix gives you some simple rules about differences in accounting principles that will enable you to begin to analyze companies from different countries. However, the appendix is designed only to give you a basic introduction to the differences that exist. It will not make you an expert in any accounting system. For those whose company or clients depend upon the quality of the analysis, much more expertise is needed.

I. BASIC ACCOUNTING PRINCIPLES

Why do differences in accounting principles exist? The differences are caused primarily by:

1. **Culture.** Accounting standards reflect a society's attitude toward business. Countries that have a distrust of business will usually require strict disclosure, and companies will be given few choices about how to do their accounting. This factor has a major impact on the accounting standards.
2. **Level of economic development.** Accounting systems generally reflect the level of economic development in the economy.
3. **Legal requirements.** Accounting systems are developed to serve the needs of those who will use the financial statements. In general, accounting systems are either mandated by law or by an institution that represents the accounting profession.[6] In countries with legally mandated systems, the government plays a dominant role in the development of the rules, and little or no differences exist between the financial and tax accounting systems. The goal is to control the corporation and collect taxes. Nonlegalistic systems are generally developed to serve groups interested in the company's performance, such as lenders and shareholders.

The accounting principles used throughout the world are relatively few. Any accounting system must report a company's liabilities and assets, its expenses and revenues. In addition, every accounting system must deal with problems created by foreign operations and inflation. Once an analyst understands the basic principles, understanding the rules for any country becomes manageable.

---

[6]   In the United States, that group is the American Institute of Certified Public Accountants, and the rules are changed by its Financial Accounting Standards Board. A detailed description of the accounting rules for each country can be obtained from the body that regulates accounting in that country.

There are many items that change from system to system. In this appendix, we will discuss asset valuation and the effects of inflation in detail.[7] Let us begin with the assets.

II. INVENTORY

A company invests in all kinds of assets. One asset that can be accounted for in a number of different ways is inventory. If the cost of any item held in inventory (e.g., raw materials used in manufacturing a product awaiting sale) changes from the time it is purchased to the time it is used to produce the goods for sale, the method of inventory valuation impacts the financial statements.[8] There are several methods that can be used to value inventory.[9]

1. **First-in, first-out** (FIFO): the cost attributed to the item removed from inventory is based on the cost of the oldest item in inventory.
2. **Last-in, first-out** (LIFO): the cost attributed to the item removed from inventory is based on the cost of the most recently purchased item in inventory.
3. **Weighted-average cost:** the cost attributed to the item removed from inventory is based on the average cost of the items in inventory.
4. **Specific identification:** the cost attributed to the item removed from inventory is the price paid for the specific item when it was purchased. This is the most accurate of the historically based methods, but it is expensive to maintain a record of prices. Thus, it is used for very large and expensive items held in inventory.

Exhibit 1A-3 shows an example of how a company's cost of goods sold and inventory accounts would look at the end of its first year of operations under these different inventory accounting methods. For the analyst, the inventory method chosen determines the allocation of the inventory's value between the income statement (cost of goods sold) and the balance sheet (inventory). Furthermore, the method chosen impacts which of two accounts, cost of goods sold or inventory, is a more accurate reflection of its actual economic value. For example, when prices for an item have risen, LIFO attributes a realistic cost to the income statement's cost of goods sold, but leaves the balance sheet's inventory undervalued. When prices are declining, the reverse would be true.

---

[7] As you read the rest of this appendix, remember that the differences in performance that come from using different accounting principles often are the result of differences in when a particular item (e.g., research and development) is reported and/or the actual value of what is being reported (e.g., how to translate foreign exchange or how to account for inflation).
[8] All inventory accounting methods assign the same value to inventory if no change has occurred in the cost of the item in inventory from the time of its purchase to the time of its sale.
[9] Several more exotic methods of inventory valuation are used in a limited number of countries, for instance, base stock, latest purchase price, and next-in, next-out. These methods are not as widely used, however, as those described in the text. Thus, the interested reader should consult the references listed at the end of this appendix for a further explanation.

EXHIBIT 1A-3   Inventory Valuation Method's Impact on Inventory and Cost of Goods Sold (as of December 31)

Method	Inventory Value	Cost of Goods Sold
FIFO	$200	$600
LIFO	100	700
Weighted average	350	450
Specific identification	150	650

Assuming:

Date	Transaction
January 1	Purchase 1,200 units for $0.50.
April 1	Purchase 200 units for $1.00.
July	Sell 600 units from the January 1 purchase.
October	Sell 600 units (500 from January 1 purchase and 100 from April 1 purchase).
December 31	Market price for each new unit, $1.25.

The differences that can result in the inventory and cost of goods sold values are wide, and the problem for the analyst can be seen when looking at performance ratios. The ratios are shown in Exhibit 1A-5 and were created from data in Exhibit 1A-4.

III. INFLATION

Thus far, the differences in the ratios we have shown are the result of differences in accounting methods. At a time of inflation, both the financial information and the actual performance can be distorted. Let's use an example to see how the distortions can occur before discussing how the data might be adapted for comparability.

Exhibit 1A-6 shows the monthly income statements for a company operating in a world where inflation is 25 percent. If you did not know that the company was in an inflationary environment, you would think that the company's sales were increasing. However, the unit volume was 10 units per month, and did not change over the period shown. Inflation has distorted our view of the real performance. We can compensate for this problem by thinking in real (adjusted for inflation) terms instead of nominal (unadjusted for inflation) terms. The real and nominal statements are shown in the last two columns of Exhibit 1A-6. Revenues started the period at $100 and, by the end of the 12 months, reached $1,455. In real terms, the value of revenues was still $100.

EXHIBIT 1A-4   Effects of Different Accounting Methods for Inventory*

	FIFO	LIFO	Weighted Average	Specific Identification
Income Statement				
Revenue	$1,000	$1,000	$1,000	$1,000
Cost of goods sold	(600)	(700)	(450)	(650)
Selling, general, and administrative	(100)	(100)	(100)	(100)
Operating profit	300	200	450	250
Depreciation	(50)	(50)	(50)	(50)
Research and development	(50)	(50)	(50)	(50)
Earnings before income taxes	200	100	350	150
Interest	(50)	(50)	(50)	(50)
Earnings before tax	150	50	300	100
Taxes	(60)	(20)	(120)	(40)
Net income	$ 90	$ 30	$ 180	$ 60
Balance Sheet				
Assets				
Cash	$ 50	$ 90	$ (10)	$ 70
Accounts receivable	250	250	250	250
Inventory	200	100	350	150
Property, plant, and equipment, net	400	400	400	400
Other assets	100	100	100	100
Total assets	$1,000	$ 940	$1,090	$ 970
Liabilities and Equity				
Accounts payable	$ 250	$ 250	$ 250	$ 250
Long-term debt	400	400	400	400
Deferred tax	0	0	0	0
Common equity	100	100	100	100
Retained Earnings:				
Beginning of year	160	160	160	160
Net income	90	30	180	60
Retained earnings, end of year	250	190	340	220
Total equity	350	290	440	320
Total liabilities and equity	$1,000	$ 940	$1,090	$ 970

* For simplicity, taxes for reporting purposes equal the actual tax liability. Differences in taxes are accounted for by changes in cash.

EXHIBIT 1A-5   Ratios That Result from Different Methods of Inventory Valuation

Method	ROS	Sales/Assets	Assets/Equity	ROE
FIFO	9%	100%	286%	25.7%
LIFO	3	106	324	10.3
Weighted average	18	92	248	40.9
Specific identification	6	103	303	18.8

This straightforward example assumes that costs rise with inflation (cost of goods sold is 50 percent each month), but this assumption is true only if the proper method for accounting for inventory is used.[10] Even then, the inventory account could be seriously misvalued. As you can see, inflation poses an especially difficult problem for accounting, since it can cause major distortions in financial performance. It is these distortions that the analyst must attempt to understand.[11]

Inflation can distort both the income statement and the balance sheet in a variety of ways, and accounting systems in different countries deal with the problem in different ways. Some ignore the problem, while others have developed sophisticated methods to correct for the distortions created by inflation.[12] The inflation-adjustment methods are, however, variations of two approaches: general price-level or specific price-level adjustments.

1. General Price-Level Adjustment

General price-level adjustments are also called constant dollar accounting. This method adjusts for decreases in the value of the currency that accompany inflation.[13] Conceptually, adjustments are made so that the revenues, expenses, assets, and liabilities are reported in units of the same purchasing power. The objective is to provide a realistic look at the performance of the company.

....

[10]   Both LIFO and the latest-purchase methods are more likely to compensate for the problems created by inflation than either FIFO or weighted-average cost. This is because they transfer goods from inventory to cost of goods sold at more current prices, and the resulting income better represents what the company actually earned. However, the inventory is not valued realistically. If a company uses a method such as FIFO in a time of inflation, unless inventory is turned over very rapidly, the cost of inventory charged to cost of goods sold misstates its real (current) cost and results in a misstatement of income.

[11]   In spite of the fact that accountants like to believe that financial statements can be made to reflect financial performance, in times of high inflation, financial statements do not provide such information.

[12]   In countries that have had high inflation for long periods of time, accountants have more sophisticated approaches to adjusting financial statements for inflation. Brazil and Argentina, for example, have well-developed inflation-accounting systems

[13]   The example in Exhibit 1A-6 shows the impact of inflation on the value of the currency.

EXHIBIT 1A-6 Impact of Inflation on Revenues, Costs, and Unit Volume: Nominal Income Statements with 25 Percent Inflation

Month	Nominal													Real
	0	1	2	3	4	5	6	7	8	9	10	11	12	12
Revenues	$100	$125	$156	$195	$244	$305	$381	$477	$596	$745	$931	$1,164	$1,455	$100
Costs	(50)	(62)	(78)	(98)	(122)	(153)	(191)	(238)	(298)	(373)	(466)	(582)	(728)	(50)
Gross income	50	63	78	97	122	152	190	239	298	372	465	582	727	50
Other costs	(20)	(25)	(31)	(39)	(49)	(61)	(76)	(95)	(119)	(149)	(186)	(233)	(291)	(20)
Earnings before taxes	30	38	47	58	73	91	114	144	179	223	279	349	436	30
Taxes	(10)	(13)	(16)	(20)	(25)	(31)	(39)	(49)	(61)	(76)	(95)	(119)	(148)	(10)
Net income	$ 20	$ 25	$ 31	$ 38	$ 48	$ 60	$ 75	$ 95	$ 118	$ 147	$ 184	$ 230	$ 288	$ 20
Unit volume	10	10	10	10	10	10	10	10	10	10	10	10	10	10
Real revenue	$100	$100	$100	$100	$100	$100	$100	$100	$100	$100	$100	$100	$100	$100

The analyst needs a basic understanding of how these adjustments are made and what impact they have on financial performance. The first column of Exhibit 1A-7 shows the statements that would be reported in the absence of adjustments for inflation. Because the company shown in this exhibit experienced 20 percent inflation over the period, the ratios do not really tell us the actual performance of the firm. Column 2 provides general price-level-adjusted statements for the same period.

2. Specific Price-Level Adjustments

This method, also called constant cost accounting, focuses on specific asset values rather than on the general change in purchasing power caused by inflation. Rather than the historical cost, the replacement value of the asset is used. This value can be determined through adjusting the historic value by multiplying it by an index reflecting subsequent inflation.[14] For example, the index used for fixed assets might be an appraisal or a construction-cost index. Any gain or loss as a result of the revaluation would be reported either as an inflation gain or loss on the income statement, or directly to the retained earnings account on the balance sheet. Exhibit 1A-7 Columns 2 through 5 show the result of specific price-level and constant dollar adjustments to one company's statements.

The general price-level or specific price-level adjustments can be used separately or together, and can be adjusted to some or all of the items on the financial statements. An analyst familiar with the two basic adjustment techniques is capable of interpreting the specific approach used in any country.

This section has provided a particularly brief introduction to the problem of understanding performance at a time of inflation. The problem the accountant faces is to adjust for inflation and to do so in a way that can be understood.[15] The critical analyst might not choose the specific revaluation approach employed in one country; however, the most important job of the analyst is to understand how financial performance is reported.

IV. THE IMPACT ON STATEMENTS OF NONDOMESTIC TRANSACTIONS

Few companies operate solely in one country. Many buy supplies or sell products outside their domestic environments, and many hold assets or owe liabilities in several countries. These transactions provide special challenges for accountants and particular problems in comparability for analysts. For assets

[14] In general, this index will be a government-calculated index reflecting the changes in wholesale or consumer prices. Just how the index is calculated varies from country to country, and even can vary over time.
[15] If inflation is not taken into account, distortions in accounting occur that can result in real changes in managers' behavior. For instance, the United States in the late 1970s, when managers turned to more service-oriented operations rather than asset-based investments since the depreciation drag was considerable.

EXHIBIT 1A-7 Effect of Different Accounting Methods for Inflation

	(1) No Adjustment	(2) Constant $*	(3) Constant $†	(4) Specific Cost‡	(5) Specific Cost§
Income statement					
Revenue	$1,000	$1,000	$1,000	$1,000	$1,000
Cost of goods sold	(600)	(600)	(600)	(600)	(600)
Selling, general, and administrative	(100)	(100)	(100)	(100)	(100)
Operating profit	300	300	300	300	300
Depreciation	(50)	(60)	(60)	(53)	(53)
Research and development	(50)	(50)	(50)	(50)	(50)
Earnings before interest and taxes	200	190	190	197	197
Interest	(50)	(50)	(50)	(50)	(50)
Earnings before taxes	150	140	140	147	147
Taxes	(60)	(56)	(56)	(59)	(59)
Inflation gains/losses	-0-	100	-0-	40	-0-
Net income	$ 90	$ 184	$ 84	$ 128	$ 88
Balance sheet					
Cash	$ 50	$ 54	$ 54	$ 51	$ 51
Accounts receivable	250	250	250	250	250
Inventory	200	200	200	200	200
Property, plant, and equipment (PP&E), net	400	470	470	417	417
Other assets	100	120	120	120	120
Total assets	$1,000	$1,094	$1,094	$1,038	$1,038

EXHIBIT 1A-7   (continued)

	(1) No Adjustment	(2) Constant $*	(3) Constant $†	(4) Specific Cost‡	(5) Specific Cost§
Accounts payable	$ 250	$ 250	$ 250	$ 250	$ 250
Long-term debt	400	400	400	400	400
Deferred tax	0	0	0	0	0
Common equity	100	100	100	100	100
Retained earnings:					
Beginning of year	160	160	160	160	160
Net income	90	184	84	128	88
Inflation adjustments	0	0	100	0	40
Retained earnings, end of year	250	344	344	288	288
Total equity	350	444	444	388	388
Total liabilities and equity	$1,000	$1,094	$1,094	$1,038	$1,038
Ratio analysis					
Return on sales	9.0%	18.4%	8.4%	12.8%	8.8%
Sales/assets	100.0	91.4	91.4	96.3	96.3
Return on assets	9.0	16.8	7.7	12.3	8.5
Assets/equity	285.7	246.4	246.4	267.5	267.5
Return on equity	25.7	41.4	18.9	33.0	22.7

* Inflation constant dollar application to long-term assets, holding gains (losses) flow through income statement, general price index = 1.2, depreciation based on revalued assets (net PP&E = $400 × 1.2 - change in depreciation).

† Inflation constant dollar application to long-term assets, holding gains (losses) flow directly to balance sheet, general price index = 1.2, depreciation based on revalued assets (net PP&E = $400 × 1.2 - change in depreciation).

‡ Inflation specific cost application to long-term assets, holding gains (losses) flow through income statement, general price index = 1.2, depreciation based on revalued assets, PP&E appraised at $417 (net PP&E = $420 - change in depreciation).

§ Inflation specific cost application to long-term assets, holding gains (losses) flow directly to balance sheet, general price index = 1.2, depreciation based on revalued assets, PP&E appraised at $417 (net PP&E = $420 - change in depreciation).

NOTE: For simplicity, financial tax for reporting purposes (40%) equals the actual tax liability. Differences in taxes are accounted for by changes in cash.

and liabilities held outside the domestic environment, the problem is how to translate the value from the local currency into that in which the company's statements are reported: assets and liabilities held or owed in a foreign country must be reported in the company's home currency. For revenues and expenses, the problem is how to report transactions that occur outside the company's domestic environment into the company's home currency.[16] All foreign currency problems occur because the company's statements are reported in just one currency, its home currency.

1. Foreign Exchange Transactions

The method of accounting for foreign transactions, as well as assets and liabilities held outside the company's domestic environment, can have a significant impact on the financial performance reported for a company. Unfortunately, accountants have devised no simple set of ways for dealing with these situations; thus, the analyst must be particularly alert to the accounting rules that are used by any company being analyzed.

To gain a perspective on the ways different countries choose to deal with the problem of foreign exchange transactions is to take what is called a transaction perspective.

One-Transaction Perspective. Accountants using this approach assume that gains or losses from changes in exchange rates should not be separated from the actions that initiated them—for instance, making sales abroad. Let us demonstrate this with an example.

> Assume that a U.S. company buys raw materials from a company in the United Kingdom for £375 when the dollar/pound exchange rate is $1.60/£1.00. At that time, the company's financial statements would show $600 of inventory and $600 in accounts payable. If, on April 1, the exchange rate is $1.75/£1.00, the financial statements would show an additional $56.25 in inventory and $56.25 in accounts payable [(1.75$/£ × £375) - (1.60$/£ × £375)]. With no further exchange rate changes, when the company pays for the goods, accounts payable and cash will be reduced by $656.25. When the inventory is sold, the cost, including any costs attributable to exchange rate changes, is charged to cost of goods sold and is reflected on the income statement.[17]

This method has a significant drawback: exchange rate gains and losses are combined with the actual cost of the company's supplies. This factor limits the

---

[16] An example of the problem is a credit sale. A change in exchange rates between the two countries will result in a loss or gain. The loss or gain will be for the seller if the product is priced in the buyer's home currency. The potential loss or gain will be the seller's if the sale is in the seller's home currency.

[17] Any exchange rate changes that occur before the accounts payable are paid are reported to cost of goods sold, even if the goods have already been used in the manufacture of the company's products and the products have been sold.

comparability of the information.[18] When using this method, the analyst is left with the question: Did skillful management of the company or did exchange rate fluctuations create the performance?

Two-Transaction Perspective. This approach allows the analyst to know whether a company's performance was based on its managers' ability to manage the business or resulted from gains or losses in exchange rates. The two-transaction perspective separates the value of the event (in our example, the purchase of materials) from any subsequent exchange rate gains or losses. To do this two new accounts are created: on the balance sheet the account is loss/gain on foreign exchange; on the income statement, the entry is foreign exchange gains or losses. To see how these statements would differ from those using the one-transaction perspective and from those of a company with no foreign purchases, see Exhibit 1A-8.[19]

2. Foreign Exchange Translation

Assets and liabilities held by the same company but in different countries present a different sort of problem. The problem is not that we have to account for a transaction, but that the value of nondomestic assets and liabilities, and their values as they change with exchange rates, must be reflected on the balance sheet. Multinational companies, with divisions or subsidiaries in other countries, have long dealt with this problem. However, as more companies operate in more than one country, the problem is becoming widespread.

The issue is to develop financial statements that reflect the company's situation fairly and in a way such that they are understandable to and useful for investors, creditors, and managers. To do this, the value of all foreign assets and liabilities are translated into the company's home currency. Whatever method a company uses, it must indicate how it both chose the exchange rate and how it accounted for exchange rate gains and losses. There are three basic translation methods: current/noncurrent, monetary/nonmonetary, and current.

1. **Current/noncurrent method.** In this method, assets and liabilities are grouped according to their maturity. Current assets and liabilities are translated at the date of the company's balance sheet; those that are noncurrent are translated at the rate in effect at the time of the transaction itself—for instance, when the liability was incurred or the asset purchased.

---

[18] This method is not used in the United States. It is used in other countries—for instance, in Brazil.
[19] The example transaction would be accounted for by showing $600 in inventory and $600 in accounts payable on January 1. On April 1, when the exchange rate changed, $56.25 would be added to accounts payable, and $56.25 to an account called "loss on foreign exchange." When the inventory is sold, on the balance sheet, inventory is reduced by $600 and loss on foreign exchange by $56.25; when the goods are paid for, accounts payable and cash are reduced by $656.25 and the income statement reflects a cost of goods sold of $600 and a foreign exchange loss of $56.25.

EXHIBIT 1A-8 Effect of Different Accounting Methods for Foreign Exchange Transactions*

	(1) Assuming No Foreign Exchange Transactions	(2) Foreign Exchange Transaction, One-Transaction Method	(3) Foreign Exchange Transaction, Two-Transaction Method
Income Statement			
Revenue	$1,000	$1,000	$1,000
Cost of goods sold	(600)	(660)	(600)
Selling, general, and administrative	(100)	(100)	(100)
Operating profit	300	240	300
Depreciation	(50)	(50)	(50)
Research and development	(50)	(50)	(50)
Exchange rate gain (loss)	0	0	(56)
Earnings before interest and taxes	200	140	144
Interest	(50)	(50)	(50)
Earnings before taxes	150	90	94
Taxes	(60)	(36)	(38)
Income from operations	90	54	56
Net income	$ 90	$ 54	$ 56
Balance Sheet			
Cash	$ 50	$ 14	$ 14
Accounts receivable	250	250	250
Inventory	200	200	200
Property, plant and equipment, net	400	400	400
Other assets	100	100	100
Total assets	$1,000	$ 964	$ 964
Accounts payable	$ 250	$ 250	$ 250
Long-term debt	400	400	400
Deferred tax	0	0	0
Common equity	100	100	100
Retained earnings:			
Beginning of year	160	160	160
Net income	90	54	54
Retained earnings, end of year	250	214	214
Total equity	350	314	314
Total liabilities and equity	$1,000	$ 964	$ 964

EXHIBIT 1A-8 *(continued)*

	(1) Assuming No Foreign Exchange Transactions	(2) Foreign Exchange Transaction, One-Transaction Method	(3) Foreign Exchange Transaction, Two-Transaction Method
Ratio Analysis			
Return on sales	9.0%	5.4%	5.4%
Sales/assets	100.0	103.7	103.7
Return on assets	9.0	5.6	5.6
Assets/equity	285.7	307.0	307.0
Return on equity	25.7	17.2	17.2

* Figures reflect assumptions in this appendix. For simplicity, financial tax for reporting purposes (40 percent) equals the actual tax liability. Differences in taxes are accounted for by changes in cash.

2. **Monetary/nonmonetary method.** Using this approach, assets are put into monetary or nonmonetary groups. Monetary or financial assets and liabilities are such things as cash receivables, payables, and long-term debt. They are any account that must be stated at current market value, and are translated at the exchange rate as of the date of the financial statement. Nonmonetary assets are translated at the rate in effect when the transaction first occurs, for instance, when the plant was purchased. A variation of this approach, called the **temporal method,** is used in the United States and other countries when accounting for the translation effects of foreign subsidiaries in high inflationary countries.

3. **Current method.** This method is the easiest and most widely used method. All assets and liabilities are translated as of the date of the financial statements.

Generally, all income statement accounts are translated at the average of the exchange rate prevailing over the period reported.[20] After the accounts are translated to reflect the effect of foreign exchange rates, a gain or loss is computed. There are two ways to account for foreign exchange translation gains or losses. Using the first method, a foreign exchange loss or gain is shown as a separate income or expense, and thus affects the income statement directly. The second method charges the gain or loss against the retained earnings account on the balance sheet. Exhibit 1A-9 shows the impact on a company of different methods of accounting for foreign exchange translations.

20 The rationales are that revenue and expenses are received and paid fairly evenly over the year and that exchange rates change gradually. This assumption is often erroneous, however.

EXHIBIT 1A-9 Effects of Different Accounting Methods for Foreign Exchange Translations

	U.S. Dollars	Income Statement Changes			Balance Sheet Changes		
		Current/ Noncurrent (yen)	Nonmon./Mon. (yen)	Current Rate (yen)	Current/ Noncurrent (yen)	Nonmon./Mon. (yen)	Current Rate (yen)
Income Statement							
Revenue	$1,000	¥145,000	¥145,000	¥145,000	¥145,000	¥145,000	¥145,000
Cost of goods sold	600	87,000	87,000	87,000	87,000	87,000	87,000
Selling, general, and administrative	100	14,500	14,500	14,500	14,500	14,500	14,500
Operating profit	300	43,500	43,500	43,500	43,500	43,500	43,500
Depreciation	50	8,250	8,250	6,750	8,250	8,250	6,750
Research and development	50	7,250	7,250	7,250	7,250	7,250	7,250
Exchange rate gain (loss)	0	(8,500)	1,500	(10,000)	0	0	0
Earnings before interest and taxes	200	19,500	29,500	19,500	28,000	28,000	29,500
Interest	50	7,250	7,250	7,250	7,250	7,250	7,250
Earnings before taxes	150	12,250	22,250	12,250	20,750	20,750	22,250
Taxes	60	4,900	8,900	4,900	8,300	8,300	8,900
Income from operations	90	7,350	13,350	7,350	12,450	12,450	13,350
Inflation gains (losses)	0	0	0	0	0	0	0
Net income	$90	¥7,350	¥13,350	¥7,350	¥12,450	¥12,450	¥13,350
Balance Sheet							
Cash	$50	¥6,750	¥6,750	¥6,750	¥6,750	¥6,750	¥6,750
Accounts receivable	250	33,750	33,750	33,750	33,750	33,750	33,750
Inventory	200	27,000	33,000	27,000	27,000	33,000	27,000
Property, plant, equipment, net	400	66,000	66,000	54,000	66,000	66,000	54,000
Other assets	100	16,500	16,500	13,500	16,500	16,500	13,500
Total assets	$1,000	¥150,000	¥156,000	¥135,000	¥150,000	¥156,000	¥135,000

EXHIBIT 1A-9 (continued)

	US$	¥	¥	¥	¥	¥	¥
Accounts payable	$ 250	¥ 33,750	¥ 33,750	¥ 33,750	¥ 33,750	¥ 33,750	¥ 33,750
Long-term debt	400	66,000	54,000	66,000	66,000	66,000	54,000
Deferred tax	0	0	0	0	0	0	0
Common equity	100	16,500	13,500	16,500	16,500	16,500	13,500
Retained earnings:							
Beginning	160	26,400	26,400	26,400	26,400	26,400	26,400
Net income	90	7,350	7,350	13,350	12,450	12,450	13,350
Dividends	0	0	0	0	0	0	0
Other	0	0	0	0	(5,100)	900	(6,000)
Retained earnings, end	250	33,750	33,750	39,750	33,750	39,750	33,750
Total equity	350	50,250	47,250	56,250	50,250	56,250	47,250
Total liabilities and equity	$1,000	¥150,000	¥135,000	¥156,000	¥150,000	¥156,000	¥135,000

Ratio Analysis

	US$	¥	¥	¥	¥	¥	¥
Return on sales	9.0%	5.1%	5.1%	9.2%	8.6%	8.6%	9.2%
Sales/assets	100.0	96.7	107.4	92.9	96.7	92.9	107.4
Return on assets	9.0	4.9	5.4	8.6	8.3	8.0	9.9
Assets/equity	285.7	298.5	285.7	277.3	298.5	277.3	285.7
Return on equity	25.7	14.6	15.6	23.7	24.8	22.1	28.2
Exchange rate gains (losses) recorded in income statement?	Not Applicable	Yes	Yes	No	No	No	No

Assumptions:

Base statements are U.S. subsidiary of Japanese parent.

Current exchange rate is ¥135:1.

Historical exchange rate of fixed assets, long-term debt, and common stock = ¥165:1.

Average exchange rate for the period is ¥145:1.

Depreciation translated at historical rate.

Other income translated at average rate.

For simplicity, financial tax for reporting purposes (40%) equals the actual tax liability.

Differences in taxes are accounted for by changes in cash.

Translation gains and losses are not real losses as transaction gains and losses are; they are estimates of what the fair value would be if an asset were sold or a liability retired at the time the financial statements are prepared. The translated income statement shows an approximation of the revenues and expenses as if they had been incurred in the home currency. Although these figures are purely estimates, they do have a profound impact on financial statements and on measures of financial performance.

V. CONCLUSION

It should be clear by now that an analyst cannot simply compare companies operating from different countries. Differences in accounting alone can make the financial statements of two companies incomparable. The analyst must move beyond the simple comparisons to adjusting for the significant accounting differences. To do this there are three steps a good financial analyst will take:

1. Define the economic event that caused the accounting transaction.
2. Determine the accounting principle that governed the transaction.
3. Determine when the event will be or was reported on the financial statements.

Exhibit 1A-10 provides a list of the various ways in which a company can account for each of the items discussed in this appendix. It is not an exhaustive list of differences in accounting principles throughout the world, but it does reflect the primary areas about which an analyst should be concerned

EXHIBIT 1A-10   Common Methods of Accounting Around the World

Method	Balance Sheet Effect	Income Statement Effect
Inventory		
a. FIFO	Inventory value based on recent prices	Cost of goods sold based on obsolete prices of inventory units sold
b. LIFO	Inventory value based on obsolete prices	Cost of goods sold based on recent prices
c. Weighted average	Inventory value based on weighted-average prices for purchases during the current fiscal year	Cost of goods sold based on weighted-average costs for inventory units sold during the current fiscal year
d. Specific identification	Inventory value based on actual historical cost of each item purchased	Cost of goods sold based on actual historical cost of each inventory item sold

EXHIBIT 1A-10 *(continued)*

Method	Balance Sheet Effect	Income Statement Effect
e. NIFO	Inventory value based on obsolete prices	Cost of goods sold based on current market prices of inventory units sold
f. Latest purchase price	Inventory value based on current market prices	Cost of goods sold based on obsolete prices for inventory units sold

Inflation

Method	Balance Sheet Effect	Income Statement Effect
a. Constant dollar, flow-through method	Various assets and liabilities revalued using a general price-level index	Inflation gains (losses) included in reported income
b. Constant dollar, balance sheet method	Various assets and liabilities revalued using a general price-level index; inflation gains (losses) recorded directly to the equity section of the balance sheet	Income statement does not reflect changes in profits caused by inflation
c. Specific cost, flow-through method	Various assets and liabilities revalued based on specific appraisals or specialized indices	Inflation gains (losses) included in reported income
d. Specific cost, balance sheet method	Various assets and liabilities revalued based on specific appraisals or specialized indices; inflation gains (losses) recorded directly to the equity section of the balance sheet	Income statement does not reflect changes in profits caused by inflation
e. No adjustments	Balance sheet accounts do not reflect changes in value caused by inflation	Income statement does not reflect changes in profits caused by inflation

Foreign Exchange Transactions

Method	Balance Sheet Effect	Income Statement Effect
a. One-transaction perspective	Receivables or payables are adjusted to reflect changes in the exchange rate prior to completion of the transaction	Gains (losses) from changes in exchange rates not separately recorded, but included with the other income statement accounts; the gain (loss) is only recorded if the transaction is completed

EXHIBIT 1A-10 *(continued)*

Method	Balance Sheet Effect	Income Statement Effect
b. Two-transaction perspective	Receivables or payables adjusted to reflect changes in the exchange rate prior to completion of the transaction	Gains (losses) from changes in exchange rates reported as a separate item on the income statement, and reflect changes in the exchange rate prior to completion of the transaction

Foreign Exchange Translation

Method	Balance Sheet Effect	Income Statement Effect
a. Current/ Noncurrent	Current assets and liabilities translated at the current exchange rate (balance sheet date); noncurrent assets, liabilities, and equity accounts translated at the rates in effect when each transaction occurred	Revenue and expenses translated using the average exchange rates for the period; depreciation expenses normally translated at the rate in effect when the asset was purchased; foreign exchange translation gains (losses) usually recorded in the current year in either a balance sheet reserve account or directly to the income statement
b. Monetary/ Nonmonetary	Monetary assets and liabilities translated at current rates; nonmonetary assets, liabilities, and equity accounts translated at historical rates	Same as current/noncurrent method
c. Current rate	All assets and liabilities translated at the current exchange rate; capital stock translated at the rate in effect when the stock was issued; ending retained earnings becomes the balancing item	Same as current/noncurrent method

when comparing the financial performance of companies from different countries. Exhibit 1A-11 provides a list of the ways in which various countries account for the major items discussed here. This list does not deal with every account or possibility, only with the most important and universal. Furthermore, due to changes in accounting rules, these rules should be verified before undertaking an analysis. The intention in providing these exhibits is to highlight the basic differences between accounting methods, and to indicate how a company from that country would deal with these major items. Exhibit 1A-11

EXHIBIT 1A-11   Accounting Methods Available in Selected Countries[§§]

Country	Inventory	Inflation	Foreign-Exchange Translation	Foreign-Exchange Transaction
United States	a, b, c, d	e	c	b
United Kingdom	a, c	e	c	b
Germany	a, b, c, d	e	a, b, c*	b[†]
France	a, b, c	d,e	b, c	b[‡]
Spain	a, b, c, d	e	b, c	b
Japan	a, b, c, d, e	e	b[§]	b
Singapore	a, b, c, d	e	b, c	b
Canada	a, c, d	e	b, c	b"
Mexico	a, b, c	a, c	c**	b**
Brazil	a, b, c	a, d	b,c	a

*   No specific requirements exist in German law or accounting principles as to which method must be used. The requirement is that whatever is chosen must be used consistently.
**   There are no published accounting principles or regulations to account for the effects of foreign currency but companies generally follow U.S. accounting practices.
†   No gains are recognized.
§   Noncurrent monetary items are carried at historical rates.
"   Unrealized gains (losses) on long-term monetary items are deferred until the transaction is completed.
§§   Refer to Exhibit 1A-10.
‡   Losses may be deferred until the transaction is completed.

is a simple matrix and does not substitute for the more detailed analysis a professional analyst should undertake.

SELECTED REFERENCES

Afteman, Allan B. *International Accounting, Financial Reporting and Analysis.* Boston, Mass.: Warren, Gorham & Lamont, 1995.

Alashim, Dhia D., and Jeffrey S. Arpan. *International Dimensions of Accounting.* Boston, Mass.: PWS-Kent Publishing, 1988.

Ball, Ray. "Making Accounting International: Why, How, and How Far Will It Go?" *Journal of Applied Corporate Finance,* Fall 1995, pp. 19-29.

Belkaoui, Ahmed. *Multinational Management Accounting.* New York: Quorum Books, 1991.

Belkaoui, Ahmed. *The New Environment in International Accounting: Issues and Practices.* New York: Quorum Books, 1988.

Choi, Frederick D. S., and Gerhard G. Mueller, eds. *An Introduction to Multinational Accounting.* Englewood Cliffs, N.J.: Prentice Hall, 1978.

Coopers & Lybrand (International). *International Accounting Summaries.* 2nd ed. New York: John Wiley & Sons, 1993.

——. *Frontiers of International Accounting: An Anthology.* Ann Arbor, Mich.: UMI Research Press, 1985.

Evans, Thomas G., Martin E. Taylor, and Oscar Holzmann. *International Accounting and Reporting.* London: Macmillan, 1985.

International Accounting Standards. International Accounting Standards Committee, London, January 1975.

Madura, Jeff. *International Financial Management.* 2nd ed. St. Paul, Minn.: West Publishing Co., 1989, chaps. 9-11.

Moffett, Michael. "Issues in Foreign Exchange Hedge Accounting," *Journal of Applied Corporate Finance,* Fall 1995, pp. 82-94.

Nobes, Christopher. *International Classification of Financial Reporting.* New York: St. Martin's Press, 1984.

Quick, Graham. *Global Reporting: A Guide.* London: Extel Financial Limited, 1989.

Samuels, J. M., and A. G. Piper. *International Accounting: A Survey.* New York: St. Martin's Press, 1985.

Shapiro, Alan C. *Multinational Financial Management.* 5th ed. Needham Heights, Mass.: Allyn & Bacon, 1996, chaps. 8-11.

C H A P T E R 2

Forecasting Future Needs

ost analysts are more concerned about a company's future performance than its history. Yet past performance can provide useful
insights about a company's strategy and its success, and can be used
to help develop forecasts for the future. A number of sophisticated techniques
are available for creating forecasts, but virtually all methods start with a thor-
ough understanding of the company's history.

Simple forecasts assume that the future is a mirror of the company's past.
To make a simple forecast, an analyst forecasts future performance that is identical to past performance, or forecasts that the trends will continue. While this
is a simple way to make a forecast, it is simplistic at best. A good analyst skillfully interprets the company's past performance, current situation, and strategy, using tools such as those described in Chapter 1, and incorporates what is
discovered into forecasts for the company's projected financial statements.

Let us be very clear. All forecasting depends upon the skill of the individual making the forecast, and skill comes from both knowledge and experience.
The first skill a financial analyst should learn and hone is the skill of interpreting and understanding the company's past and current strategy and performance. The second thing that impacts on the quality of an analyst's forecasts is
an understanding of the forces—company, industry, and economic—that will
affect the company in the future. The accuracy of any forecast depends on
proper interpretation of historical data, and the identification and extrapola-
tion of the forces. The analyst must make assumptions about the future. These
assumptions are critical to creating forecasts and to understanding the scenarios behind the forecasts. The skilled analyst knows that these assumptions
must be detailed and explicit. An inability to recognize the assumptions that
have been made and failure to test them can result in tenuous or obscure
forecasts.

The forecasts we discuss in this chapter are financial in nature. They represent the expected activity and condition of the company over time and at various points in the future, expressed in financial terms. These financial forecasts
are the explicit details about the outcomes that are expected from the company's marketing, production, and overall management. There are a variety of
forecasts financial analysts can make. External analysts typically make forecasts to anticipate a company's performance. For example, they may try to
determine what returns might be expected from an equity investment in a com-

pany, or whether a company will generate sufficient cash to remain solvent and repay its obligations. Internal analysts, on the other hand, are often concerned with forecasting needs for financial resources so that managers can plan future operations and investments. In this chapter we will focus on the types of analyses typically used by internal corporate managers. These forecasts often rely on information unavailable to external analysts.

Analysts turn forecasts into two types of financial statements. For short periods, a method known as **cash budgeting** is most often used. For longer periods of time, **projected financial statements** are developed. We will discuss each of these in turn, and then describe how the skillful analyst tests the assumptions used in creating the forecasts.

I. CASH BUDGETS

The cash budget approach to forecasting specifically focuses on the cash account of the company. This cash-based approach differs significantly from the common method of accounting in corporations, the accrual method. **Accrual accounting** attempts to match the revenues earned during a specific period with the expenses incurred, without regard to actual cash receipts or disbursements. The cash budget forecasts receipts and disbursements, with the objective of identifying whether sufficient cash will be available to meet the company's or division's financial needs or whether there is excess cash. To determine whether there is an excess or need, the analyst compares expected cash receipts with anticipated cash disbursements. The difference between cash receipts and disbursements reveals either an excess of cash or a need for additional cash.

Whether a company has excess cash or a need for cash depends upon the actual timing of the receipts and disbursements. Assuming that a company adequately prices its products, it will not need additional cash if the cash payments for its sales are received at the same time it makes payments for its production costs. However, credit sales, seasonal demand, and other factors combine to cause mismatches between disbursements and receipts. Because of these timing differences, a cash budget is a very useful internal planning tool for management.

In creating a cash budget, the analyst's first step is to choose an appropriate time period for the forecast. For the typical company a cash budget for monthly cash flows would be developed. However, in industries with highly volatile cash flows or during times of high inflation or rapid economic or industry change, cash budgets may be based on weekly or even daily cash flows. Not surprisingly, in some highly inflationary environments, companies have been known to prepare hourly cash budgets.

The analyst's second step is to choose a suitable length of time over which to forecast. The forecast horizon depends on the firm's situation. If monthly cash budgets are suitable, the company typically prepares a 12- or a 24-month forecast. Cash budgets based on smaller time periods are usually developed for correspondingly shorter forecast horizons.

After the appropriate time period and forecast horizon have been chosen, the next step is to determine what critical assumptions will underlie the forecast. Most forecasts begin with an assumption about the sales volume during the period. The forecast for sales should be developed in light of the company's current market share, its product line, and its current and future competition. Once the sales forecast has been made, the analyst can use history, along with expected changes in the future, to determine the other assumptions that will underlie the forecasts. A good place to start is with an historic performance analysis, like that described in Chapter 1. In most companies, predictions for all other variables, such as asset, liability, and expense levels, are based on the forecasted level of sales. The assumed relationships between sales and the other variables are important and need to be stated explicitly.

To demonstrate the process of developing a cash budget, let us use an example. We will develop a cash budget for Tulipline Fashions, Inc., a wholesale distributor of tennis and swimming clothing and accessories. Although Tulipline Fashions, Inc. sustained some losses during its initial operations, management expects that continuing operations will be profitable. The company has only been in existence for two years, and the owner has relied on a bank loan of $50,000 to offset the financial drain caused by the early losses. Although sales are expected to increase annually by 10 percent, the necessity of extending credit for long time periods during the peak summer sales season causes severe cash problems. To determine the severity of these problems, monthly cash budgets, commencing on September 1, 1997 and extending through August 1998, have to be prepared.

Starting with assumed sales growth of 10 percent, the analyst would prepare a set of assumptions for the cash budget. The assumptions for Tulipline are listed in Exhibit 2-1. Based on these assumptions, the expected sales volume, cash and credit sales, accounts receivable collections, and purchases of merchandise for each of the 12 months of the cash budget period are shown in Exhibit 2-2.

Using Tulipline's balances for cash, inventory, and accounts receivable at the end of August 1997, the analyst would next determine the effect of delays in receiving cash from sales and in paying cash for purchases. Equipped with this information, the analyst could then calculate the accounts receivable and payable schedules. These are shown in Exhibits 2-3 and 2-4.

On the basis of these data, the company analyst would calculate monthly cash receipts and cash disbursements, as shown in Exhibit 2-5. For each month, cash payments for expenses and supplies are subtracted from the cash generated by cash sales and collections of previous credit sales. On a cumulative basis, an excess of receipts over disbursements increases the cash balance, while a shortfall reduces it, as you can see in the cash balance forecast shown in Exhibit 2-6.

EXHIBIT 2-1   Tulipline Fashions, Inc.—1997-98 Cash Budget Assumptions

1. Sales are seasonal with the peak occurring during the summer months. Sales are expected to increase about 10 percent per year.
2. Ten percent of the sales are for cash. Credit terms are two months, and customers meet the credit terms.
3. Supplies are purchased the month prior to need. Cost of goods sold is 73 percent of sales.
4. Suppliers require payment in 30 days.
5. Selling, general, and administrative expenses are 14 percent of sales. These expenses are paid in the month in which they are incurred.
6. Fixed operating expenses are $6,500 per month. This does not include $500 per month for depreciation.
7. Lease and interest payments are $3,000 per month. This is a simplifying assumption since interest expense will depend upon the actual amount borrowed.
8. The company has tax loss carryforwards, thus no tax payments need be made in 1997-98. The fiscal year begins in September.
9. New equipment will be purchased in March 1998 for $25,000, and must be paid for two months later.
10. The bank will allow a credit line of no more than $50,000.
11. Tulipline has a $9,000 cash balance at the end of August 1997.
12. No dividends are expected to be paid.

EXHIBIT 2-2   Tulipline Fashions, Inc.—1997-98
Forecast of Sales, Purchases, and Collections

	Sales	Cash Sales	Credit Sales	Collections from Accounts Receivable	Purchases
1997					
September	$ 96.0	$ 9.6	$ 86.4	$ 136.7	$ 54.8
October	75.0	7.5	67.5	109.4	40.2
November	55.0	5.5	49.5	86.4	32.9
December	45.0	4.5	40.5	67.5	25.6
1998					
January	35.0	3.5	31.5	49.5	32.9
February	45.0	4.5	40.5	40.5	51.1
March	70.0	7.0	63.0	31.5	76.7
April	105.0	10.5	94.5	40.5	105.9
May	145.0	14.5	130.5	63.0	131.4
June	180.0	18.0	162.0	94.5	120.5
July	165.0	16.5	148.5	130.5	98.6
August	135.0	13.5	121.5	162.0	115.2
Total	$1,151.0	$115.1	$1,035.9	$1,012.0	$885.8

EXHIBIT 2-3   Tulipline Fashions, Inc.—1997-98 Accounts Receivable Schedule (in thousands)

	September	October	November	December	January	February	March	April	May	June	July	August
Beginning accts. receivable	$246.1	$195.8	$153.9	$117.0	$90.0	$72.0	$ 72.0	$103.5	$157.5	$225.0	$292.5	$310.5
Credit sales	86.4	67.5	49.5	40.5	31.5	40.5	63.0	94.5	130.5	162.0	148.5	121.5
Collection—accts. receivable	136.7	109.4	86.4	67.5	49.5	40.5	31.5	40.5	63.0	94.5	130.5	162.0
Ending accts. receivable	$195.8	$153.9	$117.0	$ 90.0	$72.0	$72.0	$103.5	$157.5	$225.0	$292.5	$310.5	$270.0

EXHIBIT 2-4   Tulipline Fashions, Inc.—1997-98 Accounts Payable Schedule (in thousands)

	September	October	November	December	January	February	March	April	May	June	July	August
Beginning accts. payable	$70.1	$54.8	$40.2	$32.9	$25.6	$32.9	$51.1	$ 76.7	$105.9	$131.4	$120.5	$ 98.6
Purchases	54.8	40.2	32.9	25.6	32.9	51.1	76.7	105.9	131.4	120.5	98.6	115.2
Payments	70.1	54.8	40.2	32.9	25.6	32.9	51.1	76.7	105.9	131.4	120.5	98.6
Ending accts. payable	$54.8	$40.2	$32.9	$25.6	$32.9	$51.1	$76.7	$105.9	$131.4	$120.5	$ 98.6	$115.2

EXHIBIT 2-5 Tulipline Fashions, Inc.—1997-98 Monthly Cash Budget (in thousands)

	September	October	November	December	January	February	March	April	May	June	July	August
Receipts												
Cash sales	$ 9.6	$ 7.5	$ 5.5	$ 4.5	$ 3.5	$ 4.5	$ 7.0	$ 10.5	$ 14.5	$ 18.0	$ 16.5	$ 13.5
Collections on accts. receivable	136.7	109.4	86.4	67.5	49.5	40.5	31.5	40.5	63.0	94.5	130.5	162.0
Total receipts	$146.3	$116.9	$91.9	$72.0	$53.0	$45.0	$ 38.5	$ 51.0	$ 77.5	$112.5	$147.0	$175.5
Disbursements												
Accts. payable payments	$ 70.1	$ 54.8	$40.2	$32.9	$25.6	$32.9	$ 51.1	$ 76.7	$105.9	$131.4	$120.5	$ 98.6
Selling, general, and admin. expense	13.4	10.5	7.7	6.3	4.9	6.3	9.8	14.7	20.3	25.2	23.1	18.9
Operating expenses	6.5	6.5	6.5	6.5	6.5	6.5	6.5	6.5	6.5	6.5	6.5	6.5
Lease and interest expense	3.0	3.0	3.0	3.0	3.0	3.0	3.0	3.0	3.0	3.0	3.0	3.0
New equipment	—	—	—	—	—	—	—	—	25.0	—	—	—
Tax payments	—	—	—	—	—	—	—	—	—	—	—	—
Total disbursements	93.0	74.8	57.4	48.7	40.0	48.7	70.4	100.9	160.7	166.1	153.1	127.0
Receipts less disbursements	$ 53.3	$ 42.1	$34.5	$23.3	$13.0	$ (3.7)	$(31.9)	$ (49.9)	$ (83.2)	$ (53.6)	$ (6.1)	$ 48.5

EXHIBIT 2-6 Tulipline Fashions, Inc.—1997-98 Cash Balance (in thousands)

	September	October	November	December	January	February	March	April	May	June	July	August
Beginning cash balance	$ 9.0	$ 62.3	$104.4	$138.9	$162.2	$175.2	$171.5	$139.6	$ 89.7	$ 6.5	$(47.1)	$(53.2)
Receipts less disbursements	53.3	42.1	34.5	23.3	13.0	(3.7)	(31.9)	(49.9)	(83.2)	(53.6)	(6.1)	48.5
Ending cash balance	$62.3	$104.4	$138.9	$162.2	$175.2	$171.5	$139.6	$ 89.7	$ 6.5	$(47.1)	$(53.2)	$ (4.7)

Using this cash budget, Tulipline's managers determined that the firm would need $47,100 additional cash in June. By July, the shortfall climbs to $53,200, but declines to $4,700 by the end of August. This short-term need for funds is typical of companies with seasonal sales. As you can see, Tulipline has a significant cash balance at the time it begins to prepare for the next selling season. By May this cash balance is almost exhausted, and in July the cash needs are greater than the bank's credit limit of $50,000. On the basis of these forecasts, management would need to change its marketing plan, or go to the bank to renegotiate an increase in the credit line to accommodate these needs.[1] If management extends the forecast for one more month, it can show the bank that Tulipline's cash need is a temporary supplement needed only to meet its seasonal needs during the summer months. Graphically, Exhibit 2-7 shows the cash balance and vividly demonstrates the impact on financing needs that can come solely from selling a product with seasonal demand.

Of course, a company's demand for cash depends not only on its seasonal needs, but also on its need for liquidity—the ready cash a company must have on hand. You will note that Tulipline management will surely have to turn to

EXHIBIT 2-7   Tulipline Fashions, Inc.—1997-98 Monthly Cash Balance (in thousands)

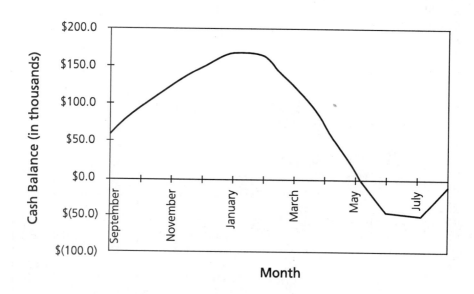

---

[1]   The forecast shows that the funds are needed because of the nature of the business, not because of poor planning or management. Thus, management should go to the bank well before the funds are needed.

the bank for a credit line exceeding the original line, and large enough to meet the need for $53,200 in July. This is because the company needs some cash on hand for is daily operations.

How much liquidity a company requires depends on its operating practices and the environment in which it operates. Companies operating in more volatile environments, with greater uncertainty about such things as sales, collections, and costs, need to maintain a higher cash balance than those operating in more stable economic conditions. The more difficult it is to forecast future events, the greater the need to maintain a high cash reserve for unforeseen needs. Note, the cash reserve need not be maintained as an actual cash balance. Adequate liquidity protection can be established with a line of credit with a bank.[2] Other kinds of companies have a need for actual cash, for instance, companies like Hannaford that have retail operations.

II. PROJECTED FINANCIAL STATEMENTS

The cash budget describes the flow of cash during the forecast period. Forecasted financial statements, like normal financial statements, provide aggregate accrual information for the forecast period, or at a point in time. Projected financial statements are summaries of the information contained in the cash budget. Cash budgets provide the details, while financial forecasts provide summaries in the more familiar financial statement format.[3] Although these forecasts could be prepared weekly or monthly, as was our cash budget, they are usually developed as quarterly or annual forecasts.

Like cash budgets, making a financial statement forecast requires defining one or more critical variables and the relationships of other variables to the critical variable(s). The relationships that underlie the forecast, and assumed by the analyst, should be explicit.

1. Developing Forecasts from Cash Budgets

While financial statement forecasts can be created directly from assumptions, because cash budget forecasts require the same information as forecasted financial statements, it is possible to derive a set of financial statements from the cash budget. The only information required to do this is the balance sheet at the beginning of the forecast period and the cash budget. With these two statements, one can calculate an end-of-period income statement, balance

---

[2]   A line of credit allows a company to borrow up to a preset limit at any time the credit line is in force.

[3]   Projected income statements forecast earnings and expenses for the period; projected balance sheets forecast assets and liabilities at the conclusion of the period; projected cash flow statements forecast funds changes over the period.

sheet, and a sources and uses of funds or cash flow statement. Let's use Tulipline to demonstrate this process.

Using the data from the cash budget for Tulipline Fashions, Inc., an income statement for the period from September 1, 1997 to August 31, 1998 is projected. This income statement is shown in Exhibit 2-8. The balance sheet for August 31, 1997, the beginning of the forecast period, and the projected balance sheet for August 31, 1998 are included in Exhibit 2-9. This exhibit also details the changes that are expected to occur in the various accounts during the forecast period. Exhibit 2-10, the sources and uses of funds, also shows the changes over the period of the forecast.

Although projections do not provide the level of detail about the ebbs and flows in the cash account that is shown in the cash budget, they do show the cash balance at the end of the forecast period. Thus, they indicate the company's financing needs at the end of the period. For companies that do not experience a significant change in cash during a year, this approach to forecasting needs is usually adequate. Because cash budgets are more time-consuming to prepare, managers of most companies elect to develop financial statement projections directly rather than on the basis of a cash budget.

2. Developing Projections Directly

To develop forecasts directly, analysts normally use an extension of ratio analysis. To do this, the analyst first determines the historical relationships among financial statement accounts for previous years. These relationships, expressed as ratios, are then adjusted to account for expected future events and trends. Finally, the analyst forecasts the various accounts on the basis of these adjusted ratios. As is the case with cash budgets, usually the first projection made is the sales account. Other accounts are then forecasted on the basis of their expected relationships with sales. These forecasts are simple, and must be adapted for anticipated company and market conditions. In addition, more sophisticated forecasting approaches may be used if warranted.

EXHIBIT 2-8   Tulipline Fashions, Inc.—1998 Income Statement (in thousands)

Sales	$1,151.0
Cost of goods sold	(840.2)
Gross profit	310.8
Expenses:	
Selling and administrative	(161.1)
Fixed operating costs	(78.0)
Depreciation	(6.0)
Lease and interest expense	(36.0)
Taxes	—
Net profit	$ 29.7

EXHIBIT 2-9 Tulipline Fashions, Inc.—1998 Balance Sheet
(as of August 31, in thousands)

	Actual 1997		Forecasted 1998
Assets			
Cash	$ 9.0	From cash budget	$ (4.7)
Accounts receivable	246.1	From accounts receivable schedule	270.0
		Plus purchases of $885.3, less cost	
Inventories	89.0	of goods sold of $840.2	134.6
Total current assets	344.1		399.9
		Plus new equipment of $25.0,	
Net equipment	42.0	less depreciation of $6.0	61.0
Total assets	$386.1		$ 460.9
Liabilities and Equity			
Notes payable	$ 10.0	No change	$ 10.0
Accounts payable	70.1	From accounts payable schedule	115.2
Total current liabilities	80.1		125.2
Long-term debt	100.0	No change	100.0
Equity	206.0	Plus net income of $29.7	235.7
Total liabilities and equity	$386.1		$ 460.9

EXHIBIT 2-10 Tulipline Fashions, Inc.—Sources and Uses Statement—
September 1997 to August 1998 (in thousands)

Sources:	
Decrease in cash	$13.7
Increase in accounts payable	45.1
Net profits	29.7
Total sources	$88.5
Uses:	
Increase in accounts receivable	$23.9
Increase in inventories	45.6
Increase in net equipment	19.0
Total uses	$88.5

A problem that bedevils the analyst when making balance sheet forecasts is that the forecasts rarely balance. Either the assets will be larger than the liability and equity accounts, indicating a need for additional financing if the asset strategy is to be followed, or the liability and equity accounts are larger than the assets, indicating that the company has additional sources of capital that may be used to increase assets or reduce liabilities and equity. One easy way to deal with this problem of balance is to include a "net financing needed" account on the projected balance sheet. This might be called a "plug" account because it is not a real account; it is used only to create the balance. If the amount in this account is positive, additional financing is needed. If the amount is negative, the company has excess funds, and additional capital is available for investment.

Because these forecasts are derived directly from specified relationships among the various accounts, the assumptions embedded in the analysis may be more obvious than those used in cash budgets. Nevertheless, it is essential to remember that the reliability of all forecasts depends on the validity of the assumptions.

III. PROJECTING FINANCIAL STATEMENTS IN HIGHLY UNCERTAIN CONDITIONS

A number of critical assumptions underlie the financial forecasts we made for Tulipline Fashions, Inc. Making such assumptions is very difficult, even in circumstances that generate confidence. Analysts feel most confident when they make forecasts for companies that:

1. Are in a reasonably stable industry.
2. Have a strong position in the industry.
3. Are not making many changes to:
   a. the products they sell,
   b. the methods used for production, or
   c. the sources of financing.
4. Are in a reasonably stable economic and political environment.

Tulipline's situation would make analysts feel reasonably confident in their forecasts. While some things about Tulipline's financial forecasts should be examined, and they will be in Section IV of this chapter, we will first look at what to do when a company does not operate in such a stable world.

Many companies operate in situations that are challenging, and while understanding the historical performance of companies that operate in highly volatile environments can be difficult, forecasting future performance can seem impossible. Let's use as an example a company operating in Brazil, a country where the economic environment has been quite volatile.

Terra Blanca operates in Brazil and binds paper into notebooks for use by schools and businesses. The early 1990s were a difficult time for the company. First, the Brazilian economy was on a roller coaster, with inflation reaching very high levels. Second, because of declines in incomes, sales of products had not met management's expectations. In addition, since some of the material Terra Blanca used to make its products came from outside Brazil, and the prices of those products were not frozen by government mandate, costs had been difficult to control. The financial performance of the company for 1993 through 1995 is shown in Exhibit 2-11. As you can see, performance was erratic.

Management, believing that planning was essential even though they had to be flexible, continued to make forecasts in spite of the volatility of the business and economy. However, the company's financial analysts were confronted with a difficult problem: historical data was so erratic that it did not provide much information to use as a basis for estimating the future. What should they do?

After looking at the past, the next thing they had to do was to assess the environment in which the company would be operating in the future. Recent events had led Terra Blanca management to believe that the Brazilian economy was under control and that a period of stability had been under way since early 1995. In this case, management determined that the current situation was normal enough to use it as a basis for making forecasts. They made explicit forecasts for inflation, as well as for the way in which Terra Blanca's business would react to the economic environment. Their analysts' forecast is shown in Exhibit 2-12.

Several things about the Terra Blanca financial statements, and financial statements for companies in similar environments, are quite different from those shown for companies like Tulipline Fashions. First, for Terra Blanca, inflation is high and has an uneven impact on revenues and costs. Second, operating profits in an uncertain and inflation-prone environment can be negative because of declines in demand brought on by decreases in real income, or because of price freezes instituted by the government to reduce inflation rapidly. Third, inflationary environments provide profit-making opportunities for companies that have cash to invest: net financing costs turn into lending profits rather than interest expenses, and the profits from financial transactions can offset product/market losses. This is what happened to Terra Blanca as infla-

EXHIBIT 2-11 Terra Blanca Sociedad Anonima Historic Income Statement Data (in thousands of reales)

	1993	1994	1995
Sales	10,100	38,500	68,540
Cost of goods sold	(20,100)	(49,450)	(82,800)
Gross profit	(10,000)	(10,950)	(14,260)
Operating expenses	(6,500)	(38,450)	(48,840)
Operating profits	(16,500)	(49,400)	(63,100)
Net financing costs	73,010	77,900	66,400
Profit before taxes	56,510	28,500	3,300

EXHIBIT 2-12   Terra Blanca Sociedad Anonima Forecasted Financial Statements (in thousands of reales)

	1996	1997	1998	1999	2000
Sales	99,109	130,625	149,174	176,324	208,415
Cost of goods sold	(67,394)	(73,150)	(82,046)	(88,162)	(104,207)
Gross profit	31,715	57,475	67,128	88,162	104,208
Operating expenses	(69,376)	(88,825)	(71,604)	(79,346)	(83,366)
Operating profits	1,982	15,675	(4,476)	8,816	20,842
Net financing costs	48,000	28,450	(22,100)	(16,000)	(12,000)
Profit before taxes	3,300	10,069	(26,576)	(7,184)	8,842
Assumptions					
Real annual sales growth rate	2.0%	5.0%	8.0%	12.0%	12.0%
Gross profit/sales	32.0	44.0	45.0	50.0	50.0
Operating expenses/sales	70.0	68.0	48.0	45.0	40.0
Inflation rate per month	3.0	2.0	0.5	0.5	0.5
Inflation rate per year	42.6	26.8	6.2	6.2	6.2
Taxes/profit before taxes	42.0	42.0	42.0	42.0	42.0
Nominal annual sales growth rate	44.6	31.8	14.2	18.2	18.2

tion dropped: Terra Blanca's profits from financial transactions declined. At that point, you will note that in the forecasts the company stops making financial gains, and borrows and incurs financing costs.

IV. MULTI-CURRENCY FINANCIAL STATEMENTS

The forecasts for Tulipline Fashions were made in dollars, because the company operates only in the United States. The Terra Blanca forecasts were in units of Brazilian currency. But what if a company made or sold products in more than one country, sourced materials outside its domestic environment, or was owned by a company in another country? How would the forecasts change? The first question concerns the proper currency in which to forecast, and the answer is: the currency in which the cash will be spent and received. For Tulipline Fashions, it is U.S. dollars, and for Terra Blanca, it is Brazilian reales. The second question concerns what to do if cash is paid or received in more than one currency. To answer that question, we need to understand how exchange rates operate.

1. The Importance of Exchange Rates

The globalization of the economic world forces us to recognize that few companies operate without dealing in more than one currency. They may owe suppliers, sell products, or get or pay dividends or interest to owners or lenders in other countries. This exposure to foreign currencies introduces a special problem when making forecasts—exchange rates. To make financial forecasts, analysts must forecast receipts and disbursements in whatever currency they occur. If the company is expected to change any of its receipts or disbursements into another currency, however, the analyst must forecast the receipt or disbursement, when it will occur, and the currency exchange rate that will be in effect at the time. Thus, to make cross-border forecasts, an analyst must have a basic understanding of foreign exchange markets, of how exchange rates affect their forecasts, and of what makes exchange rates change. In the Appendix to Chapter 1, we discussed how foreign exchange transactions and translations are handled by accountants. However, an analyst forecasting the financial performance of a company with currency exposure must understand the accounting issues, as well as foreign exchange rates and how they change.

2. Exchange Rate Theories

An exchange rate is the rate at which one currency can be exchanged for another. This is the rate at which the demand for and supply of a particular currency are equal. There are two different theories about what governs exchange rates: one theory proposes that it is relative purchasing power between the two currencies, while the other hypothesizes that it is interest rates. The first theory, **purchasing power parity**, theorizes that exchange rates render currency denomination differences irrelevant: in a free-trade world, exchange rates make the cost of goods the same in both countries. If a difference in the price of the same good offered in the two countries exists, someone will see the potential to profit and take that opportunity: they will buy the good at the lower price and offer it to buyers in the country where the good is commanding the higher price. This process is called **arbitrage**, and those acting on price differences are called **arbitrageurs**. Theoretically, exchange rates change only when there is a change in the rates of inflation in the two countries.

Purchasing power parity is simple, and it makes sense, except that it does not seem to work well in practice. The simplest version of this theory does not take into account differences in actual costs of buying, moving the product, and reselling it, or any barriers to arbitrage (e.g., tariffs) created by the two countries. Because purchasing power parity does not explain what actually occurs in the world very well, another theory was developed.

This theory, called **interest rate parity** or the **Fisher effect**, suggests that differences in real interest rates, and changes in those differences, are at the heart of exchange rates. Theoretically, exchange rates make the real returns in the two countries the same: if real rates, the rates after subtracting the rate of inflation in each country from the nominal interest rate, are not the same, the potential exists to make a profit, and an arbitrageur will move in, take the profit, and make the expected real rates of return the same. The mechanism to make the rates the same is the exchange rate between the two countries. Arbitrageurs move out of the currency of the country with the lower real rate of return, buy the currency of the country offering the higher real rate of return, and thus create a demand for that currency. An increased demand for a currency puts pressure on the exchange rate, and it changes.

In fact, exchange rates are determined by a combination of such things as the differences in real interest rates, relative inflation, growth rates in available income, and perceptions about political and economic risk in the two countries.

Most exchange rates float; that is, they can change as conditions between two countries change. A floating exchange rate can depreciate or appreciate, go down or up, relative to another country's currency. Most industrialized nations have had floating exchange rates since the early 1970s.[4]

Some exchange rates are fixed, however. A fixed exchange rate is one where the rate of exchange is set relative to some other currency—often the U.S. dollar. For example, Argentina and over 30 other countries have, or had, a currency whose value was set relative to the U.S. dollar. Fixed currency relationships can be changed by a country's governing body, usually its central bank. A decrease in the value of the currency relative to another is called a **devaluation**, an increase is a **revaluation**.

Currencies are traded. Indeed, the foreign exchange market is the largest financial market in the world. A company or individual can trade one currency for another today (**spot market**) or for some time in the future (**futures** or **forward market**).

Exchange rates are generally quoted in the home currency relative to the currency of the other country; for instance, on May 15, 1996, the spot rate for the British pound was U.S.$1.00: £0.66028, which means that you could have obtained 66 pence for a dollar, or it would cost U.S.$1.5145 to buy £1.00. To determine the exchange rate for the British pound and Japanese yen, the dollar exchange rates for those two currencies would be used. Exchange rates for major currencies are reported in the financial press daily.

There are both **bid prices**, what a seller will pay for the currency, and **asked prices**, the price at which a seller will sell the currency, quoted for large currency transactions. Small transactions cost more than large transactions.

The **futures** and **forward markets** are markets in which transactions in the future can be settled today. For example, if a company had a large payment to a supplier due 30 days from now, it could contract with a bank for the delivery of the needed currency at that time, for a price specified today. Bank forward contracts are arranged between the bank and its customer. The difference between the spot and the forward or futures rates depends on the volume of buyers and sellers of the particular currency for the date in the future and on the potential variability in the exchange rate. Forward contracts usually are for

---

[4]　While this statement is true in theory, countries' central banks often intervene to maintain the relative exchange rates between two or more countries. This intervention is usually intended to smooth otherwise rapid exchange rate changes.

less than one year. The terms and conditions are arranged between the buyer of the contract and the seller.

The customer needing to make a payment or expecting to have an excess of a particular currency in the future may also use the futures markets. The futures contract differs from a forward contract in that it is publicly traded and the contract is for a standardized quantity of the currency deliverable at a particular date. These contracts are similar to commodities futures contracts and in the United States are traded on the Chicago Mercantile Exchange. On May 15, 1996, when the spot rate between the U.S. dollar and the U.K. pound was $1.00: £0.66028, the 90-day future rate was U.S.$1.00: £0.6613. This latter rate reflected a forecast for a rise in the U.S. dollar relative to the British pound.

3. How Exchange Rates Affect Forecasts

When making a forecast for a company that has income or expenses from another country or countries, the analyst must make some assumptions about exchange rates at the time the cash will be transferred. For example, let's take the Tulipline Fashions, Inc. example and add some information about how and where the company does business: Tulipline uses fabric woven in another country to make some of its products. The assumption used to create the income statement shown in Exhibit 2-8 was that the cost of goods sold would be 73 percent of sales. However, if 21.5 percent of the cost of sales was fabric from the other country, and the exchange rate went from $1:1 to $1:0.67, there would be a significant increase in the cost of purchases. More importantly, Tulipline's need for cash would increase. These changes are shown in Exhibit 2-13. The impact on the income statement of such a cost increase is shown in Exhibit 2-14. This change in cash needed by Tulipline is a very simple example of what could occur if the exchange rate changed dramatically. Managers often insure against such dramatic exchange rate changes by anticipating the need for funds and hedging that need with a forward or futures contract.[5] The analyst would have to incorporate such hedging and its costs into forecasts.

Exchange rates do change, sometimes dramatically and sometimes slowly. Exhibits 2-15 and 2-16 show the exchange rate changes (in terms of the U.S. dollar) for Thailand's baht and Mexico's peso since early 1994. These countries export textiles and finished garments and might be places from which a company such as Tulipline would import raw materials or partially finished garments. Mexico's exchange rate, which had declined dramatically in late 1987, has risen since 1994. Over this period, forecasting for a company doing business in Mexico would have presented the analyst with a serious challenge. Thailand, relatively unstable in the late 1980s, has been relatively steady since early 1995.

---

[5]   Hedging is an activity where a future price is locked in today. There are a variety of ways to hedge.

EXHIBIT 2-13   Tulipline Fashions, Inc.—Cash Balance With
and Without Exchange Rate Change

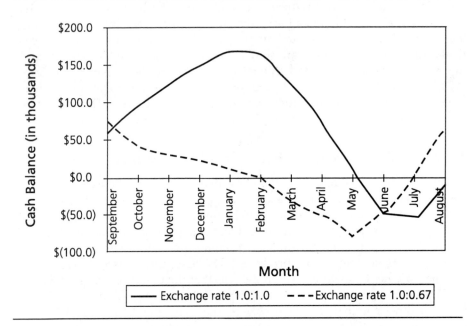

EXHIBIT 2-14   Tulipline Fashions, Inc.—1998 Income Statement (in thousands)

Sales	$1,151.0
Cost of goods sold	(929.2)
Gross profit	221.8
Expenses:	
Selling and administrative	(161.1)
Fixed operating costs	(78.0)
Depreciation	(6.0)
Lease and interest expense	(36.0)
Taxes	—
Net profit	$ (59.3)

Thailand and Mexico are classified as developing countries, and many believe that exchange rates are more volatile in developing countries with floating exchange rates. A look at the U.S. dollar exchange rates with a number of other major currencies over the same period of history (Exhibit 2-17) shows that exchange rates can be volatile regardless of the level of the country's development.

EXHIBIT 2-15 U.S. Dollar/Mexican Peso Exchange Rate (1994 to mid-1996)

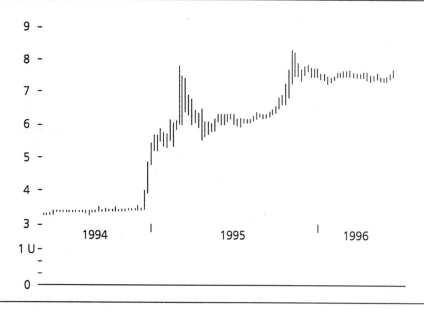

EXHIBIT 2-16 U.S. Dollar/Thai Baht Exchange Rate (1994 to mid-1996)

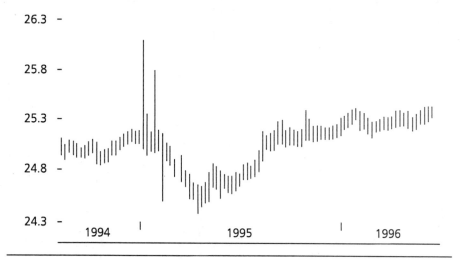

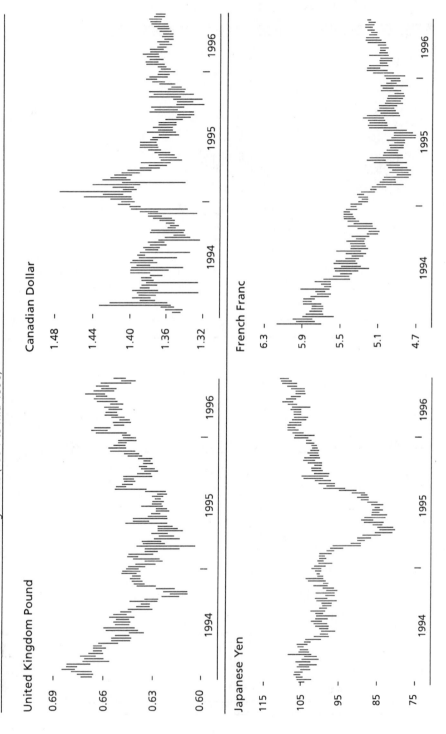

EXHIBIT 2-17 U.S. Dollar Exchange Rates (1994 to mid-1996)

For the analyst or manager, the more likely that a relevant exchange rate will change, the greater the impact that change will have on the financial viability of a company or strategy, and the more effort the manager or analyst must make to understand the potential changes and to forecast them. Because this section is only a very simple introduction to exchange rates and to what makes exchange rates change over time, the competent manager will need to know much more about exchange rates, the mechanisms governing them, and methods to hedge or take advantage of changes in them.[6]

Making forecasts in highly uncertain economic and political environments is difficult. The difficulty reinforces the need for a careful understanding of the company, its industry, and the economy in which it operates. The impact of inflation must be understood as clearly as possible, and forecasts must be based on explicit assumptions for the future. In volatile environments, these forecasts often are changed frequently as conditions change.

Note that forecasts are not irrelevant in rapidly changing environments; they are simply made more often than in stable environments. In fact, many managers contend that forecasts are more important in changing environments.

Rather than despairing about forecast relevancy, we have another way to approach uncertainty, whether that uncertainty is about the company's operations, its sales, or its environment. Let's look at how we might deal with the uncertainties we are certain to have when making forecasts.

V. ANALYZING ASSUMPTIONS

As has been stated repeatedly, any projection requires making assumptions. If the assumptions are not valid, then the subsequent forecasts are valueless. Because the true validity of an assumption is recognizable only after the fact, several procedures have been developed to assist in analyzing the reasonableness of assumptions beforehand. Let's use an example to demonstrate how assumptions impact forecasts, and how an analyst might test for reasonableness.

Design Supplies, Inc. is a distributor of drafting and architectural supplies and software. The equity investment was provided by the owner/manager of the company, and the remainder of the funding of $200,000 was provided as a no-interest loan by a friend. The lender, a friend who considered herself more a silent partner than a lender, recently requested that she become involved in the operations of the company. However, she is willing to be paid off, or will remain silent as long as there are real prospects for having her entire loan paid

---

[6] Some companies choose to insulate themselves against changes in exchange rates through certain corporate strategies. Alternatively, as noted earlier, the manager might choose to hedge risk with forward or futures contracts. Because speculating and hedging are sophisticated activities, references for further reading are provided at the end of this chapter.

off. The original agreement was that the owner/manager would, in 2000, fully repay the debt. The owner/manager hopes that Design Supplies will provide sufficient funds to allow him to do so.

To determine whether adequate funds will be available for a buyout, the minority owner has developed a five-year forecast. Exhibits 2-18 and 2-19 show the income statements and balance sheets for the previous three years and the projected statements for five more years. The assumptions used in developing the forecasts are shown at the bottom of the exhibits.

From the forecasts, it appears that the company will generate sufficient funds by 2000 to allow the manager/owner to fully pay off the debt. However, the return to the investor in 2000 would be her principal plus 6.3 percent: there are excess funds of $154,000 plus $78,600 in cash, for a total of $232,600. If the investor can wait until 2001, when the total has risen to $347,600, the full principal would be returned plus the investor would earn a rate of return of 11.7 percent. Note, the total of these accounts are sufficient to pay off the partner, but would leave the company with very little cash for operations. The owner will have to plan to have sufficient cash for operations when the loan is repaid, or delay the loan's repayment.

These forecasts look good. However, before accepting that the loan can be paid off in five years, the lender would want an explanation of the assumptions on which the forecasts are based. The first test of the assumptions would be to compare the Design Supplies' forecasts to its own recent performance or to the performance of other, similar companies.

1. Historical Comparisons

Since the relationships are typically stated as ratios, this evaluation of the assumptions is another use of the ratio analysis described in Chapter 1. Just as ratios are used to examine the historical performance of a company, so can they be used to test whether assumptions about future performance are reasonable. For Design Supplies, such a comparison of critical variables is shown in Exhibit 2-20. As an investor, you might note that the forecasted sales growth is above that obtained in 1995, but below what was experienced in 1994. This should lead to an investigation of the factors contributing to this return to higher growth: the expected decline in inflation and the increase in real sales growth. What a canny analyst would now ask is, What is the impact of inflation on Design Supplies' sales, and what would be the effect of a decline in inflation?

In addition to inflation and real growth, several other relationships are notable in the forecasts. First, company management is forecasting a major decline in operating expenses, and expects to continue to bring its current assets down relative to sales. These ratios constitute a forecast for a company that is tightly controlled, and growing. The forecasts may be overly optimistic. If the lender does not believe that these measures can be achieved, the new forecasts should be made based on the revised assumptions.

EXHIBIT 2-18 Design Supplies, Inc.—Historic and Forecasted Income Statements (in thousands)

	Actual					Forecasted		
	1994	1995	1996	1997	1998	1999	2000	2001
Sales	$1,094	$1,360	$1,402	$1,612	$1,854	$2,132	$2,452	$2,820
Cost of goods sold	(792)	(980)	(984)	(1,128)	(1,298)	(1,492)	(1,716)	(1,974)
Gross profit	302	380	418	484	556	640	736	846
Operating expenses	(244)	(290)	(351)	(376)	(402)	(430)	(460)	(492)
Profit before taxes	58	90	67	108	154	210	276	354
Taxes	(15)	(30)	(14)	(36)	(51)	(70)	(92)	(118)
Net profit	$ 43	$ 60	$ 53	$ 72	$ 103	$ 140	$ 184	$ 236

Assumptions

Sales will grow at 15 percent.
Gross margin will be 30 percent of sales.
Operating expenses will grow at 3 percent plus the expected 4 percent rate of inflation.
Taxes will be 33 percent of profit before taxes.

EXHIBIT 2-19 Design Supplies, Inc.—Historic and Forecasted Balance Sheets (in thousands)

	Actual					Forecasted		
	1994	1995	1996	1997	1998	1999	2000	2001
Assets								
Cash	$ 45.0	$ 54.0	$ 60.0	$ 64.2	$ 68.7	$ 73.5	$ 78.6	$ 84.2
Accounts receivable	118.0	168.0	165.0	177.4	204.0	234.5	269.7	310.2
Inventory	309.0	320.0	365.0	403.1	463.5	533.1	613.0	705.0
Other current assets	46.0	52.0	75.0	80.3	85.9	91.9	98.3	105.2
Total current assets	518.0	594.0	665.0	725.0	822.1	933.0	1,059.6	1,204.6
Fixed assets, net	13.0	19.0	14.0	14.0	14.0	14.0	14.0	14.0
Total assets	$531.0	$613.0	$679.0	$739.0	$836.1	$ 947.0	$1,073.6	$1,218.6

EXHIBIT 2-19 (continued)

	Actual					Forecasted		
	1994	1995	1996	1997	1998	1999	2000	2001
Liabilities and Equity								
Accounts payable	$ 41.0	$ 61.0	$ 73.0	$ 80.6	$ 92.7	$ 106.6	$ 122.6	$ 141.0
Other current liabilities	3.0	5.0	6.0	6.0	6.0	6.0	6.0	6.0
Total current liabilities	44.0	66.0	79.0	86.6	98.7	112.6	128.6	147.0
Long-term debt	200.0	200.0	200.0	200.0	200.0	200.0	200.0	200.0
Common stock	150.0	150.0	150.0	150.0	150.0	150.0	150.0	150.0
Retained earnings	137.0	197.0	250.0	322.0	425.0	565.0	749.0	985.0
Total equity	287.0	347.0	400.0	472.0	575.0	715.0	899.0	1,135.0
Subtotal	531.0	613.0	679.0	758.6	873.7	1,027.6	1,227.6	1,482.0
Net financing needed (excess funds)	—	—	—	(19.6)	(37.6)	(80.6)	(154.0)	(263.4)
Total liabilities and equity	$531.0	$613.0	$679.0	$739.0	$836.1	$ 947.0	$1,073.6	$1,218.6
Total excess funds plus cash	$ 45.0	$ 54.0	$ 60.0	$ 83.8	$106.3	$ 154.1	$ 232.6	$ 347.6

Assumptions
Receivable will be 11 percent of sales.
Inventory will be 25 percent of sales.
Cash and other current assets will increase at 3 percent plus the expected 4 percent inflation rate.
Accounts payable will be 5 percent of sales.
Other current liabilities will not change.
New fixed asset investments will equal depreciation.

EXHIBIT 2-20 Design Supplies, Inc.—Comparison of Actual
Results and Forecast Assumptions

	Actual			
Relationship	1994	1995	1996	Forecast
Sales growth	N.A.	20.0%	11.1%	15.0%
Inflation	N.A.	6.0	6.0	4.0
Real sales growth	N.A.	14.0	5.1	11.0
Receivables/sales	10.8%	12.4	11.8	11.0
Inventory/sales	28.2	23.5	26.0	25.0
Payables/sales	3.7	4.5	5.2	5.0
Gross margin	27.6	27.9	29.8	30.0
Operating expense/sales (2000)	22.3	21.3	25.0	18.8
Operating expense growth	N.A	18.9	21.0	7.0

One thing that is very useful to do is to test the impact that one factor could have on performance. For instance, let us see what would happen to the forecasts if operating expense reductions were not achieved. If operating expenses grew with sales, the operating margin would stay as a constant percentage of sales, and the investor would not be repaid by 2000. In fact, given this scenario the company would need additional financing in 2001.[7] Note that this change comes as a result of changing only one assumption.

Another way to check the validity of forecasts is to compare the assumptions with those that exist for other companies. As with any ratio analysis, the companies to be compared should be similar; that is, they should be in the same industry and have similar operating and marketing strategies. If such strictly comparable companies cannot be found for evaluation, then the analyst should adjust the comparison companies' ratios as needed.

Yet another way of using historical data to forecast future relationships is through regression analysis. This statistical technique allows the analyst to project mathematical relationships based on several past periods of data. While this method provides the security of quantitative rigor, it may be false security if the analyst has good reason to expect future relationships between various accounts to differ from their historical patterns.

2. Sensitivity Analysis

A valuable means of analyzing the assumptions is called **sensitivity analysis**. This process examines the forecast's sensitivity to changes in the assumptions.

----

[7] Note that it is growth that creates the financing need. This capital need spurred by growth will be discussed in Chapter 3.

If changing a particular assumption has little impact on the forecasts, then the assumption is not considered critical. If changing an assumption causes a major change in the projected statements, then it is considered a critical variable that warrants further analysis and careful monitoring.

Obviously, although sensitivity analysis is a fairly simple concept, it is rather time-consuming to execute properly. If the forecasts incorporate many assumptions, a considerable number of them would need to be calculated to examine adequately the sensitivity of the results to changes in each variable. To ease this process, analysts attempt to simplify the assumptions and to estimate which factors will have a critical impact on the results. The sensitivity analysis is then confined to these factors.

A frequent technique is to use three different values for a crucial assumption: the most likely, an optimistic, and a pessimistic value. Because the original projection is usually based on the most likely relationship, the analyst should then project the other two outcomes. It is important to understand that the optimistic and pessimistic forecasts are not the same as the absolute best and worst cases. The likelihood of an extremely favorable or undesirable outcome is probably remote. Therefore, it makes more sense to focus on outcomes with a greater likelihood of occurring.

Some analysts analyze only negative outcomes. Their reasoning is that while optimistic relationships may occur and create problems, those problems are easier to deal with than the problems pessimistic outcomes create. By focusing only on the downside risks, they forecast a range of potential negative results. In some cases, however, negative results arise from upside factors. For example, a large increase in sales may appear positive, but it could also result in an increased need for working capital financing, a need that should be foreseen and planned.

The risk of this simplification is that some critical assumptions might be ignored. Let us look at the outcome for Design Supplies' profits and excess funds plus cash only from changes in the sales growth rate. The chart shown in Exhibit 2-21 shows the sensitivity across a wide range of outcomes. You can clearly see that if sales growth is under 12 percent, the investor's $200,000 note cannot be paid off in 2000.

Computer-based financial modeling systems have been developed that greatly increase the analyst's ability to undertake sensitivity analysis. The analyst can determine the most significant relationships, as well as the effect that potential changes might have on performance. Not only can the modeling systems perform the calculations rapidly, they also facilitate the use of probability analysis.[8]

---

[8]   The use of these modeling systems is explained in Appendix A, "Financial Modeling." The table-building section of Appendix B, "Using Excel," describes a way to simplify sensitivity analysis of a limited number of items.

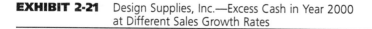

EXHIBIT 2-21 Design Supplies, Inc.—Excess Cash in Year 2000
at Different Sales Growth Rates

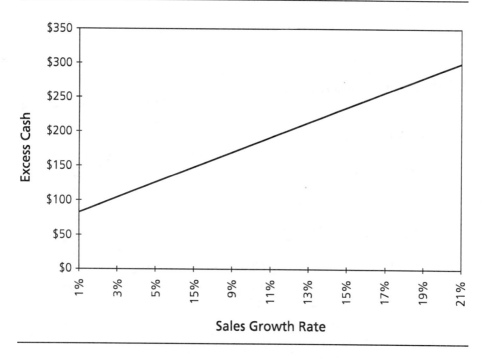

3. Probability Analysis

Probability analysis is an extension of sensitivity analysis. The analyst forecasts a range of possible values for any given variable and the likelihood that
each of the values may occur. For example, the analyst may estimate that a 7
percent sales growth has a probability of 15 percent; a 10 percent sales growth,
70 percent; and a 15 percent sales growth, 15 percent. By combining these
probabilities with those estimated for other variables—such as cost of goods
sold and rates of inflation—the analyst can calculate the overall probabilities of
all possible net financial outcomes. This series of calculations, called a **simulation**, provides more useful information than do projections relying on a single
or point estimate for each variable. For the reader interested in doing such an
analysis, suggested readings are listed at the end of the chapter.

VI. SUMMARY

Using historical relationships can aid analysts in projecting the future performance of a company. History must be tempered, however, by the analyst's

views of changes in the environment and in the company. Based on these assumptions, an analyst can estimate future cash needs using cash budgets and projected financial statements. The appropriate method depends on the needs of the company.

Projections are only as useful as the validity or reasonableness of the underlying assumptions. An important part of any forecast is testing the assumptions through sensitivity analysis. In so doing, the analyst and manager become aware of the critical assumptions and are forewarned about areas needing additional analysis and special monitoring.

One other thing must be kept in mind by those creating and using forecasts: forecasts should be constantly updated as information and conditions change. The world is not as stable as we once thought it was, and basing the future of a company on a single set of assumptions that are not kept current or tested for veracity is worse than making no forecasts at all.

SELECTED REFERENCES

For discussions of the impact of inflation on funds forecasting, see:

Seed, Allen H., III. "Measuring Financial Performance in an Inflationary Environment." *Financial Executive*, January 1982, pp. 40-50.

Vancil, Richard F. "Funds Flow Analysis During Inflation." *Financial Analysts Journal*, March-April 1976, pp. 43-56.

For a discussion of simulation, see:

Hertz, David B. "Risk-Analysis in Capital Investment." *Harvard Business Review*, September-October 1979, pp. 169-81.

For additional information on the differences between cash and accrual accounting, see:

Kroll, Yoram. "On the Differences Between Accrual Accounting Figures and Cash Flows: The Case of Working Capital." *Financial Management*, Spring 1985, pp. 75-82.

For additional discussions of forecasting financial needs, see:

Brealey, Richard A., Stewart C. Myers, and Alan Marcus. *Fundamentals of Corporate Finance*. New York: McGraw-Hill.

Ross, Stephen A., Randolph W. Westerfield, and Bradford D. Jordon. *Fundamentals of Corporate Finance*. 2nd ed. Homewood, Ill.: Richard D. Irwin, 1993, chap. 4.

Shapiro, Alan C. *Modern Corporate Finance*. 2nd ed. New York: Macmillan, 1993, chap. 24.

Weston, J. Fred, and Eugene F. Brigham. *Essentials of Managerial Finance.* 10th ed. Hinsdale, Ill.: Dryden Press, 1993, chaps. 7 and 8.

For more information on foreign exchange exposure, management, and forecasts, see:

Pringle, John. "A Look At Indirect Foreign Currency Exposure." *Journal of Applied Corporate Finance*, Fall 1995, pp. 75-81.

Pringle, John, and Robert Connolly, "The Nature and Causes of Foreign Currency Exposure." *Journal of Applied Corporate Finance*, Fall 1995, pp. 61-74.

STUDY QUESTIONS

1. In 1991 you were working for General Motors and had been assigned to study your toughest competitor, America's most successful foreign car company, Honda Motor Co., Ltd. Despite the slump in auto sales, Honda was expecting further growth in revenues. Using the financial statements for 1990 and the figures below, forecast a Honda balance sheet and income statement for 1991. In addition, to assist you in analyzing your competitor's strategic options, you should determine the change in net working capital and the current ratio for 1991. The exchange rate of the yen to the dollar for 1990 was ¥154:U.S.$1.00, but it has strengthened to ¥140:U.S.$1.00 in 1991. Your assumptions were as follows:

   - U.S. sales are expected to grow by 25 percent in dollar terms over the next year.
   - Japanese sales are expected to grow by only 5 percent in yen terms. Cost of sales is 75 percent of total revenue.
   - Research and development spending will be maintained at its current amount.
   - Total operating expenses will grow 10 percent.
   - Sales should be collected within 45 days.
   - The company is pushing for a 60-day payables period. Inventory turnover is 600 percent.
   - Management requires a minimum cash balance of 10 percent of sales. There will be no net changes in property, plant, and equipment. No dividends will be paid, and no long-term debt will be repaid. Funding will be in the form of short-term debt. The tax rate will remain at 40 percent.

HONDA
1990 INCOME STATEMENT
(in billions)

Net sales	
Japan	¥ 1,300
United States	2,200
Total net sales	3,500
Cost of goods sold	(2,625)
Research and development	(200)
Gross profit	675
Operating expenses	(500)
Operating profit	175
Taxes	(70)
Net profit	¥ 105

HONDA
1990 BALANCE SHEET
(in billions)

Assets		Liabilities and Equity	
Cash	¥ 250	Accounts payable	¥ 400
Accounts receivable	400	Other short-term debt	350
Inventory	475	Total current liabilities	750
Total current assets	1,125	Long-term debt	1,050
Net property, plant,		Common stock	75
and equipment	1,500	Retained earnings	750
Total assets	¥2,625	Total equity	825
		Total liabilities and equity	¥2,625

2. After reviewing your analysis, General Motors management believes that you are slightly optimistic about your assumptions. They expect Honda's results to be less positive, and they suggest you look into the financial statements one more time with these revised assumptions:

   - Reduce the minimum cash balance to 7 percent of sales.
   - Decrease the payables period to 45 days.
   - Increase the collection period to 60 days.

   Is the current ratio in line with the industry average of 120 percent? What are the implications of these policy changes to you as a competitor?

3. Review how your analysis would change if the ¥:$ exchange rate dropped to an unprecedented rate of ¥85:$1.00. How would such an exchange rate impact your strategy if you were Honda management? General Motors management?

4. The chief financial officer of the Top Coke Company (Top C.) is meeting with two top analysts regarding working capital management. One analyst, Charles Duncan, has suggested that a more lenient accounts receivable collection policy of 45 days would result in a sales growth of 20 percent, higher than previously forecasted. In addition, inventory turnover would increase to 600 percent and reduce bad debts to 2 percent. While management should expect operating expenses to increase 20 percent because of additional processing costs, Mr. Duncan suggests that an increase in the minimum cash balance to 20 percent of gross sales would offset any liquidity problems.

   Another analyst, Ginny Fisher, counters Mr. Duncan's argument for an aggressive working capital policy. She cites, among other issues, the recession throughout the country, and notes that this strategy could help maintain operating expenses at current levels. She estimates that reducing the accounts receivable period to 30 days would stabilize the 5 percent bad debt level and still allow sales growth of 10 percent. Although she states that the inventory turnover could decrease to 300 percent, a minimum cash balance of 15 percent of gross sales appears possible. Operating expenses would not change. Top C. has sufficient sources of short-term debt. The tax rate would remain at 40 percent, cost of goods sold at 40 percent of gross sales, and accounts payable at 114 days.

   Of course, an argument ensues between the analysts. Mr. Duncan contends that the rest of the world where Top C. operates is not suffering from a recession. Rather, the unification of Europe and the growing purchasing power of the Chinese consumer have expanded potential and current markets. Mr. Duncan argues that Top C. should attack these markets without hesitation. The financial impact on Top C. of these two strategies is not clear.

   Compute an income statement, balance sheet, net working capital ratio, and current ratio under Mr. Duncan's alternative and compare it with that proposed by Ms. Fisher.

   From the financial forecasts you have created, decide which policy changes the chief financial officer should implement. The current financial statements are as follows:

TOP C. COMPANY
(in thousands of dollars)
INCOME STATEMENT

Sales	$ 8,600
Bad debt	(430)
Net sales	8,170
Cost of goods sold	(3,500)
Gross profit	4,670
Operating expense	(3,000)
Operating income	1,670
Taxes	(668)
Net profit	$ 1,002

BALANCE SHEET

Assets		Liabilities and Equity	
Cash	$ 1,200	Accounts payable	$ 1,400
Accounts receivable	850	Other short-term debt	1,500
Inventory	800	Total current liabilities	2,900
Total current assets	2,850	Long-term debt	550
Net property, plant,		Common stock	420
and equipment	4,000	Retained earnings	2,980
Total assets	$6,850	Total equity	3,400
		Total liabilities and equity	$6,850

5. Mary Turnbull, of Mary's Ski Chalet, is attempting to plan a monthly cash budget for the coming year but is having difficulty determining her expected cash balance because of the seasonality of her sales. She has been able to accumulate the following data for 1997:

MARY'S SKI CHALET
SALES FORECASTS AND BALANCE SHEET BEGINNING BALANCES
(in thousands)

Projected Sales				Beginning Balances	
Jan.	$210	July	$ 30	Accounts receivable	$184
Feb.	175	Aug.	75	Accounts payable	173
Mar	160	Sept.	90	Cash	65
Apr.	140	Oct.	125	Inventory	50
May	50	Nov.	165	Equity	471
June	30	Dec.	230	Plant, property, and	
				equipment, net	345

- All collections and payments are made on a 30-day basis.
- 25 percent of all sales are paid for in cash.
- Cost of goods sold is 75 percent of sales.
- Selling, general, and administrative expenses are 19 percent of sales.
- Purchases are 100 percent of cost of goods sold plus 8 percent of sales for a cushion against stock-outs (safety stock).
- Interest and lease expense is $24,000 for the year.
- Depreciation expense is $12,000 for the year.
- Tax loss carryforwards will result in Mary's Ski Chalet paying no taxes in 1997.

Will Ms. Turnbull need additional financing to cover a monthly cash deficit?

6. Prepare a 1997 forecasted income statement and balance sheet for Ms. Turnbull using the information provided in Question 5.

7. Aries Corporation has entered a new market in 1997 and has asked you to prepare a five-year projected balance sheet and income statement based on the following forecasts:

- Sales growth in 1997 will be the same as in 1996. In 1998, sales growth will dip to 10 percent, and then will increase 1 percent for each year thereafter.
- Negotiations with suppliers have reduced prices, resulting in an improvement in gross margin of 12 percent, if the payment period is decreased to 60 days. Purchases made at the higher rate and included in raw materials inventory will result in an average margin of only 10 percent in 1997.
- There will be no change in the percentage of sales historical relationship for operating expenses or cash balance.
- Legislation has been passed that will reduce the tax rate to 38 percent in 1999 from its current rate of 50.7 percent.
- Inventory turnover has been historically high. Management plans to increase the turnover in 1997 to 8 times and level it out in 1999 to 6 times.
- Management does not expect any change in days' sales outstanding.
- Property, plant, and equipment—net of acquisitions, disposals, and depreciation (which is included in the cost of goods sold allocation)—will be $265,000, $291,000, $323,000, $403,000, and $513,000 for 1997 through 2001, respectively.
- Any additional financing required will be short-term (notes payable) financing.

To assist in your analysis, financial statements for 1995 and 1996 are as follows:

ARIES CORPORATION
INCOME STATEMENTS
FOR THE YEARS 1995 AND 1996
(in thousands)

	1995	1996
Sales	$ 221	$ 266
Cost of goods sold	(145)	(166)
Gross profit	76	100
Operating expenses	(38)	(35)
Operating profit	38	65
Taxes	(19)	(33)
Net income	$ 19	$ 32

ARIES CORPORATION
BALANCE SHEETS
(in thousands)

	1995	1996
Assets		
Cash	$ 22	$ 37
Accounts receivable	49	31
Inventory	47	45
Total current assets	118	113
Fixed assets	70	122
Total assets	$ 188	$ 235
Liabilities and Equity		
Notes payable	0	0
Accounts payable	$ 19	$ 34
Total current liabilities	19	34
Equity	169	201
Total liabilities and equity	$ 188	$ 235

Managing Working Capital

Most financial managers find that a significant amount of their time is spent dealing with immediate problems and opportunities. There is no doubt that the development of a comprehensive financial strategy in conjunction with a corporate business strategy is important for the long-term growth of the company. However, the financial manager must ensure that the corporation can successfully cope with the present, otherwise the long-term plan will have no value.

One of the major problems facing managers is the company's need for working capital. Working capital includes the current assets of the corporation and therefore includes inventories, accounts receivable, cash, and marketable securities. These resources are directly involved in the company's production and sales. Successful management of corporate working capital will allow managers to move their company into a prosperous future.

I. THE WORKING CAPITAL CYCLE

The term **working capital cycle**, or **production-sales cycle**, refers to the ebb and flow of funds through the company in response to changes in the level of activity in manufacturing and sales. When the company decides to manufacture a product, funds are needed to purchase raw materials, pay for the production process, and maintain inventory. If the product is sold on credit, the company also requires funds to support the accounts receivable until customers ultimately reimburse the company for the products.

The word cycle refers to the difference between the time payment is due for production expenses and the time the customer pays for the product. If the company received payment for the product at the same time it was required to pay the expenses of producing the product, there would be no working capital cycle, nor would firms have difficulty managing working capital.

This timing difference can be illustrated with a simple graph shown in Exhibit 3-1. In this highly simplified, hypothetical cycle, the raw materials are ordered on Day 0. The materials arrive and production begins. As production proceeds, workers are paid, and by Day 30, all the costs for labor and materials have been paid. The product is completed on Day 60 and is put into finished goods inventory. An order is received from a customer on Day 90, and the product is sold. Payment is received from the customer on Day 120. That

EXHIBIT 3-1   Working Capital Cycle

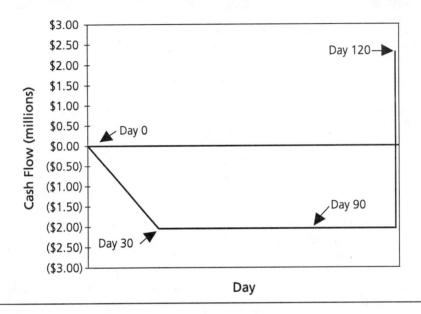

payment, presuming the company has priced its product properly, covers all the costs of production plus the profit. From a cash flow standpoint, the company has made all of the cash payments for labor and raw material costs by Day 30, but it receives no cash from the customer until Day 120. Consequently, the company requires some type of financing for more than 90 days. In this example, the working capital cycle is a total of 120 days, or four months.

The working capital cycle varies significantly among different kinds of companies. Two extreme examples are wine producers and grocery retailers. The wine producer typically stores wine for several years to age the wine. Thus, there are several years between the cash outflows for production and the receipt of cash from sales to customers. The grocery retailer usually has a rapid turnover of its perishable inventory and most sales are made for cash. Thus, the working capital cycle for the bulk of its inventory is short.

Most companies do not produce one product at a time. A grocery retailer is a good example of a company that has a variety of goods, some with short cycles, like fresh produce, others that may have a much longer shelf life, like health and beauty products. For companies like this, many products are produced and/or sold, and all are at various stages in the production-sales cycle at any given time. Thus, once a company is able to complete the start-up phase of operations successfully, it will be able to rely on a continuous flow of products through the cycle to provide funds for its needs. The company can use the cash from previous sales to pay for current production. When a company is in a stable environment with no inflation, sales growth, and changes in customer demand, lags in the working capital cycle present little difficulty. However, it is rare to find such a working capital situation. Thus, the cycle must be understood and managed.

1. The Impact of Inflation

In an inflationary environment, the cost of producing each unit increases over time. Thus, by the time the company has collected the cash from its previous sales, the production costs on subsequent units have increased. Unless the company is able to price units with sufficient profit margins, it may not be able to meet subsequent production costs with revenues from prior production.

To illustrate this problem, we will look at a simple example of a production cycle in a U.K. steel manufacturing company. The company begins with a cash balance of £450, as shown in Exhibit 3-2. This cash balance is sufficient to cover the estimated costs of manufacturing 2 tons of steel at the current price of £225 per ton. However, an unexpected outburst of inflation of 1.5 percent per month (an annualized rate of 20 percent) occurs.[1] The company sells its first ton of steel on the 120th day for £301, but it does not collect payment until 60 days later. It does not charge interest on its accounts receivable. This entire cycle is shown in Exhibit 3-2.

Note that, in spite of the fact that management initially thought it could cover its needs with its cash balance, the company must borrow to finance the production of the second ton of steel, as well as to carry the account receivable for the sale of the first ton. This is because the costs of production rose, while the amount held in accounts receivable once the sale was made did not. Management might choose to deal with this problem in a variety of ways, but identifying it is the first step.

This example is obviously highly simplified. Continual production and multiple products with varying working capital cycles and exposures to inflation complicate the analysis. Nevertheless, the conceptual framework for analyzing the increased working capital requirements caused by inflation is the same. The net effect of inflation is to increase the amount of working capital required by the company.

2. The Impact of Sales Growth

The effect of sales growth on working capital needs is similar to that of inflation. In the case of sales growth, the problem is not caused by an increasing per-unit costs, but by an increasing number of units. Although the cost per unit may be stable, total costs increase because of the increased volume.

---

[1] The annualized rate of inflation is the compound rate at 1.5 percent per month, or an annual rate of 19.56 percent. A compound rate is not the simple sum of the monthly rates. To learn more about the compounding process, see Chapter 4.

EXHIBIT 3-2   Impact of Inflation on the Working Capital Cycle—Steel Manufacturer

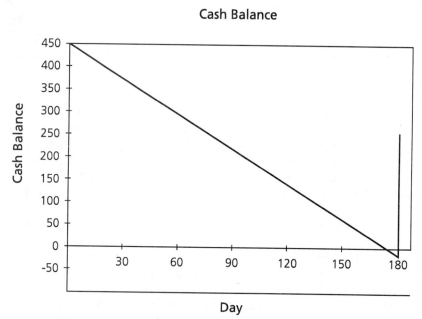

Cash Balance

Day	Activity	Cash Balance
0	Begin production of first ton.	£450
30	Complete one-third of first ton.	374
60	Complete two-thirds of first ton.	297
90	Complete production of first ton at total cost of £232.	219
90	Begin production of second ton.	219
120	Complete one-third of second ton.	139
120	Sell first ton at current price.	139
150	Complete two-thirds of second ton.	58
180	Complete production of second ton at total cost of £242.	(24)
180	Receive payment for sale of first ton at £301.	277

For example, a microcomputer producer may have been very successful in developing a market for its products. Assume that the company can produce microcomputers for a cost of $700 each. The company produces 500 computers and sells each for $800 during a particular month. The company extends credit for 30 days to buyers of the microcomputers. During the ensuing month, the demand for microcomputers is such that the company produces 600. At production costs of $700 each, the company incurs a total production cost of $420,000. However, the sales revenue collected from the previous month's sales will be only $400,000 (500 × $800). Thus, even if the company continues to charge $800 per unit, a price that allows a profit margin of 12.5 percent, the sales growth alone will result in a need for new working capital. A company in this situation will have insufficient cash inflow from collections each month to meet the expenses incurred for the production of new computers.

The microcomputer company did not misprice its products: the company's prices allowed an adequate profit margin above the costs of production. The problem stemmed from the timing differences between the payment of production expenses and the receipt of payment from sales.

This example illustrates a problem that growing a company faces. In order to grow, a company must finance that growth. A lack of adequate funding will restrict the potential growth of the company. The maximum growth rate a company can fund with its existing financing policies is termed the sustainable growth rate, discussed in Chapter 1. Sustainable growth depends on the profitability of the company, the need for assets to support sales growth, the way the company is financed, and the company's dividend policy. In general, the more rapid the actual rate of growth, the greater the need for funds to support that growth.

3. The Impact of Variable Sales Demand

The other major factor that can cause working capital problems is a varying level of sales. Changes in sales activity are of three types:

1. **Seasonal:** Peak demand occurs during particular periods of the year. Snow-skiing equipment is one example of a seasonal product.
2. **Cyclical:** Peak demand occurs during different phases of the business cycle; for instance, the demand for building materials is cyclical.
3. **Secular:** Demand fluctuates over a long period of time. Revenues from gold are secular.

These are also called cycles since they reoccur. Each of these cycles differs in duration but has a similar effect on the company's working capital. For simplicity's sake, we will focus on the seasonal cycle, because it is of short duration and its impact on working capital needs is easy to trace.

In a seasonal industry, the company may not have sold the completed units before it must incur the costs of producing additional units. To illustrate the problem, we will use the example of the snow-skiing equipment manufacturer. This business is highly seasonal: peak consumer demand occurs during fall and winter. The producer's peak sales period occurs in late summer and early fall, when retailers place their orders to have the equipment for sale during the peak snow-skiing months.

The peak sales period for the manufacturer is not, however, the peak production period. To produce skiing equipment as orders from retailers are received would be very inefficient. The manufacturer would need large production capacity, which would be idle for most of the year, and new workers would have to be hired and trained for each production season. During the peak production period the work force would be required to work overtime, and at the conclusion of the period workers would be laid off. In short, seasonal production typically is inefficient and expensive.

To avoid these problems, the ski-equipment manufacturer may produce skis all year long. During the slack sales months, in the late winter and spring, production is continued but little equipment is actually sold to retailers. The manufactured equipment is stored, and the growing inventory is used to fill sales orders as they arrive in the late summer and early fall. As inventory builds up, the company still buys and pays for the raw materials and labor needed to produce the skiing equipment.

As retailers begin to place orders in the late summer, the manufacturer ships equipment from the warehoused inventory. During this period, the manufacturer starts to draw on the finished goods inventory if orders exceed the continuing production level. However, the manufacturer still has not received payment for any of the equipment. The retailers buy from the manufacturer on credit, with perhaps 30 or 60 days in which to pay for the equipment. During this period of high but decreasing inventories, continuing production, and increasing accounts receivable, most seasonal companies experience their greatest need for working capital.

As the ski-equipment producer's selling season progresses, additional orders will be received. As these orders are filled, the large finished goods inventory is used more rapidly than it is being replenished from production. Accounts receivable increase from the credit sales, although the company does receive payment for shipments made in the late summer. By the end of the fall selling season, the company's inventory is depleted, and all of its receivables should have been collected: the company should have the cash ready to begin the next working capital cycle. The pattern of inflow and outflow of funds might exist for several seasonal peaks during a year, over a business cycle, or over a long-term secular trend. The working capital pattern in many businesses is determined by industry practice. When there is a choice (e.g., level versus seasonal production), the analytical techniques discussed in Chapter 4 are useful in determining which approach is most attractive.

II. CASH MANAGEMENT

Because financial obligations must be paid for in cash, the critical resource in dealing with the working capital cycle is cash. Corporate managers need to ensure that sufficient cash is available to meet their obligations. This has led to the development of sophisticated, automated techniques to manage a company's cash. These techniques have three objectives: to accelerate the speed of cash receipts, decelerate the speed of cash disbursements, and maximize the return on investment of cash balances. In the 1970s and 1980s, high interest rates emphasized the importance of managing cash, while the development of computers allowed managers access to the information needed for close monitoring of cash balances.

1. Managing Receipts

The process of managing cash receipts involves collecting funds as quickly as possible and concentrating them in accounts so that the financial manager can control them.

Lockboxes. The use of lockboxes speeds the collecting, processing, depositing, and reporting of payments received through the mail. A lockbox is a special post office box to which the company's customers are instructed to mail payments. The box is checked several times daily by the processing operation, which is usually operated by a bank. Checks are immediately entered into the check-clearing process to be converted into funds for the company.

Electronic Funds Transfer. A faster method of collecting funds is to require that payment be made electronically rather than with a paper check. In this system, payment is made by transferring funds directly from the payer's bank account to the recipient's account. This makes the funds immediately available and also eliminates the cost of handling paper checks. For an individual, the debit card issued by their bank acts in the same way.

Preauthorized Checks. Preauthorized checks (PACs) are preprinted, unsigned checks. For fixed, repetitive payments, companies authorize their creditors to draw checks on their accounts. The creditor sends the PAC to the bank, which then deposits the funds into the creditor's account.

Deposit Concentration. Because it is difficult to control funds in many different banks, most receipt management systems provide for transferring funds electronically into one or more large accounts. Central accounts can be more closely managed.

Note that all these systems can be used within a country and between parties in two different countries. When a payment must cross borders, the primary criterion is that the currencies of the two countries involved be freely convertible; that is, the currencies can be readily exchanged for each other at a known exchange rate. If the currencies are not freely convertible, the problem is somewhat more complex. International banks have specific expertise in dealing with payments across borders.

2. Managing Disbursements

The goal in managing disbursements is to delay payments so that funds can be used by the company as long as possible.

Managed Balance Account. A managed balance account is a special checking account that has a zero balance. As checks are presented to this account, a negative balance is created. Funds are then automatically transferred from a master account to bring the account back to zero or another predetermined balance.

In this way, all funds are centralized and no idle balances remain in the disbursing account.

Controlled Disbursement System. The purpose of this system is to maximize the time it takes for checks to clear a company's account. By making payments through geographically remote banks, the clearing time, also called "float," is increased. The purpose is to postpone the date when the company must provide funds to cover checks and to allow funds either to remain in interest-earning assets or reduce the need to borrow.

3. Investing Cash Balances

By carefully managing cash accounts, a financial manager can minimize the cash the corporation must maintain. This increases the amount of funds available to invest or reduces the need to raise additional capital. By maximizing the amount of funds available to invest in productive or working assets, the manager is operating efficiently.

Despite the efforts to control and predict disbursements, there may be unforeseen disbursements or slower than expected receipts. Therefore, companies typically maintain a positive cash balance for transaction liquidity. Having idle cash is unproductive. Good managers maximize the return on these fund balances by investing them in the money market.

The money markets match borrowers and lenders of short-term funds. Although technically money-market instruments can have a maturity of up to one year, most have shorter maturities. Money-market instruments are considered to be "near cash" because the market is quite liquid (has many buyers and sellers) and the borrowers generally are institutions with high credit ratings.

Money-market instruments in the United States include Treasury bills (short-term notes issued by the U.S. government), commercial paper (short-term notes issued by corporations), and certificates of deposit (short-term notes issued by banks). Although the returns from these short-term investments may be relatively low in comparison with longer-term, less liquid investments, the returns are superior to idle cash balances.

The short-term investment opportunities may be quite different in other countries. For instance, in smaller economies, the shorter-term market may be arranged only through banks. Very short-term investments may exist exclusively through borrowing and lending between corporations. In countries where domestic currency values are volatile, there may be instruments issued by the government or banks that are denominated in a more stable currency—for instance, U.S. dollars.

While the particular instruments available for short-term investments or to finance a company's short-term needs vary from country to country, one additional major, organized money market exists: the Eurobond market. Eurobond borrowing can be in one of several widely tradable currencies. However, much of the borrowing and lending is done in U.S. dollars, even though the market is outside the United States. A company can borrow or lend in this market from overnight up to one year. One can also borrow and lend for more than one year, a subject we will discuss in Chapter 6. Because the lending is done in dollars, the interest rates paid for Eurodollar deposits and charged on loans are similar to those of similar transactions in the United States.[2]

In order to invest in these instruments, the financial manager must know how much cash is available to invest. Cash management systems are designed to provide daily information about the amount of funds that can be invested. In many cases, investments must be made for periods as short as overnight to maximize the return available from cash balances.

In times of low interest rates and economic stability, cash by itself is not a productive asset. In such times, and in such countries, managers need to make sure that their companies have minimized the cash that is maintained in the company and that all available resources have been invested in assets being used to produce the company's products. The cash balance should be maintained at the level needed for the operations of the business alone.

Not all environments are stable or have low interest rates, however. In some circumstances, the most productive asset the company has is its cash. In situations where the company's management can lend at rates that generate higher returns than those that could be earned in the product market, management will want to adopt policies that maximize the cash at its command and invest those funds in the money market or the longer-term, capital, markets.

Opportunities to invest cash in the capital and money markets became evident to many managers around the world in the 1980s. For many companies, the returns they made on their financial transactions exceeded those earned on selling their products. In some cases, financial profits compensated for product/market losses. Periods of above-normal inflation often provide such opportunities. Terra Blanca, a company we looked at in Chapter 2, is an example of such a company.

III. MANAGING OTHER WORKING CAPITAL REQUIREMENTS

Just as a company's cash must be managed, so must other working capital investments. The general rule is to minimize working capital investments while still providing the resources required to produce quality products.

1. Accounts Receivable

The size of a company's accounts receivable is, to a large extent, determined by its competitive environment. The company often has little control over the

---

[2] This also can be done in other currencies, such as the Japanese yen.

magnitude of its credit sales. If competitors are selling goods on credit, the company may be forced to follow that practice to remain competitive. In that case, the only method of reducing accounts receivable is to ensure that credit collections are prompt. If goods or services are sold on 30-day terms, management should vigorously attempt to ensure that payment is received within the 30-day period. Any extension represents a non-interest-bearing loan by the producer to the customer. Some companies charge their customers overdue-account penalties or interest to encourage timely payment or to compensate for inflation.

A method of monitoring accounts receivable based on the due date is called **accounts receivable aging**. In this process, receivables are categorized according to the number of days they are overdue. For example, they might be categorized as 30, 60, and 90 days overdue. Collection efforts can then focus on those accounts that are most overdue. The intent is to minimize the number of accounts that are not collected punctually. Because of the costs associated with the financing of a company's working capital needs, any unnecessary increases in accounts receivable caused by lax collection of overdue accounts must be recognized as an extraneous expense for the company.

In an environment in which a company can independently determine its accounts receivable policy, the critical factor is the relationship between sales and credit policy. By reducing the financing offered to buyers, a company may be eliminating potential customers. Thus, accounts receivable may be reduced, but only at the cost of reducing total revenues. In such an environment, credit policy should be considered a marketing tool, and the cost of the resulting accounts receivable should be considered a cost of marketing the company's products.

On the other hand, extending more credit to customers may have the effect of reducing the inventory the company must keep. With easier credit terms, buyers may purchase more goods, thereby assuming some of the costs of inventory maintenance from the manufacturer. However, while the company's inventory would decline, its accounts receivable would increase.

An increased volume of credit sales has two other effects. First, it exposes the company to additional risk of uncollectible accounts. The potential cost of unpaid accounts (bad debts) must be weighed against the profits resulting from new sales generated by the easier credit terms. Second, the company extending the credit must have adequate capital to finance its customers' purchases. As you already know, and we will discuss in later chapters, money has a cost. Whether the company borrows to extend credit, or diverts resources from other uses, there is a cost. This cost is called the **cost-of-carry**.

2. Inventories

Like accounts receivable, inventory is directly related to sales volume. While maintaining too much inventory is expensive, it will have no impact on sales volume. However, too little inventory may cause stock-outs, and thus lost sales. Maintenance of an appropriate inventory level is so significant that sophisticated inventory models, including those based on neural networks and fuzzy logic, are used in inventory planning. The aim of these models is to determine the relationship between inventory levels and sales levels so the company can have the optimum production and inventory levels.

During the past decade, many managers reevaluated the size of the inventory their companies maintained. One reason for this reevaluation was high interest rates: the cost of financing additional current assets was high. A second reason for reevaluating inventory positions was the method introduced by Japanese companies called "just-in-time" inventory management. This method places the burden for inventory maintenance on the suppliers and forces both buyers and sellers to institute new inventory management procedures. In effect, this inventory method minimizes the inventory kept on hand: shipments of raw materials and goods arrive just as they are needed for production or sales. While this has the effect of reducing inventories, it does present the danger of stock-outs, not having enough inventory, in cases where a supplier falters.[3]

In sum, from the standpoint of reducing the need for working capital, the company should attempt to reduce its investment in accounts receivable and inventories. However, the company risks the loss of sales if these accounts are reduced inordinately. The managerial task is to ascertain the appropriate level for cash, accounts receivable, and inventory.

IV. FINANCING WORKING CAPITAL

Having determined the minimum level of working capital needed to carry out the production and sales cycle, the manager must then select the most appropriate method of financing. Not surprisingly, an important consideration is the cost of various sources of financing.

The most significant source of self-funding is a company's profits. If the competitive environment allows, the company may be able to price its products so that profits are sufficient to fund working capital requirements. For example, in an inflationary environment, the company might attempt to increase its prices in excess of the inflation rate in order to finance the working capital needs caused by inflating production costs. The company's ability to adjust its prices in this manner naturally depends on the competitive situation and the economic and political environment in which it operates. In a restrained political environment, above-average price increases may create excessive scrutiny and the potential for price freezes or other industry controls

---

[3]   This problem was apparent as suppliers suffered disruptions due to the major earthquake in the port and production center of Kobe, Japan, in the spring of 1995.

by the government.[4] In a highly competitive environment, the company may not have much latitude in its pricing and will need to turn to other sources.

One of the most readily available external sources of funds is the company's suppliers, through the credit terms they allow. Unfortunately, there is a limit to supplier-supplied credit: the company's suppliers may refuse to ship materials needed for production, and such refusals might force the company to stop production. This is usually the last course of action a supplier will take, however, because it results in the loss of a customer.

More often, suppliers encourage prompt payment: vendors often allow the purchaser to take a discount from the sales price if the payment is made within a specified time period. For example, suppliers may indicate payment terms of 2/10, net 30. This means that, if the purchaser pays within 10 days, a discount of 2 percent from the sales price is allowed, otherwise, the full sales price is due in 30 days. If the purchaser decides to wait 30 days to pay rather than paying within 10 days and taking the 2 percent discount, the cost of holding the funds for the additional 20 days is 43.5 percent on a compounded annualized basis.[5] Even if the purchaser decides to pay after 60 days rather than the 30 days specified by the terms of the sale, the effective cost is 15.3 percent. These figures suggest that, when a supplier offers a discount, stretching the payables period is an expensive source of funds unless payment is delayed for a long time.

In countries where tax authorities collect taxes as the profits are earned, another creditor or source of credit financing is the government. Note, however, that while some government taxing authorities may allow a temporary deferral of taxes, nonpayment of taxes is a punishable offense, thus limiting the usefulness of this source of funds.

A typically less expensive source of short-term financing is bank debt. A standard borrowing arrangement for creditworthy companies is a **line of credit** with a bank. This is an agreement that the bank will lend up to a specified amount during a specified period of time. The borrower can borrow, or draw down, against the credit line as the need arises. In situations where the borrower may not be considered a good credit risk, the bank may extend a **secured line of credit**. In this case, the bank has a claim on specific assets of the company—usually the accounts receivable and inventory—if the borrowed funds are not repaid as agreed. A standard practice is for secured lines not to exceed some portion of the value of receivables and inventory.

---

[4] Those reading this book who live and work exclusively in the United States may not recall any period of price freezes or price-induced government scrutiny, but both occurred in the 1970s—price freezes during the Nixon administration and price scrutiny of the oil industry during several periods of rapid price increases or lagging price decreases. For many readers who live in different economic and political environments, price scrutiny and price freezes are common, particularly in politically sensitive or highly visible companies or industries.

[5] If the discount is not taken, and the bill is paid on the due date in 30 days, the customer has paid 2 percent for the use of the funds for 20 days—an annualized rate of 43.5 percent. Compounding is explained in Chapter 4.

Some companies have found it advantageous to sell their accounts receivable to a financial institution. This process is called **factoring**. The company receives immediate payment for the receivables and does not have to wait until accounts are collected to have funds available. The factoring company buys the receivables at a discount from their stated, or face, value, so the company incurs a cost in selling its receivables. The advantage of factoring is that it reduces the firm's need for working capital. In addition, for a somewhat higher discount, the receivables may be sold without recourse. This means that if an account is not collectible, the financial institution, rather than the company, absorbs the loss.

Companies considered to be good credit risks have developed direct access to short-term financial markets without using commercial banks as intermediaries. These high-quality companies can issue short-term notes, called **commercial paper**, at interest rates slightly below the rates banks would have charged. Other companies, such as insurance companies, are large purchasers of commercial paper. Companies are using increasingly sophisticated and innovative methods of raising short-term funds. The objective is to obtain funds at the lowest cost.

Another method of financing for companies that have accounts receivable that are due over long periods of time is called **securitization**. It has been used primarily by companies with financial assets, such as the financing subsidiaries of large corporations and financial institutions. In general, these companies bundle a number of receivables into a package that is then sold like a security in the capital markets, hence the name securitization. The first assets that were securitized in this way were mortgages. Others, such as credit card receivables, have also been securitized.

Our focus on financing for working capital needs has, in this chapter, been short-term sources. Short-term sources generally are considered appropriate because the need is short-lived. For this reason, a company's **net working capital** is defined as current assets minus current liabilities. While a current asset (that is, a particular credit sale or product in inventory) may be short-lived, the inventory or accounts receivable balance sheet accounts are not short-lived; they are a permanent part of the assets of the company. Thus, many believe that a more appropriate way of financing working capital investments is through a more permanent form of financing. This notion of using permanent financing for working capital is especially attractive when working capital increases are secular.

If a company chooses to use short-term, temporary financing for permanent or long-lived increases in working capital, there are risks to the strategy. The risk comes when a short-term source must be renewed. At that time, the company is exposing itself to interest rate changes and the possibility that funds will not be available when needed. Financing with longer, more permanent sources of financing may be a more appropriate strategy. These sources will be discussed in Chapters 6 and 7.

V. SUMMARY

Through the normal course of business operations, companies require current assets. These assets—inventories, accounts receivable, and cash—are needed to allow the company to create and sell its products. However, because of the timing differences between the cash outflows for creating the products and the cash inflows from the sale of products, companies usually require some financing for these working capital needs.

Because of the magnitude of the amounts required for working capital, skillful managers of working capital can make a significant impact on a company's profitability. Such steps as shortening the working capital cycle or eliminating unneeded assets can reduce the need for cash. In assessing working capital needs, managers must balance reducing working capital and reducing sales and profits. Having achieved an appropriate working capital level, management's remaining responsibility is to finance working capital by taking cost and funds availability into consideration.

SELECTED REFERENCES

For a discussion of cash management and cash management systems, see:

Brealey, Richard A., and Stewart C. Myers. *Principles of Corporate Finance*. 4th ed. New York: McGraw-Hill, 1991, chap. 31.

Brealey, Richard A., Stewart C. Myers, and Alan J. Marcus. *Fundamentals of Corporate Finance*. New York: McGraw-Hill, 1995, chap. 19.

Kamath, Ravindra R., Shahriar Khaksari, Heidi Hylton Meier, and John Winklepleck. "Management of Excess Cash: Practices and Developments." *Financial Management*, Autumn 1985, pp. 70-77.

Pinches, George E. *Financial Management*. New York: Harper Collins, 1994, chap. 20.

Ross, Stephen A., Randolph W. Westerfield, and Jeffrey F. Jaffe. *Corporate Finance*. 4th ed. Homewood, Ill.: Richard D. Irwin, 1996, chap. 27.

Shapiro, Alan C. *Modern Corporate Finance*. 2nd ed. New York: Macmillan, 1994, chap. 26.

Stone, Bernell K., and Ned C. Hill. "Cash Transfer Scheduling for Efficient Cash Concentration." *Financial Management*, Autumn 1980, pp. 35-43.

Stone, Bernell K., and Tom W. Miller. "Daily Cash Forecasting with Multiplicative Models of Cash Flow Patterns." *Financial Management*, Winter 1987, pp. 45-54.

For a discussion of accounts receivable management, see:

Brealey, Richard A., and Stewart C. Myers. *Principles of Corporate Finance*. 4th ed. New York: McGraw-Hill, 1991, chap. 30.

Gentry, James A., and Jesus M. DeLa Garza. "A Generalized Model for Monitoring Accounts Receivable." *Financial Management*, Winter 1985, pp. 28-38.

Halloran, John A., and Howard P. Lanser. "The Credit Policy Decision in an Inflationary Environment." *Financial Management*, Winter 1981, pp. 31-38.

Mian, Sherzad, and Clifford W. Smith, Jr. "Extending Trade Credit and Financing Receivables." *Journal of Applied Corporate Finance*, Spring 1994, pp. 75-84.

Pinches, George E. *Financial Management*. New York: Harper Collins, 1994, chap. 21.

Ross, Stephen A., Randolph W. Westerfield, and Jeffrey F. Jaffe. *Corporate Finance*. 4th ed. Homewood, Ill.: Richard D. Irwin, 1996, chaps. 27 and 28.

Shapiro, Alan C. *Modern Corporate Finance*. 2nd ed. New York: Macmillan, 1994, chap. 25.

For information on inventory management, see:

Pinches, George E. *Financial Management*. New York: Harper Collins, 1994, chap. 21.

Shapiro, Alan C. *Modern Corporate Finance*. 2nd ed. New York: Macmillan, 1994, chap. 28.

For more information on working capital in general, see:

Emery, Douglas, and John D. Finnerty. *Principles of Finance*. St. Paul, Minn.: West Publishing Co., 1991, chap. 25.

Pinches, George E. *Financial Management*. New York: Harper Collins, 1994, chap. 19.

Ross, Stephen A., Randolph W. Westerfield, and Jeffrey F. Jaffe. *Corporate Finance*. 4th ed. Homewood, Ill.: Richard D. Irwin, 1996, chap. 25.

Shapiro, Alan C. *Modern Corporate Finance*. 2nd ed. New York: Macmillan, 1994, chap. 25.

For a discussion of state-of-the-art working capital management, see:

Gentry, James A. "State of the Art of Short-Run Financial Management." *Financial Management*, Summer 1988, pp. 41-57.

For more on cash management in an international company, see:

Madura, Jeff. *International Financial Management*. 2nd ed. St. Paul, Minn.: West Publishing Co., 1989, chap. 14.

For more on working capital management in an international company, see:

Shapiro, Alan C. *Multinational Financial Management*. 5th ed. Needham Heights, Mass.: Allyn & Bacon, 1996, chap. 14.

For additional information on money markets, see:

Brick, John R., ed. *Financial Markets: Instruments and Concepts.* Richmond, Va.: Robert F. Dame, 1981, sec. I.

Grabbe, J. Orlin. *International Financial Markets.* 2nd ed. New York: Elsevier Science Publishing, 1991.

Pinches, George E. *Financial Management.* New York: Harper Collins, 1994, chap. 22.

Ross, Stephen A., Randolph W. Westerfield, and Jeffrey F. Jaffe. *Corporate Finance.* 4th ed. Homewood, Ill.: Richard D. Irwin, 1996, chaps. 23-25.

Weston, J. Fred, and Eugene F. Brigham. *Essentials of Managerial Finance.* 8th ed. Hinsdale, Ill.: Dryden Press, 1988, chap. 10.

STUDY QUESTIONS

1. Chateau Royale International is anticipating explosive sales growth in 1997. As the company's account manager at Bank & Trust, you are concerned about the amount of short-term borrowing that will be required under current working capital policies. Forecast a balance sheet and income statement for 1997, as well as the change in net working capital and the current ratio, to assist management in understanding the effects of this increase in sales volume. Financial statements for 1996, followed by your assumptions, are given below.

CHATEAU ROYALE INTERNATIONAL
1996 INCOME STATEMENT
(in millions)

Sales	$ 375,000
Cost of goods sold	(276,150)
Gross profit	98,850
Operating expenses	(75,000)
Depreciation	(5,100)
Operating profit	18,750
Taxes	(7,500)
Net profit	$ 11,250

CHATEAU ROYALE INTERNATIONAL
1996 BALANCE SHEET
(in millions)

Cash	$ 75,000	Accounts payable	$ 23,116
Accounts receivable	46,233	Short-term debt	51,867
Inventory	93,750		
Current assets	214,983	Current liabilities	74,983
		Long-term debt	125,000
Net property, plant,		Common stock	100,000
and equipment	115,000	Retained earnings	30,000
		Total liabilities and	
Total assets	$329,983	owners' equity	$329,983

Based on your knowledge of the company and the industry, you have made the following assumptions:

- Sales will increase 60 percent. Cost of goods sold is 75 percent of sales. Operating expenses will grow 10 percent.
- Depreciation will be $8,000.
- For this analysis, common stock and long-term debt remain constant from 1996.
- Receivables will be outstanding 45 days.
- Purchases equal the cost of goods sold. Payables payment period is 30 days.
- Inventory turnover is 3 times.
- Management requires a minimum cash balance of 20 percent of sales.
- There are no purchases or disposals of property, plant, or equipment.
- The tax rate is 34 percent.
- No dividends will be issued in 1997.
- Additional funding will be in the form of short-term debt.
- Cash will be 20 percent of sales.

2. After reviewing your analysis, Chateau Royale management suggests the following working capital policy changes:

- Reduce minimum cash balance to 15 percent of sales.
- Increase payables payment period to 45 days.
- Increase inventory turnover to 400 percent.

Recompute the balance sheet and net working capital to reflect these changes. Is the current ratio in line with the industry average of 320 percent? What are the implications of these policy changes?

3. Cindy Brittain, chief financial officer of the Kurz Corporation, located in Edmonton, Ontario, Canada is meeting with her two top analysts regarding management of working capital. Tony Triano has suggested that a more lenient accounts receivable collection policy would result in higher sales. He has estimated that, by increasing the receivables collection period to 60 days, sales would be 50 percent higher than the original forecast, inventory turnover will increase to 700 percent, and bad debt will only be 2 percent of net sales. Furthermore, an increase in the minimum cash balance to 20 percent of net sales will offset any liquidity problems.

Jim Dine, however, has advised against an aggressive working capital policy citing, among other issues, the expectation of slower economic growth. He has estimated that, by reducing the receivables collection period to 30 days, there will be no bad debt expense and sales growth will still be as originally forecast at 20 percent. Although inventory turnover will decrease to 500 percent, the minimum cash balance can be reduced to 15 percent.

All additional financing will be in the form of short-term debt. The tax rate will remain at 35 percent, cost of goods sold at 75 percent of gross sales, accounts payable at 29.7 days, and operating expenses will be constant.

a. Compute an income statement, balance sheet, net working capital, and current ratio under each alternative. To assist in your analysis, the financial statements, without the strategy change, are provided.

b. Which policy changes should Ms. Brittain implement?

KURZ CORPORATION
FORECASTED INCOME STATEMENT
(in thousands of Canadian dollars)

Sales	CD $ 505,000
Bad debt	(5,000)
Net sales	500,000
Cost of goods sold	(375,000)
Gross profit	125,000
Operating expense	(90,900)
Operating profit	34,100
Taxes	(11,935)
Net profit	CD $ 22,165

KURZ CORPORATION
BALANCE SHEET
(in thousands of Canadian dollars)

Cash	CD $ 90,000	Accounts payable	CD $ 30,822
Accounts receivable	61,644	Short-term debt	86,322
Inventory	62,500	Current liabilities	117,144
Current assets	214,144	Long-term debt	110,000
Net property, plant, and		Common stock	75,000
equipment	130,000	Retained earnings	42,000
		Total liabilities and	
Total assets	$344,144	owners' equity	$344,144

4. Jose Dizon, a well-known Philippine architect, has completed the design for THE CRESCENT, to be constructed at the new financial center of the Philippines, the Ortigas Center. He has invited building contractors to bid for the work, and Pablo Lucas has won the bid for 45 million pesos. In the contract, Mr. Dizon agreed to pay Mr. Lucas P4.5 million at the beginning of construction, 20 percent of the total contract fee for every additional 25 percent of the job completed, and the final 10 percent 90 days after construction and a successful inspection is completed. Construction is expected to last one year, beginning January 1997. To start the project Mr. Lucas expects to have P1 million in cash on hand at the beginning of January 1997.

Develop a monthly cash budget for 1997 for Mr. Lucas assuming:

- Cement is now scarce because of a boom in the construction industry. As a result, it will have to be imported from Taiwan. Every other month, 33,750 bags will be needed at a cost of U.S. $3.60 per bag. A letter of credit will be used to finance the cement purchases from the Taiwanese supplier. The letter of credit will be opened with a bank one month prior to a shipment. The full value of the letter of credit must be deposited in the bank at the time the letter is obtained. The first shipment will arrive in February 1997, and the last in August 1997. The exchange rate in January 1997 is expected to be P28:U.S.$1, but it is expected to rise to P30:U.S.$1 as early as February.
- Granite tiles to be used for the building exterior must be imported from Italy. The order must be placed in May, and a letter of credit in U.S. dollars must be opened at that time. The total cost is expected to be P5 million.
- Beginning in March and ending in December 1997, 40 molded plastic window frames will be imported from Germany per month. Each window unit will cost $100. A letter of credit is required by the supplier.

- Two elevators will be ordered from Korea's Goldstar in February, at a cost of U.S. $10,000 each. Goldstar requires a letter of credit in its favor when the order is placed.
- A generator will be ordered in January. Because the producer, Caterpillar Co., has a locally operated sales office, the payment can be made in local currency. Mr. Lucas expects the generator to be delivered in April and installed and paid for in May. The cost of the generator is P2 million.
- Bathroom fixtures will be imported from Italy. A total of 130 pieces are needed at an expected cost of U.S. $150 per piece. The fixtures will take 2 months to be delivered and are needed one month before the project is completed. A letter of credit will be used to facilitate this purchase.
- Employed on the job will be 200 people with an average monthly salary and benefits of P1,875.
- Overhead expenses are expected to be P10,000 per month.
- Mr. Lucas expects to complete the job in four equal portions in May, August, October, and December.
- No taxes will be paid until 1998.

Mr. Lucas has a revolving credit line with the United Coconut Planters' Bank. The bank has asked him to provide a forecast of the amount of funds he will need and the timing of those needs during THE CRESCENT project. As his financial analyst, you are expected to provide the detailed forecasts for Mr. Lucas to take to the bank.

Valuation 1: Capital Budgeting

In Chapters 2 and 3, we discussed some simple methods of forecasting future financing needs. Most of these techniques use the history of the business to create forecasts for the future and are useful for examining the financial effects of corporate strategy and policy. However, they assume that a specific strategy has been decided on and will be undertaken. What we did not discuss in Chapters 2 or 3 was how managers choose among different investments and strategies. In this chapter, we will examine the process by which managers allocate capital among different courses of action. Because we are allocating a usually scarce resource, capital, this process of making investment decisions is called **capital budgeting**.

Capital investments can be spontaneous or long-term. In Chapter 3, we discussed the increases and decreases in current assets that can occur in businesses where sales are seasonal or cyclical. Most of these changes could be called **spontaneous**, since they do not occur as a consequence of managers' actions but are, instead, the normal results of changing sales levels. For instance, during a cyclical upturn, a manufacturing firm whose sales are made on credit needs funds for both increased inventories and larger accounts receivable. Both of these increases are investments. An investment is an outlay of funds on which management expects a return. The return comes, of course, from the profit on the expected sales increase.

Spontaneous investments often have short-term benefits and usually involve transient changes in working capital (inventory or accounts receivable) rather than capital investments. Typically, a **capital investment** is thought of as having potential benefits extending over a longer period of time, usually more than one year. It includes such things as permanent additions to working capital (such as an increase in accounts receivable as a result of a change in the company's credit policy); the purchase of land, buildings, or equipment to expand capacity; and the costs associated with advertising campaigns or research and development programs. Because capital investments are often irreversible, or the redeployment of assets comes only at considerable loss of time, money, and managerial effort, capital investments are evaluated more formally and intensely than are spontaneous investments.

In most firms, the capital budgeting process consists of five steps:

1. Generating and gathering investment ideas.
2. Analyzing the costs and benefits of proposed investments:
   a. Forecasting costs and benefits for each investment.
   b. Evaluating the costs and benefits.
3. Ranking the relative attractiveness of each proposed investment and choosing among investment alternatives.
4. Implementing the investments chosen.
5. Evaluating the implemented investments.

Of course, these five steps are continuously repeated in any company. Because financial analysts are most involved in estimating and evaluating the costs and benefits and choosing among the alternative investments, we will concentrate on steps 2 and 3 in this chapter.

I. COST-BENEFIT ANALYSIS OF PROPOSED INVESTMENTS

The goal of investing is to create value for the owners of the firm. If an investment is to do that, the expected returns from the investment must exceed its costs. In economic terms, we say that the **marginal** or **incremental benefits**—the benefits deriving solely from the investment—must exceed the **marginal** or **incremental costs**. There are several hidden difficulties with this first step. First, the very word incremental implies there is another entity or alternative. Thus, we must ask, incremental to what? The second difficulty is in choosing how to measure the costs and benefits themselves.

In estimating the value of an investment, we are only measuring costs and benefits that would not have occurred if the firm had not undertaken this particular project. To estimate the investment's benefits and costs, the analyst forecasts the cash flows associated with the investment at the time they will be received or disbursed as measured by the receipt and disbursement of cash.[1] Many companies use the accrual method of accounting: sales are recorded when an order is shipped, and obligations are recorded when incurred. Accrual accounting can trick the investment analyst. For instance, the investment may be charged with a portion of the ongoing expenses of the firm—the overhead. This is an accounting allocation of costs, not a marginal or incremental cost or benefit associated with the investment. Thus, if this investment neither increases nor decreases overhead expenses, then overhead is neither a cost nor a benefit for the purposes of the investment analysis. Only incremental, new expenses or benefits are relevant. The real benefit derived is the receipt or disbursement of cash that comes solely as a result of this investment, and it is cash that concerns the investment analyst.

---

[1] As we discussed in Chapters 2 and 3.

1. Cash Benefits

Four sources of cash benefits or receipts may be derived from an investment:

1. Cost reductions when a more efficient process is substituted for a less efficient one.
2. Cash received as a result of increased sales.
3. Cash received when replaced equipment is sold.
4. Cash expected to be received from the salvage value or sale of the new plant or equipment at the end of its useful life.

Let's illustrate these benefits by analyzing a shipping company's investment in a sail-assisted tanker. Management is considering replacing one of their diesel-fueled, ocean-going tankers with a tanker that has auxiliary metal sails to take advantage of the wind. The firm might benefit from this investment in several ways. First, the sail-assisted ship will use less fuel and thus be less expensive to operate than the diesel-powered vessel. This cost reduction will lower the operating costs for every year the ship is in operation. Furthermore, because the new ship has a larger cargo space, the tonnage carried by the ship will exceed that carried by the old tanker, resulting in increased yearly revenues. In addition to the benefits from reduced operating expenses and increased sales, the company will sell the old diesel-powered ship for cash and gain favorable tax treatment as a result of the sale. Finally, at the end of its useful life, the salvage value of the sail-assisted ship and any favorable tax effects will also be benefits.

This simple example shows that most investments offer a variety of benefits at various times throughout their useful lives. The analyst's responsibility is to identify the magnitude and timing of all benefits.

2. Cash Payments

The cash payments (costs) associated with any investment fall into three categories:

1. The initial cost (capital cost) of the investment.
2. Capital improvements made to plant or equipment during the life of the project.
3. Operating costs.

Capital costs include the initial price of making an investment (e.g., buying equipment) as well as any subsequent major outlays of cash required to extend the life of the project or equipment. In our tanker example, capital costs include the costs of obtaining the new ship, the subsequent major engine replacements, and other major repairs needed to extend the life of the vessel. Operating costs are the recurring, annual cash outlays that are required once the investment becomes a part of the company's operations. Finally, by purchasing the tanker, the company will have to cover such annual operating costs as wages, fuel, taxes, and maintenance that exceed those that would have been spent when they had the old tanker.

Any cash already expended on the investment, such as research done to develop the new tanker's sails, is not a relevant cost in this investment analysis. Instead, this type of expense is considered a **sunk cost**: it represents a past outlay of funds that has no bearing on this decision now. The manager's concern is not to recover sunk or irreversible costs but to create value from subsequent new investments. In other words, any investment being considered must have a positive marginal return.

Tax benefits and costs will also be incurred by the company as a result of making an investment. Unfortunately, the exact effect tax laws will have over the life of a given project may not be known at the time an investment is made. If current tax laws were to continue in effect during the life of the project, the impact of taxes on the costs and benefits could be determined. However, tax codes change, sometimes dramatically and quickly. For instance, during the years 1981-1991 there were three major changes in the tax code in the United States that affected the tax treatment of capital investments. From 1981 to 1986, the Accelerated Cost Recovery System (ACRS) was in use. In 1986, a new tax code was enacted that lowered tax rates, removed the investment tax credit, and lengthened depreciation schedules.[2] In 1991, the code was further adjusted and called the Modified Accelerated Cost Recovery System (MACRS).[3]

The straight-line and double-declining-balance methods of depreciation were most used under the 1980 U.S. tax codes and are widely used in other countries. With straight-line depreciation, the annual depreciation is calculated by simply dividing the investment cost by the allowed depreciable life. For example, if a company purchases a piece of equipment for $150,000 that has a depreciable life of five years, the annual depreciation expense is $30,000:

$$\text{Annual depreciation expense} = \frac{\text{Cost of asset}}{\text{Depreciable life}}$$

$$= \frac{\$150,000}{5 \text{ years}}$$

$$= \$30,000$$

[2]   Under the tax law adopted in 1986, assets were assigned to different depreciable categories depending on their expected life. Personal property was divided into six different categories (expected lives of 3, 5, 7, 10, 15, and 20 years), and real property (real estate) was divided into two groups (expected lives of 27.5 and 31.5 years).
    Capital costs in the 3-year to 10-year classes were depreciated using an accelerated type of depreciation called the double-declining-balance method, with a switch to the straight-line method permitted near the end of the life. The switch was allowed in order to optimize deductions. Costs in the 15- and 20-year categories were depreciated using a 150 percent declining-balance rate, switching later to the straight-line rate. Real estate, on the other hand, had to be depreciated using the straight-line method.
[3]   The first year is considered a half year and depreciation is 20 percent, half that under ACRS. In the following five years, the rates are 32.00, 19.20, 11.52, 11.52, and 5.76 percent, respectively.

Double-declining-balance depreciation is a little more difficult to calculate. However, this method allows a higher deduction from taxes in earlier years than does straight-line depreciation. To calculate double-declining-balance depreciation, we double the straight-line rate of depreciation and multiply it by the undepreciated investment value. Note, the first year is considered a half year.

For our example the straight-line rate of depreciation is 20 percent, based on a five-year life. Thus, the first year's depreciation using the double-declining-balance method would be twice 20 percent for a total of 40 percent. Depreciation expense is:

$$\text{First year's depreciation} = (0.20 \times 2) \times \$150{,}000$$
$$= \$60{,}000$$

This depreciation expense is twice the amount that would be expensed during this year using the straight-line method, resulting in lower taxes. That is why such a method is called **accelerated depreciation**. Exhibit 4-1 shows the rate of depreciation for this accelerated method under MACRS, the current U.S. tax code. At some times, and in some countries, the double-declining-balance rate is simply double the straight-line depreciation, and the first year is considered a full year.

Exhibit 4-1 shows the differences in depreciation using three methods: straight-line depreciation; ACRS, the method under the tax code in force from 1981; and double-declining-balance and MACRS, the method under the 1991

EXHIBIT 4-1   Depreciation Expense Under Three Methods of Depreciation

Year	Straight-Line	ACRS*	Double-Declining-Balance MACRS†	Double-Declining-Balance Traditional‡
1	$ 30,000	$ 22,500	$ 30,000	$ 60,000
2	30,000	33,000	48,000	36,000
3	30,000	31,500	28,800	21,600
4	30,000	31,500	17,280	16,200
5	30,000	31,500	17,280	16,200
6	0	0	8,640	0
Total	$ 150,000	$150,000	$150,000	$150,000

* Most machinery and equipment was depreciated over five years under U.S. ACRS rules. For those five years, depreciation was 15, 22, 21, 21, and 21 percent, respectively. An investment tax credit was allowed in the first year, generally amounting to 8 percent of the investment's cost, and the marginal tax rate was 48 percent.
† First year is considered to be a half year, regardless of the actual length of time the asset is owned during the year. The depreciation rates for the six periods are 20.00, 32.00, 19.20, 11.52, 11.52, and 5.76 percent, respectively.
‡ This is simply double the straight-line depreciation rate with a switch to straight-line depreciation when it is advantageous. In this case the switch occurs in the fourth year. At the beginning of Year 4 there is a balance remaining of $32,400 to be depreciated equally over the remaining two years.

U.S. tax code revision.[4] By comparing the depreciation expense allowed under the two recent U.S. tax codes to straight-line depreciation, a method favored by many corporations for their public reporting, you can see how the depreciation method chosen can affect the company's profitability. Because depreciation expense is much larger in the early years under the double-declining-balance method, the company's taxes will be lower during those years and its cash flow larger. It is because of this that accelerated depreciation methods are believed to encourage investment in capital projects.

There is a dark side of accelerated methods: they decrease profits. Thus, most U.S. companies do not use accelerated methods of depreciation for their financial reports, in spite of the fact that accelerated methods are used to calculate tax payments. This difference in tax and reporting methods results in financial statements that do not accurately reflect the taxes that were paid in any given year. Over time, of course, the two are equal.

Tax codes in highly inflationary environments often have a feature that an analyst must incorporate into an investment analysis: assets are revalued (that is, companies are allowed to revalue their assets to compensate for the erosive effects of inflation). An example will serve to make clear why this revaluation occurs and how the revalued asset depreciation expense will be quite different from that calculated when using an historically based asset value.

Exhibit 4-2 shows the depreciation that a company can expense in a country with 35 percent inflation, a rate reached by many countries each year, both with and without asset revaluation. (For brevity, only 3 of the 10 years are shown.) The exhibit shows the impact on a company's financial statements of asset revaluation. While profits are higher when assets are depreciated at their historical value, taxes are also higher: the depreciation tax shield has not risen to offset the changes in the value of the currency. Perhaps the most important item, the cumulative cash flow, is higher when assets are revalued to keep pace with inflation. The differences in profits, and cash flows under the two scenarios are shown most clearly in the graph in Exhibit 4-3.

Because a tax code and its effect on a project's costs and benefits are sources of uncertainty, potential changes and their impact should be assessed. Some changes in a tax code can be anticipated; others cannot. In fact, the nature of the changes and their impact can be quite unexpected.

This uncertainty is only one of the many uncertainties that face the analyst in making forecasts. Later in the chapter, we will describe methods for incorporating uncertainty into the analysis. To identify and estimate the costs and benefits associated with any investment, the analyst will call on experts in

---

[4]　In addition to changes in the method of depreciation, the U.S. 1991 tax code stipulated a lower maximum tax rate for corporations of 34 percent (the ACRS marginal rate was 48 percent). For corporations with taxable incomes of less than $75,000, the rate dropped to 25 percent, and below $50,000 the rate was 15 percent. Investment tax credits, amounting to 8 to 10 percent under ACRS, were abolished.

EXHIBIT 4-2 Inflationary Impact On Financial Performance: Depreciation With and Without Asset Revaluation—Inflation 35 Percent per Year (in units of currency)

Asset Value Based on Historical Cost

	Year 1	Year 5	Year 10
Net asset value (beginning of year)	$500,000	$ 300,000	$ 50,000
Depreciation	(50,000)	(50,000)	(50,000)
Asset value (end of year)	450,000	250,000	0
Profit before depreciation	100,000	332,151	1,489,375
Depreciation	(50,000)	(50,000)	(50,000)
Profit before taxes	50,000	282,151	1,439,375
Taxes (32%)	(16,000)	(90,288)	(460,600)
Profit after taxes	$ 34,000	$ 191,863	$ 978,775
Cumulative profit after taxes	$34,000	$506,898	$3,372,131
Cumulative taxes	$16,000	$238,540	$1,586,885
Cash flow*	$84,000	$241,863	$1,028,775
Cumulative cash flow	$84,000	$756,898	$3,872,131

Asset Value Based on Inflated Asset Value

	Year 1	Year 5	Year 10
Net asset value (beginning of year)	$500,000	$1,220,703	$3,725,295
Depreciation	(50,000)	(122,070)	(372,529)
Inflated asset value (end of year)	675,000	1,647,950	5,029,148
Asset value less depreciation			
(end of year)	625,000	1,525,880	4,656,619
Profit before depreciation	100,000	332,151	1,489,375
Depreciation	(50,000)	(122,070)	(372,529)
Profit before taxes	50,000	210,081	1,116,846
Taxes (32%)	(16,000)	(67,226)	(357,391)
Profit after taxes	$ 34,000	$ 142,855	$ 759,455
Cumulative profit after taxes	$34,000	$397,860	$2,581,534
Cumulative taxes	$16,000	$187,228	$1,214,838
Cash flow*	$84,000	$264,925	$1,131,984
Cumulative cash flow	$84,000	$808,211	$4,244,177

* For simplicity, cash flow is simply profit after taxes plus depreciation.

marketing, engineering, accounting, operations, and the economy to provide needed forecasts.

Before we conclude this section on costs and benefits, note that we have not dealt with one kind of costs and benefits—those associated with financing. It

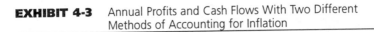

EXHIBIT 4-3 Annual Profits and Cash Flows With Two Different
Methods of Accounting for Inflation

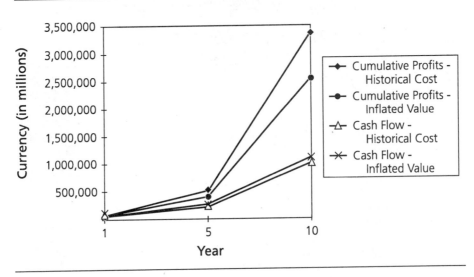

is important, however, to determine both the value created from an investment
and the value that comes from the way that investment is financed. In this
chapter we discuss only the evaluation of an investment from the point of view
of the owners of the corporation, without considering subcontracting any of
the owners' financing responsibility. Therefore, no costs or benefits associated
with financing the investment are included in the analysis. The issue of financing, since it is a complex topic, is left to Chapters 6 and 7. In Chapter 6 we will
discuss how shareholders, or managers on their behalf, decide to subcontract
some of the financing of the company to other capital providers, principally
lenders. In Chapter 7 we discuss what tools can be used to determine the proportion of financing that should be subcontracted to lenders and whether value
can be created or destroyed through judicious financing strategies. In that
chapter we show how financing costs (particularly interest payments and principal repayments) and financing benefits (primarily, new loan receipts) can be
included in the analysis of an investment.

II. EVALUATING INCREMENTAL COSTS AND BENEFITS

Once costs and benefits have been itemized, the analyst's major task is to determine the marginal or incremental effect the investment will have on the firm as
a whole. An incremental cost or benefit is one derived exclusively from the

investment and one that would not otherwise occur. To evaluate incremental costs and benefits, many analysts group investment proposals into categories that help them examine each proposal in terms of its relationship to the firm's business as a whole.

The most useful scheme is to group projects according to the degree of independence of their costs and benefits from the costs and benefits of the firm and its other investments and projects. **Independent investments** are projects that can be accepted or rejected regardless of the action taken on any other investment, now or later. **Mutually exclusive investments** are projects that preclude one another; once one project is accepted, the others become unavailable or inappropriate. Mutually exclusive projects often are designed to solve the same problem or to serve the same function. For example, managers often must choose among alternate means of adding plant capacity, or among advertising programs, or several new product lines.

There are two types of mutually exclusive and independent investments—**replacements** and investments in **new products and processes**. Replacement investments are made to modernize an existing process or to revitalize an old product line. Because estimating the net effect on the company of replacing a process or product can be especially difficult, analysts often place these investments in a separate category. They are, however, just an especially troublesome type of mutually exclusive or independent investment.

To understand the process of evaluation, we will analyze two mutually exclusive investments, but keep in mind that independent investments would be evaluated using the same tools.

Two investment proposals are being considered by the management of Betty's Better Big Boys, one of the largest franchisers of fast foods in the West. Betty's Better Big Boys sells a variety of sandwiches, drinks, and other fast foods through its 500 restaurants. Management has capitalized on the public's health concerns by offering whole-grain sandwich buns, french fries with potato skins, and tofu shakes, as well as the regular fare. Betty's Better Big Boys managers are considering either of two investments—opening their restaurants for breakfast or adding salad and pasta bars to their existing lunch and dinner menus. Because of the management effort needed to implement either project, management considers these investments mutually exclusive: it may choose one or the other, but not both projects.

1. Mutually Exclusive Investments: The Breakfast Proposal

Betty's Better Big Boys restaurants are open from 11 A.M. to 11 P.M. Because many of Betty's competitors have begun to serve breakfast, Betty's managers are considering opening from 6:30 to 11:00 A.M. to serve breakfast. They believe Betty's Better Big Boys has an edge over its competition because it pioneered the "healthy hamburger" concept. They would emphasize tasty and nutritious breakfast offerings. While the same buildings and equipment could be used for serving breakfast, the longer serving hours would increase overhead expenses. There would be added costs for ingredients, salaries of managers and employees, and advertising. Together, incremental overhead and operating expenses for all 500 restaurants are expected to total $14.25 million per year. In addition, since breakfast would be a new product, management is planning an extensive employee-training program. The program, to be completed before the company starts offering breakfast in July, would cost $1.75 million. New inventory would total $1,800 per restaurant, and all remaining inventory would be fully recovered at the end of the project in five years.[5] Betty's Better Big Boys expects to benefit from an estimated $15 million increase in sales per year to be made from the breakfast service.

The estimated costs and benefits of this project are detailed in Exhibit 4-4. Since management expects no inflation, costs and benefits are shown in real dollars. Costs and benefits are forecast for five years because management believes that the equipment used in each restaurant will last only five more years. The format in this exhibit is a useful one often employed by financial analysts.

You will note several things about the way the analysis in Exhibit 4-4 is presented. First, the effects this project will have on Betty's income statement are shown. Included in the changes are any noncash expenses, such as depreciation, that reduce taxable income and thus taxes. Because noncash charges only affect taxes, the format provides for adding noncash charges back to net income to calculate cash flow: a noncash charge does not reduce cash income, only the taxes paid on that income. You will also recall that these cash flows belong to the shareholders, because we are not introducing any financial subcontracting into the analysis.[6] Thus, there are no provisions for interest payments or principal payments or new loans in the cash flows. Because these cash flows belong to the shareholders, and shareholders have the residual claim on the company's cash flows, we call them **residual cash flows**. We will show in Chapters 6 and 7 how financial subcontracting changes an analysis.

The second set of adjustments shown to the income in Exhibit 4-4 are capital investments—cash payments for property, plant, and equipment or for working capital. Property, plant, and various items of equipment are not expensed (and thus do not affect taxes) at the time they are made but are expensed over the period allowed by the tax code. The annual capital investment expense is called depreciation. Working capital investments are expensed neither when they are made nor while the assets are used. The assumption made about cash, inventory, and accounts receivable is that these assets can be recovered by the company at its discretion, and thus they remain a part of the firm's capital.

------

[5]   Little or no inventory would remain at the end of the project's life. All perishable and nonperishable goods would have been used and not replaced, thus reducing inventory to zero.
[6]   Financial subcontracting occurs when shareholders' funds are supplemented from sources such as lenders.

EXHIBIT 4-4 Betty's Better Big Boys' Breakfast Proposal—Marginal Costs and Benefits (thousands of real dollars)

	Period					
	0	1	2	3	4	5
Income Statement Changes						
Sales	0	$ 15,000	$ 15,000	$ 15,000	$ 15,000	$ 15,000
Operating expenses	0	(14,250)	(14,250)	(14,250)	(14,250)	(14,250)
Training costs	$(1,750)					
Depreciation	0	0	0	0	0	0
Profit before taxes	(1,750)	750	750	750	750	750
Taxes*	595	(255)	(255)	(255)	(255)	(255)
Net profit	$(1,155)	$ 495	$ 495	$ 495	$ 495	$ 495
Noncash Charges						
Depreciation		0	0	0	0	0
Capital Investments						
Property, plant, and equipment	(900)					
Inventory	0	0	0	0	0	900
Residual net cash flow	$(2,055)	$ 495	$ 495	$ 495	$ 495	$ 1,395

* Positive taxes are a tax reduction in the rest of the business due to the training expenses in the year prior to start up. This benefit occurs only if the company has profits in other parts of its business.

2. Mutually Exclusive Investments: Salad and Pasta Bar Proposal

As an alternative to adding breakfast, managers at Betty's Better Big Boys are considering adding all-you-can-eat salad and pasta bars to their existing lunch and dinner menus starting in July. They have already spent $600,000 in developing the salad and pasta bar concept in limited test-marketing. To introduce the product into all of their restaurants, they estimate that personnel would have to be trained at a cost of $832 per restaurant and that display cases would have to be bought and installed at $2,800 per bar. The managers expect that the display cases would be scrapped in five years and that the value of the scrap would be offset by disposal costs. Incremental (marginal) operating expenses include the cost of ingredients, additional refrigeration, and the salary of one additional employee per restaurant to stock the salad and pasta bar. On the basis of test market results, the marketing staff estimate sales of salad and pasta at $15 million per year and operating expenses at $13.934 million. New inventories would be $1,800 per restaurant. These inventories could be sold for close to their full value at any time.

The diverse effects these two proposals would have on Betty's Better Big Boys illustrate the usefulness of categorizing investments as independent or mutually exclusive. Managers consider the two proposed investments to be mutually exclusive because they do not believe that they could adequately oversee both projects at the same time. The breakfast option would be independent of Betty's existing business because it would extend the existing product line. The salad and pasta bar, however, would be a partial replacement since it would affect existing sales of sandwich meals at lunch and dinner. In fact, the marketing staff estimate that half of the salad and pasta bars' sales would come from customers who would otherwise have purchased sandwiches and french fries. Thus, while total salad and pasta sales would be $15 million, incremental sales would be only half, $7.5 million per year.

The salad bar's status as a partial replacement would be responsible not only for lower net cash receipts but also for lower incremental overhead and operating expenses than the breakfast project. Unlike the breakfast option, it would add less to current overhead and operating expenses because it would be offered during existing hours and manned by existing employees. If the analyst did not realize that the salad and pasta bar option would be a replacement investment, he or she might erroneously include a portion of the costs of buildings and equipment as part of its incremental costs, or include its total sales of $15 million as a benefit, rather than the $7.5 million incremental sales. The net cash flow for the salad and pasta bars is the net profit plus any noncash charges that were deducted from profit before taxes for the purpose of calculating taxes.

Details of this evaluation of the net benefits of the project appear in Exhibit 4-5. Note that the $600,000 in expenses incurred in developing and test-marketing the salad and pasta bar concept are not included. They are sunk costs: cash already spent and not relevant in making this new decision.

EXHIBIT 4-5   Betty's Better Big Boys' Salad and Pasta Bar Proposal—Marginal Costs and Benefits (thousands of real dollars)

				Period			
	0	*1*	*2*	*3*	*4*	*5*	*6*
Income Statement Changes†							
Sales		$ 7,500	$ 7,500	$ 7,500	$ 7,500	$ 7,500	0
Operating expenses		(6,967)	(6,967)	(6,967)	(6,967)	(6,967)	0
Training costs	$ (416)						
Depreciation		(280)	(448)	(269)	(269)	(161)	$ (81)
Profit before taxes		253	85	264	264	372	(81)
Taxes‡	141	(86)	(29)	(90)	(90)	(127)	28
Net profit	$ (275)	$ 167	$ 56	$ 174	$ 174	$ 245	$ (53)
Noncash Charges							
Depreciation		280	448	269	269	161	81
Capital Investments							
Property, plant, and equipment	(1,400)						
New Inventory	(900)	—	—	—	—	900	—
Residual net cash flow	$(2,575)	$ 447	$ 504	$ 443	$ 443	$ 1,306	$ 28

† The development cost is not included since it is a sunk cost.

‡ Positive taxes that result from the expense of training are a tax reduction. This tax reduction is a benefit only if the company has profits from other businesses and these losses can offset the profits and lower the company's total taxes.

Now that the incremental costs and benefits for the two projects have been estimated, Betty's management must decide whether to accept one or the other of the plans or reject both projects and seek other opportunities. To make these decisions, the managers need a method of measuring the relative value of the two proposals.

III. CHOOSING AMONG INVESTMENTS

The relative attractiveness or value of investments may be ranked in a number of different ways. Each of these methods has advantages and disadvantages.

1. Simple Valuation Methods

Benefit/Cost Ratio. The easiest way to compare two investments is to compare their benefit/cost ratios. If the benefits of an investment exceed the costs—if the benefit/cost ratio is greater than 1.0—the project is deemed acceptable using this measure. To choose among acceptable investments, managers select the project with the highest benefit/cost ratio. For the proposed investment in breakfast service, the benefit/cost ratio is calculated as follows, using the residual net cash flow figures in Exhibit 4-4.

$$
\begin{aligned}
\text{Benefit/cost ratio} \; &= \; \frac{\text{Benefits}}{\text{Investment}} \\[6pt]
&= \; \frac{\$495 + \$495 + \$495 + \$495 + \$1,395}{\$2,055} \\[6pt]
&= \; \frac{\$3,375}{\$2,055} \\[6pt]
&= \; 1.64
\end{aligned}
$$

A comparable analysis of figures in Exhibit 4-5 for the salad and pasta bar yields a ratio of 1.23 ($3,171/$2,575).

Average Payback Period. A similar measure is called average payback period or just average payback. Quite simply, average payback is used to measure the number of years before the annual benefits of the project are equal to its initial cost. For the breakfast proposal, the average payback period is calculated as follows:

$$
\begin{aligned}
\text{Average payback} \; &= \; \frac{\text{Investment}}{\text{Average yearly benefit}} \\[6pt]
&= \; \frac{\$2,055}{\$675} \\[6pt]
&= \; 3.0 \; \text{years}
\end{aligned}
$$

A similar analysis of the salad and pasta bar proposal yields an average pay-back of 4.1 years, using five years to average the benefits.[7]

Payback Period. The payback period is a similar calculation, except that the actual yearly benefits, rather than the average, are used to calculate the pay-back. This method is widely used. Exhibit 4-6 shows the payback calculation for the breakfast option. For the salad and pasta bars, the payback is 4.56 years.

Whether a payback of 4.05 years is adequate or not is a decision for Betty's managers. Ordinarily, managers set a limit on the length of the average pay-back period and reject those investments with longer paybacks. To choose among several projects with acceptable payback periods, managers select the project with the fastest payback period.

Payback can be useful as a quick approximation of a project's relative attractiveness or can be used to indicate whether a firm can recover the project costs in time to make another planned investment, before the product or process becomes technologically or competitively obsolete, or before the polit-ical and economic environment changes dramatically. The method ignores all benefits that are received after the payback date, and thus it can arbitrarily exclude potentially attractive investments that have longer lives.

Let's look at an example to illustrate the problem. Vast Resources, Inc. (VR) has two projects in which it can invest the $1.5 million it has available. VR man-agement uses a payback criterion of three years and will not accept a project that fails to meet this standard. Exhibit 4-7 presents data for the two projects. On the basis of this data, management has chosen to invest in Project A and reject Project B. Do you agree with this choice? Note that unless VR needs the $1.5 million in the first year for another investment or to pay an obligation,

EXHIBIT 4-6 Betty's Big Boys' Payback Calculation for Breakfast Option (in thousands)

Period	Investment	Cash Flow	Remaining Investment
0	$2,055		$2,055
1		$495	1,560
2		495	1,065
3		495	570
4		495	75
5		$1,395	$(1,320)

Payback = 4.054 years where the remaining investment in the fourth year takes 0.054 ($75/$1,395) years to cover.

---

[7] We use five years of benefits since the depreciation shield that occurs in the sixth year is a con-vention under MACRS. The sixth year has no other benefits from the project.

EXHIBIT 4-7 Vast Resources, Inc.—Alternative Investments (in millions)

	Project A	Project B
Cost	$1.5	$1.5
Residual cash flows:		
Year 1	$1.6	0
2	0	0
3	0	0
4	0	0
5	0	$8.0
Payback	0.94 years	4.19 years
Benefit/cost ratio	107%	533%

Project B eventually provides a much larger cash flow and should be the most attractive to management.

The VR example points out obvious problems that can occur when using payback. Similar problems can occur using benefit/cost analysis. Neither method takes the timing of cash flows into account. The benefit/cost ratio treats cash received at all points in time as equivalent, but we know that investors prefer equivalent amounts of cash received sooner to those received later. The payback method attempts to take investors' preferences for early cash flows into account, but it ignores cash flows beyond the payback period. We know later cash flows are not irrelevant, particularly if they are large. In summary, the benefit/cost ratio and the payback method evaluate investments solely on the size or speed of their returns, and thus neither adequately incorporates the investor's **time value of money**.

2. Dealing With the Timing of Cash Flows: Discounting Techniques

Investors want to be rewarded for waiting for future returns. They need a method for evaluating investments that will take into account their time value of money and will compensate them for temporary lack of liquidity by promising increased returns for more distant cash flows. There is a very straightforward way of determining the value of later cash flows. It is called **future value**. Exhibit 4-8 illustrates this method. In the exhibit you see that the value at the end of five years of $6.27 million invested at an annual rate of 5 percent is $8.002 million. This is the sum that the investor will have if all the annual earnings are reinvested.

In Exhibit 4-8 we compounded each year's cash flow to the end of Year 5 to calculate the amount that we expect to receive in five years. This task is not easy, especially when dealing with a more complex situation than we showed in this example.

EXHIBIT 4-8 Future Value of an Investment at a 5 Percent Annual Rate of Return (in thousands)

	Year				
	1	*2*	*3*	*4*	*5*
Investment value (beginning of year)	$6,270	$6,584	$6,913	$7,259	$7,622
Interest (@ 5%)	314	329	346	363	381
Investment value (end of year)	$6,584	$6,913	$7,259	$7,622	$8,003

An easier method exists for calculating the future value of a sum invested today. To take a shortcut, we create a factor that can be used as a multiplier.

$$\text{Future value factor} \quad = \quad (1 + R)^n$$

where
R = The rate of return
n = The number of years

The process for creating this future value factor for an investment made for five years at a 5 percent compound rate of return is:

$$
\begin{aligned}
\text{Future value factor} \quad &= \quad (1 + R)^n \\
&= \quad (1 + .05)^5 \\
&= \quad (1.05)^5 \\
&= \quad 1.276
\end{aligned}
$$

Let's look at an example to see how this multiplier factor can be used. If you put $6.27 million in a savings account today at a 5 percent annual compound rate of return, in five years you will have $8 million. This future value is calculated as follows:

$$
\begin{aligned}
\text{Future value} \quad &= \quad (1 + R)^n \times (CF) \\
&= \quad (1 + .05)^5 \times \$6,270,000 \\
&= \quad 1.276 \times \$6,270,000 \\
&= \quad \$8,000,520
\end{aligned}
$$

This process is called **compounding**.

We can use an adaptation of the compound value process to determine what a series of future cash flows would be worth today. Today's worth, or value, is called **present value**, or **discounted present value**. The process of **discounting** is simply the reverse of compounding.

To determine the present value discount factor, if you do not have access to a discount factor table or financial calculator, first calculate the future value factor. You can divide this factor into the future cash flow to get its present value. Alternatively, you can create a present value factor as follows:

$$\text{Present value factor} = \frac{1.00}{(1 + R)^n}$$

$$= \frac{1.00}{(1.05)^5}$$

$$= \frac{1.00}{1.276}$$

$$= 0.78$$

The 0.78 figure means that a dollar received five years from now is worth 78 percent of its present value, or $0.78, today. To calculate the value of more than $1.00 received in the future, multiply the cash flow received in the future by the present value factor. For instance, to calculate the present value of $8 million received in five years, multiply it by the present value factor of 0.78. The present value is $6.24 million.

Fortunately, one does not have to go through the laborious process of calculating compound value factors. Lists of factors are available in most finance textbooks. Moreover, all but the simplest modern calculators perform compounding and discounting functions quite painlessly, thus generally rendering the direct use of discount factors an unnecessary step.

Present Value Payback. The most simplistic use of discounting is present value payback. To calculate a present value payback, discount each residual net cash flow to its equivalent present value. These discounted present values are summed until the total equals the amount of the original investment. Exhibit 4-9 provides the data needed to calculate the discounted payback for the breakfast project. Using 5 percent as the discount or **hurdle** rate, the discounted payback value of this project is 4.27 years. The salad and pasta bar project's discounted payback is 4.9 years, using 5 years as the project life.

While including the time value of money, the discounted payback still ignores cash flows beyond the payback period. This is a particularly critical fault when projects with large future returns, such as new products, are being considered. It is neither necessary nor appropriate to discriminate arbitrarily against projects with returns in the more distant future.

Net present value and internal rate of return are two frequently used discounting techniques that take all cash flows into consideration. Either method provides a better measure of value than do the simpler ranking methods. We will describe and point out the advantages and disadvantages of each method.

EXHIBIT 4-9   Breakfast Proposal—Present Value Payback (in thousands)

Year	Residual Net Cash Flow	Present Value Cash Flow	Remaining Investment
0	$(2,055)	$(2,055)/(1.05)^0 = $(2055.00)	$2,055.00
1	495	495/(1.05)^1 = 471.43	1,583.57
2	495	495/(1.05)^2 = 448.98	1,134.59
3	495	495/(1.05)^3 = 427.60	706.99
4	495	495/(1.05)^4 = 407.23	299.76
5	1,395	1,395/(1.05)^5 = 1,093.02	

The total present value payback is 4.27 years. The 0.27 is calculated thus:

$$\frac{\$299.76}{\$1,093.02} = 0.274$$

Net Present Value.   The net present value is the lump sum value today of all the current and future benefits less the present value of all current and future costs. The net present value can also be described as the present value of the net worth an investment will contribute to a firm by the end of its useful life.

Net present value (NPV) is calculated by using a discount rate. The discount rate is used to adjust each year's returns according to the time between it and the date of the initial investment. The discount rate is better known as the investors' **required rate of return**. Net present value is calculated as follows:

$$NPV = \left(\frac{NCF_1}{(1 + R)^1} + \frac{NCF_2}{(1 + R)^2} + \ldots\ldots + \frac{NCF_n}{(1 + R)^n} \right) - I$$

where

NCF	=	The net cash flow per year (cash flow benefits minus cash flow costs)
R	=	Annual discount rate
1, 2, . . ., n	=	Years from the date of original investment
I	=	Amount of initial investment

While we described the discounting and compounding processes in terms of annual rates of return and years, any period can be used. For instance, shorter periods are useful when cash flows vary over the year. This can be especially true in development projects and in inflationary environments. The analyst using different periods must, however, make sure that the rate of return is for a period equivalent to the length of the periods being used in the cash flows. For instance, if the analyst is evaluating the project over quarters, the rate of return would be a quarterly rate of return. In our example, the annual 5 percent rate of return would be equivalent to a 1.25 percent quarterly rate. This latter rate would be used to discount or compound quarterly cash flows. Rates of return are discussed in Chapters 6 and 7 in more detail.

For Betty's Better Big Boys, the net present value of the breakfast option using 5 percent as an annual discount rate is calculated as follows:

$$
\begin{aligned}
NPV &= \frac{\$495,000}{(1 + .05)^1} + \frac{\$495,000}{(1 + .05)^2} + \frac{\$495,000}{(1 + .05)^3} + \frac{\$495,000}{(1 + .05)^4} + \\
&\quad \frac{\$1,395,000}{(1 + .05)^5} - \$2,055,000 \\
&= \$793,260
\end{aligned}
$$

The NPV of $793,260 is the present value of the net worth the breakfast project will contribute to Betty's by the end of the investment's five-year life. The NPV of the salad and pasta bar project is $101,274 at a 5 percent discount rate. The process is quite simple when a calculator with a net present value function or a computer spreadsheet is used.

The NPV approach offers a logical method of evaluating investments. It takes into account the timing of cash flows by placing a higher value on those received immediately than on those to be received in the future. Once the timing of cash flows has been taken into account, acceptable investments are those with net present values equal to or greater than zero.

Present Value Index.   Some managers prefer to use the profitability or present value index (PVI) rather than net present value. The PVI is simply an adaptation of the benefit/cost ratio:

$$
\text{Present value index} = \frac{\text{Present value of net benefits}}{\text{Present value of investment costs}}
$$

Calculating the present value index is simple and straightforward. Using the breakfast option as an example, and the 5 percent discount rate, the index is calculated as follows:

$$
\begin{aligned}
PVI &= \left(\frac{\$495,000}{(1 + .05)^1} + \frac{\$495,000}{(1 + .05)^2} + \frac{\$495,000}{(1 + .05)^3} + \frac{\$495,000}{(1 + .05)^4} + \right. \\
&\quad \left. \frac{\$1,395,000}{(1 + .05)^5} \right) / \$2,055,000 \\
&= \frac{\$2,848,260}{\$2,055,000} \\
&= 1.36 \text{ or } 136 \text{ percent}
\end{aligned}
$$

In other words, for each dollar of investment, the breakfast proposal returns a present value of $1.36 of benefits. The present value index for the salad and pasta bar project is 1.03. As is the case with any method using a discount rate, the magnitude of the present value index will change if the discount rate is changed.

Internal Rate of Return. A second discounted cash flow technique is internal rate of return (IRR). This method is used to measure the average rate of return that will be earned over the life of the project. To calculate the IRR, the same formula as that for calculating net present value is used except that the net present value is set equal to zero and we solve for R.

Solving for R is somewhat more difficult than solving for the NPV. To solve for R we must use a trial-and-error method, or the computer must do so. We start by choosing an arbitrary discount rate, say 5 percent, and calculating the NPV. If the resulting NPV is positive, a higher discount rate is next selected, and the NPV is recalculated. We continue choosing discount rates until we find the discount rate that yields an NPV of zero. With the Betty's Better Big Boys' breakfast project, the IRR is obviously larger than 5 percent since, at that rate, the NPV is $793,260. Exhibit 4-10 provides a graph of the results of this trial-and-error approach for both Betty's projects. The graph is also called a **net present value profile** because it depicts the project's net present value at various discount rates. Note that at a discount rate of zero, the net present value is the simple sum of the undiscounted cash flows. For the breakfast project, the IRR is 15.9 percent. For the salad and pasta bar project, the IRR is 6.2 percent, and at all discount rates it provides a lower NPV than does the breakfast pro-

EXHIBIT 4-10   Net Present Value Profile: Salad and Pasta Bar and Breakfast Options

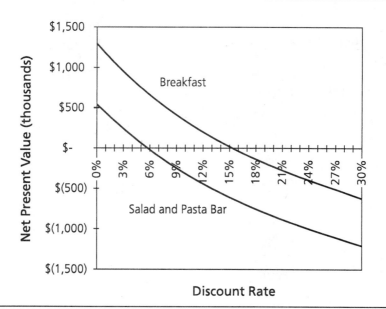

ject. An acceptable IRR for a risk-free project is a return that equals or exceeds its required rate of return. Here we have used 5 percent. Thus, both projects would be acceptable, but the breakfast option clearly is superior.

While the IRR method is purported to be equivalent to the net present value method, it poses special problems for the user. If the investments are of quite different sizes, if the timing of the cash flows is different for each project under consideration, or if negative and positive net cash flows alternate over the life of the project, the internal rate of return can give results that are misleading or difficult to interpret. Our sail-assisted tanker project is such a situation. In evaluating the project, we noted there would be significant investments at several points over the useful life of the tanker. First, the tanker would be purchased, and later, extensive engine overhauls would be needed. Thus, its net cash flows would be negative in the first year and again in the future. During the intervening years, cash flows would be positive. As a result of alternating negative and positive net cash flows, several different discount rates would allow the NPV to equal zero. In other words, the project would have several IRRs. Exhibit 4-11 shows the net present value profile for the sail-assisted tanker project. There are IRRs of both 8.1 and 21.0 percent. Does this mean that for companies using discount rates below 8.1 and above 21 percent, the project is acceptable? Yes, and if the required rate of return is between 8.1 and 21 percent, the investment should be rejected. If the analyst had solved only for the IRR and not plotted the net present value profile, the project might have been rejected rather than accepted. Most simple computer models and calculators are designed to solve for one IRR, but the analyst with one IRR may erroneously believe he or she has the complete information necessary to analyze

EXHIBIT 4-11 Net Present Value Profile: Sail-Assisted Tanker

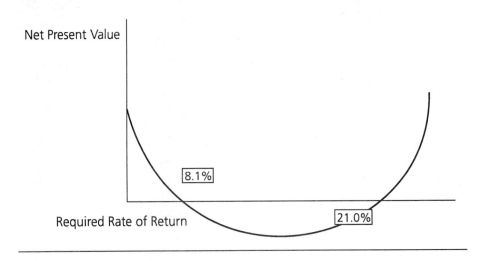

the project. Net present value profiles yield more complete data. For these and other reasons, the net present value technique is the preferred approach.

We have summarized in Exhibit 4-12 the results of using six ranking methods for Betty's two projects. The benefit/cost ratio and payback period take into account the size of the residual cash flows, but not their timing. The net present value and internal rate of return take into account both the size and timing of the residual cash flows. Fortunately for Betty's Better Big Boys, all our methods indicate that the breakfast option is the more attractive.

3. Ranking Projects

So far, we have assumed that if an investment creates value it should be accepted—the company can and should invest in all attractive projects. If that is not true, investments must be ranked by their relative value, and the firm should invest in those with the greatest values until its resources are exhausted. In most circumstances, that means management will choose the investments with the highest relative values.

For the manager in a company with more projects than resources, projects must be ranked from highest to lowest in value. Our preference is the use of the net present value method or the present value index to rank projects. This method provides a ranking consistent with value creation. For Betty's Better

EXHIBIT 4-12   Value of Breakfast Versus Salad and Pasta Bar Option
(dollars in thousands)

Method	Breakfast	Salad and Pasta Bar	Decision Rule
Benefit/cost ratio	1.64	1.23	B/C>= 1.0
Average payback period	3.0 years	4.1 years	Average payback period>= management minimum
Payback period	4.1 years	4.6 years	Payback period>= management minimum
Present value payback	4.27	4.92	PV payback>= management minimum
Net present value (in thousands), at discount rate of:			
5%	$793.26	$101.274	NPV>= 0
10%	$380.27	$(288.05)	
Present value index, at discount rate of 5%	1.36 or 136%	1.03 or 103%	PVI>= 1.0
Internal rate of return	15.9%	6.2%	IRR>= hurdle rate

Big Boys' management, does this mean that the breakfast proposal is one it should choose? Maybe, but the breakfast proposal is riskier: customers may not come. The salad and pasta bar seems less risky since it merely supplements the present sale of sandwiches, a product line and meal in which the restaurants are firmly established. Since risk is obviously an issue, how should we include it in our analysis?

4. Dealing With Risk

Our first question must be, what do we mean by risk? Risk means that our residual cash flow forecasts might be wrong. Over- or underestimated residual cash flows result in higher- or lower-than-expected returns. Investors, in addition to preferring large, rapid returns, also prefer certain returns: they do not like to take risks unless rewarded to do so. To induce the typical risk-averse investor to invest in risky projects, larger returns must be anticipated. The higher the risk, the larger the return premium required.

Of all the problems facing the investment analyst, risk is the most troublesome. To date, we have not found the ideal method for incorporating risk into the measurement of an investment's value. However, several methods are currently being used by managers. None of these methods is flawless: all are attempts at dealing with a very complex problem.

In most analyses, we assume that the project's risk is the same as that of the company as a whole: the cash flows for the project are as predictable as those from the firm's current business. Once that assumption is made, we can use the firm's average required return as a discount rate. We will discuss how this return is estimated in Chapters 6 and 7.

What if the risk of the investment is higher or lower than the corporate average? In this situation, many managers adjust for risk by increasing or decreasing the corporate rate of required return to compensate for the difference. The rate that includes the risk differential is called a **hurdle rate**. As the hurdle rate increases—that is, as investors require greater returns as compensation for greater risks—the net present value of an investment diminishes dramatically. Exhibit 4-10 illustrates this decline. When the discount rate is 5 percent, the breakfast and salad and pasta bar options provide net present values of $793,260 and $101,274, respectively. If a discount rate of 10 percent is used, the net present values diminish dramatically, as indicated in Exhibit 4-12.

Even after adjusting for risk by discounting the breakfast investment's cash flows at a higher rate, the breakfast project still offers greater value to Betty's shareholders. But these calculations again assume that the risks of the projects are equivalent. On the contrary, opening for breakfast is more risky than adding salad bars. New employees must be hired, a new advertising campaign must be undertaken, new food items will be offered, and a large unrecoverable investment in training is required. The fact is that Betty's Better Big Boys' managers could be wrong in their forecasts of potential sales and costs of the breakfast option. Salad and pasta bars, on the other hand, add little to the risk of the firm. The initial investment is small and a portion of it is recoverable, training costs are low, and few additional employees must be hired. The two projects have different levels of risk. How can these differences be included in the comparison?

So far, neither academics nor business practitioners have answered that question very well, although several techniques are currently being used. One approach is to present the problem of risk directly to the managers. Using the firm's required rate of return as a discount rate, managers can determine for themselves whether the net present value compensates for the risk of the project. For instance, the net present value of the breakfast option at a discount rate of 10 percent is greater by $668,320 than that of the salad and pasta bar alternative. Is this amount adequate, in the managers' view, to compensate for the differences in risk between the two investments? It is up to them to decide.

This approach, however, is often not scientific enough for managers who prefer a more structured method. Another approach is to modify the discount rate according to the apparent risk of the investment. For example, new products may be considered to have greater risks than the risk of the firm as a whole. Consequently, management will set a higher hurdle rate for new products than the firm's marginal cost of capital. A scheme such as the one shown in Exhibit 4-13 is used by many firms to categorize investments.

Managers who use this scheme believe that investments in cost reductions are less risky than their firm's average risk and that new products are more risky. Using this scheme, Betty's management might discount the salad and pasta bars' cash flows at a rate of 5 percent, but, since breakfast is a new product and is considered riskier, its cash flows might be discounted at an even higher rate, for instance 10 percent.

While this scheme is often used, it leads to predictable results: new products are less attractive, whereas cost-reduction projects are usually acceptable. These conclusions may or may not be appropriate for the specific firm or investment. Furthermore, it is difficult to determine the appropriate changes to make to the discount rate.

EXHIBIT 4-13 Risk Categories for Investment Analysis

Investment Category	Risk Level	Hurdle Rate
Cost reduction	Less than firm's average risk	Lower than firm's required rate of return
Plant expansion	Average risk	Marginal average required rate of return
New products	Higher than average risk	Higher rate than required rate of return

Managers with a number of divisions or lines of business have attempted to adapt their corporate discount rates for the specific risks of the division or product line. Because the required rate of return for a division is not available, a number of methods are used to estimate the appropriate discount rate. Most often the rate is calculated by using information about a number of publicly traded proxy firms—firms with similar characteristics. These proxy methods are imprecise, but hold more promise, than using a single rate for businesses with very different levels of risk in their various investments.

Some suggest that manipulating cash flows is more appropriate than varying the discount rate for risk. The most simplistic method of revising the cash flows for risk is conservative forecasting, which typically involves overestimating costs and underestimating revenues. Rather than being conservative, it is wrong. Such estimates permit an inaccurate picture of the real potential (upside and downside) of the project. While such conservatism is broadly practiced, the good analyst will seek the most accurate forecasts and analyze risk using a different method.

There are two methods for incorporating risk directly into investment valuation. Both are based on the analyst forecasting several probable outcomes (costs and benefits), or multiple scenarios, for an investment. The analyst then incorporates this information into the investment analysis.

In the simple use of multiple scenario analysis, an analyst forecasts just three alternative outcomes—optimistic, pessimistic, and most likely—for each of the project's costs and benefits. The result of this analysis is three forecasts and three sets of measures of value for each investment. For instance, the management of Betty's Better Big Boys might decide that the breakfast proposal has a possibility of much greater success as well as real potential for failure. Its success or failure will depend on whether the customer will perceive a fast-food restaurant as a place for breakfast. The forecasts made for the breakfast project (shown in Exhibit 4-4) were the most likely estimates, but the managers were quite uncertain about what would occur if they opened their restaurants for breakfast. If sales from the new breakfast menu exceeded the most likely estimate of $15 million, the operating costs as a percentage of sales might be expected to be slightly lower, since some costs (for instance, maintenance) would not increase with sales. Likewise, if sales were lower than expected, operating costs would not decrease as fast as sales and the net profit might be lower. Exhibit 4-14 provides the annual residual cash flows for the optimistic, most likely, and pessimistic scenarios for the breakfast proposal. The net present value for each scenario is given at the bottom of the exhibit. The investment cost of $2.055 million remains the same regardless of the success of the project.

Quite obviously, if the breakfast project is not successful, the value to Betty's is negative: the costs will exceed the benefits. Using a higher discount rate makes the net present value even lower. However, if customers find the new breakfast menu appealing, the project could be quite a boon to Betty's and its

EXHIBIT 4-14 Betty's Better Big Boys' Breakfast Proposal—Annual Residual
Cash Flows (in thousands of real dollars)

	Pessimistic	Most Likely	Optimistic
Incremental sales	$ 3,300	$ 15,000	$ 26,000
Operating expenses*	(3,168)	(14,250)	(24,440)
Depreciation	0	0	0
Pretax profit	132	750	1,560
Taxes (34%)	(45)	(255)	(530)
Profit after taxes	85	495	1,030
Noncash charges	0	0	0
Residual net cash flow[†]	$ 85	$ 495	$ 1,030
Net present value (@5%)	$ (982)	$ 793	$ 3,110

* Operating expenses are projected by management to decline as sales increase. Management expects them to be 96, 95, and 94 percent of sales, respectively.
† This assumes that each year's cash flows follow the pattern shown in Exhibit 4-4.

shareholders: the net present value would be very attractive. To decide whether to proceed with the breakfast proposal, management must decide on the likelihood of the pessimistic scenario occurring and whether the most likely and optimistic scenarios could create enough value to offset this danger.

Most managers who use this three-scenario analysis approach implicitly assume that each scenario is equally likely, and they use the information to decide whether the company could afford the project if the pessimistic scenario occurred. However, the worst (or best) outcomes possible for every cost and benefit typically result in a forecast that is possible but improbable. Possible but not probable forecasts give managers very little information on which to base decisions. Therefore, in making these forecasts, the analyst must take care that all three sets of forecasts are probable, not just possible.

When creating the scenarios, managers do not need to believe that each of the outcomes is equally likely to occur. Using the breakfast proposal as an example, the management of Betty's might think it most likely, based on the experience of other fast-food restaurants in introducing a breakfast menu, that the breakfast proposal would have sales of $15 million as predicted in Exhibit 4-4. While $15 million is a good estimate of the expected sales, there is a reasonable chance that the innovative menu Betty's management is planning will be very successful. The analyst could estimate the probabilities associated with the potential outcomes. For instance, instead of only three scenarios, the analyst might estimate five or more scenarios and the probability that each might occur. In Exhibit 4-15, the Betty's Better Big Boys' analyst has estimated five alternative outcomes for the breakfast proposal and the likelihood that each will occur.

EXHIBIT 4-15 Probabilistic Analysis—Breakfast Proposal (in thousands of real dollars)

Probability	Net Present Value	Weighted Value
15%	$ (977)	$(147)
20	(102)	(20)
30	793	238
20	2,100	420
15	3,105	466
Expected value (weighted average)		$ 957

To put the forecasts into perspective, the analyst weights the net present value for each scenario by the probability that it will occur to obtain what is called an **expected value**—the probability-weighted net present value. Exhibit 4-15 provides the result of such an analysis. While the net present value of $957,000 is not one that the analyst explicitly forecasted, it represents a sort of average for the project. The analyst also could compute a standard deviation to obtain a measure of risk.

In a more complex investment analysis, where there are numerous costs and benefits for which an analyst could assess probabilities, computer-assisted analysis, especially simulation, provides a good means for analyzing complex data and estimating the expected value and standard deviation for a project.

One word of caution in the use of multiple scenario, expected value analysis: the veracity of this method depends on the company engaging in a number of projects at the same time, or over time, in order for the net present value to represent the average net present value the firm will receive from its projects. If only one project is undertaken, only one outcome can occur: no other projects exist to average the results. Thus, probabilistic analysis can yield rich information for a knowledgeable user, but holds dangers for the naive. Thus, it is best used to gain insight, not to make mechanistic decisions.

Simulation analysis is used by an increasing number of companies. Managers find that the discipline of deciding what might occur for each of the various costs and benefits keeps their assumptions reasonable and makes the analysis useful. Although this technique is time-consuming and requires a computer, the increasing use of microcomputers has made multiple scenario simulation and analysis more accessible and useful for managers.

All forms of risk analysis that we have described in this chapter treat risk as a negative attribute: increases in risk require increased attention and increases in the required return; decreases in risk reduce the required return. All these investments have the possibility that their cash flows, and thus their value, could be either higher or lower. Not all investments have these same sort of upside and downside possibilities, however. In some cases, management can avoid some or most of the downside—the negative cash flows—by purchasing insurance or arranging a partnership with another company. Eliminating the downside typically has a cost, however, and managers will want to be certain that the cost is appropriate.

How does a manager or analyst evaluate an investment where the potential losses have been reduced or eliminated?[8] The usual approaches to risk analysis require that roughly equivalent upside and downside cash flow potentials exist.[9] Some analysts have adapted option-pricing techniques to value the investment with these characteristics. The method developed for use in valuing options in the securities markets has real potential for analyzing certain kinds of capital investments. Those investments are called **contingent claims** or **options**. A contingent claim is a right to buy a particular set of assets at a particular price, or the right to continue or abandon the project if certain things occur. When those things occur, the person who has the claim can use or exercise the claim, that is, buy or continue making the investment.

What is the advantage to owning a contingent claim, or option, rather than making the investment? First, the cost for this claim is much smaller than the cost of making the full investment. Second, the investor can choose to exercise the claim on the investment or not: if the investor chooses not to exercise the claim, the only cost is the initial cost of the option. Thus, for a small price, the investor has the right, but not the obligation, to make the investment.

As an example, consider the following: Strike-It-Rich Oil Co. has just heard that the government is going to sell drilling rights in the interior of the country, in a remote jungle area. From satellite maps, the area appears to have the necessary conditions for oil, so Strike-It-Rich management is interested. If it buys the right to drill in the area, management can decide later, or after more exploration, whether to make the investment in complete exploration and development of oil wells. The cost of the drilling right is small, the cost of developing wells is large, but Strike-It-Rich does not have to drill.

If we used discounted cash flow analysis, we would discount all the costs associated with this investment and all the benefits that might accrue. Strike-It-Rich management can stop investing at any point, however, and walk away from the project. Thus, there is a limit to the losses, and it is up to management's discretion whether they will invest or not. It is the dynamic decision making that discounted cash flow analysis does not take into account. Discounted cash flow analysis is static; the outcomes are presumed to be without management discretion once the investment is made. However, contingent claims or options analysis is dynamic, and thus more realistic. One of the critical differences is that a static technique like NPV does not adequately consider the risk of projects that have embedded options, options to be taken later at the discretion of management. When the investor has an option, high potential variability is attractive: it increases the possibility of reaping the rewards from

---

[8]   One way that losses can be reduced in a project that is not developing as it was forecasted is to stop investing and abandon the project.
[9]   To be specific, a normal distribution of outcomes.

the investment. NPV analysis treats variability as risk, assigns it a cost, and discounts the higher risk (more variable) cash flows at higher rates than the rate at which it discounts more certain cash flows. The result is that NPV analysis often unduly penalizes the value of investments that are contingent claims. In a dynamic world, they should not be penalized.

Option-pricing techniques are one form of capital investment analysis that allows us to value dynamic projects where decisions about what will happen can be made later. Since these techniques are rather new in their application to capital investment analysis, we have not included a detailed description of how they are implemented in this chapter. Rather, we have placed this information in an appendix to this chapter. Whether you have a fleeting or in-depth knowledge of this type of analysis, the forward-thinking analyst should know that discounted cash flow analysis deals with limited-loss projects very poorly, and that option-pricing methods lend themselves well to analyzing such problems. Thus, analysts and managers who are faced with analyzing investments that have such characteristics should read further. Option-pricing methods and a brief description of their use can be found in the references at the end of this chapter, and in the appendix to this chapter.

None of the widely available risk-adjustment methods is completely satisfactory. Therefore, while new methods for incorporating risk into capital investment decision making are being developed or learned, some managers assign different hurdle rates to divisions or strategic business units that are exposed to different levels of risk. Other managers attempt to quantify risk differences for each individual investment. Still others use statistical techniques, such as probabilistic simulation analysis, to estimate directly the riskiness of investments. To date, risk is the most difficult problem in assessing value.

IV. OTHER CONSIDERATIONS IN CREATING VALUE

Not all investments are as complex or as risky as our Betty's examples. Some are simple replacements of old, antiquated, or technologically inferior equipment. Analysis of one of these replacement investments will allow us to examine the impact of such things as different methods of depreciation and taxes on an investment's cash flows and its value.

1. The Impact of Taxes and Depreciation on Value

Betty's Better Big Boys' management is considering a replacement investment—microwave ovens. Currently, each of Betty's restaurants uses conventional electric ovens to heat some foods. Such ovens are large, take an average of 10 minutes to heat the food and, because they warm up slowly, must be kept hot whether they are being used or not.

Microwave ovens have been proposed to replace these ovens. They are small, cook much more rapidly and, because the method of heating and cooking is totally different, need only be turned on when actually in use. Thus, the primary savings would be in the expense for electricity.

Management has made the following estimates of the costs and benefits associated with each new oven.

1. Microwave ovens can be purchased, fully installed, for $630 by July.
2. The old ovens can be sold to a used-equipment dealer for their book value of $25 each.
3. While annual usage and costs of electricity vary from restaurant to restaurant, the average cost per year per oven has been $300. The new ovens would use about one-third the electricity, for a cost of $100 per oven per year.
4. The new ovens are expected to be fully useful for five years. After that time, the ovens will be obsolete or in need of substantial repair. Management believes the ovens would have no salvage value at the end of the fifth year. Management would depreciate the new ovens over six years, according to MACRS.

This is a very straightforward problem. As you can see in Exhibit 4-16, reduced costs are treated the same as increased income. The IRR that results from this analysis is 13.95 percent and the NPV (at a 10 percent discount rate) is $61.02 per oven, seemingly a reasonable investment opportunity.[10]

However, there are changes within management's discretion that can increase the value of the investment. As an example, under certain tax codes management could have elected to use another rapid method of depreciation or straight-line depreciation. Different tax codes use different accelerated methods. Let's examine the effect of using other depreciation methods on the value of the microwave oven investment.

The yearly depreciation changes that would result from using other methods of depreciation and the effect on the net cash flow of using other methods is shown in Exhibit 4-17. The double-declining-balance method yields the largest increase in the project's value.

At first glance, this may seem like numerical black magic, but it is, in fact, a real change in the value of the investment to the company. While the same total depreciation is taken, the amount taken in each year is different. Thus the timing of the taxes paid by the firm is different. Since the discounting process deems earlier cash flows to be more valuable, and since accelerated depreciation methods result in larger, earlier cash flows, the method of depreciation chosen by or allowed to management can create value. As shown in Exhibit 4-17, the present values under each tax code are different. The 1991 MACRS depreciation table provides the most favorable benefit.

....

[10] An analysis for ovens for all 500 restaurants would yield the same IRR of 13.95 percent, but an NPV of $30,700 (500 × $61.4).

EXHIBIT 4-16 Betty's Better Big Boys' Microwave Oven Investment Analysis—Per Oven (in thousands)

				Period			
	0	1	2	3	4	5	6
Income statement changes:							
Revenues		0	0	0	0	0	0
Electricity:							
Old oven		$(300.0)	$(300.0)	$(300.0)	$(300.0)	$(300.0)	0
New oven		(100.0)	(100.0)	(100.0)	(100.0)	(100.0)	—
Electricity cost decrease		200.0	200.0	200.0	200.0	200.0	—
Depreciation:							
Old depreciation		—	—	—	—	—	—
New depreciation*		(126.0)	(201.6)	(121.0)	(72.6)	(72.6)	$(36.3)
Depreciation increase		(126.0)	(201.6)	(121.0)	(72.6)	(72.6)	(36.3)
Change in pretax profits		74.0	(1.6)	79.0	127.4	127.4	(36.3)
Taxes (@ 34%)**		(25.2)	0.5	(26.9)	(43.3)	(43.3)	12.3
Profit after taxes		48.8	(1.1)	52.1	84.1	84.1	(24.0)
Noncash charges:							
Net depreciation		126.0	201.6	121.0	72.6	72.6	36.3
Asset changes:							
Property, plant, and equipment:							
Microwave oven	$(630.0)						
Old oven salvage value	25.0						
Net cash flow	$(605.0)	$174.8	$200.5	$173.1	$156.7	$156.7	$12.3

Net present value at 10% = $61.4
Internal rate of return = 13.95%

* MACRS depreciation schedule.
** Negative taxes are a tax credit against earnings in some other portion of the business.

EXHIBIT 4-17 Yearly Depreciation Charge—Different Depreciation Methods for the Microwave Oven Investment (in thousands)

				Period			
	0	*1*	*2*	*3*	*4*	*5*	*6*
Straight-line*							
Cash flow	$ (630.0)	$126.0	$126.0	$126.0	$126.0	$126.0	
Net present value (@ 10%)	$57.8						
Internal rate of return	13.7%						
Double-declining-balance†							
Cash flow	$ (630.0)	$252.0	$151.2	$90.6	$68.1	$68.1	
Net present value (@ 10%)	$69.1						
Internal rate of return	14.7%						
Sum-of-years' digits‡							
Cash flow	$ (630.0)	$210.0	$168.0	$126.0	$84.0	$42.0	
Net present value (@ 10%)	$68.1						
Internal rate of return	14.6%						
U.S. ACRS§							
Cash flow	$ (630.0)	$94.5	$138.6	$132.3	$132.3	$132.3	
Net present value (@ 10%)	$56.0						
Internal rate of return	13.5%						
MACRS§§							
Cash flow	$ (605.0)	$126.0	$201.6	$121.0	$72.6	$72.6	$36.3
Net present value (@ 10%)	$61.4						
Internal rate of return	14.0%						

*   The depreciation rate is calculated by dividing 100% by the number of years. In this case, the depreciation rate is 100/5 = 20% per year. To determine yearly depreciation, multiply the purchase price, minus the salvage value, by the depreciation rate.

†   Double the straight-line depreciation rate is multiplied by the full depreciated value of the asset. A switch to straight-line depreciation occurs when it is larger.

‡   To calculate the sum-of-the-years' digits factor:
   a) Sum the numbers of the years, in this case 5 + 4 + 3 + 2 + 1 = 15.
   b) For each year, divide the number of remaining years by the summed years. In this case, the depreciation factor for the first year is 5/15 or 0.33.
   c) Multiply the depreciable value by this factor.

§   Five-year U.S. ACRS rates are 15 percent the first year, 22 percent the second year, and 21 percent the remaining three years.

§§ MACRS depreciates at the following rates: 20, 32, 19.2, 11.52, 11.52, and 5.76 percent, for years one through six, respectively.

Changes in the tax laws illustrate the impact external factors can have on the operations and decisions of the company. With the tax shield having a significant impact on the attractiveness of a project, the analyst should always be informed of not only current tax regulations but pending legislation as well. Keeping abreast of the economic, social, and political environment is essential for the analyst in order to analyze managerial decisions properly.

2. Including Investment-Size Considerations

We have looked at three investments Betty's Better Big Boys could make—the breakfast service, the salad and pasta bar, and installing microwave ovens. Each has a different net present value. While the breakfast option appears to be the best choice, we have failed to take note of one other thing: Betty's investments will require different amounts of capital. Thus, if we simply compare the net present values of the three alternatives, we have ignored the invested capital. As an example, all 500 microwave ovens require a net investment of only $302,500, while the breakfast proposal requires $2.055 million. On this basis alone we cannot make a decision because we do not know what use management could make of the difference in the two investments: if only the microwave ovens were bought, the difference would be $1.752 million. That means that management would have $1.7 million in funds to use elsewhere. Thus, if we simply compare net present values, or any other measure of relative return for that matter, we could make a bad decision. In essence, by failing to take into account the investment of all the capital, we would be comparing different corporate strategies.

Must managers have an intended use for the extra capital in order to compare the projects? No. They can examine the value the added investment would create for the owners. To do this, the analyst must first determine the differences in the initial costs and the annual residual cash flows of each of the two investments. A simple method is to subtract the annual residual cash flows of the smaller investment from those of the larger investment. Exhibit 4-18 shows the results of this analysis of differences between the breakfast and microwave oven options for Betty's Better Big Boys. By looking at the last column in the exhibit, you can see that the breakfast option would require an additional investment of $1.7 million beyond that required for installing microwave ovens in all the restaurants.

What does Betty's get for its investment? To determine the benefit, we can discount the differences between the two sets of cash flows. The discounted value is $349,800, as shown in column 3 of Exhibit 4-18, a significant contribution to the shareholders' value. Of course, Betty's management will want to compare this present value with the present values generated by other investments that it might make with the $1.7 million. However, whatever use it might have for the capital, the exhibit clearly shows that the return would have

EXHIBIT 4-18 Betty's Better Big Boys Residual Net Cash Flows—
Two Alternatives (in thousands)

	(1) Breakfast Option	(2) 500 Microwave Ovens	(1) - (2) Difference
Net investment	$ 2,055.0	$ 302.5*	$ 1,752.5
Annual net cash flows, year:			
0	$(2,055.0)	$(302.5)	$(1,752.5)
1	495.0	87.4	407.6
2	495.0	100.3	394.7
3	495.0	86.6	408.4
4	495.0	78.3	416.7
5	1,395.0	78.3	1,316.7
6	0	6.2	(6.1)
NPV (at 10%)	$380.27	$30.5	$349.8
IRR	15.9%	13.95%	16.2%

* This is the net present value per oven from Exhibit 4-16 times 500 ovens, one for each restaurant.

to be 17 percent to render any other use equal to the breakfast investment. Management would likely conclude that the incremental return on the added investment in the breakfast option is attractive.[11]

3. Incorporating Expected Inflation

Inflation can have a neutral, positive, or negative effect on the value of an investment, depending on whether managers can pass on their costs in the form of prompt price increases. If cost increases can be passed on immediately and fully, the relative value of the project will remain the same regardless of the level of inflation. If there is a lag between the time the company's costs increase and the time when it can raise prices, however, inflation can have a very negative effect on the value of a project. Of course, if management can raise prices more than inflation, or has cash it can invest, the company can prosper from inflation.[12]

Inflation can have yet other effects. Revenues themselves may rise or fall depending on the rate of inflation. For instance, if more people eat breakfast at fast-food restaurants than at traditional restaurants when inflation and prices rise, Betty's Better Big Boys may find that its revenues rise in both real terms

....

[11] If Betty's Better Big Boys had a number of investments of different sizes, the comparisons made in Exhibit 4-18 would have to be repeated for each pair of investments.
[12] Terra Blanca, an example used in Chapter 2, showed such inflation-related gains.

(more customers are eating breakfast) and in nominal terms (prices rise to account for the increased costs of producing the same number of breakfasts).

The effects of these increases should be well understood by the manager. Up to now, all the cash flows Betty's management forecasted for its investments were in real terms; they did not include inflation. Exhibit 4-19 provides a forecast for the salad and pasta bar proposal that Betty's Better Big Boys management is considering, with 10 percent inflation. In this example there is no real increase in revenues and unit sales remain the same; the only increases arise from the expected inflation. Inflation alone decreases the net present value loss from this project (at a discount rate of 10 percent) from $288,050 to a loss of $109,676.

Before you conclude that inflation has increased the value of this project, remember that we discounted these cash flows at 10 percent, the same rate we used on the cash flows before we introduced inflation. Investors do not ignore inflation. If the required return for this project was 10 percent before inflation, investors certainly will expect a higher return once they expect inflation. Using a more appropriate discount rate of 20 percent results in an NPV loss of $555,065.[13] Obviously, inflation's effect on value in this case is negative, not positive.[14]

You might have noted depreciation did not change at all in Exhibit 4-19, especially if you compared the cash flows with those shown in Exhibit 4-5. This is because, in many countries, depreciation schedules for capitalized property are calculated on the basis of historical cost, and companies are not allowed to revalue assets to incorporate inflation-driven changes. As a result of this situation, as the rate of inflation increases, depreciation does not change, and neither do the taxes that are deferred by the depreciation tax shield. Thus, the investment is less valuable. This inflation drag is one of the insidious costs of inflation. In some countries, particularly those with high rates of inflation that have persisted for some time, companies are allowed to increase the book value of fixed assets to keep pace with inflation. As the book value rises, the depreciation increases too, keeping pace with inflation.[15] For companies operating in these environments, profits actually increase at a rate comparable to that of inflation.

V. SUMMARY

Good investments are critical to the future of a company. The analyst's job is to gather and analyze the relevant information and present it in a way that

---

[13]   We will discuss the impact of inflation on discount rates in Chapter 6.
[14]   Ten percent required rate of return and 10 percent for expected inflation is a fair estimate of the combined required return.
[15]   It depends upon the index used to calculate the inflation adjustment. The adjustment usually is statutory.

EXHIBIT 4-19 Betty's Salad and Pasta Bar Proposal—Marginal Costs and Benefits with Annual Inflation of 10% (thousands of dollars)

				Period			
	0	1	2	3	4	5	6
Income Statement Changes							
Sales		$ 8,250	$ 9,075	$ 9,983	$ 10,981	$ 12,079	
Operating expenses		(7,673)	(8,440)	(9,284)	(10,212)	(11,233)	0
Training costs	$ (416)						
Depreciation	—	(280)	(448)	(269)	(269)	(161)	$ (81)
Profit before taxes	(416)	297	187	430	500	685	(81)
Taxes	141	(101)	(64)	(146)	(170)	(233)	28
Net profit	$ (275)	$ 196	$ 123	$ 284	$ 330	$ 452	$ (53)
Noncash Charges							
Depreciation		280	448	269	269	161	81
Capital Investments							
Property, plant, and equipment	(1,400)						
New inventory	(900)					—	
Residual net cash flow						900	
	$ (2,575)	$ 476	$ 571	$ 553	$ 599	$ 1,513	$ 28
Net present value @ 5%	$573.11						
Net present value @ 10%	$(109.68)						

allows managers to make informed decisions. Analysts have three major problems in assessing potential investments. First, the appropriate cash costs and benefits must be determined. That process, as we have suggested, can be difficult, particularly when evaluating replacement investments or when operating in an inflationary environment. The analyst's second problem is to evaluate the relative attractiveness of the investment's net marginal benefits. This book suggests that the NPV method is the most appropriate technique to use in measuring this value.[16] Third, the particularly vexing problem of incorporating risk into the evaluation of any investment must be dealt with. If all of the investments are of a risk similar to that of the firm, an appropriate method is to use the firm's marginal required return as a hurdle rate. If the investment is more or less risky than the firm, the analyst may leave it to the managers to decide subjectively whether the return is adequate to compensate for the risk. Some managers find the information from multiple scenario or simulation analysis to be useful in making their decisions; others prefer to adjust the required return to compensate for risk. While understanding and incorporating risk into an analysis is one of the most difficult things that faces investors, ignoring it is not a sensible approach. Determining the investments a company makes is challenging, and critical.

SELECTED REFERENCES

For comprehensive reviews of the capital budgeting process, see:

Bierman, Harold, Jr., and Seymour Smidt. *The Capital Budgeting Decision.* 7th ed. New York: Macmillan, 1988.

Levy, Haim, and Marshall Sarnot. *Capital Investment and Financial Decisions.* Englewood Cliffs, N.J.: Prentice Hall International, 1990.

For corporate strategy and capital budgeting, see:

Shapiro, Alan. "Corporate Strategy and the Capital Budgeting Decision." *Midland Corporate Finance Journal*, Spring 1985, pp. 22-36.

Shapiro, Alan. *Modern Corporate Finance.* 2nd. ed. New York: Macmillan Publishing Co., 1993, chap. 10.

For an analysis of the capital budgeting and planning process in one firm, see:

Bower, Joseph. *Managing the Resource Allocation Process: A Study of Corporate Planning and Investments.* Homewood, Ill.: Richard D. Irwin, 1970.

---

[16]   Augmented by contingent claims analysis when appropriate.

For descriptions of various approaches to risk analysis, see:

Bower, Richard S., and J. M. Jenks. "Divisional Screening Rates." *Financial Management,* Autumn 1975, pp. 42-49.

Hertz, David B. "Risk Analysis in Capital Investment." *Harvard Business Review,* September-October 1979, pp. 169-81.

Weston, J. Fred. "Investment Decisions Using the Capital Asset Pricing Model." *Financial Management,* Spring 1973, pp. 25-33.

For information on the effects of inflation on capital budgeting analysis, see:

Rappaport, Alfred, and Robert A. Taggart, Jr. "Evaluation of Capital Expenditure Proposals Under Inflation." *Financial Management,* Spring 1982, pp. 5-13.

Shapiro, Alan C. *Modern Corporate Finance.* New York: Macmillan Publishing Co., 1989, chaps. 6-8.

For more on international capital budgeting, see:

Madura, Jeff. *International Financial Management.* 2nd ed. St. Paul, Minn.: West Publishing Co., 1989, chaps. 5-11.

Pinches, George E. *Financial Management.* New York: Harper Collins, 1994, chap. 27.

Ross, Stephen A., Randolph W. Westerfield, and Bradford D. Jordon. *Fundamentals of Corporate Finance.* 3rd ed. Homewood, Ill.: Richard D. Irwin, 1995, chap. 21.

Shapiro Alan C. *Modern Corporate Finance.* New York: Macmillan Publishing Co., 1989, chap. 31.

Shapiro Alan C. *Multinational Financial Management.* Needham Heights, Mass.: Allyn & Bacon, 1989, chaps. 5-11.

For information on capital budgeting in general, see:

Aggarwal, Raj. *Capital Budgeting Under Uncertainty.* Englewood Cliffs, N.J.: Prentice Hall, 1993.

Brealey, Richard A., and Stewart C. Myers. *Principles of Corporate Finance.* 5th ed. New York: McGraw-Hill, 1996, chaps. 5 and 9-12.

Brigham, Eugene, and Louis Gapenski. *Financial Management.* Fort Worth, TX: Dryden, 1994, chaps. 9-11.

Levy, Haim, and Marshall Sarnat. *Capital Investment and Financial Decisions.* 4th ed. New York: Prentice Hall, 1990.

Pinches, George E. *Financial Management.* New York: Harper Collins, 1994, chaps. 7, 8, and 10.

Ross, Stephen A., Randolph W. Westerfield, and Jeffrey F. Jaffe. *Corporate Finance.* 4th ed. Homewood, Ill.: Richard D. Irwin, 1996, chaps. 3, 4, 6, 7, and 8.

Ross, Stephen A., Randolph W. Westerfield, and Bradford D. Jordon. *Fundamentals of Corporate Finance*. 3rd ed. Homewood, Ill.: Richard D. Irwin, 1995, chaps. 7-9.

For information on discounting, see:

Brealey, Richard A., and Stewart C. Myers. *Principles of Corporate Finance*. 5th ed. New York: McGraw-Hill, 1996, chaps. 2 and 3.

Ross, Stephen A., Randolph W. Westerfield, and Bradford D. Jordon. *Essentials of Corporate Finance*. 3rd ed. Homewood, Ill.: Richard D. Irwin, 1995, chaps. 5 and 7.

STUDY QUESTIONS

1. In December 1996, Metalwerks' management was considering the development of a new assembly line. The necessary machinery was estimated to cost 1.4 million deutsch marks. The tax code would allow the equipment to be depreciated in 20 years, its useful life, using the double-declining-balance method of depreciation with a switch to straight-line depreciation when advantageous. Management estimated that the costs associated with owning and running the machinery (gas, minor repairs, etc.) would be constant over time and total DM 260,000 over its 20-year estimated life. Twenty people would be required to work the assembly line. These would be new employees, each earning an average of DM 24,000 a year in salary and benefits. Sales from the new assembly line were estimated to total DM 1.625 million a year, with raw materials representing 37 percent of that amount. No other costs specific to the project were anticipated. Metalwerks had a 34 percent tax rate and a required payback period of four years on all new projects. Should the company develop the assembly line? What is the project's benefit/cost ratio?

2. The SUN Company is considering an investment that will cost 200,000 lira initially. The new equipment is estimated to have a useful life of five years but will require an additional investment of 60,000 lira in the second year for specialized equipment. The initial investment will be depreciated under the tax code for five years. The second investment will meet the guidelines for the three-year class. Sales specific to the project are forecasted at 120,000 lira in year one, increasing 15 percent a year to year five. Necessary raw materials, labor, etc., are estimated at 39 percent of sales.

    The tax code allows the following depreciation schedules.

Year	5-Year Schedule	3-Year Schedule
1	15%	26%
2	22	32
3	21	42
4	21	
5	21	

a. Compute the project's net present value using a 10 percent discount rate and a 34 percent tax rate.

b. What is the major factor creating the project's net present value?

3. The Cloud Frame Company operates in an environment where capital is scarce. Management is trying to decide between the two capital projects described below. Evaluate each of the projects on the basis of their payback period, benefit/cost ratio, and net present value. Which project would you recommend Cloud Frame Company undertake? Why?

Project 1: Expand existing production by acquiring new machinery costing Libra 800,000 and having a productive life of 10 years:

- Incremental sales = Libra 500,000 a year
- Cost of goods sold = 49 percent of sales
- Advertising = Libra 50,000 a year
- Depreciation computed using double-declining-balance for 10 years.

Project 2: Expand product line by undertaking a project estimated to cost Libra 600,000 for production facilities, Libra 200,000 for production training for employees, and depreciable using double-declining-balance for its 10-year life. Cloud Frame management has already funded Libra 100,000 worth of market research, which documented the product's sales potential. Cloud Frame management hopes to recoup this outlay through further sales.

- Sales in year 1 are estimated to be Libra 350,000, increasing 10 percent a year in years 2-4, 15 percent a year in years 5-7, and 10 percent a year in years 8-10
- Cost of goods sold is projected at 50 percent of sales
- Advertising is to be 25 percent of sales for first three years and to level off at Libra 100,000 thereafter

  Cloud Frame has a 34 percent tax rate and uses a 10 percent discount rate to evaluate all projects.

Real Options and Capital Investing

Net present value analysis is a fine method for analyzing investment opportunities, when we know what the outcome will be. However, if we do not know the outcome, and we can take some action to change the outcome that does develop, net present value analysis is not the best way to value an investment opportunity. Net present value analysis should be used for a **static decision**: a decision where the outcome cannot be altered. If, however, all the decisions about the future are not made, and a manager has future discretion, the investment is a **dynamic decision**, and it is not appropriate to use net present value to analyze the investment.

Options for action are all around us. Every time we use the phrase "if. . . . then," we are talking about a contingency, an optional choice, something we can do if something else happens. For managers making investments, there are a number of different kinds of options that can exist:

1. To abandon a project or strategy in the future if it is not proceeding as desired. These are called **abandonment** or **bail-out options**.
2. To increase the investment or commitment to an investment or strategy, if it is attractive to do so. These options usually offer the opportunity to grow, and are called **growth options**.
3. To acquire or use something that currently has little or no value, when conditions change. These are called **investment options**.

An investment project can have both static and dynamic features. Some things about an investment may be unchanging and unchangeable once the investment is made. Other features are optional. In some cases these options are a natural part of the investment; in other situations management designs the investment project to incorporate future choices. Because the option or options are bundled together with an investment project, these options generally are called **embedded options**.[1] An example will make this clear.

The RAPTOR Group needs a new plant to build its products. The primary reason that it needs to expand is a new product developed by the Mesozo Division. The new product was the brainchild of their hot new designer, but it is so revolutionary the marketing staff is not sure just how many the company

---

[1] In this appendix, we limit ourselves to real options, options to invest, disinvest, or grow. The company also can use options in its financing activities.

will sell. If the market is as large as the Mesozo Division head has forecasted, they will need a large plant with special technology, for this product, labeled the X Design. If, however, most customers decide to stay with the old technology, the company's current plants will be adequate, and any new plant built would have to be sold.

Management has been presented with two possible ways to satisfy X Design's production needs: Build a small plant that can be expanded in three years, or build a large plant now. The smaller plant plus the later expansion would cost more than the large plant, but it would allow management to test the market's acceptance of the revolutionary new product. However, if the market does not develop, management would stop production of X Design, scrap the original plant, and ignore the addition. If management chooses the larger and more sophisticated plant and the market does not develop, the company would have a large, expensive, little-used plant that would be harder to sell. The option embedded with the smaller plant is to expand later. There is no option embedded in the larger plant investment. Before proceeding, management needs to know the value of each of the investments.

In this appendix we will show how net present value analysis is not up to the task of valuing the small-plant-with-later-expansion option. Through an example it will be clear that using net present value to compare the two investments is not appropriate, and we will present an explicit approach to real option valuation. First, we must set the groundwork and look at options where they are valued most frequently, in the capital markets.

I. FINANCIAL OPTIONS

While options exist all around us, the formal valuation of options has been more highly developed in the capital markets where standard option contracts are used. Because of the magnitude of the markets for these options, standard approaches have been developed to deal with them. These methods can be used for the custom options that accompany capital budgeting decisions.[2]

There are options on a variety of financial instruments designed to suit the insurer or the owner. There are two kinds of **financial options**: call and put. **Call options** give the owner the right, but not the obligation, to buy a specific thing (the **underlying**) at a specific price (the **strike price**) at, on, or before a specific time (the **exercise date**). An option that can be exercised from the date it is purchased until it expires is called an **American call**. One that can only be exercised on a specific date is called a **European call**. Embedded options can be of either type. **Put options** allow the owner to sell a specific thing, at a specific price, on or before a specific time. They are the reverse of a call option.

---

[2] In this appendix we will use the most general of the option-valuation methods, the binomial model. Other models, most notably the Black-Scholes option-pricing model, require more stringent conditions than exist for most corporate investments.

In the capital markets both put and call options are traded. Not all securities have either or both. The options that are freely traded are listed on an organized exchange, like the Chicago Board Options Exchange (CBOE).

These options allow the investor to take later action. For instance, a call option on common stock allows an investor to acquire a particular number of shares of stock at a later date at a specified price. Exhibit 4A-1 shows the call prices listed for Philip Morris shares in August 1996. The last date on which the call can be used, the date it expires, is listed in the third column. As you can see, at any time, there are a variety of call dates available. The second column is the strike or exercise price, the price for which the stock can be acquired. You will note that the exercise prices are near the stock price of $90. The calls at the various strike prices allow the owner of the call to purchase shares later, or sell the option to someone who wants the shares, at $90. However, the owner of the call does not have to buy them now. They can wait, conserving their capital, in the hopes that the actual price will be higher, and a profit can be earned. The value of the call as the stock price rises is the difference between the price of the call and the market price. The put options allow the owner to sell shares at $90 on or before the put expiration date. Notice that call prices at exercise prices below $90 are rather high. These are called in-the-money options: the exercise price is below the current stock price. Put options become more valuable as the strike price rises above $90.

To understand the real value of options, let's look at what can happen to the value of a put and call option, and the underlying shares of Philip Morris common stock, at the moment of expiration.

Value of a stock is the current market price. That price could be much higher or lower in October. That is because many things can happen to the company, its competitors, and the economy, between August and October 1996. The more time that exists between the time the option is purchased and the exercise date, the more that can happen to the stock price.

The value of an option is the difference between the exercise price of the option and the market price of the stock. If the exercise price of a call option is below the stock price, the option is worth the difference between the market price of the share and the exercise price of the option. In other words, the call-option holder gains the upside from share price increases. However, if the exercise price is above the stock price, the option is worthless. The option holder has limited the downside, and the total cost to the holder of holding the call is the price of the option. The put option has value when the exercise price is above the market price. The put-option holder then can sell shares with a lower market price at the higher strike or exercise price.

Thinking about these options, we can see that the value of the option, the price for which it would sell, depends upon five things.

1. The price of the underlying. If the price rises, the value of a call (put) option rises (falls). If the price declines, the value of a call (put) option falls (rises).

EXHIBIT 4A-1 Options on Philip Morris Stock—August 14, 1996

Option	Strike Price	Expiration	Call	Put
90	80	Sept	11.00	1.00
		Dec	12.75	2.63
		Sept	7.25	2.25
		Dec	9.38	4.25
		Mar	N.Av.	5.75
	90	Aug	1.56	1.38
		Sept	4.25	4.25
		Dec	7.25	6.63
	95	Aug	0.25	4.63
		Sept	2.06	7.25
		Dec	4.63	9.06
		Mar	6.50	10.13
		Aug	0.06	9.50

Option	Strike Price	Expiration	Call	Put
90	100	Sept	0.06	9.50
		Dec	1.00	11.25
		Mar	3.25	N.Av.
		Aug	4.38	N.Av.
	105	Sept	0.44	4.88
		Dec	2.13	16.50
		Mar	3.50	N.Av.
	110	Aug	0.06	20.00
		Sept	0.25	N.Av.
		Dec	1.25	N.Av.
		Mar	2.50	20.06
	115	Aug	0.06	N.Av.
		Sept	1.00	N.Av.
		Dec	1.25	N.Av.

N.Av. means that there are no options at this price.

2. The exercise price. Given a particular price of the underlying, the higher (lower) the exercise price, the lower (higher) the price of the call (put).
3. The time until the option expires. The longer the life of the option, the greater its value. As we said before, more things can happen, and there is, therefore, a greater possibility that the option will be exercised.
4. The variability of the price of the underlying investment. The more variable the price, the greater the possibility that the price will change and that the option will be exercised.
5. The current market interest rate. The higher the rate, the more valuable the option. This is because in owning the option rather than the underlying investment, we have avoided investing the full value of the underlying investment, and we invest in the option alone. Since the option has a small value, and the underlying investment a much larger value, we defer making the investment, and can invest the difference. Thus, the higher the interest rate, the more we earn on this investment. This is the reverse of net present value analysis where the higher the discount rate, the less valuable the investment. Exhibit 4A-2 summarizes this.

There are four things that we know about the value of an option on a stock.

1. The option price is never greater than the stock price.
2. The option price cannot drop below zero.
3. The option price is never below the value that could be earned if the option were exercised.
4. The option price, less the present value of the price paid for the option, will approach the stock price when there is a large stock price increase.
5. Because an option has a small price relative to the stock, the price volatility is higher than the stock's price volatility. The higher the price of the stock and option, the lower is the option's volatility. The lower the price of the stock and option, the higher the volatility. Thus, the risk of an option is always higher than that of the stock, but it changes and the change depends upon the relationship between the stock and exercise prices.

EXHIBIT 4A-2   Price Changes from Changes in Critical Variables

Increase in Critical Variables	Impact on Call Option Price	Impact on Put Option Price
Stock price	Positive	Negative
Exercise price	Negative	Positive
Volatility of stock price	Positive	Positive
Time to expiration	Positive	Positive
Interest rate	Positive	Positive

These variables impact the price of an option differently than the price, usually called the value in corporate capital investing, of an investment that is valued using net present value techniques. The major differences are shown in Exhibit 4A-3.

Financial options often come in bundles. There may be several puts and/or calls contained in one instrument. These combinations of options are usually called synthetic securities. We will discuss these briefly in Chapter 7.

Options on such things as common stocks are called **financial options**; options embedded in corporate investment decisions are called **embedded** or **real options**. In this chapter, we take what we know about market options and apply it to corporate investments.

II. REAL OPTIONS

Real options allow managers to increase their potential returns and limit potential losses. In the past, many managers, without the proper tools to value the option, called these strategic or intangible investments. They intuitively knew that these options had a value, but net present value analysis did not allow a value to be placed on them. Thus, managers would argue for an investment with a negative net present value on strategic grounds. Purists would say that anything could be valued; realists knew that net present value analysis did not provide a complete valuation.[3]

Let us return to the plant expansion example to see what the valuation differences might be between net present value and an option valuation method. RAPTOR can build a new plant now for $11.5 million. The analysis of this alternative is shown in Exhibit 4A-4.

The net present value of investing in the larger plant today is $36.9 million. The net present value of building a smaller plant now and waiting to build the remainder until the market is better known, in three years, is $35.3 million, as shown in Exhibit 4A-5. Based on this traditional net present value analysis,

EXHIBIT 4A-3   Impacts on Option and Net Present Values from Changes in Critical Variables

Variable	Option Value	Net Present Value
Risk-free rate rises	Increases value	Decreases value
Variability of outcomes increases	Increases value	Decreases value
Life of investment lengthens	Increases value	Decreases value

---

[3]   One such option is clearly valuable. That is complying with health and safety or pollution requirements imposed by the government. While it is hard to justify cost savings, if the standards are not met, the company may be closed. The option is to avoid closure, and that has a very high value.

EXHIBIT 4A-4   Net Present Value Analysis of RAPTOR Large Plant Expansion

		Period		
	0	*1*	*2*	*3*
Sales		$ 7,962,400	$ 9,395,632	$11,086,846
Variable costs		(3,821,952)	(4,509,903)	(5,321,686)
Depreciation		(1,000)	(1,000)	(1,000)
Fixed costs		(5,000)	(5,000)	(5,000)
Earnings before taxes		4,134,448	4,879,729	5,759,160
Taxes		(1,653,779)	(1,951,891)	(2,303,664)
Net profit		$ 2,480,669	$ 2,927,837	$ 3,455,496
Depreciation		1,000	1,000	1,000
Operating cash flow		2,481,669	2,928,837	3,456,496
Plant	$(11,500,000)			
Terminal value		—	—	69,129,917
Residual cash flow	$(11,500,000)	$ 2,481,669	$ 2,928,837	$72,586,413
Net present value	$ 36,884,887			

Assumptions:

Operating characteristics (Year 1):

Sales volume (units)	592,000
Sales price per unit	$13.45
Variable cost per unit	48.0%
Fixed costs	$5,000
Depreciation	$1,000
Sales growth rate	18.0%
Terminal value growth rate	5.0%
Marginal tax rate	40.0%
Initial cost	$10,000,000

Non-operating factors:

Exercise price (price to expand)	$1,000,000
Periods till option expires	3
Risk (annual change)	40.0%
Required rate of return	18.0%
Risk-free rate of return	7.0%

EXHIBIT 4A-5 Net Present Value of Wait-and-See Plant Expansion

		Period		
	0	1	2	3
Sales		$ 7,962,400	$ 9,395,632	$11,086,846
Variable costs		(3,821,952)	(4,509,903)	(5,321,686)
Depreciation		(1,000)	(1,000)	(1,000)
Fixed costs		(5,000)	(5,000)	(5,000)
Earnings before taxes		4,134,448	4,879,729	5,759,160
Taxes		(1,653,779)	(1,951,891)	(2,303,664)
Net profit		$ 2,480,669	$ 2,927,837	$ 3,455,496
Depreciation		1,000	1,000	1,000
Operating cash flow		2,481,669	2,928,837	3,456,496
Plant	$ (10,000,000)	—	—	(5,000,000)
Terminal value		—	—	69,109,917
Residual cash flows	$ (10,000,000)	$ 2,481,669	$ 2,928,837	$67,566,413
Net present value	$ 35,329,560			

RAPTOR management would choose to build the larger plant now, rather than to wait and see how the market develops.

In spite of the higher net present value from building the larger plant today, there is a value to being able to wait before building the rest of the plant. The value comes from being able to expand the plant only if the market materializes.

Our analysis in Exhibits 4A-4 and 4A-5 presumes that the company will proceed with the plant expansion and product, whether the new market develops or not. A decision tree, with a branch for the potential upside and downside net profit, is shown in Exhibit 4A-6.[4] The primary difference between this set of forecasts and the forecasts contained in Exhibit 4A-5 is that we are showing the potential upside and downside for the sales over the three periods. Each branch of the tree describes the possible profits that might result for each of the three years. The weighted average of each period's branches, shown at the bottom, is identical to that period's net profit reported in Exhibit 4A-5.[5]

Exhibit 4A-7 shows the net present value decision tree. The probabilities, identical to those shown in Exhibit 4A-6, are not shown. The initial investment of $10 million is subtracted from the present value to determine the net present value. The net present value is identical to that from the analysis in Exhibit 4A-5, since the probability-weighted sum of the branches is our forecast shown in Exhibit 4A-5.

However enthusiastic the division management might be, it is unlikely that RAPTOR management would expand the plant in the third year if the second

---

[4]   There are a number of models that provide formulas for valuing options. These methods depend upon relatively strong assumptions about how the cash flows behave over time. For most corporate investment decisions, the model we use here, based on the binomial option pricing model, is appropriate.

[5]   Exhibit 4A-5 lists the assumptions underlying these exhibits. The forecasts are just like those we have been making in Chapters 2 and 4. However, there is one thing that is different. That is the probabilities. To create the probabilities for each of the branches, we must make an assumption. That assumption is that the investor, in this case RAPTOR management on behalf of its shareholders, would be satisfied with the risk-free rate of return on a riskless investment. This is the same as saying that investors want more return for taking more risk, and that risk and return are related. Once we make this assumption and estimate the risk-free rate expected by investors and the potential variation in the values, we can use a simple formula to calculate the probabilities for each branch.

Upside change	$= e^{(s\,h)} - 1$
Downside change	$= e^{(-s\,h)} - 1$
Probability of upside change	$= \dfrac{r_f - d}{u - d}$

Where
- e = 2.718, the base for natural logarithms
- h = number of periods
- u = upside change
- d = downside change
- r_f = risk-free rate of return

EXHIBIT 4A-6 Decision Tree of Net Profits for Wait-and-See Investment

	Period		
	1	*2*	*3*
Net profit			$5,524,783
Probability of occurrence		$3,702,340	38.50%
	$2,480,669	62.05%	$2,480,669
		$1,661,724	47.10%
		37.95%	$1,112,747
			14.40%
Weighted average profit	$2,480,669	$2,927,926	$3,455,672

year's net profits were $1.7 million and declining, like those shown in the lower branch of the tree.[6] Indeed, the plant would not be built, and the branch would cease to exist at that point, and the plant would be sold for some value far less than its cost, certainly no more than $8 million.

There is a big difference between the net present values that result from the assumption that the project continues and where the project is terminated at the end of the second year. Exhibit 4A-8 shows the differences. In part A the present value is the present value of the cash flows each year and a terminal value that assumes that management will continue the operation. This value was determined by presuming the cash flows in the third year would continue and grow at 5 percent forever. We now know that management would, if the

EXHIBIT 4A-7 Decision Tree of Net Present Values for Wait-and-See Investment

	Period		
	1	*2*	*3*
Net present value			$67,571,082
		$2,659,681	
	$2,103,109		$28,663,498
		$1,194,143	
			$11,179,744
Weighted present value of annual flows	$2,103,109	$2,103,509	$41,125,257

....

[6] This is from sales of $5.3 and $3.6 in years 2 and 3 respectively. In our analysis we assume that the last year's sales, and thus the cash flows, would grow at 5 percent. However, with profits declining each year along this branch, this is unlikely.

EXHIBIT 4A-8   Net Present Value of Lowest Sales Forecast Branch

A. Present Value of Continuing Cash Flows as Terminal Value

	Period			
	0	1	2	3
Sales		$7,962,400	$5,337,578	$3,578,034
Net income		2,480,669	1,661,724	1,112,747
Residual cash flow*	$(10,000,000)	$2,481,669	$1,662,724	$9,681,032
Net present value	$ (810,574)			

B. Sale of Plant for $8 million in Year 2 as Terminal Value

	Period			
	0	1	2	3
Sales		$7,962,400	$5,337,578	
Net income		2,480,669	1,661,724	
Residual cash flow**	$(10,000,000)	$2,481,669	$9,662,724	
Net present value	$ (957,273)			

*   Terminal value is operating cash flow/(discount rate - rate of perpetual growth).
**   Terminal value is the sale value of the plant for $8 million at the end of the second year.

second year's cash flows are weak, abandon the project and sell the plant for $8 million. Those cash flows are shown in Part B. Our traditional net present value analysis shown in Exhibit 4A-4 did not take this into account.

Given these differences, Exhibit 4A-9 shows the net present value of the decision tree as if the project continues and with the lower branch severed at the end of the second year.[7]

The value of the option is the difference between the two net present values: the value assuming that management continues operations and builds the plant regardless of the product's success and abandoning the product and selling the plant if the product does not do well. Since the option is worth $1.6 million, management should build the smaller plant and wait to see if the market develops. Management should only exercise the option to expand the plant if the market for X Design shows promise after two years.

---

[7]   If the project ceased to exist after the second year, the present value of the two years of cash flows would be $4.1 million, less the initial cost for the plant of $10 million. Of course, management might sell the plant, or find some other use. However, for this project, the value of the plant is diminished if the sales decline and the product is scrapped.

EXHIBIT 4A-9 Residual Cash Flows and Net Present Value
With and Without Abandonment

Without Abandonment

	Period		
	1	2	3
			$67,571,082
		$2,659,681	38.50%
	$2,103,109	62.05%	$28,663,498
		$1,194,143	47.10%
		37.95%	$11,179,744
			14.40%
Weighted present value of annual flows	$2,103,109	$2,103,509	$41,125,257
Net present value	$35,331,875		

With Abandonment

	Period		
	1	2	3
	—	—	$67,571,082
	—	$2,659,681	38.50%
	$2,103,109	62.05%	$28,663,498
	—	$1,194,143	47.10%
	—	37.95%	0
	—	—	14.40%
Weighted present value of annual flows	$2,103,109	$2,103,509	$39,515,374
Net present value	$33,721,992		
Value of option	$1,609,883		

III. CONCLUSION

This is the briefest of introductions to the basics of embedded or real options. As you can see, this is a powerful, realistic analysis that is and should be gaining widespread acceptance. The mathematics of the methodology, particularly some of the shortcut methods, like the widely used Black-Scholes option-pricing model, can be daunting. However, using this decision tree approach, also called the binomial method, can be straightforward, portray decisions as they are likely to be taken by management, and incorporate into the valuation of an investment the likely courses of action. More and more corporate managers are recognizing that net present value analysis depends upon static, unchanging, outcomes—outcomes that are unlikely even at the outset of an investment. Managers already knew that many investments held options to abandon, expand, or grow. What they did not have with option analysis was a method for analyzing the options. Analyzing and valuing embedded options is a skill analysts must gain. Creating the options is the job of good managers.

SELECTED REFERENCES

On options in general, see:

Brealey, Richard A., and Stewart C. Myers. *Principles of Corporate Finance.* 5th ed. New York: McGraw-Hill, 1996, chap. 20.

Brigham, Eugene, and Louis Gapenski. *Financial Management.* Fort Worth, TX: Dryden, 1994, chap. 22.

Ross Stephen A., Randolph W. Westerfield, and Jeffrey F. Jaffe. *Corporate Finance.* 4th ed. Homewood, Ill.: Richard D. Irwin, 1996, chap. 21.

Ross, Stephen A., Randolph W. Westerfield, and Bradford D. Jordon. *Fundamentals of Corporate Finance.* 3rd ed. Homewood, Ill.: Richard D. Irwin, 1995, chap. 23.

On real options, see:

Brealey, Richard A., and Stewart C. Myers. *Principles of Corporate Finance.* 5th ed. New York: McGraw-Hill, 1996, chap. 21.

Dixit, Avinash K., and Robert S. Pindyck. "The Options Approach to Capital Investment." *Harvard Business Review*, Boston, Mass.: May-June 1995.

Pinches, George E. *Financial Management.* New York: Harper Collins, 1994, chap. 10.

Leuhrman, Timothy A. "Capital Projects as Real Options: An Introduction." Boston, Mass.: Harvard Business School Case Series, 1994.

Ross, Stephen A., Randolph W. Westerfield, and Jeffrey F. Jaffe. *Corporate Finance.* 4th ed. Homewood, Ill.: Richard D. Irwin, 1996, chap. 7.

Ross, Stephen A., Randolph W. Westerfield, and Bradford D. Jordon. *Fundamentals of Corporate Finance.* 3rd ed. Homewood, Ill.: Richard D. Irwin, 1995, chaps. 10 and 20.

Valuation 2: Acquisitions and Divestitures

A nalyzing a corporate strategy—whether the investment is in property, plant, or equipment; a line of business; or a whole company—requires valuation tools. The only real differences between capital budgeting and corporate valuation lie in the scope and availability of the data needed to create estimated cash flows and discount rates. Because acquisitions and divestitures are large, are strategically important, and seem to require special analytical approaches, we consider their analysis as a separate topic in valuation.[1]

Merger activity in the United States by domestic and nondomestic firms burgeoned during the late 1960s and the 1980s. In the early part of the 1990s, as shown in Exhibit 5-1, merger activity dropped precipitously, and did so for non-U.S. firms as well as U.S. firms. One might have expected that U.S. companies, on the trail of global business partners, would have taken their acquisition activity outside the United States. The decline in worldwide merger activity may well have been the result of a backlash to the merger boom of the 1980s and the recession that was spreading around the world. In addition, acquisitions by Japanese companies in the United States declined in the early 1990s because of the recession and the steep decline of the Japanese stock market that reduced Japanese investor liquidity. Merger activity revived again in 1993, expanding further in 1994. Much of the renewal in mergers can be attributed to the rebound of the U.S. economy and increases in stock market valuations.[2] Exhibit 5-2 shows, however, that acquisitions of non-U.S. companies by U.S. companies declined dramatically in 1995.

Managers engaged in merger activity have given a number of reasons for making acquisitions. They report mergers are attractive to:

1. Lower financing costs.
2. Diversify and thus reduce risk.

---

[1] In the past, the words merger and acquisition were used to denote different forms of corporate combinations. In general, the word merger now is used to designate the physical combining of companies after acquisition is complete.

[2] Perhaps much of the decline in activity in 1995 may be due to stock market valuations in the U.S. in the mid-1990s.

EXHIBIT 5-1 Acquisitions of U.S. Companies by U.S. and Non-U.S. Companies

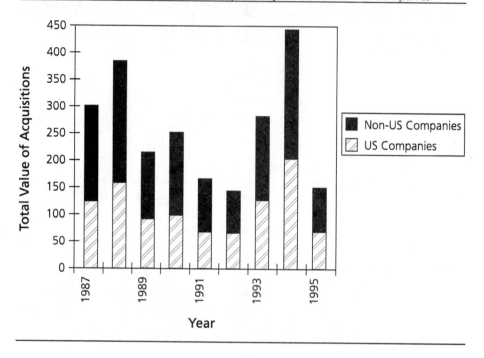

EXHIBIT 5-2 Acquisitions of Non-U.S. Companies by U.S. Companies

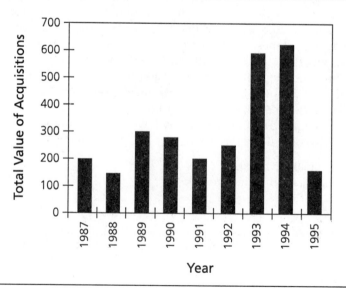

3. Increase the earnings per share of the acquiring firm.
4. Use excess funds.
5. Provide needed funds.
6. Purchase an undervalued company.
7. Take advantage of economies of scale or size.
8. Enter a business or market.
9. Gain market share or presence.

These are quite different reasons for an acquisition or merger. However, all these reasons can be reduced to one: to create value for the acquiring company's shareholders. This creation of value comes only as the result of synergy between the merging firms. Synergy comes from combining unused capacity in one company with a need for that capacity in another. Value for an acquiring firm's shareholders can be the result of paying less for the targeted company than it is worth. However, real synergy may come from combining or better using such things as plant capacity, sales forces, distribution systems, equity or debt-market access, brand presence, or management talent. Synergy could also come from the willingness of one company's owners to take risk, combined with another's too-conservative approach. Acting on potential synergies can result in the creation of value, the goal of shareholders.

Creating value is a familiar goal, one that was discussed in relation to capital investment decisions in Chapter 4. The goal is the same with the sale or purchase of businesses. Although a business is usually larger than the typical capital investment, the acquired firm, division, or line of business must still generate an adequate return for the acquiring company's shareholders. Thus, the tools used in Chapter 4 apply here. We make the case that an acquisition is just like any other corporate investment. Why then do we devote another chapter to its discussion?

There are five reasons.

1. Since acquisitions usually require large investments, firms frequently have a separate staff of acquisition analysts.
2. Merger analysts often borrow the analytical tools of stock analysts, using them instead of or as a supplement to traditional valuation (capital investment) techniques and criteria. The stock analyst's approach is used because many acquisitions are made by purchasing the stock of the acquired firm with cash or securities of the acquiring firm. Because stock often is used or exchanged in the transaction, stock analysis techniques appear appropriate.
3. Acquisitions are a separate topic because the real benefits of an acquisition can be difficult to identify and awkward to evaluate, since the costs and benefits are unusually influenced by tax and accounting issues.
4. Companies often rely on outside advisers, such as investment bankers or business brokers, to identify, analyze, and value potential acquisitions or divestitures. These outside analysts may use special language to

describe their analysis and special tools to value a business. Managers who are acquiring or divesting a business should be aware of the basic valuation concepts and how experts use and interpret them.

5. The acquisition decision is an excellent example of the way a manager can create or destroy value for a company's owners.

Despite difficulties with valuing companies or divisions, an acquisition is essentially a complex capital investment. Thus, the capital investment framework presented in Chapter 4 can be used to determine whether a potential acquisition will create value for the acquiring firm's owners. In this chapter, we will recommend and describe present value analysis of cash flows as a method for valuing and pricing a business. We will then discuss some of the other valuation techniques currently used by analysts. Note that while an acquisition is our primary focus, a divestiture is the same transaction seen through the seller's eyes, and the approach to the analysis is the same.

Acquisitions are done to create value. There are two ways in which value can be created in making an investment. First, value can be created by finding unusual benefits that accrue from the investment itself. Second, value can come from the way the investment is financed. Because these sources of value are quite distinct, the analysis of these sources should also be distinct. In Chapter 4 we discussed the methods for valuing an investment, but we did not consider whether special forms of financing might enhance or detract from this value. In this chapter we follow the same process, saving our discussion of how a company should finance itself and how that financing might affect the value of capital investments, including mergers, for Chapter 7. In the appendix to that chapter we will discuss leveraged mergers, also called leveraged buyouts.

Before we begin to look at how capital budgeting tools are adapted to value businesses, a word of warning: the combination of poor analysis, misuse of tools, and overenthusiasm among buyers creates a dangerous situation. Buyers can let their enthusiasm for a merger cloud the analysis of the potential costs and benefits of the merger. When enthusiasm overwhelms judgment, management can overvalue the benefits and misjudge the costs. Therefore, in the United States, the stock price of an acquirer is often negatively affected by the announcement of a pending merger, whereas the shareholders of the company being acquired often find positive and significant returns from their shares.

A major consulting firm, McKinsey and Company, verified this stock market impact in a study it conducted of 200 acquisitions made by the largest U.S. public corporations in the late 1970s and early 1980s. McKinsey found that 70 percent of the acquirers failed to earn the required return on their investments. Few, it found, added value for the acquiring company's shareholders.[3] In fact,

[3]   Reported in "Establishing the Failure Factor," *Euromoney Corporate Finance Supplement,* February 1987, p. 14.

many mergers during the period studied provided returns below those of very low-risk U.S. Treasury securities. This result is disheartening. Because of findings like these, it is critical that the analyst evaluating the purchase of another business do so with great care.

Now, armed with our knowledge about basic valuation techniques gained in Chapter 4, we are ready to value lines of business, divisions, or whole companies.

I. PRESENT VALUE ANALYSIS OF CASH FLOWS

The analyst must follow two steps in valuing an acquisition:

1. Identify the value of the equity of the company to be acquired (NPV_A).
2. Identify the present values of the synergies that may result as the acquired firm's business is joined with that of the acquirer (NPV_S).

The marginal value of the acquisition depends both on the value of the company to be acquired and on the value of the synergies:

$$\text{Acquisition value} = NPV_A + NPV_S$$

Let's follow an example to demonstrate the analysis of an acquisition, using these two steps and the problems an analyst will face in performing the analysis.

1. Calculating the Value of an Acquisition Without Synergy

The management of Lifelike Cabinet Co., a manufacturer of kitchen cabinets, has identified another company that is an interesting acquisition, Tract Company. Tract Co. is a printer, binder, and distributor of books for little-known religious organizations whose beliefs are based on early Greek mythology. Since the demand for Tract's books has been level for years and is not expected to rise, the current cash flow for Tract is expected to continue without change into the foreseeable future. Management expects Tract Company's 1997 sales to be $10.3 million, operating expenses to be 92 percent of sales, depreciation to be $50,000, equipment purchases to be $50,000, and taxes to be 34 percent of income before taxes. Net income is expected to total $511,000. Income and costs are not expected to grow, and there is a widely held view that there will be no inflation. Using these assumptions, management has produced the forecasted income and residual cash flow forecast shown in Exhibit 5-3.

Some acquisition and stock analysts discount earnings rather than cash flows. We do not use earnings: earnings reflect the impact of accounting rules on the timing of expense and revenue recognition, but do not necessarily show

EXHIBIT 5-3   Tract Co. 1997 Income and Residual Cash Flow Forecast (in thousands)

	1997
Sales	$10,300.00
Operating expenses	(9,476.00)
Depreciation	(50.00)
Income before taxes	774.00
Taxes	(263.16)
Income after taxes	510.84
Depreciation	50.00
Change in property, plant, and equipment	(50.00)
Annual residual cash flow	510.84
Terminal value	—
Residual cash flow	$ 510.84

when cash inflows or outflows occur. If the tax authorities allowed companies to recognize revenues when customers paid for their orders and costs when the company had to pay for purchases, earnings and cash flows would be identical. Since few, if any, tax authorities allow companies to do this, cash flow is best recognized when cash is received and available to pay expenses or give to the company's owners. In some circumstances, for some companies, earnings and cash flow are the same. This is coincidence. Under no circumstances should the earnings of a company be discounted to estimate the value of a business, only the cash flows.

To estimate Tract's value, we could forecast the cash flows for each year and discount them at the investors' required rate of return on equity, the discount rate. If the cash flows are expected to be the same each year, however, as they are with Tract, we can use a shortcut. We simply divide the annual cash flow by the discount rate to obtain an estimate of the value of the cash flows from that point forward. This is the perpetuity method of valuation.[4] Note that this shortcut works only if we are expecting the unchanging cash flows to last a long time. If we were expecting the cash flows to last only a few years and then terminate, we would have to forecast each year's cash flows and discount each of them to estimate the net present value.

In the case of Tract, because the residual cash flow will remain the same every year in perpetuity, we can use the following formula to calculate the net present value of the whole company:

$$NPV_A = \frac{NCF_A}{R_{eA}}$$

---

[4]   If you are not certain that the two methods are equivalent, try it yourself.

where

R_{eA}	=	Investors' required return on equity for a company
NCF_A	=	Yearly residual net cash flow for a company
NPV_A	=	Net present value of equity cash flows for a company

Because management expects no growth and investors require a return of 13.8 percent, the value of Tract is:

$$NPV_T \quad = \quad \frac{NCF_T}{R_{eT}}$$

$$= \quad \frac{\$510,840}{0.138}$$

$$= \quad \$3,701,739$$

The question is, however, at a value of \$3.7 million, should Lifelike acquire Tract? The answer is, it depends upon the price.

If Lifelike pays a fair price for Tract, there is no expected benefit or loss to the owners of either firm. A fair price for Tract is one that neither creates nor destroys value—one that exactly equals the present value of the benefits from Tract, \$3.7 million. That is, by fair price we mean that the Lifelike owners pay a price equal to the value of Tract. For Tract's owners, \$3.7 million is what the cash flows are worth to them if they continue to own the company. If by skillful negotiation, however, Lifelike management can acquire Tract for less than \$3.7 million, Lifelike's owners will gain value, while investors holding Tract stock will lose value. A simple formula can be used to show the important relationship between price and value:

$$NRC_A \quad = \quad Price_A - NPV_A$$

where

NRC_A	=	The net real cost to acquire a company
$Price_A$	=	The purchase price of a company
NPV_A	=	The present value of a company, with no synergistic benefits

If Lifelike pays \$3.7 million for Tract, the value created for Lifelike's owners will be zero.

$$NRC_T \quad = \quad \$3.7 - \$3.7$$

$$= \quad \$0$$

If Lifelike pays more than \$3.7 million, its owners should expect to lose value. For instance, if the price were \$4.0 million, the expected loss would be \$300,000, as shown:

$$NRC_T = \$4.0 - \$3.7$$
$$= (\$0.3) \text{ million, or } (\$300,000)$$

This loss to Lifelike's shareholders is a gain to the shareholders of Tract. However, if Lifelike management negotiated skillfully and paid $3.4 million for the $3.7 million in benefits expected from Tract, $300,000 in expected value would be transferred to Lifelike's shareholders.

This example shows clearly that, in the simplest case, managers face two problems in making an acquisition or selling a business. First, managers must place a value on what is being acquired, and second, a price must be determined. The two are not the same.

2. Calculating the Marginal Benefit of an Acquisition With Synergy

Our calculations thus far have assumed that the acquisition offers no new benefits, no synergies. What if the combined companies were expected to have cash flows in excess of those the two firms would have had without each other? The increase in the cash flows might come from a variety of synergies. For example, Tract might be operating at full capacity with a large backlog of orders for its products. Lifelike might have an empty manufacturing facility that could be used, with little change, to produce products for Tract's customers. Lifelike's unused capacity combined with Tract's need for capacity would increase cash flows without incurring fully offsetting costs: more pamphlets could be printed and sold without adding to the combined firm's plant capacity. Thus, because of the synergy, the combination of Tract and Lifelike would provide a value that is greater than the value the two companies would have if they were operating alone.

Synergies clearly have a value. There are two ways Lifelike's analysts might go about estimating the value of such synergies. First, the analysts could forecast the cash flows associated with the synergies and discount them. To do this, they would need to estimate the increase in Tract's sales, the marginal costs incurred in using Lifelike's plant, and any other new costs associated with producing, selling, and delivering the additional pamphlets. This is an analysis we might have done in Chapter 4.

Let's assume that the managers of Lifelike and Tract have met and have forecasted the costs and revenues expected from printing additional pamphlets for Tract customers in the unused space at Lifelike's plant. Revenues from the sales of the new booklets are expected to be $350,000 per year, and new expenses, expenses not already being incurred by either company, will be $85,000, including taxes on incremental net income. There will be no new equipment needed: Tract has equipment that is not being used and the skilled workers to install it.

Tract management is quite certain that all the new product can be sold, but it does not expect sales to grow. Since management believes that these sales are more certain than Tract's regular business, management estimates investors' required return for these cash flows of 13 percent. Using the perpetuity method, the present value of the synergies is:

$$NPV_S = Cash\ flows_s/R_{es}$$
$$= \frac{\$350,000 - \$85,000}{0.13}$$
$$= \$2,038,462$$

To determine the total value of the potential merger, the value of the synergies would be added to Lifelike's estimate of Tract's value. The total value of Tract plus the synergies that result from the merger of Tract with Lifelike is $5.7 million.

For analysts who find estimating the value of synergies difficult, there is another way to make the forecast. As shown in Exhibit 5-4, the analyst first would estimate the present values of Lifelike and Tract operating alone. The analyst would then estimate the value of the combined firms after the merger, then would subtract the two. What would remain from these steps is the value of the synergies. As you can see from Exhibit 5-4, the synergies are worth $2.0 million, the same amount we just calculated directly. Of course, whether the Tract shareholders, or those from Lifelike, will actually receive the value of the synergies depends upon the purchase price.

Because the value of Tract without synergies is $3.7 million and the synergies' value is $2.0 million, Lifelike management could offer up to $5.7 million for Tract. However, if Lifelike offered $5.7 million, no value would be created for its owners: the full value of Tract plus the synergies would be paid to the Tract owners. At a price of $4.7 million, the buyer and seller share the synergies equally, and at a price of $3.7 million, Tract's owners are not paid for their contribution to the synergies. The graph shown in Exhibit 5-5 shows the relative positions of the two sets of owners at a variety of prices. As you can see, the price that will be paid in a merger is critical in determining whether the acquirer can create value with its investment.

We made the analysis of the Lifelike-Tract merger and its synergies deceptively straightforward by assuming that the benefits and the resulting present values had already been determined. The practicing analyst must estimate these benefits. Projecting the costs and benefits of the synergies of the combined companies is often subject to even greater forecasting error than is fore-

EXHIBIT 5-4 Net Present Value of Combined Firms: Synergistic Benefits

	Lifelike	Tract Co.	Combined Companies
Residual net cash flow per year	$600,000	$510,840	$1.376 million
Investors' required return	12.0%	13.8%	12.8%
Net present value	$5.0 million	$3.7million	$10.750 million

EXHIBIT 5-5   Value to Owners of Tract and Lifelike at
Different Purchase Prices for Tract

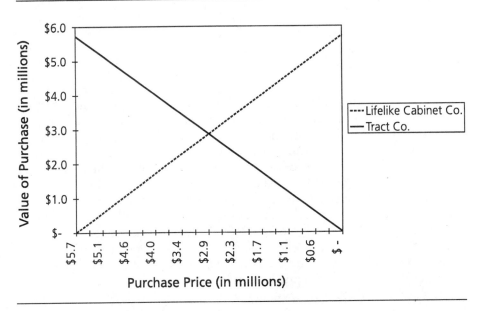

casting the cash flows for the original entities. For example, we said that Tract might benefit by using Lifelike's excess capacity. However, the benefits of using that space could depend on such factors as the availability of local labor, the suitability of the space, and unpredictable conversion costs. The benefits may be quite different from those originally forecasted. Most acquisitions provide far greater forecasting ambiguity than does our example.

Risk and the impact of an acquisition on risk are also difficult to estimate. In the Lifelike-Tract example, we made the analyst's life simple by assuming that the business risk of the new firm was the average of the firms' risks prior to acquisition plus the risk associated with the synergies. This simplifying assumption rarely holds true in practice. For example, joining a cyclical to a countercyclical firm will greatly reduce the risk of the combined firm, all other factors being equal, but joining two firms with the same cycle would not have the risk-reducing effect.

3. Calculating the Marginal Benefit of an Acquisition With Growth

Both analyses of Tract assumed that the company was not anticipating any growth in its future cash flows. However, forecasts by industry experts suggest that growth in splinter religions is expected to increase from 1997 until the end of the millennium. Management believes that this means that Tract will experience growth in the sales of its products: growth in sales could be as high as 10 percent for the next five years, before it drops to zero. Management knows that the current equipment would not be adequate to sustain this growth, and added investments would be necessary. Management must consider both the cash flows that might result from the change, as well as the following questions about the impact on value.

1. What is the value given this change in the expected growth of the company?
2. What is the least Lifelike should pay if it acquired Tract?
3. What is the most Lifelike should pay to acquire Tract?

The analysis shown in Exhibit 5-6 was prepared by management, based on the assumption that Tract sales will grow at a rate of 10 percent to 2002, and will not grow thereafter. [5] The present value of this growing Tract is just over $4.6 million.[6] The present value exceeds that calculated with no growth. The value would be even greater if management could grow without investing in the new assets needed to support that growth.

To value Tract, Lifelike's analyst forecasted the cash flows for six years: five years with growth of 10 percent and one year with no growth. Once Tract's growth stops, we can use the perpetuity method to value the cash flows that are expected in the ensuing years. Thus, in this case, the perpetuity method is used to value the cash flows for 2003 onward.

The calculation for the perpetuity value for 2003 and onward is shown at the bottom of Exhibit 5-6. This value, $6.1 million, is added to the cash flow of $835.9 thousand forecasted to be received in 2002. The sum of these two cash flows, $6.9 million, is discounted back to its present value, the value at the beginning of 1997, to determine the value of a growing Tract Co.

Terminal value is a curious concept. In general, it means the value of an investment at the time the investment is liquidated (later in this chapter, we will discuss liquidation value). In valuing a business, however, the terminal value usually means the present value of an investment's cash flows from that point onward. The terminal value is estimated at the point in the forecast when the analyst can use a shortcut to estimate the value of cash flows extending into the future. When can an analyst use this shortcut? The answer to that question is: when the cash flows are not expected to change for a very long time into the future. When no growth in the cash flows is forecasted, the perpetuity method of valuation can be used.

There is one other circumstance in which the perpetuity method may be used: when the cash flows are expected to grow at a constant rate for a very

---

[5]   However, in this case we simplified what is usually a more complex analysis by forecasting that the capital investments would equal the depreciation, and there would be no other investments, even with the growth.
[6]   The analysis shown is the same sort we used in Chapter 4 to value capital investments.

EXHIBIT 5-6 Tract Co. Income and Residual Cash Flow With Growth (in thousands)

	1997	1998	1999	2000	2001	2002
Sales	$ 11,330.0	$ 12,463.0	$ 13,709.3	$ 15,080.2	$ 16,588.3	$ 16,588.3
Operating expenses	(10,423.6)	(11,466.0)	(12,612.6)	(13,873.8)	(15,261.2)	(15,261.2)
Gross income	906.4	997.0	1,096.7	1,206.4	1,327.1	1,327.1
Depreciation						
Original	(50.0)	(50.0)	(50.0)	(50.0)	(50.0)	(50.0)
Growth-induced	(0.5)	(1.1)	(1.7)	(2.3)	(3.1)	(3.4)
Income before taxes	855.9	945.9	1,045.0	1,154.1	1,274.0	1,273.7
Taxes	(291.0)	(321.6)	(355.3)	(392.4)	(433.2)	(433.1)
Income after taxes	564.9	624.3	689.7	761.7	840.8	840.6
Depreciation						
Original	50.0	50.0	50.0	50.0	50.0	50.0
Growth induced	0.5	1.1	1.7	2.3	3.1	3.4
Change in property, plant, and equipment						
Original	(50.0)	(50.0)	(50.0)	(50.0)	(50.0)	(50.0)
Growth-induced	(5.0)	(5.5)	(6.1)	(6.7)	(7.3)	(8.1)
Working capital change	(206.0)	(226.6)	(249.3)	(274.2)	(301.6)	—
Annual cash flow	354.4	393.3	436.0	483.1	535.0	835.9
Terminal value						6,057.6
Residual cash flow	$ 354.4	$ 393.3	$ 436.0	$ 483.1	$ 535.0	$ 6,893.5

Net present value at 13.8% = $4,653.299

Assumptions:
1. Working capital is 20% of the change in sales.
2. Terminal value is the perpetuity value of the annual residual cash flow in 2002 at a discount rate of 13.8% [$835.9/(0.138 - 0.0)].
   The growth is zero from 2002 onwards.

long time. By constant rate, we mean a rate that does not change. Since the rate of growth will not change for a very long time, that implies that the rate must be relatively low.[7] That is what is expected to happen with Tract Co. Let's use an example of how to use this concept of **constant growth perpetuity**.

Suppose you were making an investment in a company that was expected to return $100 forever, and the required return for its level of risk was 10 percent. What would it be worth, what price would be fair for this investment? Using the perpetuity approach, your answer would be $1,000 ($100/0.10). Suppose someone told you that you could have an investment that, while otherwise identical to the first investment, would provide $100 the first year and would increase by 3 percent for every year thereafter. What would this investment be worth?

To value it, we will use an adaptation of the perpetuity shortcut that is called a **constant growth valuation**:

$$\frac{\text{Constant growth}}{\text{present value}} = \frac{\text{Annual cash flow}}{\text{Investors' required} - \text{Growth in residual}}$$
$$\text{rate of return} \quad \text{cash flows}$$

$$= \frac{\$100}{0.10 - 0.03}$$

$$= \$1,428.57$$

The question of when an analyst can use one of the perpetuity shortcuts is one that is widely debated. Analysts often use a shortcut to value cash flows long before the cash flows are either steady or growing at a steady, slow rate. This is generally because the analyst's fear of forecasting overcomes common sense: they just do not know what the cash flows are likely to be. Fear, however, is not a good reason to use a shortcut, especially when it can lead to significant errors in value. One general rule about when a shortcut can be used can be developed from the concept of sustainable growth rate described in Chapter 1: When the expected growth rate of the company into the future is equal or very close to its long-term sustainable rate of growth, the analyst can use a perpetuity shortcut.

One other factor that affects the value of a company is important: inflation. Inflation affects both the cash flows and the discount rate—sometimes not in the ways you might expect. In the appendix to Chapter 1, we discussed the impact of inflation on depreciation. When the tax code requires that assets be depreciated at their historical cost, depreciation does not keep up with inflation: depreciation is calculated based on a currency value that has changed. In Chapter 2 we showed an example of the problems that one encounters in making a forecast in a highly inflationary environment. Inflation also affects value.

....

[7]   At a high rate of growth into perpetuity, the company would eventually be unrealistically enormous. Thus, when high growth is expected for some time, the cash flows must be forecasted annually until the abnormal growth is exhausted.

Exhibit 5-7 shows cash flow forecasts for Tract with 10 percent inflation from 1997 to 2001. Compare the depreciation shown in Exhibit 5-7 with the depreciation when there was real growth of 10 percent (Exhibit 5-6). You can see that the depreciation is lower and the taxes higher under inflation. This is the depreciation penalty of inflation.

Inflation has another impact on the value of a company. It increases the investors' required rate of return. A higher discount rate reduces the value of any given set of cash flows, as you can see by looking at the net present values shown in Exhibits 5-6 and 5-7. The higher discount rate better reflects the rate that investors would require in a world with 10 percent inflation. The twin impacts of inflation on cash flows and on the investors' required rate of return point out a critical element in valuation: the forecasts for the discount rate and the cash flows must both rest on the same assumptions for the future.

II. EARNINGS-VALUATION METHOD

To avoid elaborate projections of cash flows, risks, and required rates of return, some analysts use the relationship of a firm's projected earnings to its present stock price to calculate a crude approximation of an acquisition's value or of a cash flow terminal value. To use this approach, the analyst first estimates the earnings of the firm to be acquired (or uses historical earnings as an estimate of future earnings) and estimates the relationship between those earnings and the stock price, known as the price/earnings ratio (P/E). From this ratio, the analyst estimates the price per share for the business to be acquired as follows:

$$\text{Price per share} = \text{EPS} \times \text{P/E}$$

where

    EPS = Earnings per share

    P/E = The firm's estimated price/earnings ratio after acquisition

Or the price for the whole company would be:

$$\text{Price} = \text{Earnings} \times \text{P/E}$$

where earnings are equal to annual net income.

Now suppose that Tract's earnings over the next 12 months are expected to be $510,840 and that 100,000 shares of stock are outstanding.[8] Earnings per share are forecasted to be $5.11. Tract is not publicly traded, however, and thus it has no market price or P/E ratio to use as a starting point. To overcome this lack of information, analysts often use the average P/E for a group of similar

---

[8] As shown in Exhibit 5-3.

EXHIBIT 5-7 Tract, Inc. Cash Flow With No Real Growth and 10% Inflation for Five Years and No Inflation or Growth Thereafter (in thousands)

	1997	1998	1999	2000	2001	2002
Sales	$ 11,330.0	$ 12,463.0	$ 13,709.3	$ 15,080.2	$ 16,588.3	$ 16,588.3
Operating expenses	(10,423.6)	(11,466.0)	(12,612.6)	(13,873.8)	(15,261.2)	(15,261.2)
Gross income	906.4	997.0	1,096.7	1,206.4	1,327.1	1,327.1
Depreciation						
Original	(50.0)	(50.0)	(50.0)	(50.0)	(50.0)	(50.0)
Growth-induced	—	—	—	—	—	—
Income before taxes	856.4	947.0	1,046.7	1,156.4	1,277.1	1,277.1
Taxes	(291.2)	(322.0)	(355.9)	(393.2)	(434.2)	(434.2)
Income after taxes	565.2	625.0	690.8	763.2	842.9	842.9
Depreciation						
Original	50.0	50.0	50.0	50.0	50.0	50.0
Growth-induced	—	—	—	—	—	—
Change in property, plant, and equipment						
Original	(50.0)	(50.0)	(50.0)	(50.0)	(50.0)	(50.0)
Growth-induced	—	—	—	—	—	—
Working capital change	(206.0)	(226.6)	(249.3)	(274.2)	(301.6)	—
Annual cash flow	359.2	398.4	441.5	489.0	541.3	842.9
Terminal value						6,107.7*
Residual cash flow	$ 359.2	$ 398.4	$ 441.5	$ 489.0	$ 541.3	$ 6,950.6

Net present value at 13.8% = $4,698.3
Net present value at 23.8% = $3,107.8

* Since there is no inflation from 2002 onwards, and Tract is not expected to grow, the perpetuity value is $842.9/(0.138 - 0.0).

but publicly traded firms as a proxy for this unobtainable P/E. To use this proxy method, the analyst must assume that firms in the same industry or with similar earnings records are equally risky and that the market will pay a standard multiple of earnings for stocks of equivalent risk. However, these assumptions are not always valid. The price/earnings multiples of comparable stocks in comparable industries can be very different. As an example, Exhibit 5-8 shows varying P/E ratios for an industry similar to Tract's, the publishing industry.

If the analyst estimates a price/earnings ratio for Tract equal to the 1996 industry average of 11.4, the estimated price per Tract share would be:

$$
\begin{aligned}
\text{Price per share} \;&=\; \text{EPS} \times \text{P/E} \\
&=\; \$5.11 \times 11.4 \\
&=\; \$58.25
\end{aligned}
$$

At a price per share of $58.25, the total price for the company would be $5.83 million ($58.25 × 100,000 shares). This price is higher than any of the net present values we calculated for Tract using the cash flow projection method. There can be a number of reasons why this is so. Tract is different than many of the companies listed in Exhibit 5-8. It is not publicly traded, sells different products and to different customers, and has had virtually no growth in the recent past. Perhaps the most important difference is the size: Tract is quite small while the publicly traded companies on the list are large. Thus, the universe of competitors listed in Exhibit 5-8 is not reflective of the character of Tract. Several have P/Es that are much higher than what Tract might command if it were publicly traded.[9]

EXHIBIT 5-8   Selected Publishing Companies' Average Annual P/E Ratios

	1995	1996
Banly	6	7
Brown Inc.	8	4
C.C.&H.	8	6
Delfin	6	7
Grants Industries	19	28
Hightower	24	21
John Howard	11	12
McDougal	8	6
Average	11.3	11.4

[9]   If the analyst knew more about why Grants Industries and Hightower P/Es were so high, or why Brown Inc. had a P/E of only 4 in 1996, they might be excluded as noncomparable. Others might be candidates for exclusion based on their lack of comparability on the basis of such things as company size or lines of business.

The price/earnings method requires a P/E estimate, which can be difficult to make. The method is easiest to use with a company that is not growing and is unlikely to create synergies with its merger partner. Such a target is rare. Most interesting acquisitions (and divestitures, for that matter) are growing and will provide opportunities for synergies. The fact that we found Tract's value using the cash flow and the earnings methods to be quite different is typical.

Several other factors can make us question the validity of the P/E ratio method for valuation. First, in using this approach we assume that recent earnings represent the real earning power of the firm. In the past, the reported earnings of U.S. corporations have become less and less representative of the companies' economic earnings. The effects of inflation, and the accounting treatment of those effects, combined with changes in accounting methods for such items as retiree health benefits, have made the reported earnings of U.S. corporations resemble only vaguely the firms' real earning power. As for the veracity of earnings of companies in other countries, they vary greatly.

Second, this method also assumes that the price/earnings ratio is a reliable indicator of value. While the current P/E of a publicly traded firm reflects its shareholders' present estimates of its future as an independent company, it is just the relationship between the market price of the company's stock and its earnings. It does not reflect the potential synergies that might result from a merger. To estimate the value of synergies using the earnings-valuation approach, the analyst must forecast the new earnings after the merger and forecast the P/E ratio if the merger were known to investors. The current P/E reflects prospects without a merger, and a P/E reflecting the potential for a merger is difficult to estimate. If the acquisition is expected to create value, the analyst is justified in using a higher estimate. The problem is that no simple method exists for making this estimate.

There are still other assumptions behind the earnings-valuation method: that the earnings stream will remain constant over time; that short-term earnings and market prices are good indicators of value. The NPV method, on the other hand, assumes that any acquisition with a positive marginal value will increase the value of the acquiring company and that the increased value will eventually be reflected in the market price of its stock. The logic behind the NPV method is clear and powerful.

While we would dismiss the P/E multiple method as the sole approach to valuing an acquisition, it can be put to good use by the analyst. It can be used to put the present value analysis into a capital market perspective. We can compare the P/E that is implied by a present value analysis to a P/E estimated using the earnings analysis. In Exhibit 5-3 we determined the 1997 earnings and cash flows, and in Exhibit 5-6 we determined the present value. Exhibit 5-9 summarizes the information.

The implied price/earnings ratio is equal to the present value per share divided by the earnings per share as computed on the following page.

EXHIBIT 5-9   Tract Co. Valuation Information

Cash flow per year	$510,840
Earnings per year	$510,840
Discount rate	13.8%
Net present value with 10 percent growth for five years (Exhibit 5-6)	$4.7 million
Number of shares	100,000

$$
\begin{aligned}
\text{Implied P/E} &= \frac{\text{PV/Share}}{\text{Earnings/Share}} \\
&= \frac{\$4{,}653{,}945/100{,}000}{\$510{,}840/100{,}000} \\
&= \frac{\$46.54}{\$5.11} \\
&= 9.1 \text{ times}
\end{aligned}
$$

The implied P/E is lower than the average ratio for three of the companies in the group in Exhibit 5-8. There are several possible reasons for the discrepancy: (1) our predicted cash flows and their underlying growth may be less than what the market is forecasting, (2) our predicted risk incorporated in the required rate of return may be higher than the market's prediction, (3) we might have made an error in our inflation forecasts, or (4) the P/E of Tract could be lower than that of the industry because of its size, markets, products, or prospects. The good analyst would return to the analysis to determine which cause is likely, and adjust the analysis or conclusions where needed. With Tract, the growth is lower than the industry over the long run due to its concentration in the religious publishing business. Thus, a lower P/E is justified.

III. OTHER VALUATION TECHNIQUES

Several other valuation techniques are used by acquisition analysts. These methods should be used only as supplements to the present value analysis, not as substitutes for it.

1. Book Value

This valuation technique is quite simple and lacks any but the most simplistic reasons for its use. Book value (net assets minus liabilities), calculated by using the balance sheet figures, is a poor estimate of economic value for several reasons. Book value:

1. Depends on the accounting practices of a firm. It is usually only a vague approximation of the real economic value of the firm.
2. Ignores intangible assets. Intangibles—copyrights, trademarks, patents, franchise licenses, and contracts—protect a company's right to market its goods and services and thus have value. If the book value of the assets is less than the present value of the cash flows of the firm, intangible assets can account for the discrepancy.
3. Ignores liabilities not reflected on the balance sheet. These liabilities may be such things as lawsuits pending against the company or employee retirement benefits that are not reported on the balance sheet.
4. Ignores the price appreciation of real assets. Since assets are valued on the balance sheet at their depreciated costs, some assets (for instance, land, precious metals, and mineral reserves) may be valued far below even their liquidation value.

Particularly with privately or closely held firms, owners may believe that book value is the least they should receive when selling the company. When this is true, book value often provides a floor below which a successful price offer is unlikely to go. It is not always a floor value. The book value may overstate the value of the company.[10]

2. Liquidation Value

Liquidation value is the cash value the acquirer would receive if the assets of the acquired firm were sold. This method of valuation is useful if the acquirer intends to sell the assets of the acquired firm. It may also be used to aid in determining the fair book value of under- or overvalued assets. Analysts sometimes use liquidation value as a floor price for an acquisition. If liquidation value exceeds the present value, the company is worth more if its assets are sold. Liquidation value can also be used as a terminal value in valuing a company when its products or services have a definite life. This valuation method might be useful, for instance, in valuing the patent protection on prescription drugs.

3. Replacement Cost

Replacement cost is a measure of the cost of replacing the assets of the potential acquisition. While some analysts use it to set a ceiling price on the acquisition, replacement cost estimates can be difficult to make.

---

[10] Overstating occurs when management has invested and still holds, at book value, assets that are obsolete, worthless, or worth less than what was paid for them.

4. Market Value

The market value of the firm's stock is often a good starting point in estimating an acquisition's price. If the stock is publicly traded, its market value is simply the market price per share times the number of shares. The reason market value is only a starting point should be clear from the present value analysis we performed for Tract and Lifelike. If the acquisition is expected to increase value for the shareholders of one or both firms, this increase in value is unlikely to be reflected in the public price of the common stock of either firm.[11] Thus, if there are synergies and value will be created, the current market prices underestimate the present value of the merging firms. Still, the market price of the stock is a benchmark from which the analyst can begin.

Under a certain set of circumstances, all these values should be the same. Liquidation value should reflect what a buyer is willing to pay for the earning power of the firm's assets. Thus, a liquidation value, if it can be obtained, should be close to the value estimated using present value analysis. Likewise, book value, if it truly reflects the economic value (the earning power of the assets), will be similar. Only because of estimation errors and accounting conventions, coupled with inflation's impact, are the values different.

IV. SUMMARY

There is only one purpose in making an acquisition. That purpose is to create value for the owners. Value can be created through increased returns or reduced risk. In general, an increase in value comes from increased capacity being matched with a need for that resource—a matching that cannot occur unless the two firms merge. The analyst's task is to estimate the effect of a merger on a firm's return and risk characteristics. Since projected earnings are, at best, only a vague indication of real earning power of the company, the analyst should project cash flows with and without the benefits of the merger, and discount them to determine the value. Other valuation techniques, such as earnings analysis, should be used merely to corroborate the present value analysis.

SELECTED REFERENCES

For methods of analyzing a merger, see:

Brealey, Richard A., and Stewart C. Myers. *Principles of Corporate Finance.* 5th ed. New York: McGraw-Hill, 1996, chap. 33.

Brealey, Richard A., and Stewart C. Myers. "A Framework for Evaluating Mergers." In *Modern Developments in Financial Management.* New York: Frederick A. Praeger, 1976.

---

[11]   Of course, the expectation of increased value may be reflected in the price once the merger becomes public knowledge.

Brigham, Eugene, and Louis Gapenski. *Financial Management.* Fort Worth, TX: Dryden, 1994, chap. 24.

Myers, Stewart C. "The Evaluation of an Acquisition Target." *Midland Corporate Finance Journal*, Winter 1983, pp. 39-46.

Pinches, George E. *Financial Management.* New York: Harper Collins, 1994, chap. 26.

Ross, Stephen A., Randolph W. Westerfield, and Jeffrey F. Jaffe. *Corporate Finance.* 4th ed. Homewood, Ill.: Richard D. Irwin, 1996, chap. 29.

Ross, Stephen A., Randolph W. Westerfield, and Bradford D. Jordon. *Fundamentals of Corporate Finance.* 3rd ed. Homewood, Ill.: Richard D. Irwin, 1995, chap. 20.

Salter, Malcolm S., and Wolf A. Weinhold. *Diversification Through Acquisition.* New York: Free Press, 1979, part II.

Shrives, Ronald E., and Mary M. Pashley. "Evidence on Association between Mergers and Capital Structure." *Financial Management*, Autumn 1984, pp. 39-48.

Weston, J. Fred, Kwang S. Chung, and Susan E. Hoag. *Mergers, Restructuring and Corporate Control.* Englewood Cliffs, N.J.: Prentice Hall, 1990.

For more on shareholder value creation, see:

Finegan, Patrick T. "Maximizing Shareholder Value at the Private Company." *The Journal of Applied Corporate Finance,* Spring 1991, pp. 30-45.

Rappaport, Alfred. *Creating Shareholder Value.* New York: Free Press, 1986.

Shapiro, Alan C. *Modern Corporate Finance.* 2nd ed. New York: Macmillan, 1994, chap. 11.

For more on takeovers and takeover waves, see:

Shapiro, Alan C. *Modern Corporate Finance.* 2nd ed. New York: Macmillan, 1994, chap. 30.

Shleifer, Andrei, and Robert W. Vishny. "The Takeover Wave of the 1980s." *Journal of Applied Corporate Finance,* Fall 1991, pp. 49-56.

For more on estimating divisional required returns, see:

Fuller, Russell, and H. Kerr. "Estimating the Divisional Cost of Capital: An Analysis of the Pure Play Technique." *Journal of Finance*, December 1981, pp. 997-1009.

Gup, Benton E., and Samuel W. Norwood, III. "Divisional Cost of Capital: A Practical Approach." *Financial Management*, Spring 1982, pp. 20-24.

Harrington, Diana R. "Stock Prices, Beta, and Strategic Planning." *Harvard Business Review*, May/June 1985, pp. 157-164.

Harris, Robert S., Thomas J. O'Brien, and Doug Wakeman. "Divisional Cost-of-Capital Estimation for Multi-Industry Firms." *Financial Management*, Summer 1989, pp. 74-84.

Shapiro, Alan C. *Modern Corporate Finance.* 2nd ed. New York: Macmillan, 1994, chap. 9.

For studies on the relative values of mergers, see:

Cusatis, Patrick, James Miles, and J. Randall Wooridge. "Some New Evidence That Spinoffs Create Value." *Journal of Applied Corporate Finance*, Summer 1994, pp. 100-107.

Mueller, D. C. "The Effects of Conglomerate Mergers: A Survey of the Empirical Evidence." *Journal of Banking and Finance*, December 1977, pp. 315-48.

Rappaport, Alfred. "What We Know and Don't Know About Mergers." *Midland Corporate Finance Journal*, Winter 1983, pp. 63-67.

Rumelt, Richard. *Strategy, Structure and Economic Performance.* Boston: Harvard Business School Press, 1986.

STUDY QUESTIONS

1. Magnus Corporation and Carr Company both operate in the same industry, and although neither is experiencing any rapid growth, both provide a steady stream of earnings. Magnus's management is encouraging the acquisition of Carr because of its excess plant capacity, which it hopes to use. Carr Company has 50,000 shares of common stock outstanding, which are selling at about $6.00 per share. Other data are shown in the following table.

	Magnus Corporation	Carr Company	Combined Entity
Profit after taxes	$48,000	$30,000	$92,000
Residual net cash flow/year	$60,000	$40,000	$120,000
Required return on equity	12.5%	11.25%	12.0%

CARR COMPANY
BALANCE SHEET

Assets		Liabilities and Owners' Equity	
Current assets	$273,000	Current liabilities	$134,500
Net PP&E	215,000	Long-term liabilities	111,000
Other	55,000	Owners' equity	297,500
		Total liabilities and	
Total assets	$543,000	owners' equity	$543,000

Compute the maximum price the management (for the shareholders) of the Magnus Corporation should be willing to pay to acquire the Carr Company, and the minimum price Carr's management should accept.

2. Smyth Instrument Company wishes to acquire Robinson Research Lab through a merger. Both companies are Canadian and operate exclusively in Ontario Province. Smyth Instrument expects to gain operating efficiencies from the merger through distribution economies, advertising, manufacturing, and purchasing.

   The required rates of return for Smyth and Robinson are 16.2 percent and 14.5 percent, respectively. Neither company has any long-term debt outstanding. The effective required rate of return after the merger is estimated to be 15.5 percent. The projected real growth rate for each of the firms is 4 percent per year, and management expects that growth rate to continue when the two companies are merged. All revenues and costs are expected to keep pace with inflation of 4 percent annually. The current net cash flow per year is Canadian $6.45 million for Smyth and Canadian $2.2 million for Robinson. Based on an analysis of the synergies for the combined company, the combined net cash flow would have been Canadian $10.92 million if the two had been combined for the past year.

   Calculate the price Smyth Instrument should offer to acquire Robinson Research and the price above which Robinson should accept the merger offer.

3. Action Corporation makes cardboard boxes for a wide range of clients. The industry is experiencing a severe slowdown in terms of sales. Several substitute products are threatening to win over Action's major clients. In spite of the fact that entry into the industry is relatively cheap, fixed assets account for a large percentage of the total expenses. Thus, volume is important, and there is pressure on margins.

   In late 1996, Action was approached by a large packaging company that wanted to add a cardboard box manufacturer to its portfolio of companies.

   Mr. Santiago, CFO at Action, was concerned about the price he should expect for this acquisition and wondered how best to maximize the return to Action's owners.

   Action was rated by Moody's as a moderate risk. Mr. Santiago believed that Action's owners would demand at least an 11.2 percent return on their investment. Sales in 1996 were $250 million and were expected to grow at 5 percent annually until 2003, and 3 percent thereafter; cost of sales is 75 percent of sales; and selling, general, and administrative expenses are 10 percent of sales. Taxes are 34 percent. Depreciation is fixed at $7 million per year, and PP&E and working capital investments total $7 million per year. The company has no debt. In the past, Action paid dividends of 10 percent of net income, and the return on the investment was about 3.4 percent. At what price should Mr. Santiago sell to provide the owners a fair return?

The Required Rate of Return on Equity

In Chapter 4, we followed the financial analyst through the evaluation of investment opportunities for Betty's Better Big Boys. We used two projects as examples for our investigation of incremental cash flow analysis and to demonstrate several methods for evaluating the value of those investments to a company's owners. We showed that the net present value (NPV) technique is both intuitively acceptable and unambiguous.[1] While there can be confusion about whether an investment is appropriate when other ways of valuing and ranking investments are used, there is no doubt about whether value will be created by the investment when net present value is used as the criterion. Investments with a positive net present value are expected to create value. Those with a zero net present value are expected neither to create nor destroy value. Those with a negative NPV should be rejected, and available funds should be used for value-creating investments or returned to the shareholders, the owners. The shareholders could do better by investing those funds in other securities in the capital markets than by allowing Betty's Better Big Boys to make unacceptable investments. Exhibit 6-1 shows the NPV criteria graphically. Remember that any net present value depends on the quality of the cash flow forecasts.

In Chapter 5, we delved deeply into valuation. We found that the methods we used in Chapter 4 to value capital investments applied to valuing whole companies and divisions, and the same rules could be used to determine whether a merger or acquisition could be expected to create value. To evaluate investments using the NPV method, we needed two estimates: (1) the expected cash flows from the investment and (2) a rate at which to discount those cash flows. In Chapter 4, we first used a discount rate designed to compensate investors only for the timing of cash flows. We later augmented this rate to compensate investors for risk. In Chapter 5 we used the equity investors' required rate of return from their investment in the company to value a com-

---

[1]   If you have read the appendix to Chapter 4, you know we are talking about deterministic investments. However, whether you are using net present value or option valuation methods, a required rate of return is needed for discounting.

EXHIBIT 6-1 Value-Creation Criteria

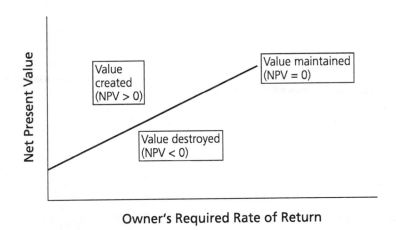

Owner's Required Rate of Return

pany or division, but we did not discuss how we might estimate that rate. In this chapter, we discuss how to estimate this required return on equity.

There are two things that contribute to the magnitude of an investor's required return: the premiums for liquidity and risk. Since investors are inconvenienced by no longer having funds available to spend at will, they require a rate of return that compensates them for not being able to use their money whenever they choose. This **illiquidity premium**, or the **time value of money**, is what an investor would expect to make on a riskless investment while his or her money is unavailable. If the investor expects inflation to erode the value of money, we can be certain that the illiquidity premium will include a return to compensate for the expected inflation. We saw this increase in the required return when inflation struck Tract Co. in Chapter 5. When the investors' required return includes a premium for inflation, we call it a **nominal return**. A return that does not include compensation for inflation is called a **real return**.

There is a second part of an investor's required return: a premium that compensates for risk—that is, the possibility that the invested funds will never be regained. The riskier the investment, the higher its expected return must be. That is why common stocks have higher expected returns than debt or preferred stock, both of which have claims on the firm's earnings and assets that supersede the claims of common shareholders.

The return required by an investor is compensation for both illiquidity and risk. This fair return for risk, or **market price of risk**, is so difficult to determine that, in order to estimate it for a company, we turn for help to the experts— those who determine the fair return for different levels of risk all the time—

those who are buying and selling securities in the capital markets. The most direct information the capital markets give us about the market price of risk for any company is the return required by those investing in the company, in particular, its equities.[2] To understand required return better, and to see how investors determine the return they require on their investments, a brief discussion of the capital markets will be helpful. It is in these markets that the users of funds (corporations) and the providers of funds (investors) meet.

In this chapter, we discuss the return required by the company's owners, its shareholders.[3] In Chapter 7 we discuss how and why investors in a company might subcontract some of their financing obligations to others such as lenders, the lenders' required return, and whether value is created through different financing arrangements.[4]

I. CAPITAL MARKETS

The markets for long-term funds for corporations are called **capital markets**. Capital markets differ from the money markets discussed in Chapter 3: money market funds are short-term investments with maturities of under one year; capital market funds are long-term investments, exceeding one year. In addition to providing debt funds with a stated **maturity**, the date when they come due and must be fully repaid, capital markets provide equity funds that have no stated maturity.

Equity capital markets exist on two levels, the **primary markets** and the **secondary markets**. Primary market transactions occur when companies issue equity to investors. Typically, these securities are sold through investment bankers, who, through their relationships with brokers, act as agents for the companies selling the instruments. The proceeds from the sales of financial instruments, minus the investment bankers' commissions, are paid to the issuing companies.[5] The primary markets are the major source of new equity capital for companies. New equity issues by companies that have never raised equity in the public markets are called **initial public offerings**, or **IPOs**.

After the securities have been sold initially, the purchaser of the securities may then trade them in the secondary markets. Financial instruments may be sold individually or bundled together and then traded between individuals or institutions who may have no relationship with the original issuing company.

---

[2]   Required returns can be used as discount or hurdle rates so long as the investments being considered are as risky as the firm. If the investment is more or less risky than the company at the moment, the required return for that particular level of risk must be independently determined.

[3]   The company's cost of equity is the return required by shareholders for the risk that the company is taking with their equity.

[4]   Also called the company's cost of borrowing.

[5]   The sale can be "best efforts," where the sales proceeds are delivered to the company, or on a contractual basis, where the proceeds are guaranteed. Obviously the cost of the transaction would depend upon the risk being taken by the intermediary.

While the company does not gain direct benefit from this trading, it is not indifferent to activities in the secondary markets. Prices of its securities may change as a result of changing prospects for the company, its industry, and the economy. The prices for secondary market trading of securities are reported in such U.S. publications as *The Wall Street Journal* and *Barron's*, in U.K. publications such as *The Financial Times*, and in the major financial or daily newspapers in other countries.

In recent years, derivative instruments, such as options and futures contracts, have been widely traded in mature markets and in some emerging markets.[6] These instruments, which are designed to provide a means of protecting investors against price movements in the capital markets, are all secondary market instruments. They are not a source of capital for corporations.[7] Company treasurers and investment bankers have gained a real appreciation of the attractiveness of the features of some of these new instruments, however, and have included some of their characteristics into new forms of corporate securities. For those working in corporate treasury offices or in investment banks, or considering investing in synthetic or exotic securities, careful review of the features of each security is critical.[8]

Trading in capital market instruments can take place in organized market exchanges or over the counter (OTC). Organized exchanges such as the New York Stock Exchange (NYSE) and the American Stock Exchange (AMEX) in the United States, as well as stock exchanges around the world, allow trading only in listed securities. To achieve listed status, companies must meet specific qualifications of the exchange, including such things as the size of the company, the total market value of the publicly traded shares, and the amount of trading in the company's securities. Trading on these exchanges can only be done by members of the exchange. Members are typically brokerage companies who buy and sell securities for their customers. Increasingly, large blocks of securities can be and are traded between buyer and seller using an electronic trading system.[9] Comparable, but not identical, arrangements exist in other countries.

Unlike the exchanges, which have a specific location where trading takes place, the **over-the-counter market** consists of numerous traders located

---

[6] Derivative instruments are those based on another instrument. For instance, a call option on a common stock gives the owner of the option the right to buy shares at a particular price within a given time period. Put options are the right to sell. These two option types are the basic forms of derivatives. More exotic securities can be fashioned from bundles of these.

[7] For corporations, options and futures are used for hedging risk and, sometimes, speculating.

[8] Synthetic securities are those that mimic the characteristics of some other instrument or security. Exotic securities, which have a variety of features, are generally the special creation of a particular investment bank for one issuer or a group of issuers, and they are generally in vogue for a short period of time.

[9] Some exchanges themselves are electronic (for instance, the Singapore exchange), and in some areas (for instance, Europe) the electronic trading systems compete for trades with organized exchanges. These electronic trading networks are becoming increasingly important.

throughout a country. These traders do what is called making a market. That means that they buy, sell, and keep an inventory in one or several securities. Brokerage firms are market makers. In the United States, a computerized network called NASDAQ, sponsored by the National Association of Securities Dealers, ties these various market makers together. Many more securities are traded OTC than on the exchanges. Because listed companies tend to be larger, however, the average trading volume for the securities listed on the exchanges is much greater than for the OTC trades.

While most countries have equity markets, the level of individual equity ownership varies substantially. For instance, in the United Kingdom most securities are owned by institutions. In Germany, banks own many of the securities of companies. In Japan, cross-ownership, where shares of two or more companies are owned by each other, is common. Institutional investors such as mutual funds, insurance companies, and pension funds are the largest investors in the equity markets worldwide.

Most countries have a small or nonexistent public bond market. There are several reasons for this. First, in many countries the issuing and selling of new bonds is either directly controlled by the government or by banks. In other countries companies may issue bonds or stock into the public debt or equity market. While many restrictions exist, the increasing integration of the world's capital markets has led to significant increases in the volume of nondomestic securities issued in some countries, and in the number of issues that are placed simultaneously in more than one market.

In spite of the fact that equity is the fundamental core of capital for a company, equity investors often subcontract some of their financing obligations to others.[10] Most often, the subcontracting is done with lenders, and the additional capital is in the form of debt. Some instruments, however, combine characteristics of debt and equity through convertible provisions. Convertible instruments typically allow an investor to convert a debt or preferred stock instrument into common stock at a specified conversion price and, usually, for a particular period of time.

There are two types of equity, **common stock** and **preferred stock**. Preferred stockholders do have a preferential position over common stockholders, hence the name preferred stock. While the company does or will pay dividends to common shareholders, it has no contractual obligation to do so.[11] Dividends may be paid to equity investors, but only after all obligations have been paid to bondholders. The dividend that is to be paid on preferred stock

---

[10] In publicly held companies, management, along with its advisors, makes the decision. However, shareholders' opinion about the level of debt is reflected in the pricing of the equity. It is their way of "having their say."

[11] In some cases, rather than paying dividends, the company repurchases some of its outstanding shares. This is done for one of two reasons: (1) to reduce the amount of equity outstanding or (2) to provide a tax-advantaged way for investors to receive some income by selling some of their shares.

is a stated amount. Preferred stock usually provides that the preferred dividend must be paid before any dividend can be paid to the common shareholders. If the company has insufficient funds to pay the dividend, however, the dividend may be omitted without causing a default. Usually, any previously omitted preferred dividends must be paid before dividends can be paid to common shareholders. Preferred stock with this provision is termed **cumulative preferred**. Because the dividend is stated, like an interest payment, preferred stock is similar to debt. On the other hand, because the company has no obligation to pay the dividends, the preferred shareholder's return is uncertain; thus, it is also similar to equity.

After the required preferred dividend has been paid, the common shareholders may receive any dividend that management deems appropriate and the board of directors approves. Many investors buy common stock in the expectation that the company will grow and prosper and, therefore, the stock price will increase. These increases in price come when investors revise their expectations for the company: investors increase or decrease their estimates of the company's dividend payments in the future. A change in the market price of the stock is termed **capital appreciation** if the change is positive. In addition to owning the residual or remaining income of the company, common shareholders, unlike owners of preferred shares, elect the board of directors.

Determinants of changes in stock prices are not easy to isolate. Factors that affect the general economy, such as changes in interest rates and the rate of economic growth, affect stock prices. In addition, the market price may be affected by a revised industry outlook as well as by changes in prospects for the specific company.

Dividends are the only source of income from equity investments.[12] Of course, if expectations change regarding future dividends, and the stock price changes, the equity holder can sell some stock and capture these revised dividend forecasts. The relative importance of the dividend or capital gain depends on how long the investor has held the shares. However, since future return is uncertain at the time the equity is purchased, investors must determine the return they require and decide if the current market price is fair, that is, if the cash flows that are expected to be generated from their investment will provide the return they want.

II. DETERMINING THE SHAREHOLDERS' REQUIRED RETURN

Investors expect to earn a return on the funds they provide—a return that compensates them for both the time that the funds are made available to the com-

---

[12] Companies may liquidate some or all of themselves by paying an unusual dividend, selling to another buyer, or returning the equity investors' capital.

pany and the risk that the firm will not provide the expected return. Returns on common stock come from the dividends the common shareholders receive over the term of their investment in the stock and from any gains realized by the investors on the sale of the stock that result from increases in its market price.

How do analysts estimate the returns shareholders require? If the firm were owned by a single shareholder or a small group of shareholders, the analyst could simply ask them, "What return do you expect this firm to earn on your behalf?" If the shareholder replied, "Fifteen percent would satisfy me; with that return, I would not want to buy a larger share of the firm, nor would I want to sell the ownership position I already have," the analyst would know that the shareholder's required return was 15 percent. However, companies whose stock is bought and sold on the stock exchanges do not have such limited ownership. As a result, we must find a way to estimate the return required by a large number of dispersed shareholders.

There are two categories of methods used to estimate the required return. The first category places a value on the cash the company generates for its shareholders. The second group of approaches could be called **capital market estimates**. Capital market methods categorize all securities into risk classes and then use the classifications to estimate the owners' required return. Note that we have been calling the return the owners' required return. From the company's perspective, it is its cost of equity.

1. Cash Flow Valuation: The Dividend-Discount Method

To determine the fair value of a share of common stock, its price (MP_0), we must first forecast the cash flows the investor will receive from the share of stock now and in the future. We made such cash flow forecasts in Chapter 5 when we valued the acquisition of Tract Co. To value Tract, we forecasted the residual cash flows (RCF) the company would generate in the future, discounted them at the investors' required return (R_e), and estimated a fair value for Tract. The formula we used was

$$\text{Net present value} = \frac{RCF_1}{(1 + R_e)^1} + \frac{RCF_2}{(1 + R_e)^2} + \frac{RCF_3}{(1 + R_e)^3} \cdots + \frac{RCF_n}{(1 + R_e)^n}$$

We also used a shortcut, a perpetuity version of the formula, when a company's residual cash flow was growing at a low, constant growth rate (g) for a long period:

$$\text{Net present value} = \frac{RCF}{R_e - g}$$

When we used these formulas in earlier chapters, we solved for the net present value. Let's think about using these formulas in a slightly different way. Let's solve for the shareholders' required return (R_e). Knowing a little algebra, you know that we can have only one unknown in any formula. Thus, if we are going to solve for R_e, we must "know" the net present value. Making one assumption, we can substitute the price of the company's stock for the net present value. The assumption that we must make is that capital markets are efficient.

In an **efficient market**, all available information known to market partici-pants is reflected in the current market price of a company's stock. While a market price may change, and frequently does so, often quite dramatically, in an efficient market the price changes only when the market participants gain new information or change their attitude about the company. Completely effi-cient markets are markets in which no one can forecast changes in stock prices, at least not at a cost that allows them to make money repeatedly.

Research has shown that the capital markets are relatively efficient, espe-cially the major markets, even though some studies conclude that the market may have some inefficiencies that an astute investor can exploit.[13] By assum-ing that equity markets are relatively efficient, we can use a company's current stock price as the net present value investors have placed on the company's future cash flows. By doing this, we have two of the formula's unknowns, and that is all we need to solve for the required rate of return.

Let's use an example to see how to estimate the required return on equity using one of these formulas. For our example, we will use National Presto Industries, Inc., a company that manufactures pressure cookers and small elec-trical appliances. The company's stock is traded on the NYSE in the United States. Since our first step is to forecast the future cash flows, we need to look at the prospects for sales of National Presto's products. As in previous analy-ses, we first analyze the past performance of the company to gain insight into the company and its performance. Exhibit 6-2 shows National Presto's histor-ical financial performance.

As you can see from the financial statements, National Presto has had a decline in performance in the last few years. This decline in performance is vividly reflected in the stock price, shown in Exhibit 6-3. The changes came as a result of a number of different factors. First, National Presto produces a group of very traditional products, and small, special purpose, kitchen appliances. In 1991, it introduced a curly french fry maker, a product that became a big seller during the holiday season. Since that time, the company has had some prob-lems. First, it has not had another innovative and popular new product intro-duction like the curly french fry maker since 1991. Second, management over-estimated inventory needs in 1992, and lost revenues from the closing of a

---

[13] The question of whether stock price changes can be forecasted is controversial. Most researchers conclude, however, that the markets are relatively efficient.

EXHIBIT 6-2   National Presto's Historic Performance

	1990	1991	1992	1993	1994	1995
Revenues (millions)	$127	$162	$128	$119	$128	$120
Net income (millions)	29	37	26	19	22	19
Dividends/Share	4.15	2.70	3.80	2.55	1.90	2.15
Annual cash flow	$30.30	$38.00	$27.10	$19.80	$22.60	$21.50
Ratios						
Operating income	23.2%	27.1%	23.9%	18.4%	19.8%	13.8%
Net income/Sales	22.8%	22.8%	20.3%	16.0%	17.2%	15.8%
Sales/Assets	52.5%	60.9%	49.2%	42.0%	44.0%	42.1%
Long-term debt/Assets	2.1%	1.9%	2.0%	1.8%	1.8%	0.0%
Assets/Equity	120.4%	122.0%	83.5%	83.0%	119.8%	115.4%
Dividend/Net income	105.3%	54.2%	107.6%	100.0%	65.1%	82.4%
Return on equity	14.4%	16.9%	8.3%	5.5%	9.1%	7.7%
Sustainable growth rate	-0.8%	7.7%	-0.9%	0.0%	3.1%	1.4%
Inventory days	97.8	78.4	105.0	110.9	100.2	105.5
Payables days	99.6	98.0	120.7	109.3	90.0	72.3
Receivables days	84.5	72.5	86.6	77.7	90.7	112.4

EXHIBIT 6-3 National Presto Industries Stock Price 1985-1996

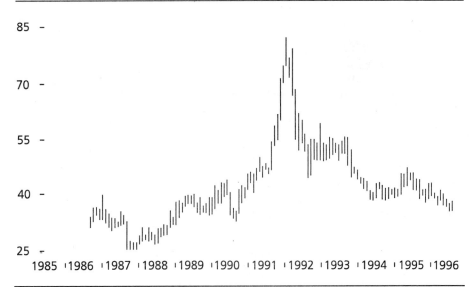

SOURCE: Bridge Information Systems.

munitions manufacturing plant. Third, it had problems with one of its major channels of distribution, Kmart: first it lost Kmart as a customer, then regained it just as Kmart developed its own problems. Finally, National Presto had to learn to deal with just-in-time inventory systems put in place by its major customers, including Wal-Mart. As a consequence of all these things, the company's receivables have lengthened; income has declined; returns on sales, assets, and equity have been reduced; and a decline in growth rates for three of the last five years has occurred.

Once history has been reviewed, the question that the analyst must next address is: What is the likely growth in the future? Relying on what we discussed in Chapter 1, we might turn to the sustainable rate of growth for some information about potential growth. From the basic ratios for National Presto in Exhibit 6-2, we see that its recent sustainable growth rate is about 2 percent. If you look at earlier history, and consider the 1990s data aberrant, the sustainable growth rate was about 6 percent. Most analysts in mid-1996 are forecasting a recovery in the retail sector that should return National Presto to a steady but low rate of growth, a likely average growth rate at or above inflation. This rate might be expected to be about 2.5 percent for the long-term. The growth rates forecasted by one readily available analysis service are shown in Exhibit 6-4.

In mid-May of 1996, National Presto's stock price was $41.87, thus there was a total equity value of $306 million with 7.3 million shares traded. The

EXHIBIT 6-4   National Presto Industries' Historic and Forecasted Growth Rates

	Historic		
Growth Rates in	10 Years	5 Years	Forecast
Revenues	2.0%	2.0%	11.0%
Cash Flow	3.0	Neg.	14.0
Earnings	4.0	Neg.	13.5
Dividends	5.0	3.0	5.0

Source for data: *Value Line.*

cash flow an analyst might expect in the future was $4.00 per share.[14] Using these numbers, and substituting the market price for the net present value, we find that the required return on equity for National Presto would be:

$$\text{Net present value} \quad = \quad \frac{RCF}{R_e - g}$$

$$\text{Market price} \quad = \quad \frac{RCF}{R_e - g}$$

$$\$41.87 \quad = \quad \frac{\$4.00}{(R_e - 0.025)}$$

$$R_e \quad = \quad 0.121 \text{ or } 12.1\%$$

The shareholders' required return and National Presto's cost of equity is 12.1 percent.

In our example, we discounted the company's residual cash flow, the cash flow that belongs to the shareholders. Some of this cash flow will be received by the investors in the form of dividends. The remainder, however, will be reinvested in the company to benefit the shareholders at a later date. Because the shareholders receive only dividends, not residual cash flow, many analysts use a version of the cash flow discount model that discounts dividends only. The model is called the **dividend-discount model**. The first step in using this model is to forecast the dividends the company will pay. These dividends then are compared with the current market price in order to determine the return that the shareholders require. The process is similar to the one we used in dis-

---

[14]   This is a forecast made by *Value Line* analysts. Because we use such a forecast as a part of our example does not suggest that this is the only or best forecast source. Consensus forecasts, the average of forecasts made by stock analysts, have earnings growing at almost 15 percent in 1996 and 12.7 percent in 1997. In spite of these forecasts for recovery, it is unlikely that the long-term growth rate will average such a high number.

counting cash flows, except the cash flows in this case are the dividends alone. The company's earnings per share and the dividends shareholders received in the past 16 years are shown in Exhibit 6-5.

In forecasting the future dividends, there are several things to note about National Presto. First, the dividend rate over a year has not been level, as it is in many companies. National Presto's board has generally declared an extra dividend in December, depending upon the year's results. The special dividend is reflected in the rapid growth in dividends in the early 1990s that reflected the earnings gains. However, the dividend appears to have returned to its more normal range, and an analyst might expect the future growth in dividends to be equal to the long-term earnings growth rate of 5 percent.[15] Our forecasts in Exhibit 6-4 show that one group of analysts are forecasting a dividend growth rate of 5 percent.

Estimates by analysts place National Presto's dividend for 1996 at $2.72 per share (a total of $19.9 million).[16] Using a growth rate of 5 percent, and the constant growth dividend-discount model, the investors' required return is found to be 11.5 percent, as shown on the following page.

EXHIBIT 6-5   National Presto Industries Historic Earnings and Dividends Per Share

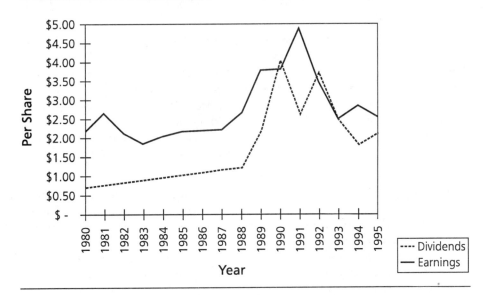

[15]   There are a variety of forecasts that could be made, as there inevitably are. However, the forecast of 5 percent growth in dividends is consistent with the forecast we are making for the company's growth. This growth is higher than cash flow growth.

[16]   We use the dividend anticipated in the next year, not last year's dividend, to estimate the value of the dividend in perpetuity.

$$\text{Market price} \quad = \quad \frac{\text{Dividend}}{R_e - g}$$

$$\$41.87 \quad = \quad \frac{\$2.72}{R_e - .05}$$

$$R_e \quad = \quad 0.115 \text{ or } 11.5\%$$

This required rate of return is close to the required return we calculated using the residual cash flow valuation model. These estimates should be quite close *if* the forecasts for cash flows and dividends are consistent and reflect a reasonable scenario for growth and dividend payment for National Presto. If the rates had been quite different, we would know that our forecasts were inconsistent and required further analysis and thought.

The dividend-discount model is in widespread use. Thus, its limitations must be recognized by an analyst. The constant growth dividend-discount model cannot be used when:

1. The firm pays no dividends. When this situation exists, the company's revenues, earnings, cash flows, and eventual dividend policy must be forecasted to estimate the required return on equity.
2. The expected rate of growth is higher than the discount rate, or the rate of growth is not constant. These situations signal that the company is entering an abnormal growth phase; thus, explicit, annual forecasts must be made for it.

One thing is clear: it would be impossible for the dividend growth rate to exceed the cash flow discount rate over a very long time. Eventually the dividends would greatly exceed the cash flows. For some companies the disparity between the cash flow and dividend growth rates is so wide, the perpetuity versions of the valuation models cannot be used. We must use different models. To deal with abnormal growth, we would make year-by-year forecasts and compare them to the current market price. Using the information about National Presto's prospects for future sales, earnings, and cash flows, we could devise the following scenario:

1. For years 1-5, growth will come from cost cutting and higher-than-usual sales arising from the recessionary conditions in the United States: National Presto's sales of its kitchen appliances seem to increase during periods of recession.
2. For years 6-10, growth will be lower than in years 1-5, but still higher than a company could sustain for a long period of time. In addition, dividend growth will increase as the company's growth in sales declines and its need for funds decreases.
3. For years 11-15, sales, earnings, and cash flow growth will slow further and dividends will grow (reflecting a continuing decline in the company's need for additional capital for growth). By the end of the 15 years, the dividends, earnings, and cash flow will be virtually identical.

The growth rates and resulting forecasts are shown in Exhibits 6-6 and 6-7.[17] This kind of forecasting is frequently done by Wall Street stock analysts.

Because, in this scenario, National Presto will grow at a low constant rate from 2010 onward, we can use the perpetuity method to estimate the value of the company from 2010 onward. Our value in the 15th year is the present value of the cash flows from year 15 onward.[18] The value, like all values in the cash flow forecast, then must be discounted to the present. The model is similar to that used in Chapter 4.

$$\text{Market price} = \frac{RCF_1}{(1 + R_e)^1} + \frac{RCF_2}{(1 + R_e)^2} + \frac{RCF_3}{(1 + R_e)^3} + \frac{RCF_n/(R_e - g)}{(1 + R_e)^n}$$

Using this formula and the cash flows we forecasted for National Presto, we estimate that the shareholders have a 15.8 percent required return on equity.[19] If we were to add a forecast for the company's dividend policy, we could use the dividend-discount model to develop yet another estimate of the investors' required return on equity.[20]

In addition to the cash flow and dividend-discount models, analysts use numerous abbreviated approaches to estimate shareholders' required return— that is, the company's cost of equity. Many of the approaches rely on earnings, or the relationship between earnings and the market price. The most wide-spread method is called the **implicit required return on equity** or **cost of equity**. For National Presto, the implicit required return on equity is calculated on page 215.

EXHIBIT 6-6   National Presto Industries, Inc., Forecasted Growth Rates in Sales, Earnings, Cash Flows, and Dividends

Period (years)	Sales	Earnings	Cash Flow	Dividends
1-5	9.50%	9.50%	9.50%	12.00%
6-10	5.00	5.00	6.50	18.00
11-15	3.50	3.50	3.50	11.00
16 onward	2.50	2.50	2.50	2.50

....

[17] As with any set of forecasts, different analysts will make different forecasts. These forecasts are consistent with the history of National Presto and its current market position.

[18] We discussed terminal value in Chapter 5. When dealing with common stock, analysts use a variety of other approaches to estimate the terminal value. One of the most common is to forecast the market price at some time in the future, often by multiplying an estimated price/earnings ratio by the forecasted earnings and discounting it—at best, however, a very difficult task.

[19] To estimate the owners required return, we used the same method we used in Chapter 4 when we were estimating the internal rate of return.

[20] The formula is the same as the cash flow discount model, but uses forecasted dividends in place of cash flows.

EXHIBIT 6-7 National Presto Industries, Inc., Forecasted Financial Performance (dollars in millions)

	1996	1997	1998	1999	2000	2001	2002	2003	2004	2005	2006	2007	2008	2009	2010
Sales	$138	$151	$165	$181	$198	$208	$219	$230	$241	$253	$262	$271	$280	$290	$300
Earnings	22	24	26	29	32	33	34	36	38	40	41	43	44	45	48
Cash flow	22	24	26	29	32	34	36	39	41	44	45	46	48	50	51

$$R_e = 1/(\text{Market price/Earnings per share})$$

or

$$= \text{Earnings per share/Market price}$$

$$= \frac{\$19{,}000{,}000/7{,}279{,}693}{\$41.87}$$

$$= \frac{\$2.61}{\$41.87}$$

$$= 0.062 \text{ or } 6.2\%$$

The implicit cost of equity is well below the shareholders' required return estimated using the other methods we have used thus far. The discrepancy arises because the implicit required return on equity does not have any provision for growth in the future. This approach is similar to the other models only when the company does not grow, that is, it (1) either pays out all earnings to its shareholders or (2) does not create value for its shareholders with any funds that it retains. In other words, the equation assumes that the net present value of a company's investments is zero.

Only for the most mature companies in stable and highly competitive industries would the implicit required return on equity be anything more than a rough approximation. For companies in declining industries, investors may believe that today's earnings and dividends are higher than they will be in the future. For new companies in growing markets, present earnings and dividends are often less than investors expect to gain in the future. When a portion of the company's earnings will be reinvested in the firm, and these investments will create (or destroy) value for the owners, a simple approach to determining the required return on equity that fails to account for growth is useless.

2. Capital Market Estimations: Risk Premium Methods

The cash flow and dividend-discount models use cash flow and dividend forecasts and the current stock price to calculate the shareholders' required return on equity. These forecasts can be difficult to make. An analyst can, however, use a different approach, one that estimates the required return according to the risk of the security in comparison to other investments in the market.

The market is the great arbitrageur of risk and return. Investors, both large and small, and security traders monitor the market constantly looking for profit-making opportunities. In doing so, these market participants constantly compare the returns they are getting with the risk they are taking. We can use this same process of arraying securities by their relative levels of risk, on the understanding that riskier securities must promise higher levels of return to be attractive. This approach, called **capital market estimation**, assumes that investors require additional return to compensate them for added risk. This additional return is known as the **risk premium**. The concept can be expressed mathematically thus:

$$R_e \; = \; R_f + R_p$$

where

 R_e = The total return investors require
 R_f = The return received on a hypothetical risk-free security
 R_p = The risk premium

There are several different ways to use this simple concept to estimate the cost of equity. We will discuss two methods: the stock-bond yield spread method and the capital asset pricing model.

The Stock-Bond Yield Spread. This simple model estimates the cost of equity by means of two key variables: (1) the firm's marginal pretax cost of debt and (2) the historical difference between the firm's costs of debt and equity. Expressed mathematically,

$$R_e \; = \; \overset{o}{R_d} + \overset{o}{(R_e} - R_d)$$

where

 R_e = The required return on equity
 R_d = The required return (pretax) on debt, for instance, the yield to maturity on the firm's bonds
 o = Indicates historical data

Let us use this formula to calculate National Presto's shareholders' required return on equity. If National Presto's historical equity/debt cost difference (the spread) has been 6.0 percent and the company's marginal required return on debt is 7.0 percent,[21] we can calculate National Presto's shareholders' required return on equity in this way:

$$
\begin{aligned}
R_e \; &= \; \overset{o}{R_d} + \overset{o}{(R_e} - R_d) \\
&= \; 7.0\% + 6.0\% \\
&= \; 13.0\%
\end{aligned}
$$

This percentage is almost 1 percent above the cost of equity we calculated with the cash flow discount model. These two methods usually do not yield exactly

----

[21] National Presto has no debt.

the same results. If they do not, the difference in results may be because the difference between the yields of stocks and bonds is not always constant. Panel A of Exhibit 6-8 shows annual returns on the Standard & Poor's (S&P's) 500 Index and a high-grade corporate bond index. Panel B of this exhibit shows that the differences between stock and bond returns are not as constant as the stock-bond yield spread method implies. This approach provides a quick estimate, but it should not be used, therefore, unless its results are to be verified by another method.

EXHIBIT 6-8   Realized Returns on Common Stock and Corporate Bonds (1926-1995)

Panel A: Returns on Bonds and Stocks

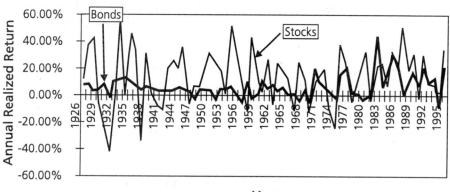

Panel B: Equity Risk Premium*

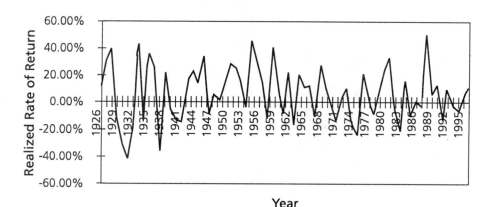

* Realized stock returns minus bond returns.

The Capital Asset Pricing Model. The simple risk premium model we just described could be rewritten to include a term denoting the difference between the average risk of all securities in the market and the risk of one firm's security. We would write the new equation thus:

$$R_{ej} \;=\; R_f + X_j(R_m - R_f)$$

where

j	=	Term to denote a particular company's stock
X	=	Measure of the risk for a stock
R_m	=	The return required on an asset of average risk
R_f	=	The return required on a hypothetical risk-free security

This formula could also be called the **relative risk premium model**, because it contains a factor, X, to indicate the relative risk of the particular security. Notice that in this formula, only X_j changes; all other factors remain constant from company to company.

The capital asset pricing model (CAPM) is a very intriguing adaptation of this basic relative risk premium approach. The model describes a particular relationship between risk and return. In fact, the relationship is one where the higher the risk, the higher the expected return. Exhibit 6-9 depicts this relationship. Since investors require a return for illiquidity, the line starts at R_f, the return required from a riskless security. The solid line represents the return required at each level of risk. This risk/return concept seems quite realistic: investors do expect greater rewards for taking greater risks, and the expected

EXHIBIT 6-9   Risk/Return Trade-Off

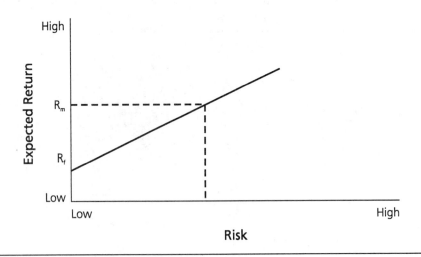

return for the common stock of any company is relative to its risk. However, in order to use this method, we must define and measure risk.

The CAPM is an attempt to make the relative risk premium model usable. In the CAPM, risk is defined as the covariance of a stock's returns with those of an asset of average risk. This definition is a bit different from the usual definition of risk as total variability. Covariance rests on a simple idea: it is not the total variability of the returns of each security that is important to the investor. Instead, what is important is how each security's variability contributes to the total variability of the investor's total portfolio. We could, for instance, place a security with cyclical returns (such as an automobile company's common stock) with a security whose returns are countercyclical (such as an automobile replacement parts manufacturer's common stock). Both of these stocks have risky returns. As shown in Exhibit 6-10, when the auto manufacturer is doing well, the replacement parts manufacturer is experiencing a slump. The reverse is also true: replacement parts sell when people defer new car purchases. As you can see, returns from the portfolio containing both stocks would be quite stable: that is, they would not be very risky according to the CAPM's definition of risk even though the returns from each are quite risky. Note our optimism about these stocks since we show the returns for both the companies growing, not diminishing, over time.

The only difference between the relative risk premium formula and the CAPM is that the CAPM defines risk as the covariability of stock returns with those of the asset market.[22] The CAPM is illustrated on the following page.

EXHIBIT 6-10 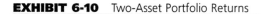 Two-Asset Portfolio Returns

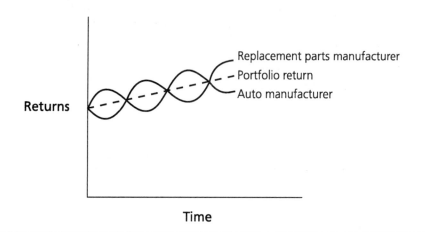

---
[22] Covariance or covariability is the correlation of the two assets multiplied by the variance of each asset.

$$R_{ej} = R_f + \beta_j (R_m - R_f)$$

where:

β_j = beta, a measure of the covariance between the total returns (dividends plus capital gains) of the asset market and those of company j's stock

The relative risk premium model does not define risk. To estimate National Presto's cost of equity based on the CAPM approach, first we must have estimates for the risk-free rate of return, the expected return on the average asset, and the covariability of the returns on National Presto's stock with those on the average asset sometimes called "the market."[23] To use the CAPM, therefore, we need forecasts for R_f, R_m, and β.

R_f is the risk-free rate of return. In theory, this return should entail no risk, including any risk of purchasing power loss from the impact of inflation on prices. In practice, however, most analysts choose a proxy that includes inflation. For investors in U.S. assets or securities, the proxy probably would be a U.S. Treasury instrument. Sensibly, the analyst would choose a Treasury bond that would be outstanding for a period similar to the life of the asset being evaluated. Because equity securities have long lives, a longer-term U.S. Treasury bond is a good choice. More precisely, since, as you can see in Exhibit 6-11, the typical U.S. Treasury yield curve has an upward slope to 7- to 10-year maturities and is rather flat thereafter, many analysts choose a U.S. Treasury bond with 7 to 10 years to maturity as an appropriate proxy.

EXHIBIT 6-11   Treasury Security Yields (week ending June 14, 1996)

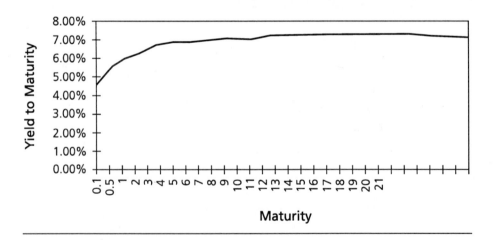

---

[23] Considerable controversy surrounds the theory and use of the CAPM. The reader should become familiar with the problems before becoming a frequent user. Since these problems are lengthy and complex, they are beyond the scope of this book.

When analyzing the required return on non-U.S. assets, including compa-nies, another proxy might be more appropriate than a U.S. Treasury bond. The rate on a U.S. Treasury bond contains an estimate of the real rate of return, gen-erally thought to be about 2.5 percent, and a return to compensate for domestic inflation. Assets in other countries must return enough to compensate for the domestic inflation rate in those countries. The differences in various countries' treasury securities can be seen in Exhibits 6-12 and 6-13. Exhibit 6-12 shows rates at the short end of the yield curve; Exhibit 6-13 shows longer-term rates.

R_m is the expected return on an asset of average risk. Analysts have used two ways to determine the average expected return. One is a risk premium approach: the long-term historical return on the risk-free asset is subtracted from the historical return on a proxy for all assets.[24] In the United States, ana-lysts have often used data like that shown in Exhibit 6-14 to estimate the pre-mium. At year-end 1995, the 40-year premium of U.S. equities above U.S. Treasury bonds was 7.6 percent.[25]

Analysts also use an estimate of the expected market premium. This esti-mate may come from information derived from security analysts working in money management companies whose job it is to make forecasts for individual stocks. Putting all their forecasts together produces a consensus estimate of the expected U.S. stock market return.[26]

EXHIBIT 6-12   Government Rates, Various Countries

	1-Year	2-Year
Canada	4.7%	5.2%
France	N.Av.	4.0%
Germany	3.2%	3.7%
Italy	N.Av.	6.8%
Japan	1.1%	0.8%
Netherlands	0.0%	3.6%
United Kingdom	5.8%	6.1%
United States	5.9%	6.3%

N.Av. = not available.

....

[24] Equities are used as a proxy for the average risk asset because, if you consider all possible investments that an investor can make, equities are rather average in risk.
[25] There is considerable controversy over what is the right period of history to use as a proxy for the future. Some argue that a period longer than 40 years should be used and, because the data are easily available, they use data from 1926 to the present. Others choose a period of history as much like the future they foresee as possible. Others argue that realized returns, however long-term, are not a good proxy for expectations.
[26] The analyst forecasts and the historic returns can be quite different. For instance, when his-toric data would have shown a market return of 12.1, in late 1991 the analysts' estimates for the long-term expected rate of return for U.S. equities ranged up to 14 percent.

EXHIBIT 6-13   Government Bond Rates, Various Countries

	10-Year	30-Year
Canada	7.3%	7.8%
France	6.2%	7.1%
Germany	6.9%	7.0%
Italy	8.0%	8.4%
Japan	3.0%	N.Av.
Netherlands	6.1%	6.8%
United Kingdom	7.7%	8.1%
United States	6.7%	7.1%

N.Av. = not available.

EXHIBIT 6-14   Basic Series: Summary Statistics of Annual Returns (1926-1994)

Series	Geometric Mean	Arithmetic Mean	Standard Mean	Distribution
Large Company Stocks	10.2%	12.2%	20.3%	
Small Company Stocks	12.2	17.4	34.6	
Long-Term Corporate Bonds	5.4	5.7	8.4	
Long-Term Government Bonds	4.8	5.2	8.8	
Intermediate-Term Government Bonds	5.1	5.2	5.7	
U.S. Treasury Bills	3.7	3.7	3.3	
Inflation	3.1	3.2	4.6	

| -90% | 0% | 90% |

SOURCE: © Computed using data from *Stocks, Bonds, Bills & Inflation 1997 Yearbook*™, Ibbotson Associates, Chicago (annually updates work by Roger G. Ibbotson and Rex Sinquefield). Used with permission. All rights reserved.

The typical method of estimating a beta is to use a version of the simple linear regression and the monthly total rates of return for the stock and for an index like the S&P 500:

$$R_j - R_f = a_j + \beta_j (R_m - R_f) + e_j$$

where
a	=	The intercept of the linear regression
β	=	The slope of the line
e	=	The errors that occur because the fit of the line to the data is not perfect
j	=	The designated stock or portfolio

A regression created for National Presto is shown in Exhibit 6-15. Each dot shown on the graph represents the returns for National Presto and the Standard and Poor 500 for one period. The line that minimizes the distance of the dots from the line, shown by the middle line of the three, is called the **security characteristic line**.

As any financial analyst knows, however, using history as a predictor for the future is dangerous. The danger is no less here than elsewhere. Thus, even when you calculate a historical beta, it is only a guideline for what the beta might be in the future. Several companies calculate and publish betas for a number of publicly traded U.S. common equities. Standard and Poor's *Industry*

EXHIBIT 6-15 National Presto and Standard & Poors 500
Security Characteristic Line[27]

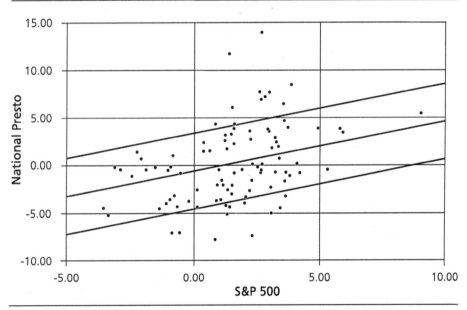

SOURCE: Bridge Data Services.

....

[27] For those of you with such an interest, the regression statistics from this regression are shown below. For those of you seeing this for the first time, the mystery of regression can be deciphered in many of the readings listed at the end of this chapter.
  $Y = -0.714 + 0.518X$, with an R^2 (a measure of fit) of 0.29.

Survey and Value Line's *Investment Reports* are two sources that are widely available. In addition, many money management companies estimate and sell proprietary versions.

However, neither the betas nor the historical data needed to calculate an historical beta are available when analyzing a company that is privately held or operates and/or sells its securities outside the United States. Does this mean that you cannot use the CAPM? You can use it, but you must use judgment about what the beta will be when good historical data does not exist to begin an analysis. To do this, you must understand on what beta depends. It depends on the company's sensitivity to changes in factors that, to a greater or lesser degree, negatively or positively affect the returns from all assets worldwide. Examples of such factors are inflation, worldwide industrial production, and investors' propensity to take risk. Companies that are highly sensitive to changes in these factors will have a higher-than-average beta. An average beta is 1.0, and most betas are from 0.5 to 1.8.

To demonstrate how the analyst might use the model, we will use 6.98 percent as the current yield on a 10-year U.S. Treasury bond for R_f, and 7.6 percent, the historical return premium of equities over long-term U.S. government bonds, for R_m. For the covariability, or risk, of National Presto's returns, the beta, we will use 0.70, an estimate based on the historical relationship of National Presto's returns with those of the S&P 500, adjusted by industry analysts for changes anticipated in the systematic risk of the company.[28] Using these estimates, we can calculate National Presto's required return on equity as follows:

$$
\begin{aligned}
R_{ej} &= R_f + \beta_j \, (R_m - R_f) \\
R_{Presto} &= 6.98\% + 0.70 \times (7.60\%) \\
&= 12.3\%
\end{aligned}
$$

While the CAPM provides a result that is quite close to those of other methods in this case, that is not always true. The analyst is wise to use several approaches to corroborate any cost of equity estimate.

The method we just described uses data from a publicly traded company in the U.S. markets. The CAPM is not a model that can be used only with publicly traded companies, however, or only with companies that operate in the United States. The model is universal, and the global analyst will consider the level of risk of a company based on how sensitive its returns will be to macroeconomic, systemwide (systematic) economic events. These returns are affected by where a company sources materials and where it sells its products. The fact that many analysts use historical data to calculate betas for publicly traded U.S. companies should not mislead one into thinking that this is the only, or even the best, way to estimate the future relative risk of a company.

---

[28] Systematic risk is the risk relative to the market, not risks specific to the company. Specific risks are also called unsystematic risk.

References at the end of this chapter and Chapter 7 include advanced readings on the topic.

III. REQUIRED RETURN ON EQUITY FOR PRIVATE, NON-U.S., OR CHANGING COMPANIES

The analysis we have performed thus far was for National Presto, a U.S. company that is traded on the NYSE, the largest stock exchange in the world. Considerable data are available for such companies, and there are stock analysts whose job it is to know as much about public companies as possible. Much of the writing about how to use the methods was based on the U.S. market and meant for students and practitioners in the United States. The models are equally applicable to any company, however, whether it is public or private, operates in a developed or developing country, is stable or undergoing considerable change. To estimate the required return on equity for such companies may require more ingenuity and judgment than most analysts are used to exercising. However, with experience in estimating required return on equity, an analyst will gain skill in dealing with more varied situations where information is not available, and where an analyst's judgment is critical.

IV. SUMMARY

In this chapter we looked at what returns shareholders expect to earn on their investments. We call this return the required return on equity or the company's cost of equity. The models used to estimate what investors require are attempts to replicate the methods investors themselves use to price an equity security. These models can be used with publicly traded companies for which there are considerable data, or they can be applied, using proxies or analogy, to companies that are privately held or are in small or developing markets.

The required return on equity is the rate that is used to discount the residual cash flows—that is, the cash flows to equity shareholders, the owners of the company. In many companies, however, the shareholders have chosen to share their financing obligation with others, especially with those investing in debt instruments. What happens to the company's required return when the shareholders share their rights and obligations with lenders is the subject of Chapter 7.

SELECTED REFERENCES

For information on equity markets, see:

Ball, Ray. "The Theory of Stock Market Efficiency: Accomplishments and Limitations Values." *Journal of Applied Corporate Finance*, Spring 1995, pp. 4-17.

Bodie, Zvi, Alex Kane, and Alan Marcus. *Investments.* 3rd ed. Homewood, Ill.: Richard D. Irwin, 1996, chaps. 2 and 3.

Haugen, Robert A., *Modern Investment Theory.* 3rd ed. Englewood Cliffs, N.J.: Prentice Hall, 1993, chap. 2.

Ibbotson, Roger G., and Gary P. Brinson. *Investment Markets.* New York: McGraw-Hill, 1987, Part 2.

Malkiel, Bernard. *A Random Walk Down Wall Street.* 5th ed. New York: W. W. Norton & Co., 1990.

For information about equity valuation methods, see:

Bodie, Zvi, Alex Kane, and Alan Marcus. *Investments.* 3rd ed. Homewood, Ill.: Richard D. Irwin, 1996, chaps. 17 and 18.

Brealey, Richard A., and Stewart C. Myers. *Principles of Corporate Finance.* 5th ed. New York: McGraw-Hill, 1996, chap. 4.

Brigham, Eugene, and Louis Gapenski. *Financial Management.* Fort Worth, TX: Dryden, 1994, chap. 19.

Haugen, Robert A. *Modern Investment Theory.* 3rd ed. Englewood Cliffs, N.J.: Prentice Hall, 1993, chap. 21.

Levy, Haim. *Introduction to Investments.* Cincinnati, OH: South-Western College Publishing, 1996, chap. 18.

Ross, Stephen A., Randolph W. Westerfield, and Jeffrey F. Jaffe. *Corporate Finance.* 4th ed. Homewood, Ill.: Richard D. Irwin, 1996, chap. 5.

Ross, Stephen A., Randolph W. Westerfield, and Bradford D. Jordon. *Fundamentals of Corporate Finance.* 3rd ed. Homewood, Ill.: Richard D. Irwin, 1995, chap. 6.

Shapiro, Alan C. *Modern Corporate Finance.* 2nd ed. New York: Macmillan, 1994, chaps. 12 and 13.

Sharpe, William F., Gordon J. Alexander, and Jeffery V. Bailey. *Investments.* 5th ed. Englewood Cliffs, N.J.: Prentice Hall, 1995, chaps. 18 and 19.

Woolridge, J. Randall. "Do Stock Prices Reflect Fundamental Values?" *Journal of Applied Corporate Finance*, Spring 1995, pp. 64-69 and 102.

For more on warrants and convertible securities, see:

Brigham, Eugene, and Louis Gapenski. *Financial Management.* Fort Worth, TX: Dryden, 1994, chap. 22.

Shapiro, Alan C. *Modern Corporate Finance.* 2nd ed. New York: Macmillan, 1994, chap. 20.

Ross, Stephen A., Randolph W. Westerfield, and Jeffrey F. Jaffe. *Corporate Finance.* 4th ed. Homewood, Ill.: Richard D. Irwin, 1996, chap. 22.

Ross, Stephen A., Randolph W. Westerfield, and Bradford D. Jordon. *Fundamentals of Corporate Finance.* 3rd ed. Homewood, Ill.: Richard D. Irwin, 1995, chap. 12.

For information about how companies issue securities, see:

Brealey, Richard A., and Stewart C. Myers. *Principles of Corporate Finance.* 5th ed. New York: McGraw-Hill, 1996, chap. 15.

Brigham, Eugene, and Louis Gapenski. *Financial Management.* Fort Worth, TX: Dryden, 1994, chap. 19.

Ross, Stephen A., Randolph W. Westerfield, and Jeffrey F. Jaffe. *Corporate Finance.* 4th ed. Homewood, Ill.: Richard D. Irwin, 1996, chap. 19.

Ross, Stephen A., Randolph W. Westerfield, and Bradford D. Jordon. *Fundamentals of Corporate Finance.* 3rd ed. Homewood, Ill.: Richard D. Irwin, 1995, chap. 13.

For general information about the stock market, see:

Fogler, H. Russell, Frank Fabozzi, and Diana Harrington. *Analyzing the Stock Market.* 2nd ed. Chicago: Probus Publishing, 1988.

Haugen, Robert A. *Modern Investment Theory.* 3rd ed. Englewood Cliffs, N.J.: Prentice Hall, 1993.

Levy, Haim. *Introduction to Investments.* Cincinnati, OH: South-Western College Publishing, 1996.

Sharpe, William F., Gordon J. Alexander, and Jeffery V. Bailey. *Investments.* 5th ed. Englewood Cliffs, N.J.: Prentice Hall, 1995.

For those with a further interest in the capital asset pricing model and discounted cash flow methods of equity valuation, see:

Harrington, Diana R. *Modern Portfolio Theory, The Capital Asset Pricing Model and Arbitrage Pricing Theory: A Users Guide.* 2nd ed. Englewood Cliffs, N.J.: Prentice Hall, 1987.

Kothari, S.P., and Jay Shanken. "In Defense of Beta." *Journal of Applied Corporate Finance,* Spring 1995, pp. 53-58.

For historical data from the stock and bond markets and information about comparable firms, see:

Arnold Bernhard & Co., Inc. *Value Line Investment Survey.*

Dun & Bradstreet, *Key Business Ratios.*

Ibbotson Associates. *Stocks, Bonds, Bills and Inflation, 1996, Yearbook.*

Robert Morris Associates, *Annual Statement Studies.*

For information on estimating the risk premium, see:

Harrington, Diana R. *Modern Portfolio Theory, The Capital Asset Pricing Model and Arbitrage Pricing Theory: A Users Guide.* 2nd ed. Englewood Cliffs, N.J.: Prentice Hall, 1987.

Sharpe, William, and Katrina Sherrerd. *Quantifying the Market Risk Premium Phenomenon for Investment Decision Making.* Charlottesville, VA: Institute of Chartered Financial Analysts, 1989.

STUDY QUESTIONS

1. Bakelite Company is a commercial bakery specializing in biscuit-making and located in rural Ohio. Recent substantial declines in grain prices have resulted in significant raw material savings. Since prices do not need to be cut, because Bakelite is already at the low-priced end of the market, cash reserves have built up well beyond historical levels. This wealth of cash spurs management, with the support of the board, to consider some capital investments they have long deferred. The various division heads have been asked to propose capital investments to Carl Borg, vice president of finance. Mr. Borg has the job of evaluating the projects and making recommendations to the board. Because it has been years since Bakelite made any really significant investments, Mr. Borg is concerned about choosing the right ones. To get some advice about making these decisions, he calls an old college friend, Jane Wilson, now a finance professor at a nearby university. Professor Wilson says that, since Mr. Borg already has cash flow forecasts from the divisions, the only thing left to be done is to discount the flows at the appropriate discount rate.

   Bakelite is too small a company to be followed by investment services like *Value Line*. However, a regional investment banker has just published a brief report on the company. It includes the following information: Bakelite's beta is 1.32 and the analyst's estimates for Bakelite's nominal long-term growth is 4.9 percent, a figure with which management agrees. The company has been paying a $3 dividend, and its current market price in the over-the-counter market is $25. At present, U.S. Treasury seven-year bonds are yielding 8.9 percent and 90-day Treasury bills are yielding 6.5 percent. Historically, the stock market has yielded about 8.5 percent above Treasury bills and 6 percent above longer-term Treasury bonds. Its taxes are 34 percent. Bakelite's balance sheet is shown below.

BAKELITE CORPORATION
(in millions)

Assets		Liabilities and Equity	
Cash	$0.2	Accounts payable	$1.4
Marketable securities	2.3	Taxes payable	0.3
Accounts receivable	1.1	Total current liabilities	1.7
Total current assets	3.6	Common stock	1.2
Net property, plant,		Retained earnings	1.9
and equipment	1.2	Total equity	3.1
Total assets	$4.8	Total liabilities and	
		equity	$4.8

What is Bakelite's owners' required return on equity, using:

a. the dividend-discount model, where g = (1 - Payout)(Return on equity)?

b. the capital asset pricing model?

2. Kelly Services is one of the largest U.S. providers of temporary personnel for large companies. The temporary help business has been suffering from contract-building practices and the U.S. recession. In spite of this, the company's growth has been a relatively steady 4.2 percent. With U.S. Treasury seven-year bonds yielding 6.3 percent and 90-day Treasury bills at 3.8 percent (on average 8.9 percent below the U.S. stock market), what is Kelly's cost of equity? The company pays a $3.00 dividend per year; its stock price is $36.00; and *Value Line* reports a beta of 0.95.

CHAPTER 7

Obtaining Outside Capital

In Chapter 6 we learned how to estimate the fair return that should be expected for an equity investment. We found that all investors require a return for:

1. *Illiquidity:* the time that money is invested.
2. *Inflation:* losses caused by changes in the purchasing power of money.
3. *Risk:* the chance that the returns from an investment may be higher or lower than was expected.

We used the following formula to determine this required return:

Required return = Risk-free rate + Inflation premium + Risk premium

We used the rate from a U.S. Treasury security as an estimate of the return required for both the time value of money and inflation for U.S. investors. As for risk, we know that investors expect more return for increased risk, and we asked capital market experts what they believed was a fair return for risk, their market price of risk. Notice, that up to this point, we have assumed that all our investments have been financed by the owners of the company alone. However, we know that companies rarely are financed by the owners, the shareholders, alone. Many of these owners, or the managers on their behalf, have decided to subcontract some of their financing obligations to others, particularly others who prefer investments that have predetermined repayments and pay a rent for the use of the money. These financing subcontractors are called **lenders**, the investment is called **principal**, and the annual rent is called **interest**. We used a variety of methods in Chapter 6 to estimate the investors' required return (the company's cost of equity capital) for National Presto Industries, Inc. National Presto's balance sheets indicate that its shareholders have chosen to subcontract little or none of their financing responsibilities to lenders. While debt has not played much of a role in the financing of National Presto, for most other companies the lenders provide some portion of a company's capital.

How do shareholders, or managers on their behalf, decide if they want to use debt in financing their company? The answer is, if subcontracting increases the shareholders' value, they will subcontract to lenders. However, if it makes no difference at all in the value of the shareholders' position, then they can subcontract or not, it really does not matter. The question is, can subcontracting some of the financing obligations to lenders create value for the shareholders?

Let us start with two things that we know. First, shareholders want managers to create value for them. Second, to create value, managers must make decisions that will increase the present value of the company by either reducing risk, increasing cash flow, or both. Keeping the shareholders' objectives in mind, let us see if financing the corporation with some mixture of debt and equity can actually make the company worth more than financing it without the debt.

I. THE VALUE OF LEVERAGE

To decide whether a particular capital structure can enhance shareholders' value, let's look at Greenway Corporation. Greenway currently has no debt and is located in a country where interest is not tax-deductible. Greenway's cash flows and their value are shown in Exhibit 7-1.

In Column 1 of Exhibit 7-1 you can see that the residual cash flow per share is $1.00. Discounted at the shareholders' required return, the company's market value, or the shareholders' value, is $66.67 million, or $6.67 per share.

Now let's see what happens when Greenway borrows enough to repurchase 10 percent of its equity. The value of the company does not change because the risk and return, the cash flows, of the company remain unchanged as debt is added.[1] However, the company's cash flows, because of the lenders' contract, belong first to the lenders: the company must pay the lenders $0.67, 10 percent on the capital borrowed. While this payment to the lenders reduces the shareholders' residual cash flow to $9.4 million, on a per-share basis it rises to $1.04 per share for the nine remaining shareholders. With an increase in the required return, the shareholders' total value declines to $60.0 million, but, on a per-share basis it has risen to $6.67 per share.

Exhibit 7-2 illustrates, more dramatically, why the shareholders' return requirements increase with increased leverage. The exhibit shows the shareholders' returns (ROE) as the company's earnings change from those originally forecasted in Exhibit 7-1 to those earned under other circumstances. Without leverage, the maximum return is 24.8 percent. With only 10 percent of the company's capital from lenders, the shareholders' maximum expected return increases to 26.3 percent. Increase the leverage even more than the 10 percent,

---

[1]   Note that we said value of the company, not the portion of the value that comes to each group. The company's value depends upon the company's cash flow and risk. The lenders' or shareholders' portion of the value depends upon cash flows and risks that have been assigned to them. Clearly their risk and return change with changes in leverage.

EXHIBIT 7-1   Greenway Corporation Earnings, Cash Flow, and Value: No Tax
Deduction for Interest Expense (in millions, except per-share data)

	100% Equity Financed	10% Debt/Capital (Equity Cost 15.6%)
Profit before taxes	$15.0	$14.3
Taxes	(5.0)	(4.9)
Profit after taxes	10.0	9.4
Depreciation	5.0	5.0
New plant and equipment	(5.0)	(5.0)
Added working capital	0.0	0.0
Cash flow to all capital providers	$10.0	$ 9.4
Number of shares outstanding	10.0	9.0
Debt cost	0.0	$0.67
Residual cash flow per share	$1.00	$1.04
Book value of firm	$66.67	$66.67
Book value of equity	$66.67	$60.00
Book value of debt	0.0	$6.67
Return on book equity	15.0%	15.0%
Required return on equity	15.000	15.667
Required return on debt (interest)	10.0%	10.0%
Interest expense	0.0	$0.67
Equity market value*	$66.67	$60.00
Equity market value per share	$6.67	$6.67
Total market value†	$66.67	$66.67

* Total market value calculated using the nongrowth perpetuity method of valuation described in previous chapters:

$$\text{Value of company} = \frac{\text{Residual cash flows}}{\text{Required return}}$$

$$\$66.67 = \frac{\$10.00}{0.15}$$

† The market value of the total firm also can be calculated as the sum of the value of the equity and debt, $66.67.

and the ROE increases even further. In bad times, of course, leverage increases the downside for the shareholders. It is this range of outcomes, which they cannot know beforehand, that shareholders recognize as risk, and for which they expect the higher return of 15.5 percent.

As leverage increases, the combined return required by all Greenway's investors (a return of 15 percent) does not change. This is because the company's risks and cash flows do not change with leverage. However, the risks and cash flows for each capital provider do change as the returns required by lenders and shareholders rise as each of their risks increases. The process for

EXHIBIT 7-2 Greenway Corporation Forecasted Earnings and Cash Flows: Three Outcomes With and Without Leverage (dollars in millions)

	Bad Times	Most Likely	Good Times
Profit before taxes	$ 5.0	$15.0	$25.0
Taxes	(1.7)	(5.0)	(8.5)
Profit after taxes	3.3	10.0	16.5
Depreciation	5.0	5.0	5.0
New plant and equipment	(5.0)	(5.0)	(5.0)
Added working capital	0.0	0.0	0.0
Cash flow	$ 3.3	$10.0	$16.5
Without Leverage			
Net income and cash flow to:			
All capital providers	$3.3	$10.0	$16.5
Shareholders	$3.3	$10.0	$16.5
Book value of equity	$66.67	$66.67	$66.67
Return on debt	10.0%	10.0%	10.0%
Return on equity	4.95%	15.00%	24.75%
10% Debt/Total Capital			
Net income and cash flow to:			
All capital providers	$3.3	$10.0	$16.5
Shareholders	$2.6	$9.3	$15.8
Book value of equity	$60.00	$60.00	$60.00
Return on equity	4.33%	15.50%	26.33%

calculating the average, or weighted-average, cost of capital for a company is as follows:

$$\begin{aligned} \text{Weighted-average} \atop \text{cost of capital} \;&=\; \begin{array}{l}\text{[Cost of debt (1 - Tax rate)](Debt proportion) +} \\ \text{Cost of equity (Proportion of equity)}\end{array} \\ &=\; \{[0.10(1 - 0)]0.10\} + (.156 \times 0.90) \\ &=\; 0.15 \text{ or } 15\% \end{aligned}$$

Leverage does not change the average cost of capital for the company or the company's value. At low levels of debt, lenders charge less than do equity providers because the lenders are protected by contracts, while shareholders, now in a less advantageous position, require a higher return. As debt increases the return required by each rises, as seen in Exhibit 7-3.[2]

....

[2] Appendix 7A to this chapter discusses a shortcut method of valuation that depends on a company's capital structure remaining constant. The method uses a weighted-average cost of capital to discount the cash flows to all capital providers. It is a quick alternative to forecasts that include the financing of cash flows in determining the value of an investment. It is only useful, however, under certain conditions.

EXHIBIT 7-3   Greenway Corporation: Costs of Capital in a Tax-Free World

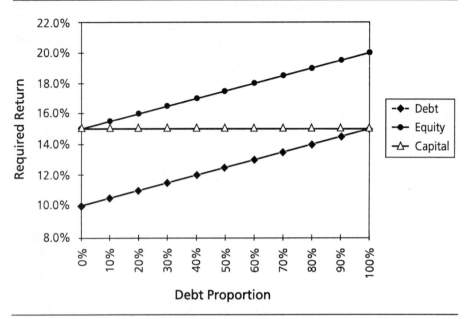

There is an exception to the rule that leverage does not affect shareholders' value. Value will be changed if leverage changes the company's cash flows, its risk, or both.[3] One thing that can change cash flows is taxes, or rather the deductibility of any debt financing expense. In many countries, interest is a deductible expense for tax purposes. Thus, interest payments lower the taxes a company pays, increasing the company's cash flows, with no change in the company's overall risk. This makes debt more attractive to borrowers than it would otherwise be: the cost of the debt to the borrower is the lenders' required return less the taxes saved. Exhibit 7-4 shows the impact of this feature of the tax code on Greenway's cost of capital and its shareholders' value. Exhibit 7-5 shows graphically the effect of taxes on the cost of capital. You can see that when interest is tax-deductible, although debt and equity costs rise as lenders finance an increasing proportion of a company, the cost of the company's capital declines, and the value of the company rises. Since this is so, in a world where there are taxes, why don't companies finance themselves with more debt?

There is no definitive answer to why there seems to be a limit to a company's financial leverage. One of the most interesting theories is the notion of

---

[3]   This is not a change in cash flows to any of the providers of capital, but to the company as a whole.

EXHIBIT 7-4   Greenway Corporation Tax Effect of Capital Structure Changes With 10 Percent Debt/Total Capital (dollars in millions except per share value)

	Cash Flow and Value With and Without Deductible Interest	
	Interest Not Deductible	Interest Deductible
Profit before interest and taxes	$15.0	$15.0
Interest	0.0	(0.7)
Earnings before taxes	15.0	14.3
Taxes (34%)	(5.0)	(4.9)
Profit after taxes	$10.0	$ 9.4
Depreciation	5.0	5.0
New equipment	(5.0)	(5.0)
Added working capital	0.0	0.0
Cash flow to equity shareholders	$10.0	$ 9.4
After-tax cost of equity	15.6%	15.6%
After-tax cost of debt	10.0%	6.6%
Weighted-average capital cost	15.0%	14.7%
Corporate value	$66.67	$68.61
Debt value	$6.67	$6.67
Equity market value*	$60.00	$61.94
Value per share	$6.67	$6.88

* Calculated as in Exhibit 7-1 ($9.4/0.147 = $68.61).

financial distress.[4] Financial distress occurs when a company cannot pay the interest or principal on its debt. The failure to pay its lenders can result in bankruptcy: the contract with the lender is broken, and the lender, because it has a contract, can require debt payment. Shareholders have no such contract, and thus cannot force the company into bankruptcy. Obviously, shareholders are not happy when a company is financially distressed, but they have no contract, only expectations. When shareholders' expectations are not met, they can sell their shares and the price of the shares will decline, or they can use their voting rights to change the board of directors.

In the case of a company with modest amounts of debt, most lenders do not worry about the possibility of bankruptcy. As the amount of debt rises, however, bankruptcy becomes more probable, and lenders begin to incorporate the expected costs of possible bankruptcy into their required return. Thus, at the point when lenders begin to be concerned about bankruptcy, they appear to

---

[4]   A company that is financially embarrassed is unable to pay the interest on its debt. If it is financially distressed it can pay neither interest nor principal.

EXHIBIT 7-5   Greenway Corporation: Costs of Capital in a Taxable World
Without Bankruptcy

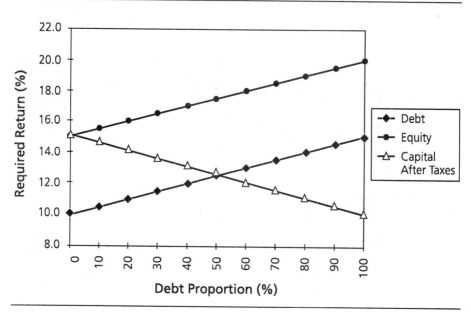

have added an extra charge to the cost of debt. Exhibit 7-5 shows what happens to a company's cost of capital when lenders and shareholders are not concerned about bankruptcy. With bankruptcy, the costs of debt and equity jump and the cost of capital starts its rise. Exhibit 7-6 shows the sort of rise that can occur.

We have suggested that the lender's return increases when the probability of bankruptcy becomes real. This is only one theory that may explain a jump in the cost of capital as leverage increases. Other theories have been used to explain the phenomenon.[5] Whatever the reasons, there does appear to be a point at which the weighted-average cost of capital begins to rise, and the value of the company thus starts to decline. The point just before this increase is where the company has the lowest capital cost. The capital structure at this point is called **optimal capital structure**. It is optimal because, beyond this point, as the cost of capital rises the value of the company and the shareholders' value both decline.

_____

[5]   Another possible explanation for the rise in capital costs is the impact that the company's agents have on decisions. Agents are those who work on behalf of the shareholders but are not owners of the company. Managers and lenders are agents. Those who work for lenders, acting in their personal best interests, may become wary of lending to a company long before their employer would be: the impact of a loss on the lending agent is considerable, while the impact on the lending institution may be negligible.

EXHIBIT 7-6   Required Return and Capital Cost With and Without Bankruptcy
Considerations

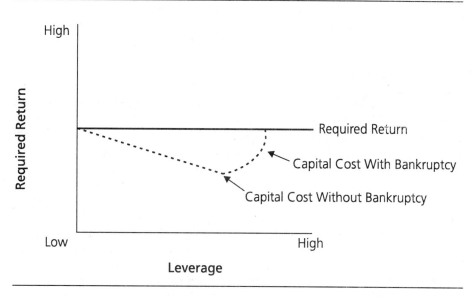

The manager must consider all the risks and returns in determining the appropriate mix of debt and equity. In some ways, this task is a marketing problem: the manager has several different products (the company's financial securities) and several different markets (potential investors in the company). The financial manager must match securities with investors in a way that creates the greatest value for the company. He or she does so by analyzing the potential effects of various financing alternatives on the total market value of the company. To understand the decisions that face managers as they consider the appropriate capital structure for their company, a basic understanding of debt and debt markets is important.

II. SOURCES OF DEBT FINANCING

Most companies are financed with a combination of equity and debt. Debt is different from equity in that it is contractual, typically specifying the amount to be borrowed, the interest charged for the money, and the time at which the money will be returned. The debt contract may also have some **covenants**, which are provisions that restrict the company's activities (e.g., allow no further increase in debt) or require that certain standards be met (e.g., a particular current ratio). Lenders' claims appear before the shareholders' residual claim both on the balance sheet and in law.

In addition to the public markets for debt, which are similar to those for equity described in Chapter 6, capital can be raised through **private placements**.[6] Public issues are regulated by the Securities and Exchange Commission (SEC) in the United States and by similar commissions in other countries. They require the issuing company to disclose specific information about the company's business activities, the financial instrument being issued, and the use of the proceeds. Such disclosure provides the public with information that facilitates subsequent trading in the secondary market. Private placements are direct placements of the securities with investors such as large insurance companies. They are not registered and generally are not traded in the secondary market. However, because the issuer can negotiate directly with the investor, private placements allow more complicated and specialized financial arrangements between borrower and lender (company and shareholder) than are available in the public capital markets. In general, debt and debt with some equity characteristics are placed privately.

Private institutional investors such as mutual funds, insurance companies, and pension funds are the largest investors in the capital markets. Although precise data are difficult to obtain, estimates suggest that well over half of publicly traded securities in the United States are owned by these institutions. Individual shareholders account for the remainder. In other countries, the level of institutional ownership is quite different, and can be much higher.

While the two primary types of securities used by companies to raise long-term capital are debt and equity, some instruments combine the two types through "convertible" provisions. **Convertible instruments** typically allow the investor to convert debt or preferred stock into equity, usually common stock, at a specified price and usually during a particular period of time.

1. Debt Markets

Long-term debt instruments are frequently called **bonds**. A bond is a contractual debt obligation to repay a stated amount on a specified date, termed the **maturity**, and to make periodic interest, or **coupon**, payments. The stated amount is called the **principal** or **par value**. The par value is typically a standard amount in each country. For instance, in the United States the usual par value is $1,000. Specific features of the bonds issued are described in a contract called an **indenture agreement**. The stated interest or coupon payments are determined by a specified interest rate or coupon rate at the time the bond is issued. If the contractually obligated payments are not made, the bond is in

---

[6]   The market for certain bonds can be much less liquid than markets for equity issues. This even can be true for bonds of large companies. This is because a company may have many different debt instruments (bonds), each with a different set of characteristics, and because one or a few large investors own large quantities of a particular debt instrument, making trading infrequent.

default and the bondholders may have to call on, or take, some or all of the assets of the company as compensation.

For most bonds, the coupon rate is fixed for the life of the bond. Because of large fluctuations in interest rates in recent years, some bonds have been issued with variable, or floating, interest rates. For **variable-rate bonds,** the interest rate is restated at specified intervals based on a particular market index of interest rates—for example, LIBOR (the London Interbank Offer Rate) or the prime rate, the rate charged the best customers of a bank. These bonds are also called **floating-rate bonds** or **floaters.**

For fixed-coupon bonds, changes in interest rates subsequent to the date of issue affect the bond price in the secondary market but do not affect the cost to the company. If general market interest rates go up (or down), the price of the bond will go down (or up) in order to continue to provide a fair rate of return in the subsequent interest rate environment. These adjustments occur so that the bond's **yield to maturity** (return from interest plus principal repayments) will approximate the current market rate of interest for bonds of similar maturity and quality and other features. Thus, the price that an investor is willing to pay for a bond is a function of the par value of the bond, the coupon rate, the maturity, and prevailing interest rates. The formula shown below for determining the proper secondary price of a bond is similar to the present value calculations discussed in Chapters 4 and 5.

$$P = \frac{CP_1}{(1 + R)^1} + \frac{CP_2}{(1 + R)^2} + \dots + \frac{CP_m}{(1 + R)^m} + \frac{PAR}{(1 + R)^m}$$

where

P = Market price of the bond
CP = Periodic coupon payment (interest payment)
R = Current market interest rate
PAR = Par value of the bond
m = Maturity period of the bond

If, for instance, a company had issued $2 million in bonds at 12.0 percent and the rate of interest on bonds of a similar maturity and quality rose from 12.0 to 15.7 percent, the market price of the bonds with two years remaining until maturity would drop from $2 million to under $1.9 million in order to provide a 15.7 percent yield to new purchasers:

$$P = \frac{\$240,000}{(1 + 0.157)^1} + \frac{\$240,000}{(1 + 0.157)^2} + \frac{\$2,000,000}{(1 + 0.157)^2}$$
$$P = \$1,880,762$$

Conversely, if market rates dropped to, say, 10 percent, the bond price would rise to over $2 million:

$$P = \frac{\$240{,}000}{(1 + 0.10)^1} + \frac{\$240{,}000}{(1 + 0.10)^2} + \frac{\$2{,}000{,}000}{(1 + 0.10)^2}$$

$$P = \$2{,}069{,}422$$

Present values (prices) of bonds with longer maturities are more affected by interest rate changes than are values of bonds with short maturities.

If the market price of a bond is known, but the effective interest rate (the yield to maturity) is not, it is possible, using the same formula, to calculate the yield to maturity. The method for determining the yield to maturity is like that used in Chapter 4 for calculating the internal rate of return. A calculator is all you need.

For conventional bonds, the amount the company borrows is the same as the principal or par value of the bond, net of issue costs, of course. This statement is not true for **zero-coupon bonds**. These bonds do not require any periodic coupon payments. Instead, the par value of the bond is much larger than the amount originally borrowed (the cost of the bond to the investor): essentially, interest is accrued during the bond's life and paid at the time the initial principal is repaid as a part of the final payment. Determining the return on these bonds is a simplification of the yield-to-maturity calculation, because there are no coupon or interest payments. The following simplified formula would be used:

$$\text{Price} = \frac{\text{PAR}}{(1 + i)^m}$$

Where:
  i = yield to maturity

Using this formula, if a firm issues a zero-coupon bond today at a price of $275 per bond returning $1,000 in 10 years, the effective yield, or yield to maturity, is 13.8 percent ($275 = $[1{,}000/(1 + x)^{10}]$).

In the 1980s, we saw the explosion of a relatively new version of debt. This debt was called junk bonds. There had always been a market for bonds of companies that had fallen into disfavor after their debt was issued, and whose debt-quality ratings had declined. These bonds, sometimes called fallen angels, were traded at discounts to their original issuing price.[7] **Junk debt** was, however, debt of companies that were not highly rated or of companies that were issuing unusually high levels of debt for their size or risk. The debt carried very high interest rates and was issued at a discount to its par value; thus, it was called **original issue discount (OID) debt**.

Not all bonds retire the entire principal amount at the specified maturity date of the bond. Many bonds require the company to make periodic principal

---

[7]   This discount existed with no marketwide change in interest rates.

reductions, called a **sinking fund**. The purpose of these sinking funds is to reduce the risk that the borrower will not be able to repay the par amount. While the amount going into the sinking fund may be placed in a trust account to be held until the maturity date, this practice is not typical today. It is more likely that, when the sinking fund payments are due, the company will retire a portion of the issued bonds, even though they have not reached maturity. The way in which bonds are chosen to be purchased or retired before maturity is specified at the time the bonds are first issued by the company and noted in the indenture agreement. For publicly traded bonds, commonly the company will simply purchase some of the existing bonds in the market, thus reducing the total amount of bonds outstanding.

In addition to reducing the amount of bonds outstanding to meet sinking fund requirements, companies may choose to retire the bonds before the specified maturity. This process is termed **refunding** or **calling** the bonds. Companies are especially interested in refunding when interest rates fall. The existing bonds can be called, retired, and refinanced with lower cost debt. To protect against this possibility, many bonds have **call protection**: the bonds cannot be called for a specified period of time or may be called only if a stated premium is paid to the bondholders. Call provisions are specified in the indenture agreement.

As a further protection for bondholders, the bond contract or indenture may limit the company in other ways. Frequently the company will be required to maintain certain levels of assets or to limit its total amount of debt. Often these restrictions, or covenants, are specified in the form of ratios—the kind we discussed in Chapter 1. If any of the bond covenants are violated, the bond is deemed to be in technical default and is immediately due for payment. It is up to the bondholder whether the company will be forced to pay or whether the covenant will be waived or rewritten.

The general risk to the borrower is reflected in the **bond rating**. Bond ratings are important because bonds with higher potential for default (lower ratings) must have a higher coupon (that is, pay a higher interest rate) to compensate investors for the increased risk. Several organizations publish bond ratings; Moody's and Standard & Poor's (S&P) are the two most widely known in the United States. Based on these independent organizations' assessments of the general credit risk of the borrower, bonds are assigned a rating, with Aaa (Moody's) or AAA (S&P) indicating the most creditworthy bonds—those with the lowest risk of default. The ratings decrease through Aa/AA, and so on, to high-risk bonds rated Caa/CCC or below. A bond's rating may be changed because of changes in the issuer's situation.

A company may have several kinds of debt at the same time. The debt may have been issued to different lenders, at different times, and under different market conditions. The indenture agreement stipulates the differences: the amount of debt, the coupon rate of interest, payment terms, specific assets on which the lenders may call in event of default, the priority in which the lenders' claims will be settled, and criteria the company must meet in order to have the debt without covenant revision. Debt that holds claim to specific assets in event of default is usually called **mortgage debt**. Debt that, by contract, allows other debt precedence in event of default is called **subordinated debt**. Different issues of debt are listed separately on a company's balance sheet. The balance sheet and the accompanying notes describe the major differences in each debt instrument. Bond guides such as S&P and Moody's in the United States provide more detail for the potential investor or company analyst.

III. DETERMINING THE COST OF DEBT

Most firms use debt to finance a portion of their assets. The proportion of debt used by U.S. firms has changed dramatically over rather short periods of time, as shown in Exhibit 7-7. In the 1990s, equity has regained favor with investors, as shown in Exhibit 7-8. Not only does the debt proportion change, so do interest rates. At a high in the early 1980s, they have, until the past year, declined. Exhibit 7-9 shows the market rates of interest during the last 12 years on publicly traded debt of varying qualities. Note that the interest rate on the best quality corporate debt is higher than that on government debt of the same maturity, and that the lower the corporate debt is rated, the higher the interest rate—the lender's required return.

EXHIBIT 7-7   Annual Growth of Capital Structure and Its Composition
(all nonfinancial business corporations)

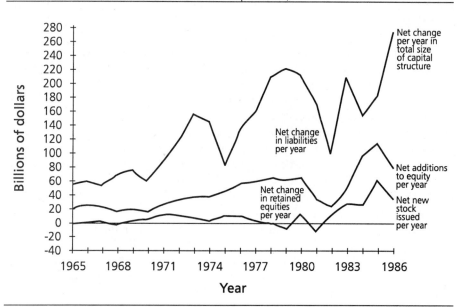

EXHIBIT 7-8 Growth in Equity Financing

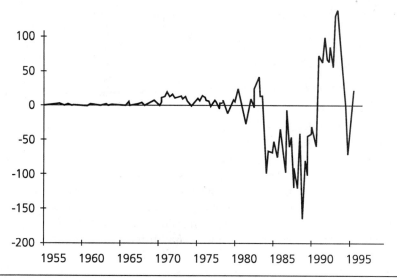

SOURCE: Mathias, Edward J., *Economic and Investment Environment, Washington, D.C.: The Carlyle Group., 1995.*

EXHIBIT 7-9 Interest Rates for Debt of Different Qualities—1984-1995

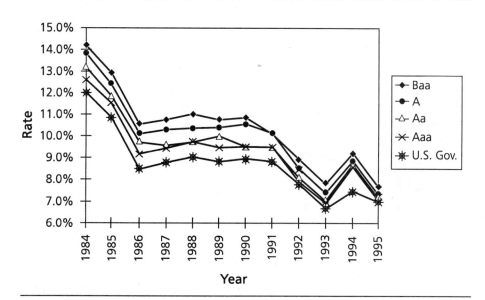

Just as the reliability of the borrower affects the interest rate, so does the length of time the borrower wishes to use the principal. Exhibit 7-9 shows the market rate of interest on debt of the same quality but different maturities at several points in time. The normal line is upward sloping like that shown for early September 1996. An upward slope is normal because lenders who provide capital for longer times require, quite logically, more return. At some points in time, this upward-sloping curve, the **yield curve**, does not exist. This has been particularly true in periods of high inflation. For instance, during the 1970s, the relationship between the market rate of interest and debt of different maturities was sometimes perverse. Exhibit 7-10 shows two typical yield curves and two inverse yield curves (March 1, 1981, and December 1, 1981). The rapidity of the change, coupled with the change from a normal to an inverse yield curve, has not been repeated since that time.

In addition to interest payments, a number of special features may be required by the lender. For example, specific assets may be pledged to support the loan; the lender may require seniority over others' claims in the case of bankruptcy, or the loan may be convertible into common or preferred stock under certain conditions. Each feature offers the lender different levels of protection from risk and thus carries a somewhat different cost, which is reflected in the interest rate.

EXHIBIT 7-10   Interest Rates for Debt of Different Maturities

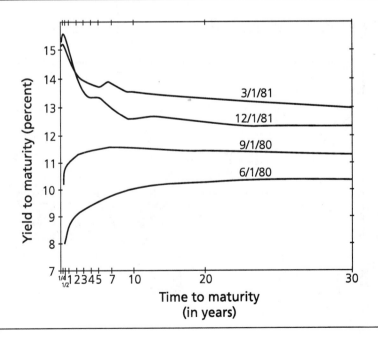

Earlier we showed that the lenders' required return on debt was the ratio of the interest rate to the principal amount of the debt.

$$K_d = \frac{\text{Interest payment}}{\text{Debt principal}}$$

However, the company's interest expense is tax-deductible, making the company's cost of debt (K_d).

$$K_d = \frac{\text{Interest payment (1 - Tax rate)}}{\text{Debt principal}}$$

Let's use an example. If a company wanted to borrow $2 million, and the lender expected interest payments of $163,000 per year, the investor's required return would be 8.15 percent ($163,000/$2,000,000), but the company's cost of debt would be

$$K_d = \frac{\text{Interest payment (1 - Tax rate)}}{\text{Debt principal}}$$

$$= \frac{\$163,000 \ (1 - 0.34)}{\$2,000,000}$$

$$= \frac{\$107,580}{2,000,000}$$

$$= 0.054 \text{ or } 5.4\%$$

This formula applies whether the company issues bonds at par or at a discount. If the company issues zero-coupon bonds, however, there are no interest payments during the life of the bond, and the investor's return comes from the difference between the price paid and the principal returned at maturity. Following our example, if the company's lenders' required yield-to-maturity was 8.5 percent on zero-coupon bonds, and it wanted to borrow $2.0 million for 10 years, the principal returned at the maturity of the bonds would be $4.5 million, not $2.0 million.[8]

IV. RICHS ANALYSIS

The capital markets are complex and ever-changing. Deciding to add debt to a company's all-equity capital structure adds risk, and potential return, to their owners' position. How do a company's owners, or the managers on the own-

....

[8] To determine the $4.5 million principal to be repaid, compound $2.0 million by 8.5 percent for 10 years.

ers' behalf, decide whether to subcontract some of their financing responsibilities? A convenient framework for analyzing the many different, and sometimes conflicting, forces that affect the capital structure decision is provided by the RICHS process. This acronym is used to represent five major factors that should be considered:

R — Risk
I — Income
C — Control
H — Hedging
S — Speculating

These factors are not listed in order of priority or importance; for each firm, and in different economic environments, the relative importance of the factors will differ. However, the manager should ensure that all factors have been considered.

The process of making the decision about a company's capital structure is not a strictly mechanical process in which computational abilities can be substituted for analytical skill and judgment; the manager must interpret the results of the analysis. For this reason, the RICHS analytical process can best be explained through a specific example—Greenway Corporation's decision about whether to finance a $6 million expansion in production capacity through a public equity offering or through a privately placed debt issue.

Greenway is the leading producer and marketer of sand trap graders for golf courses. The company was a market leader in both the manufacture and sale of graders until the rising value of the dollar made it economically attractive for Greenway to sell its production plants and produce the needed parts in a joint venture with a Japanese firm. Up to 1997, parts for the graders were manufactured in Japan and assembled and sold in the United States by Greenway. Recently the value of the dollar has declined relative to the Japanese yen and it has become economically attractive to manufacture as well as assemble the grader parts in the United States. Greenway has thus decided to buy a parts manufacturing plant, and one that is readily adaptable is available. Exhibit 7-11 shows historical and forecasted income statements and balance sheets Greenway managers made for the company in 1997, not including the new plant the company is considering purchasing. Exhibit 7-12 shows the forecasts including the new plant investment. The increased earnings before interest and taxes and cash flows shown in Exhibit 7-11 are expected to come from a reduction in transportation and manufacturing costs. Greenway management also expects to pay $2.0 million in dividends per year.

To make the investment, Greenway will need a total of $6.4 million: $4.5 million to pay for plant and equipment and $1.9 million for new working capital (to be invested largely in inventory). Greenway will need the money in January 1997, and the new plant will start operations shortly thereafter.

EXHIBIT 7-11 Greenway Corporation—Historic and Forecasted Financial Statements Without the New Plant (dollars in millions)

	Actual			Forecast		
	1996	1997	1998	1999	2000	2001
Income Statement						
Sales	$ 32.72	$ 36.00	$ 38.48	$ 41.12	$ 44.00	$ 47.12
Manufacturing expenses	(26.99)	(29.70)	(31.75)	(33.92)	(36.30)	(38.87)
Depreciation	(1.64)	(1.80)	(1.92)	(2.06)	(2.20)	(2.36)
Earnings before interest & taxes	4.09	4.50	4.81	5.14	5.50	5.89
Interest	(0.70)	(0.70)	(0.70)	(0.70)	(0.70)	(0.70)
Earnings before taxes	3.39	3.80	4.11	4.44	4.80	5.19
Taxes (@34%)	(1.15)	(1.29)	(1.40)	(1.51)	(1.63)	(1.76)
Net earnings	2.24	2.51	2.71	2.93	3.17	3.43
Cash Flow						
Depreciation	1.64	1.80	1.92	2.06	2.20	2.36
New property, plant, and equipment	(1.00)	(1.00)	(1.00)	(1.00)	(1.00)	(1.00)
New working capital	(0.64)	(0.80)	(0.92)	(1.06)	(1.20)	(1.36)
Principal payments or new debt	0.00	0.00	0.00	0.00	0.00	0.00
Residual net cash flow	$ 2.24	$ 2.51	$ 2.71	$ 2.93	$ 3.17	$ 3.43
Ratios						
EBIT/interest	584%	643%	687%	734%	786%	841%
Cash flow/interest	320%	358%	388%	419%	453%	489%
Balance Sheet						
Total current assets	$ 27.72	$ 28.52	$ 29.44	$ 30.50	$ 31.70	$ 33.06
Net property, plant, and equipment	15.00	14.20	13.28	12.22	11.02	9.66
Total assets	$ 42.72	$ 42.72	$ 42.72	$ 42.72	$ 42.72	$ 42.72
Total current liabilities	$ 7.24	$ 6.30	$ 4.85	$ 3.08	$ 0.98	$ 0.00
Long-term debt	7.20	7.20	7.20	7.20	7.20	7.20
Equity	28.28	28.79	29.50	30.43	31.60	33.02
Subtotal	42.72	42.29	41.55	40.71	39.78	40.22
Net financing needed	0.00	0.43	1.17	2.01	2.94	2.50
Total liabilities and equity	$ 42.72	$ 42.72	$ 42.72	$ 42.72	$ 42.72	$ 42.72

EXHIBIT 7-12   Greenway Corporation—Historic and Forecasted Financial Statements With the New Plant (dollars in millions)

	Actual		Forecast			
	1996	1997	1998	1999	2000	2001
Income Statement						
Sales	$ 32.72	$ 42.40	$ 44.64	$ 46.96	$ 49.36	$ 51.92
Manufacturing expenses	(26.99)	(34.98)	(36.83)	(38.74)	(40.72)	(42.83)
Depreciation	(1.64)	(2.12)	(2.23)	(2.35)	(2.47)	(2.60)
Earnings before interest & taxes	4.09	5.30	5.58	5.87	6.17	6.49
Interest	(0.70)	(0.70)	(0.70)	(0.70)	(0.70)	(0.70)
Earnings before taxes	3.39	4.60	4.88	5.17	5.47	5.79
Taxes (@34%)	(1.15)	(1.56)	(1.66)	(1.76)	(1.86)	(1.97)
Net earnings	2.24	3.04	3.22	3.41	3.61	3.82
Cash Flow						
Depreciation	1.64	2.12	2.23	2.35	2.47	2.60
New property, plant, and equipment	(1.00)	(4.50)	(1.00)	(1.00)	(1.00)	(1.00)
New working capital	(0.64)	(2.70)	(0.83)	(0.86)	(0.89)	(0.95)
Residual net cash flow	$ 2.24	$ (2.04)	$ 3.62	$ 3.90	$ 4.19	$ 4.47
Ratios						
EBIT/interest	584%	757%	797%	839%	881%	927%
Cash flow/interest	320%	-291%	517%	558%	599%	639%
Balance Sheet						
Total current assets	$ 27.72	$ 30.42	$ 31.25	$ 32.11	$ 33.00	$ 33.95
Net property, plant, and equipment	15.00	17.38	16.15	14.80	13.33	11.73
Total assets	$ 42.72	$ 47.80	$ 47.40	$ 46.91	$ 46.33	$ 45.68
Total current liabilities	$ 7.24	$ 7.24	$ 7.24	$ 7.24	$ 7.24	$ 7.24
Long-term debt	7.20	7.20	7.20	7.20	7.20	7.20
Equity	28.28	29.12	25.86	27.77	29.96	32.43
Subtotal	42.72	43.56	40.30	42.21	44.40	46.87
Net financing needed	0.00	4.24	7.10	4.70	1.93	(1.19)
Total liabilities and equity	$ 42.72	$ 47.80	$ 47.40	$ 46.91	$ 46.33	$ 45.68

Greenway currently has 20 percent of its $36 million of long-term capital in the form of debt issued in 1992. The coupon, or interest rate, on that debt is 9.74 percent. It is 30-year debt with no principal repayments due until 2002. Greenway can get the $6 million it needs from either debt or equity—the sale of common stock.

Common Stock. Greenway has 926,376 shares outstanding. The market price of the shares is $27.17 per share. To obtain the needed capital, Greenway's investment banker has said that the company can issue up to 230,769 new shares at $26.00 per share.[9] Greenway has paid its shareholders, and expects to continue to pay, $2.40 per share. This dividend represents a payout ratio of almost 100 percent. The high payout ratio reflects the wishes of the company's founder and family. They hold the single largest block of stock in the company, about 30 percent of the outstanding shares. The rest of the shares are widely held in the locale in which the company operates.

Bonds. Greenway already has some debt. Any new debt would be subordinated to the old debt—that is, it would not have as strong a contract. The investment banker believes that Greenway would have to offer a coupon of 12 percent to attract buyers. These would be 20-year bonds, with interest and principal to fully amortize the debt beginning in 2002. To decide which is better, management will want to look at all the important factors, and determine which financing method will increase the value of the company more. First, let's look at the impact on the first factor in RICHS, risk.

1. Risk to Lenders

Affordability—Interest Payments. To ensure that the company can meet its debt obligations, management should determine how much cash is available to meet interest and principal payments, that is, to service the debt. The cash that will be available sets an upper limit on the amount a company should borrow. Companies that take on obligations in excess of their ability to service them readily court disaster.

In assessing how much debt a company can bear, its **debt capacity**, the manager must first forecast the company's future financial performance. While the size of the future cash flows are important, so is their variability: companies with steady, predictable cash flows can bear more debt than companies with more volatile cash flows. Because periods of cash flow shortage can

---

[9]   An investment banker assists company management in designing the security to be issued, determining when the security should be issued, how much should be sold, and at what price. In addition, the investment banking company, along with others, provides marketing and distribution, also called syndication. In the U.S. and in other countries, firms such as Morgan Stanley, Merrill Lynch, Credit Suisse, Goldman Sachs, and Morgan Granfells provide such services.

impair the company's ability to service its debt, a manager will want to be sure to forecast financial performance for the company in lean times, times of cash flow shortages.

The factors that might lead to a cash shortage will be different for each business. For some companies, an unusual demand for its products, with the resulting need for cash to finance growth, might be the time when more cash, and thus greater debt financing, is needed. For other companies, an economic recession with a decline in sales might cause cash problems. Whatever the case for the particular company, the managers should examine the cash flows under the maximum likely cash shortfall in order to determine the business's ability to meet debt payments and remain solvent.

There may be actions a company can take to free up cash during difficult periods. For example, during a recession, a company might postpone capital investments. If the cash shortfall is caused by rapid growth, management might decide to tighten credit terms and thus decrease accounts receivable. After evaluating the impact of all the cash-freeing alternatives, management can determine how much cash will be available to pay the company's debt obligations. The amount of debt this cash can service (cover interest and principal payments), should establish a company's debt limit or debt capacity.

Companies may decide to borrow less than their capacity. The actual debt level that management decides to attain is termed the **debt policy**. While debt capacity is limited by the ability of the company to service the debt, the debt policy is determined by management's judgment of the markets' reactions. The objective of debt policy is to maximize the market value of the company by minimizing its cost of capital. Let's use Greenway to see how this might work in practice.

To measure Greenway's ability to meet its cash obligations, management could use the coverage ratios discussed in Chapter 1. These ratios focus on the relationship between the company's fixed obligations, primarily debt service, and the resources Greenway has available to meet them. Obviously, the higher the ratio, the more margin for error. As shown in Exhibit 7-11, projected earnings before interest and taxes in 1997 will cover interest, with room to spare, and will do so through 2001.

$$\text{Earnings-interest coverage} \quad = \quad \frac{\text{EBIT}}{\text{Interest}}$$

$$= \quad \frac{\$4.5}{\$0.7}$$

$$= \quad 6.43 \text{ or } 643\%$$

The coverage ratios are high regardless of whether we evaluate the EBIT or cash flow relative to interest payments. Note that because Greenway does not have any principal payments until 2001, the cash flow/interest and cash flow/debt-service ratios are identical.[10]

Interest is not the only payment Greenway management wants to make. Dividends, because of the Greenway family's policies, are a high priority. Therefore, management may want to add dividends to the payments to be covered. This adjustment would reduce the EBIT coverage ratio in 1997 to 166 percent from 643 percent. This resulting figure allows EBIT to decline by 66 percent before Greenway management would have to consider revising its dividend payment plans.

Exhibit 7-13 shows what will happen to the ratios of earnings to interest coverage if Greenway chooses either debt or equity. Because the projected cost savings are not certain, it also shows what will happen to the ratio if EBIT is only $4.5 million. If the company finances its need with debt, the ratio is lower by half, but interest expense can still be covered easily. When management includes dividends, however, the contractual payment coverage ratios are just over 100 percent if new earnings do not materialize. Even if earnings do materialize, the coverage ratios leave little room for error the first year the new plant is owned and operated.

If the forecasted earnings materialize, the company can cover its debt obligations and dividend payments. In later years, because management expects EBIT to grow, coverage ratios will improve. We can conclude that lenders will feel assured that their interest payments can be met—or can we? In 1999, EBIT covers interest more than eight times. Is this enough of a cushion to comfort

EXHIBIT 7-13   Greenway 1997 Interest Coverage Ratios: Alternative Financing Schemes (dollars in thousands)

	Old EBIT		New EBIT	
	Debt	*Equity*	*Debt*	*Equity*
EBIT	$4,500	$4,500	$5,300	$5,300
Old interest	700	700	700	700
New interest	720	0	720	0
Total interest	$1,420	$ 700	$1,420	$ 700
EBIT/interest	316.9%	642.9%	373.2%	757.1%
Dividends	$2,223	$2,777	$2,223	$2,777
EBIT/contractual payments	123.5%	129.9%	145.5%	152.4%

....
[10]   The cash flow/Debt-service ratio is:

$$\frac{\text{EBIT} + \text{Depreciation} - (\text{PP\&E changes} + \text{Working capital changes})}{\text{Interest} + [\text{Principal}/(1 - \text{Tax rate})]}$$

Note that principal payments are not tax-deductible expenses and are, therefore, adjusted to a before-tax basis.

lenders? That depends on how volatile Greenway's earnings might be. Lenders to companies with very volatile earnings will want a larger cushion than lenders to companies whose earnings are quite stable.

The most common source of risk, and thus unstable earnings, is the impact of business cycles. Cyclical expansions and contractions strain a firm's ability to service product demand, maintain proper inventories, and control its resources adequately. These strains are most vividly seen in their effects on earnings and cash flow. As economic conditions deteriorate, companies are pressed to find adequate cash flow to meet their obligations.

In addition to the problems caused by business cycles, companies face other types of risks. In some industries, strikes occur with almost the same regularity as business cycles. These disruptions cause problems not only for the companies experiencing strikes but also for their suppliers and customers. There are other unforeseeable problems, such as periodic market gluts and shortages of basic raw materials, that can affect particular industries or companies. In each of these situations, a company's ability to marshal its cash resources is critical to its ability to service debt.

Greenway's earnings and revenues have been very stable in the past. Management has been able to secure equipment orders far in advance of delivery and has not been badly hurt by previous recessions. Thus, the coverage ratios should hearten lenders, if not shareholders. However, regardless of the financing method chosen, Greenway will be somewhat more risky in 1997 than it was, or than it would be without the new plant. Therefore, of the two methods, common stock financing provides better coverage in 1997.

Note that these calculations provide only an approximation of the cash available to service obligations during an adverse cycle. Greenway may be able to generate additional cash internally through astute management of inventories, accounts payable, accounts receivable, and capital expenditures. Thus, cash could increase during periods of declining sales and decline during periods of increasing sales. This strategy is, in fact, what most companies have discovered. The critical factor in the management of a company is to identify the economic situation and respond quickly to minimize any adverse impact it may have on the cash position of the company.

Affordability—Principal Repayments. Lenders are concerned not only with interest payments; they want to be certain the principal they have lent can be repaid. Since a lender's business is to make money by lending money, the lender does not want the money returned since that means the loss of interest income or creates the need to find another customer. What a lender wants is to be sure the money could be repaid. When firms are financially embarrassed, they cannot pay the interest on their debt; when they are distressed, they cannot repay the principal. To determine whether they could lose their principal, lenders often use ratios that measure the relative proportion of the company's capital they have provided. The ratio of debt to total capital is a good measure of the exposure of a lender's principal to loss.

Greenway currently has 20.3 percent of its capital in the form of debt. Exhibit 7-14 shows what will happen when Greenway adds $6 million in either debt or equity. Greenway's ratio of debt to total capital increases to 31.8 percent if it uses debt. The ratio drops to 17.4 percent if equity is raised. Increased leverage does increase the lender's risk, but does it raise it beyond a level that is acceptable?

To determine what the impact of leverage might be and whether it is acceptable, analysts often examine what others in the same industry are doing. Exhibit 7-15 provides information on others in Greenway's industry. Producers of lawn and garden equipment obtain about one-third of their capital from

EXHIBIT 7-14   Greenway Corporation Debt-to-Total Capital: Alternative Financing Methods (dollars in thousands)

	Debt Financing	Equity Financing
Total capital:		
Old	$35,480	$35,480
New	6,000	6,000
Total	$41,480	$41,480
Debt outstanding:		
Old	$ 7,200	$ 7,200
New	6,000	0
Total debt	$13,200	$ 7,200
Debt/total long-term capital:		
Old	20.3%	20.3%
New	31.8%	17.4%
Debt/equity:		
Old	25.5%	25.5%
New	46.7%	21.0%

EXHIBIT 7-15   Industry Comparisons

	Interest Coverage	Debt/Total Capital
Lawn and garden equipment producers		
RideRite Enterprises	310.3%	33.1%
Topflight Irrigators	253.7	34.3
General Cropharvester, Inc.	304.5	46.0
Greenway Corporation	642.0	31.8
Golf course equipment producers		
Fairway Products, Inc.	1,430.3	11.2
Greenskeepers Corporation	2,103.1	18.1
Sam Speed, Inc.	1,836.1	15.3
Greenway Corporation	642.0	31.8

lenders—more debt than Greenway will have if it raises $6 million in debt. In addition, Greenway's net EBIT/interest ratio would be above others in that industry. Based on these comparisons, if Greenway raises debt, it would still be following a conservative financing plan.

Greenway does not really fall into the lawn and garden equipment industry, however. A better comparison is with producers of golf course equipment. In this case, Greenway would be following a more aggressive strategy.

Based on these comparisons, management must ask itself, "Why do golf course equipment producers have less debt and higher coverage ratios?" The likely answer is that they are more affected by economic cycles than sellers of lawn and garden equipment. Lenders have thus decided that they require more protection and will lend less to producers of golf equipment.

While Greenway may well be stronger and more able to handle higher levels of debt than others in its industry, following a different financing plan is likely to cause lenders to scrutinize Greenway very carefully. Therefore, we must be certain that debt financing will indeed be better than equity financing for Mr. Greenway and the rest of the shareholders. How about the shareholders? Which would they prefer? Which alternative will create more value?

2. Income

One of the obvious impacts of debt financing on shareholder value is its effect on their income—the I in RICHS. If a particular form of financing increases the riskiness of the firm, the risk could be offset by increased income. New funds are generally invested in productive assets, with the benefits from investment accruing to the lenders and shareholders. Because the debt holders' claim, although senior, is fixed, the residual benefits belong to the common shareholders. That is why management should analyze income and value from the shareholders' point of view. Such an analysis is also consistent with the concept that management should create value for the shareholders.

In determining the impact the financing decision will have on the income of shareholders, two general costs need to be considered: first, the explicit cost of the financing—the impact on the earnings and cash flow per share; second, the implicit cost—the impact on the market price of the stock.

Cash Flow Impact. To determine explicit cost, as reflected in cash flow per share, Greenway managers will estimate the effect that each financing alternative would have on the company's cash flow per share. This analysis is similar to the coverage analysis that was undertaken to estimate the impact of risk on the company. The result is shown in Exhibit 7-16.[11] The only changes in the

---

[11] You may have noted that we are doing our analysis on a per-share basis. This is because different numbers of shares will be outstanding depending on whether management chooses debt or equity financing.

EXHIBIT 7-16 Impact on Greenway's 1997 Earnings and Residual Cash Flow of Proposed Financing Schemes (dollars in thousands except per-share)

		Old EBIT	
		Proposed Financing	
	Before Financing	*Debt*	*Equity*
EBIT	$ 4,500	$ 4,500	$ 4,500
Old interest	(700)	(700)	(700)
New interest	0	(720)	0
Profit before taxes	3,800	3,080	3,800
Taxes	(1,292)	(1,047)	(1,292)
Profit after taxes	2,508	2,033	2,508
Depreciation	1,800	1,800	1,800
Change in property, plant, and equipment and working capital	(1,800)	(1,800)	(1,800)
Residual cash flow	$ 2,508	$ 2,033	$ 2,508
Number of shares	926	926	1,157
Earnings per common share	$2.71	$2.20	$2.17
Earnings dilution	0	19%	20%
Residual cash flow per share	$2.71	$2.20	$2.17

		New EBIT	
		Proposed Financing	
	Before Financing	*Debt*	*Equity*
EBIT	$ 5,300	$ 5,300	$ 5,300
Prior interest	(700)	(700)	(700)
New interest	0	(720)	0
Profit before taxes	4,600	3,880	4,600
Taxes	(1,564)	(1,319)	(1,564)
Profit after taxes	3,036	2,561	3,036
Depreciation	2,120	2,120	2,120
Change in property, plant, and equipment and working capital*	(2,120)	(2,120)	(2,120)
Residual cash flow	$ 3,036	$ 2,561	$ 3,036
Number of shares	926	926	1,157
Earnings per common share	$3.28	$2.77	$2.62
Earnings dilution	0	16%	20%
Residual cash flow per share	$3.28	$2.77	$2.62

* New investment not included.

results from those existing before financing (the first column) are caused by the alternative financing plans.

Comparing the impacts of the two alternatives indicates that the equity alternative, the issuance of common stock, lowers cash flow per share for 1997 more than the debt alternative, with and without new earnings. Although total EBIT for Greenway is expected to increase to $5.3 million from $4.5 million as the company uses its new capital, the additional shares issued dilute the impact of increased cash flow on individual shares. Each owner now holds a smaller piece of the company, although the total size of the company has increased. A reduction in cash flow per share is a common occurrence as additional common stock dilutes the benefits of stock ownership. Still, the higher the EBIT, the more attractive debt will look, because once the debt's fixed cost (interest) is covered, the residual goes to the shareholders.

There is one more thing to notice about this analysis before we use it to help Greenway management make its decision—we focused on cash flow per share, not earnings. We did this because cash flows are the basis for valuation. However, many analysts and investors are acutely aware of earnings and how earnings change. For Greenway, the earnings and cash flow are the same: depreciation offsets new investments. However, even when this is not the case, earnings are highly related to cash flows since the new working capital and PP&E investments are the same. Whether the investments are financed with debt or equity does not make a difference.

The effects of different financing methods on the shareholders are often shown graphically in a cash flow per share/EBIT or an earnings per share/ EBIT chart. Exhibit 7-17 shows this comparison for Greenway. Each line shows cash flow or earnings per share (EPS) for a financing alternative under different EBIT levels. Since the relationships are linear, only two points are necessary to plot each of the lines. Typically, analysts determine the **break-even point—** that is, the EBIT level at which the cash flow per share or EPS figures are equivalent for the financing alternatives—and one other point. For Greenway, at any EBIT level above $4.3 million, the debt alternative will provide greater cash flow and earnings per share. The cash flow and earnings per share at the break-even point are $2.05, calculated by using this formula:

$$\frac{(EBIT - I_n - I_o)(1 - t) - P}{CS_d} = \frac{(EBIT - I_n - I_o)(1 - t) - P}{CS_e}$$

where

EBIT = Break-even EBIT level
I_o = Interest payments on old debt
I_n = Interest payments on new debt
t   = Tax rate
P   = Preferred dividends applicable to the alternative under consideration
CS_d = The number of common shares outstanding with the debt alternative
CS_e = The number of common shares outstanding with the equity alternative

The break-even formula can be solved for the EBIT level as follows:

$$\text{EBIT} = \frac{(CS_d \times I_o) - (CS_e \times I_o) - (CS_e \times I_n)}{CS_d - CS_e} + \frac{P}{(1 - t)}$$

Although cash flow (and earnings) is higher with debt financing, in only one of the past years, 1996, has Greenway surpassed the break-even levels above which debt is preferable. While debt financing does provide higher EPS for the growth rate projected, Greenway has recently passed the point at which debt financing would have resulted in lower earnings per share. Thus, there is some danger.

The cash flow per share/EBIT chart, Exhibit 7-17, demonstrates the results of leverage. As can be seen, the slope of the debt financing line is greater than the slope of the equity financing line. In other words, for the same growth in EBIT, the growth in cash flow and earnings per share under debt financing exceeds that under common stock financing. This increased rate of change is the primary advantage of using leverage, or increased debt, in financing a firm. The bigger the difference in the slopes of the two lines, the faster the rate of change and the greater the impact of leverage on earnings and cash flow.

EXHIBIT 7-17 Greenway Corporation Cash Flow/EBIT or Earnings per Share/EBIT Chart

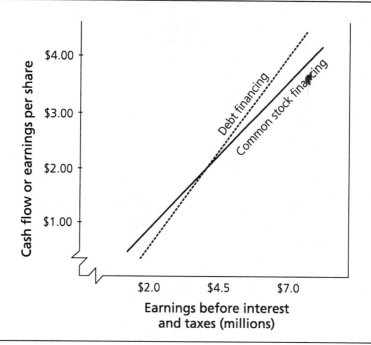

Although our focus has been on the benefits of leverage, note that below the break-even point, leverage works against shareholders. When the EBIT falls below this point, the impact of the leverage will be reversed and shareholders will suffer. The same analysis can be used to study the effect of financing alternatives on dividends per share at different EBIT levels when the payout ratio is kept constant.

Risk of Increased Leverage to Shareholders. We have seen that income increases with debt. We also concluded that lenders should see that the probability of bankruptcy is not large. The question remains, how will Greenway's shareholders see the increase in risk?

Leverage certainly affects shareholders' risk. Greenway will have higher fixed costs, and while its EBIT will not be any more sensitive to changes in economic conditions after financing costs than before, earnings and cash flows will be more sensitive. These changes affect the safety of the shareholders' returns.

In Exhibit 7-2 we saw that the value of the equity rose and fell as leverage increased. Because shareholders' risk increases with added leverage, so should the shareholders' required return. Using the two models from Chapter 6, the capital asset pricing model (CAPM) and the dividend-discount model, let us look at the effect of leverage on Greenway shareholders' required return.

Think for a moment about how changes in leverage would affect the factors used in the capital asset pricing model. Only one factor in the CAPM is company specific, the beta.[12] If Greenway takes on fixed-rate debt, the beta will increase because the after-tax earnings of the company will become more volatile. The increased volatility comes from deducting a fixed charge, interest, from the potentially volatile EBIT. Currently, Greenway's beta is 1.3. Using a theory about how leverage impacts beta, we can estimate a beta at any other capital structure. The theoretical relationship is:

$$\beta \text{ of Leveraged Firm} = \beta \text{ of Unleveraged Firm} \times \{1 + [\text{Debt/Equity} \times (1 - \text{Tax rate})]\}$$

Using this relationship, we can determine the beta under the different possible capital structures. Exhibit 7-18 shows the results. Greenway's required return on equity is that shown in the last column of Exhibit 7-18. In calculating the required return, we have assumed that lenders are willing to lend $6 million to Greenway for 12 percent, the yield on a 7-year U.S. Treasury security is 7.5 percent, the market premium is 6 percent, the tax rate is 34 percent, and that the formula above represents the relationship between capital structure and beta.

Before seeing how beta re-leveraging would affect the company's and its shareholders' value, let's double-check our CAPM estimate using the dividend-discount model as shown on the following page.

---

[12] The nominal risk-free rate of return and market premium are common factors for all risky assets.

EXHIBIT 7-18 Greenway's Beta at Different Capital Structures

Debt/Equity	Beta	CAPM Required Return on Equity
0.0%	1.11	14.2%
21.0	1.26	15.1
25.5	1.30	15.3
46.7	1.45	16.2
60.0	1.55	16.8

$$\text{Shareholders' required return} \ = \ \frac{\text{Dividends}}{\text{Market price}} + \text{Growth}$$

Because of the increase in leverage, Greenway will have to pay more interest. This fixed cost can affect the company's ability to raise its dividend, so investors' estimates of dividend growth should change. Currently Greenway pays $2.40 per share in dividends. This dividend is highly related to earnings. Greenway is mature and has had few uses for its profitability inside the company, and the Greenway family has expressed a need for the money. Before the financing, earnings growth was expected to be 5.2 percent, as shown in Exhibit 7-19. After financing, growth will increase to 6.8 or 6 percent, with debt and equity financing respectively. Given this increase in growth, shareholders might expect that management will increase dividends, perhaps at the earnings and cash flow growth rate of 6.8 percent. Using this information, if Greenway finances with debt, the dividend-discount model cost of equity would be:

$$\begin{aligned} \text{Shareholders' required return} \ &= \ \frac{\text{Dividends}}{\text{Market price}} + \text{Growth} \\ &= \ \frac{\$2.40}{\$25.50} + 0.068 \\ &= \ .162 \text{ or } 16.2\% \end{aligned}$$

This is virtually the same as the cost of equity we calculated using the CAPM.

Value. We have determined and verified the shareholders' required returns. What is the value of the company to its shareholders if the $6 million is debt- or equity-financed? To discover that answer, we need to discount the residual cash flows, shown in Exhibit 7-12. Since the two different financing methods result in different shares outstanding, the best way to see the impact on the shareholders' value is on a per-share basis. Exhibit 7-20 shows the cash flow per share under the different financing scenarios. We will discount the normalized 1998 cash flows using the perpetuity method. The normalized cash

EXHIBIT 7-19   Greenway Corporation EBIT and Cash Flow Forecasts

	1997	1998	1999	2000	2001	Compound Rate of Growth
EBIT (millions)	$5.30	$5.58	$5.87	$6.17	$6.49	5.2%
Earnings and cash flow per share:						
Without financing	3.28	3.48	3.69	3.90	4.13	5.9
Debt financing	2.76	2.97*	3.17	3.38	3.61	6.9
Equity financing	2.62	2.78*	2.95	3.12	3.30	5.9

* Earnings adapted to normal, ongoing operations.

EXHIBIT 7-20   Greenway Equity Value per Share—Two Different Financing Plans

	Equity Financing	Debt Financing
Equity required return	16.2%	15.1%
Cash flow growth rate	6.9%	5.9%
1998 residual cash flow per share	$2.78	$2.97
Value per share	$26.44	$29.00

flows eliminate unusual or one-time charges to get a forecast of what could occur over the long-term. Greenway's 1998 cash flows have been normalized by assuming that depreciation will offset capital investments and there will be no working capital increases.[13] These, plus the 1998 and 1997 annual cash flows are discounted to obtain the per share value.

The value per share if the company finances itself with debt or equity is shown in Exhibit 7-20. Clearly, given the shareholders' concern for value creation, debt financing is the preferred alternative. The per-share difference in the values is $2.56.

Debt financing increases shareholders' returns. Since the increase in income is not fully offset by increased risk, the value of Greenway increases. Thus, given our analysis, the best alternative appears to be debt financing. A debt-to-total-capital ratio of 31.8 percent should not be considered too extreme

---

[13]   Net earnings in 1998 are expected to be $3.22 million. With no new additions to working capital, and all capital investments offset by depreciation, the cash flow also would be $3.22 million. We adapt the 1998 cash flows so we can use the constant growth method of valuation from 1998 onwards. We could also have discounted the 1997 - 2001 cash flows plus a terminal value in 2001. We chose the constant growth method for brevity.

by lenders: with the addition of debt, the cost of capital should decline, and shareholder value should increase. The result will be an increased price for the shareholders' stock; and the price/earnings ratio, often a measure of the relative value of a company, should increase under debt financing, as shown in Exhibit 7-21.[14]

3. Control

Equity Financing. In addition to diluting cash flow and earnings per share, issuing equity involves a potential loss of ownership control—the "C" in RICHS: a new issue of new common stock can expand the existing ownership and dilute voting control of the current owners of the company. Whether this dilution is important depends on the distribution of ownership of the company. For companies with a significant proportion of ownership in the hands of an individual or a small group of shareholders, where the existing owners wish to maintain a dominant voting position without buying the new stock, then an equity issue may not be appropriate. Typically, the dilution issue is critical at three levels of ownership: when the ownership block will be reduced below 100, below 50, and below 25 percent.

The problem of introducing outside owners for the first time is usually more a psychological problem than a managerial one. If the original owners can still maintain an ownership position greater than 50 percent, they are in a position to continue control of the affairs of the company. The primary change will be that outside owners now have an interest in the operations of the company and may create additional accounting, reporting, and legal requirements.

In spite of the desire to own the company, there may be compelling reasons for issuing outside equity. Not the least of these is the need to develop a market for the equity to provide for liquidity in the owners' holdings. This is particularly true with owners who are aging, and whose family members are not interested in an active role. Another factor that may force a company to admit outside owners is rapid growth accompanied by capital needs that exceed the

EXHIBIT 7-21 Impact of Financing on Greenway's Price/Earnings Ratio

		New Plant	
	No New Plant	*Debt Financing*	*Equity Financing*
Earnings per share	$2.71	$2.76	$2.62
Market price per share	$26.83	$29.00	$26.44
Implied price/earnings ratio	9.9 X	10.5 X	10.1 X

---

[14] Given the strength of the ratios, it is possible that even higher leverage could be considered.

company's debt capacity or the owner's ability to provide new equity. For these or other reasons, the owner or ownership block may believe that selling equity to outsiders is necessary.

Once outside owners are involved, the original owners can maintain operating control only so long as they own 50 percent of the voting common stock. Thus, the 50 percent hurdle is a very difficult one for many owners to pass. Usually the need for outside equity must be severe before the controlling owners will relinquish their 50 percent position.

For publicly held companies with a widely distributed ownership position, effective control can usually be maintained with an ownership block of 20 to 25 percent. Through solicitation of proxy votes, an insider group with a significant minority position can dominate managerial decisions and control the operations of the company.[15] Because dilution of this block through the issuance of additional shares could eliminate effective control, dilution below this level is another critical point in evaluating equity control.[16]

Other than at these critical points, the dilution of control is not usually a significant issue when issuing equity. Obviously, for the company with a widely dispersed ownership and no significant ownership blocks, the control issue is moot.

Debt Financing. Although the control issue is more easily assessed when financing with equity, debt financing may also create some control issues. Lenders frequently impose restrictions on company operations in the form of debt covenants. These covenants may specify certain actions the company may or may not undertake, or may limit other actions. For example, loan covenants may require the company to maintain specific levels of working capital, to limit additional borrowings, or to limit the amount of dividends. The purpose of the covenants is to protect the lender's investment, but their effect may be to restrict the ability of owners or managers to operate the company as they believe necessary.

Jim Greenway and the Greenway family own 30 percent of the stock of Greenway Corporation. Since the rest of the shares are held by a large number of people, the Greenway family effectively controls the company. They certainly will be concerned about what happens to their control under different financing alternatives.

Greenway has 926,376 shares outstanding. If the company were to finance its needs with equity, 230,769 new shares would be sold. Jim Greenway and his family would then own:

---

[15] Proxy votes are the right to vote shares on behalf of the shares' owners.

[16] Companies can use equity dilution as a means of thwarting unwanted takeover bids. Through issuing new stock, the company dilutes the ownership an unfriendly suitor may have gained, thereby making the takeover more difficult. Poison pill covenants, where new stock is automatically issued upon an unfriendly takeover attempt, are often designed to create this situation.

$$\text{New proportion} = \frac{\text{Old proportion} \times \text{Old shares}}{\text{Total shares}}$$

$$= \frac{0.30 \times 926{,}376}{1{,}157{,}145}$$

$$= 0.24 \text{ or } 24\%$$

If even one person were to buy all the new shares, he or she would only control 20 percent of the company. The family would not lose effective control if the new equity were issued. Even so, the issue of control, when coupled with the fact that debt financing will increase the value of the company, should lead management to choose debt to finance the company.

4. Hedging/Speculating

Hedging and speculating, the final factors in the RICHS analysis, are actions that most of us think of in connection with the commodities or securities markets. However, hedging is really a mechanism for investors to use to insulate themselves from a change in price. One way to hedge is in the futures markets. A futures contract is a contract to deliver a particular quantity of a commodity (including Treasury bills, bonds, and stock market indices) at a particular time at a given price. A producer or owner of the commodity can lock in the price at which it will be sold (hedged) by selling a futures contract that is large enough to cover the commodity held, such as the crop expected to be harvested. Regardless of what happens to the price between the time the future is sold and the date the commodity is to be delivered, the hedger has a guaranteed price; he or she has "hedged the risk."

The same futures contract can be used to speculate. For example, a speculator, believing a commodity price will decline in the future, can sell a futures contract (without owning the commodity) and, if the price declines, cover the obligation to deliver with another, less expensive futures contract. The speculator gains the difference between the price at which the first contract was sold and the price for which the covering contract was bought.

Investors who are satisfied with the current price can hedge by locking in the price and eliminating price volatility. Investors willing to bet on the upward or downward direction of prices can speculate. Corporate managers do the same thing every time they make a financing decision. Implicitly or explicitly, they bet on the direction of interest rates and stock market levels, and they either hedge or speculate. In the past, managers have used a simple rule: match the maturity of the need (e.g., new plant to be used for a long time) with that of the financing instrument (e.g., long-term debt or equity). Using this matching principle, financing decisions were made by default. While the rule is reasonable in environments where interest rates and the stock market are relatively stable, management must make a decision whether to speculate or hedge when markets are not stable. Decisions by default can be costly.

For risk-averse managers who believe interest rates are going to change, options and futures contracts can provide protection. Change is the operative word in making this decision. Changes create opportunities for speculation or hedging. Hedging provides insurance that can be bought in the futures or options markets.

A risk-taking manager might decide to try to capture gains from cheaper financing later. For instance, if Greenway's managers believe interest rates will fall, they might choose to finance the needed $6 million with short-term money—such as commercial paper or an existing bank line of credit—and refinance later, deliberately mismatching the lives of the asset and the liability for a short time. If the managers' bet is wrong, however, and rates go up, the speculating managers will be forced to borrow later at higher rates rather than making the expected profit.

Managers deciding to finance with equity face the same hedging-speculating dilemma. Their question is, Should we issue stock at the going price, or wait until the market rises and fewer shares need to be issued to raise the same money? Typically, managers are tempted to delay issuing new equity as long as possible because they believe that, in a growing company, earnings will steadily increase, and the stock price will follow. In that case, a stock issue should be delayed to take advantage of the impact of increased profitability on the stock price.

In considering whether to hedge or speculate, management has three primary concerns: (1) the use of long-term versus short-term financing, (2) the sequencing of financing methods over time when the company needs money continuously, and (3) how to deal with multiple-currency financing. With the increased integration of the global capital markets, other questions must be faced.

1. Should nondomestic currency obligations be matched with debt borrowed in the same currency?
2. Should the manager take advantage of perceived opportunities for reduced-rate financing?
3. Should the manager take advantage of profit-making (arbitrage) opportunities that appear to present themselves to the financing corporation?

Whenever a financing decision is made, these questions must be addressed. Forecasting interest rates and market prices is difficult, and the consequences of incorrect forecasts are especially severe in planning capital structure. If forced to raise capital in unfavorable markets, a company will bear the impact of that decision for several years. Exhibit 7-10 showed the rapidity with which short-term rates can change. Rate changes in the last 20 years have been especially severe and rapid. For most growing companies, the problem is not whether to issue debt or equity, but when to do so. Growth brings with it a continuous need for funds, and most companies find that they are unable to finance growth solely through internal sources. Recognizing that the use of external capital is inevitable, companies should seek the most opportune time to enter the markets.

The implicit and explicit speculating and hedging activities involved in financing corporations today are increasingly complex.[17] A wise manager will call on experts inside the firm and at the company's bank and investment bank to explore hedging and speculating in:

1. The general level of interest rates.
2. The level of the stock market.
3. The company's stock price.
4. The quality rating of the company's debt.
5. Multiple capital markets.

These are just a few of the difficult issues that concern present-day managers. These issues are complex, increasing, and continuously changing. Because of these uncertainties, the financing decision lends itself to the sort of multiple-scenario analysis we discussed in Chapter 4. Let's use Greenway's decision to demonstrate the process.

Suppose the treasurer of Greenway decided to issue debt to obtain the $6 million the company needs, but he believed that rates would decline in the future. The treasurer would consider three probable scenarios:

1. Interest rates do not decline and the money must be renegotiated later at the same cost.
2. Interest rates decline and the money is borrowed later at the lower rate.
3. Interest rates rise and the money is borrowed later at a higher rate.

Using the framework described earlier, the manager would find that each of the three scenarios would result in a different debt cost and different values for Greenway's shareholders. Greenway's treasurer must balance the value gained if rates decline against the value lost if rates rise. In addition, the probability that each scenario will occur must be considered. This analysis can become complex and sophisticated.

5. Greenway's Financing Decision

Now back to Greenway. On the basis of Risk, Income, Control, Hedging, and Speculating, what should Greenway management choose to finance the company's needs? Since good managers create value—they add to their sharehold-

---

[17]   We also know from a number of examples that some managers who believed they were hedging were in fact speculating, or did not understand the limits of their hedging activities. Major U.S. banks and others have been involved in both unexpected activities, and in lawsuits that have resulted from these activities. The references listed at the end of the chapter provide further reading into some of these situations.

ers' RICHS—Greenway management should borrow: value will be created for its shareholders without subjecting them to undue risks.

Greenway managers should decide to use debt. Because the company was growing slowly, management would not believe it would need much other new financing in the near future and thus should not feel the need to retain much debt capacity for future use. In addition, management was likely to believe that interest rates, lower than they had been in the recent past, were unlikely to drop much further. On the basis of the analysis, management should conclude that the shareholders would prefer debt and that the risk the added debt created was not excessive.

6. Leasing

Greenway management considered one other way to finance a part of the company's needs: it could lease new equipment for the fabrication operation in the new plant. It may seem peculiar to be discussing leasing in a chapter on financing, but leasing is a form of financing. There are some who believe that the decision management should make is whether to lease or to buy equipment. That is not the decision facing management. Management must determine whether, once it has decided to get the equipment, it should use equity or debt financing to purchase the equipment or lease.

Greenway's new equipment would cost $446,975 of the total $4.5 million needed for the new plant. Greenway could, of course, borrow this amount at 12 percent, but the equipment manufacturer's representative has suggested that the company might want to lease it for $76,000 a year for 10 years. To analyze the decision, we will use net present value analysis. The discount rate would be 7.92 percent (12 percent after taxes) to compare leasing to the cost of debt.[18] If leasing provides a higher net present value, Greenway should lease the equipment. However, if borrowing yields a superior net present value, borrowing is the way it should be financed.

Exhibit 7-22 illustrates an analysis of the alternative financing schemes. By purchasing the equipment and borrowing the money, Greenway gets tax shields from deductions for both depreciation and interest. By leasing the equipment, Greenway benefits from the fact that lease payments are tax-deductible expenses. The total after-tax cost of the lease over its life is less than that from borrowing. However, these payments are level, and the costs from borrowing and owning the equipment are not: they start lower and rise. Thus, borrowing and buying the equipment is superior to leasing since the present value of the costs is lower. In fact, the present value of the lease payments is $2,538 higher. Thus, management should borrow money to buy the equipment.

---

[18]   There is considerable disagreement about the best way to analyze the lease-borrow decision. There are references at this chapter's end for those who want further reading.

EXHIBIT 7-22 Analysis of Borrow and Buy Versus Lease

| | Borrow and Buy | | | | | Lease | |
Year	Loan Payment (1)	Interest (2)	Depreciation (3)	Tax Shield [(2) + (3)] × 0.34	After-Tax Cash Cost (1) - (4)	Payment (5)	After-Tax Lease Cash Cost (5) × 0.66
1	$79,107	$53,637	89,395	$48,631	$ 30,476	$76,000	$ 50,160
2	79,107	50,581	71,516	41,513	37,594	76,000	50,160
3	79,107	47,157	57,213	35,486	43,621	76,000	50,160
4	79,107	43,323	45,770	30,292	48,815	76,000	50,160
5	79,107	39,029	36,616	25,719	53,388	76,000	50,160
6	79,107	34,220	29,293	21,594	57,513	76,000	50,160
7	79,107	28,834	29,293	19,763	59,344	76,000	50,160
8	79,107	22,801	29,293	17,712	61,395	76,000	50,160
9	79,107	16,044	29,293	15,415	63,692	76,000	50,160
10	79,107	8,477	29,293	12,842	66,265	76,000	50,160
Total					$522,103		$501,600
Net present value (@ 7.92%)					$335,258		$337,796

V. LEVERAGE IN ACQUISITIONS

We began this long chapter by discussing whether leverage can create value for shareholders and, if so, where that value comes from. It is clear that unused debt capacity reduces shareholder value. Companies that do not fully use their debt capacity are less risky for their shareholders, but they provide lower returns. These companies also are prey for acquirers willing to take more risk and use unused debt capacity.

In Chapter 5 we discussed the valuation of acquisitions and divestitures. What we did not discuss was the value of debt capacity in making an acquisition. Leveraged buyouts are examples of acquisitions in which value is created when the acquirer permanently or temporarily increases the leverage of the target. Appendix 7B discusses the evaluation of leveraged corporate acquisitions.

VI. SUMMARY

This chapter introduced you to the markets for debt and methods for determining whether using debt capital can create value for the firm's shareholders. We determined that to create value, a company's owners (or managers on their behalf) must find debt financing that increases the company's after-tax cash flows per share or reduces the company's risk. We identified one potential source of value—the tax deductibility of interest payments. With the tax advantages of debt comes increased risk to the shareholders, however. We asked, therefore, given these opposing forces, how should management determine the best financing mix for their firm?

To investigate the decisions that had to be confronted by managers, we used the RICHS analysis, looking specifically at the risk, income, and control aspects of the financing decision, and whether management, given the financing alternatives, should hedge or speculate. To see how the RICHS analysis works in practice, we examined the decision facing Greenway management. We then used net present value to determine the best choice. However, Greenway's decision was a simple one, and each decision about financing is different. The current and future capital market conditions, coupled with the company's size, condition, and its current and future needs, require analysis, insight, and judgment. The tools discussed in this chapter help the manager confront the decisions.

SELECTED REFERENCES

For information about the effects of different financing instruments on capital costs, see:

Smith, Clifford W. "Raising Capital: Theory and Evidence." *Midland Corporate Finance Journal*, Spring 1986, pp. 6-22.

For more on capital structure and its value, see:

Brealey, Richard A., and Stewart C. Myers. *Principles of Corporate Finance.* New York: McGraw Hill, 1996, chaps. 17 and 18.

Brigham, Eugene F., and Louis C. Gapenski. *Financial Management.* Fort Worth, TX: Dryden, 1994, chaps. 12 and 13.

Fruhan, William E., Jr. *Financial Strategy.* Homewood, Ill.: Richard D. Irwin, 1979.

Miller, Merton H. "Leverage." *Journal of Applied Corporate Finance*, Summer 1991, pp. 6-12.

Miller, Merton H. "The Modigliani-Miller Propositions after Thirty Years." *Journal of Applied Corporate Finance*, Spring 1989, pp. 6-18.

Patrick, Steven C. "Three Pieces to the Capital Structure Puzzle: The Cases of Alco Standard, Comdisco, and Revco." *Journal of Applied Corporate Finance*, Winter 1995, pp. 53-61.

Pinches, George E. *Financial Management.* New York: Harper Collins, 1994, chaps. 11 and 12.

Ross, Stephen A., Randolph W. Westerfield, and Jeffrey F. Jaffe. *Corporate Finance.* 4th ed. Homewood, Ill.: Richard D. Irwin, 1996, chaps. 15-16.

Ross, Stephen A., Randolph W. Westerfield, and Bradford D. Jordan. *Fundamentals of Corporate Finance.* 3rd ed. Homewood, Ill.: Richard D. Irwin, 1995, chap. 15.

Shapiro, Alan C. "Guidelines for Long-Term Corporate Financing Strategy." *Midland Corporate Finance Journal*, Winter 1986, pp. 6-19.

Shapiro, Alan C. *Modern Corporate Finance.* 2nd ed. New York: Macmillan, 1994, chaps. 14 and 15.

For more on the characteristics of debt and debt markets, see:

Brealey, Richard A., and Stewart C. Myers. *Principles of Corporate Finance.* New York: McGraw Hill, 1996, chaps. 23 and 24.

Brigham, Eugene F., and Louis C. Gapenski. *Financial Management.* Fort Worth, TX: Dryden, 1994, chap. 20.

Bodie, Zvi, Alex Kane, and Alan Marcus. *Investments.* 3rd ed. Homewood, Ill.: Richard D. Irwin, 1996, chaps. 2, 3, and 4.

Fabozzi, Frank J., and T. Dessa Fabozzi. *Bond Markets, Analysis and Strategies.* Englewood Cliffs, N.J.: 1989.

Haugen, Robert A. *Modern Investment Theory.* 3rd ed. Englewood Cliffs, N.J.: 1993, chaps. 2, 12-14.

Madura, Jeff. *International Financial Management.* 2nd ed. St. Paul, Minn.: West Publishing Co., 1989, chap. 18.

Pinches, George E. *Financial Management*. New York: Harper Collins, 1994, chap. 16.

Ross, Stephen A., Randolph W. Westerfield, and Jeffrey F. Jaffe. *Corporate Finance*. 4th ed. Homewood, Ill.: Richard D. Irwin, 1996, chaps. 14 and 20.

Shapiro, Alan C. *Modern Corporate Finance*. 2nd ed. New York: Macmillan, 1994, chaps. 18 and 19.

Shapiro, Alan C. *Multinational Financial Management*. 5th ed. Needham Heights, Mass.: Allyn & Bacon, 1996, chaps. 20 and 21.

Sharpe, William F., Gordon J. Alexander, and Jeffery V. Bailey. *Investments*. chap. 14.

For more on financing strategy, see:

Barclay, Michael, J., Clifford W. Smith, and Ross L. Watts. "The Determinants of Corporate Leverage and Dividend Policies." *Journal of Applied Corporate Finance*, Winter, 1995, pp. 4-19.

Brealey, Richard A., and Stewart C. Myers. *Principles of Corporate Finance*. New York: McGraw Hill, 1996, chap. 19.

Pinches, George E. *Financial Management*. New York: Harper Collins, 1994, chap. 14.

Shapiro, Alan C. *Modern Corporate Finance*. 2nd ed. New York: Macmillan, 1994, chap. 16.

Shapiro, Alan C. *Multinational Financial Management*. 5th ed. Needham Heights, Mass.: Allyn & Bacon, 1996, chap. 22.

For more on leasing, see:

Brealey, Richard A., and Stewart C. Myers. *Principles of Corporate Finance*. New York: McGraw Hill, 1996, chap. 26.

Brigham, Eugene F., and Louis C. Gapenski. *Financial Management*. Fort Worth, TX: Dryden, 1994, chap. 21.

Pinches, George E. *Financial Management*. New York: Harper Collins, 1994, chap. 18.

Ross, Stephen A., Randolph W. Westerfield, and Jeffrey F. Jaffe. *Corporate Finance*. 4th ed. Homewood, Ill.: Richard D. Irwin, 1996, chap. 23.

Ross, Stephen A., Randolph W. Westerfield, and Bradford D. Jordan. *Fundamentals of Corporate Finance*. 3rd ed. Homewood, Ill.: Richard D. Irwin, 1995, chap. L.

Shapiro, Alan C. *Modern Corporate Finance*. 2nd ed. New York: Macmillan, 1994, chap. 21.

For more on finance theory and financial practice, see:

Myers, Stewart C. "Finance Theory and Finance Strategy." *Midland Corporate Finance Journal*, Spring 1987, pp. 6-13.

Wruck, Karen Hopper. "Financial Policy as a Catalyst for Organizational Change: Sealed Air Corporation's Leveraged Special Dividend." *Journal of Applied Corporate Finance*, Winter 1995, pp. 20-37.

For more on financing corporate growth, see:

Cornell, Bradford, and Alan C. Shapiro. "Financing Corporate Growth." *Journal of Applied Corporate Finance*, Summer 1988, pp. 6-22.

For additional information about leasing analysis, see:

Bayless, Mark E., and J. David Diltz. "An Empirical Study of the Debt Displacement Effects of Leasing." *Financial Management*, Winter 1986, pp. 53-60.

Brick, Evan E., William Fung, and Marti Subrahmanyam. "Leasing and Financial Intermediation: Comparative Tax Advantages." *Financial Management*, Spring 1987, pp. 55-59.

Schall, L. "The Evaluation of Lease Finance Options." *Midland Corporate Finance Journal*, Spring 1985, pp. 48-65.

For more on international capital structure issues, see:

Jacque, Laurent, and Gabriel Hawawini. "Myths and Realities of the Global Capital Markets." *Journal of Applied Corporate Finance*, Fall 1995, pp. 81-94.

Shapiro, Alan C. *Multinational Financial Management*. Upper Saddle River, N.J.: Prentice Hall, 1996, chap. 17.

STUDY QUESTIONS

1. Management at Zumar, Inc., a chain of gourmet food stores located primarily in New York, was planning to expand its main store in Manhattan. By expanding, Zumar management could add an imported beer and wine section. This $15 million addition, management believed, would increase sales by 20 percent, to $120 million in the next year, 1997. The new EBIT/sales would be the same as Zumar had on its current product lines, 13 percent, and once the new beer and wine lines were established, management expected overall growth to go back to its traditional 2 percent. Taxes were expected to be 34 percent. Zumar currently had $40 million in 7 percent coupon long-term debt. While principal payments on this debt were $2.8 million per year, management expected to keep debt at this level and thus borrowed whenever principal payments were due. In addition to the debt, Zumar had 2 million shares of stock outstanding, with a par value of $2. The current balance sheet for the company follows.

ZUMAR, INC.
1996 BALANCE SHEET
(in millions)

Assets

Cash	$ 54
Long-term assets	80
Total assets	$ 134

Liabilities and Equity

Current liabilities	$ 40
Long-term debt	40
Common stock ($2 par)	4
Retained earnings	50
Total debt and equity	94
Total liabilities and equity	$ 134

To finance the $15 million needed for expansion, management had two alternatives:

a. Borrowing $15 million of 10-year, 10 percent coupon debt with annual principal payments beginning after 5 years.

b. Issuing equity of 750,000 common shares, netting, after issue costs, $20 per share.

Prepare an EPS-EBIT table and chart using the existing and proposed levels of EBIT. What is the break-even EBIT? How do you interpret these data?

2. Zumar management currently had a policy of increasing dividends about 5 percent per year. In 1996 the dividend per share was $0.75. Analyze and compare the present dividend coverage with that likely under both debt and equity financing schemes at the projected level of sales.

3. Which of the two financing schemes is expected to create more value for Zumar's shareholders assuming that:

a. there will be no changes in net working capital, and corporate expenditures will be equal to depreciation? (These aspects are typical of a low-growth company.)

b. the required return on equity is 16.9 percent if the expansion is financed with debt, and 15.4 percent if the expansion is financed by equity?

The Weighted-Average Cost of Capital and Free Cash Flow Valuation

Throughout this book, the perspective has been that of the company's owners or management working for the owners. Even when discussing how to finance the company, we took the owners' (shareholders') point of view: we treated the introduction of debt into a company's capital structure as a subcontracting of the owners' financing obligation to those with different needs, like lenders.

To value capital investments, acquisitions, and financing schemes, we made forecasts of the residual cash flows. Since residual cash flows belong to the shareholders, we discounted them at the owners' required return on equity. To incorporate the costs of this subcontracted financing, we included them into the residual cash flow analysis. An example of such residual cash flows is given in Exhibit 7A-1.

Exhibit 7A-1 shows the cash flows for Tai Chin, Inc., a company that expects sales and costs to grow at 11 percent for five years before they level off to a growth rate of 7 percent. The company currently has $7 million in debt and is in a stable market where debt levels often exceed its current 70 percent level. Management expects to continue providing 30 percent of the company's capital from owners.

In valuing a company like Tai Chin, we can discount the cash flows by the required return of equity holders, 20 percent, to obtain a value of $3 million. However, in cases like this we can take a shortcut. The shortcut is possible because the company is not expected to change its capital structure, and the required returns on debt and equity are expected to stay the same over time. When these conditions exist, we can eliminate the cash flows attributable to debt from the cash flow forecasts and include the debt financing costs in the required return on capital. This new lender and shareholder required return is called the cost of capital. The cash flows, without the financing costs deducted, are called the free cash flows, or cash flows to all capital providers. We call this the cost of capital: lenders have a required return on their capital, but because companies in many countries are allowed to deduct interest as a tax-deductible expense, the company's cost of debt is less than the lenders' required return on

EXHIBIT 7A-1   Tai Chin, Inc. Residual Cash Flow Forecast

TAI CHIN, INC.
(in thousands)

	1997	1998	1999	2000	2001
Revenues	$10,000	$11,100	$12,321	$13,676	$15,181
Operating expenses	(6,420)	(7,126)	(7,910)	(8,780)	(9,746)
Operating income	3,580	3,974	4,411	4,896	5,435
Depreciation	(1,600)	(1,776)	(1,971)	(2,188)	(2,429)
Interest	(980)	(1,088)	(1,207)	(1,340)	(1,488)
Earnings before taxes	1,000	1,110	1,233	1,368	1,518
Taxes	(400)	(444)	(493)	(547)	(607)
Net income	$ 600	$ 666	$ 740	$ 821	$ 911
Depreciation	1,600	1,776	1,971	2,188	2,429
Capital expenditures	(2,689)	(2,985)	(3,314)	(3,679)	(3,479)
Changes in					
Working capital	(11)	(12)	(13)	(14)	(13)
Debt principal*	770	855	949	1,053	744
Annual residual cash flows	270	300	333	369	592
Terminal value**					4,873
Residual cash flows	$ 270	$ 300	$ 333	$ 369	$ 5,465

Net present value (@ 20%) = $3,000

*   Since revenues grow at 11 percent with a constant capital structure with 30 percent debt, there will be annual increases in debt. Interest payments reflect these changes.
** In 2001, growth will slow to about 7 percent per year Thus, the value of the cash flows from 2001 onwards is $4,873 ($592 × 1.07)/(0.2 - 0.07).

their capital. To use this shortcut, the analyst must first determine the cost of capital (WACC) and, second, the free cash flows.

I. CALCULATING THE WEIGHTED-AVERAGE COST OF CAPITAL

The cost of capital to a company is the weighted average of all the sources of capital, calculated by multiplying the costs of debt and equity by the respective portions to be raised by the company. Remember, because the cost of debt to the company is partially offset by the tax effect, that effect must be taken into account.

$$R_{WACC} = (R_d \times D/V) + (R_e \times E/V)$$

where

R_{WACC}	=	Weighted-average cost of capital
D	=	Amount of debt expected in the firm's capital structure
E	=	Amount of equity expected in the firm's capital structure
V	=	D + E, the value of the firm's capital
R_d	=	Marginal after-tax cost of debt
R_e	=	Marginal cost of equity

Let's use Tai Chin to demonstrate how to calculate the WACC for a company. Lenders making new loans to Tai Chin say that they would require a return of 14 percent. Using the methods described in Chapter 6, Tai Chin analysts have determined that the equity holders require a return of 20 percent for their investment in the company. Management does not expect the company's current tax rate of 40 percent to change. Using these assumptions, Tai Chin's weighted-average cost of capital is 11.88 percent:

$$R_{WACC} = \{[0.14 \times (1 - 0.40)] \times 0.7\} + (0.20 \times 0.30)$$
$$= 0.1188 \text{ or } 11.88\%$$

Note that in calculating the WACC we used the marginal cost of debt, not the embedded cost, and we assumed that all the equity would come from new retained earnings. The marginal cost of debt is the cost of debt that the company will be using to finance its future operations. The embedded cost, in contrast, is the price the company has paid on debt that it took on in the past. The marginal required return on debt will be obvious if the company is in the process of arranging for new debt. If it is not, however, an analyst might use the yield-to-maturity on the company's debt that is trading in the capital markets.[1] As for equity, if the company expected to raise new equity in the capital markets, the cost would be higher than that for new retained earnings—these are costs of marketing new stock.[2]

While calculating the amounts of debt and equity used to finance the firm might appear to be quite simple, it is, like most of the analyst's jobs, not completely straightforward. The capital structure we want to use in calculating the weighted-average cost of capital is what investors believe will be the way funds are raised by the company in the future, not the proportions currently held by the company.[3] Some analysts would prefer to use the company's marginal or "target" capital structure—that structure wherein sufficient capital is

---

[1]   If there is no publicly traded debt, the analyst might use the yield-to-maturity on the debt of a comparable company or companies as a proxy. The yield-to-maturity is the rate of return that equates interest and principal payments to the current market price of the debt.

[2]   This was described in Chapter 6.

[3]   The current proportions on the balance sheet represent the cumulative impact of all past financing actions. This may or may not represent the proportions that management will use in the future.

raised to finance all value-creating investments, presuming that is the capital structure that investors will expect the company to use. For some companies, the target capital structure is one in which the cost of capital is at its minimum. For other firms, the marginal capital structure reflects a management decision to keep the leverage within a certain range. However you go about determining the marginal capital structure, it is a challenging task, since it is expected, not actual.

For simplicity, we assumed that Tai Chin's current book value capital structure was the same as its market value and target capital structures. The **book value** capital structure is the percentage of debt and equity currently financing the assets of the firm. It can be calculated directly from the balance sheet. The **market value** capital structure is calculated by taking the current market values of the company's debt and equity and recalculating the same percentages. In Tai Chin's book value capital structure, 30 percent of the capital was equity and 70 percent was debt.

We made the Tai Chin example especially easy by assuming that the book, the market value, and management's target capital structure were all the same. If they were not, we might use the current market value to provide a clue to investors' expectations, we might turn to statements made by management about its future intentions, or we might examine the financing activities of similar companies to gain insight about their practices.[4] In spite of the vagueness of the marginal capital structure, and our love of facts and ease, it is not appropriate to use either book value or market value capital structures in the calculation of WACC if they differ from the target expected for the future.

The analyst is faced with two other considerations in calculating WACC. First, the analyst has to estimate the marginal costs of debt and equity at a time when the company may be issuing neither. Even a company in need of capital usually does not simultaneously issue debt and equity securities just to fit its target capital structure. Rather, the firm would issue first one and then the other, depending on market prices and available investors in the capital markets. Over time, however, the firm would issue sufficient debt and equity to achieve its targeted capital structure.

Second, a company may be expecting to issue several different kinds of debt over time. Some debt may be placed with banks or insurance companies, and other debt may be sold to the public. Each kind of debt would have different features. The differences in such things as maturity, coupon, and security will result in different interest rates, even if it were all issued at the same time.

The marginal debt cost is an average of the costs of several kinds of debt used by the company. Most analysts exclude short-term (current) debt from the

---

[4]   While many firms use their book value structure as the target, analysts are concerned with the market value of the marginal capital raised. If the target is the same as the book value capital structure, the market value of the capital raised will be in the same proportions as the book value, regardless of the market value of the capital already in use by the firm.

calculation of the marginal cost of debt, primarily because it will be repaid within one year. Analysts have reconsidered the exclusion of short-term debt because it has become an important source of funds for many firms, either because the borrowers use it as a stopgap financing source while they wait for long-term rates to drop or because lenders prefer it in order to monitor the borrower or to frequently revise rates. The best rule for an analyst to follow in dealing with short-term debt is to exclude it if it is being used to supply temporary needs (such as seasonal inventory buildup) but to include it and its cost if the short-term funds represent permanent financing for the firm's assets.

II. FREE CASH FLOWS

The second piece of information we must have to use this shortcut is the free cash flows, the cash flows available to all capital providers. These cash flows are different from the residual cash flows, those available to shareholders. The free cash flows do not include the costs of debt or the debt principal inflows or repayments. Interest and principal flows will be taken into account in the discount rate, the WACC.

To contrast the residual and free cash flows, compare Exhibit 7A-1 with Exhibit 7A-2. The difference between the two exhibits is that the interest expense and principal payments are eliminated from the cash flows in the second exhibit. The free cash flow shown in Exhibit 7A-2 belongs to both shareholders and lenders.

We value the free cash flows by discounting them by the WACC (less any expected growth in capital, of course). In our example, the free cash flow value of Tai Chin is $10,000, which is $7,000 higher than the value we calculated using the residual cash flows and the cost of equity. In spite of the fact that it does not appear to be equal to our residual cash flow valuation, it is. The free cash flow valuation values the total company to lenders and shareholders. Thus, to obtain the value of the company to its shareholders, the value of the debt must be deducted. For Tai Chin, the free cash flow value is $10,000, and the debt value is $7,000. The resulting value of the equity of $3,000 is identical to the value we estimated from the residual cash flow valuation.

For the two valuations to be the same, both must use all the same assumptions. If they are the same, the only difference in the two methods is where the costs of debt are incorporated: in the residual cash flow, we incorporated the debt activity in the cash flows; in the free cash flow method, they were incorporated in the discount rate.

One thing that may bother you in looking at these calculation is taxes. In the residual cash flows, interest is a tax-deductible expense. In the free cash flows, the interest expense and its impact on taxes is taken into account in the discount rate. As for the new debt inflows or the repayment of debt, in the free cash flows any debt repayments would be offset by new debt. Remember, the capital structure does not change in the WACC.

EXHIBIT 7A-2   Tai Chin, Inc. Free Cash Flow Forecast and Valuation

TAI CHIN, INC.
(in thousands)

	1997	1998	1999	2000	2001
Revenues	$10,000	$11,100	$12,321	$13,676	$15,181
Operating expenses	(6,420)	(7,126)	(7,910)	(8,780)	(9,746)
Operating income	3,580	3,974	4,411	4,896	5,435
Depreciation	(1,600)	(1,776)	(1,971)	(2,188)	(2,429)
Earnings before taxes	1,980	2,198	2,440	2,708	3,006
Taxes	(792)	(879)	(976)	(1,083)	(1,202)
Net income	1,188	1,319	1,464	1,625	1,804
Depreciation	1,600	1,776	1,971	2,188	2,429
Capital expenditures	(2,689)	(2,985)	(3,314)	(3,679)	(3,479)
Changes in working capital	(11)	(12)	(13)	(14)	(13)
Annual free cash flow	88	98	108	120	741
Terminal value*					16,183
Free cash flows	$ 88	$ 98	$ 108	$ 120	$16,924

Net present value of free cash flows (@11.8%)	$10,000
Value of debt	(7,000)
Value of equity	$ 3,000

* In 2001 growth will slow to about 7 percent per year.

There is one other way we have valued a company, the dividend-discount model. If we do this for Tai Chin, and it is based on the same assumptions about the company, we should obtain the same valuation. Exhibit 7A-3 shows the dividend valuation for Tai Chin. Of course, we made the example simple for clarity, but no matter how complex the situation, if the forecasts and discount rates are based on the same assumptions, all three methods will result in the same valuation of the company's equity.

III.   WHEN TO USE FREE CASH FLOW VALUATION

Because they believe that it frees them from having to determine the explicit debt-service schedule associated with any investment, many people choose to use the free cash flow valuation exclusively. However, the WACC includes an implicit forecast of the capital structure and costs. We believe explicit forecasts are superior to error-prone shortcuts, and thus suggest that the residual cash

EXHIBIT 7A-3   Tai Chin, Inc. Dividend Forecast and Valuation

TAI CHIN, INC.
(in thousands)

	1997	1998	1999	2000	2001
Revenues	$10,000	$11,100	$12,321	$13,676	$15,181
Operating expenses	(6,420)	(7,126)	(7,910)	(8,780)	(9,746)
Operating income	3,580	3,974	4,411	4,896	5,435
Depreciation	(1,600)	(1,776)	(1,971)	(2,188)	(2,429)
Interest	(980)	(1,088)	(1,207)	(1,340)	(1,488)
Earnings before taxes	1,000	1,110	1,233	1,368	1,518
Taxes	(400)	(444)	(493)	(547)	(607)
Net income	$ 600	$ 666	$ 740	$ 821	$ 911
Payout ratio	0	0	0	0	0
Dividends	270	300	333	369	410
Terminal value					5,055
Total dividend flows	$ 270	$ 300	$ 333	$ 369	$ 5,465

Net present value of dividends (@ 20%) = $3,000

flow valuation method is superior. Using the free cash flow method of valuation exclusively is a mistake.[5]

The free cash flow valuation is an acceptable shortcut under certain circumstances. Those circumstances are when the company's capital structure, costs of debt and equity, and the tax rate are not expected to change. If they are expected to change, then the residual cash flow method is much better. There is a rational use of the WACC—to value small investments that a company frequently makes, where managers find the time and effort needed to make explicit forecasts of the financing arrangements prohibitive. While it eases the pain of valuing the myriad of small investments companies make, the result of using this shortcut in this way is to discount some investments at a rate that is too low and others at a rate that is too high. In an effort to deal with the problem and still use the free cash flow valuation, managers have adapted discount rates for risk—grouping investments into so-called risk classes. We showed such a risk class scheme in Chapter 4. In spite of its ease, except for the small projects a company evaluates, one would do better to avoid such arbitrary hurdle rates. The residual cash flow valuation is explicit. The magnitude of the

---

[5] The analyst could, of course, change both the costs of debt and/or equity or their proportions in the WACC calculation. However, if the analyst is making explicit forecasts of costs and capital structure changes, they can be incorporated directly into the residual cash flows. In many ways the WACC is an artifact of a time when analysts' tools were pencil and paper, not a calculator or computer.

potential errors when using free cash flows can be significant. These errors can be seen in such valuations as those done in leveraged acquisitions. Appendix B to this chapter describes such valuations.

IV. SUMMARY

In estimating the weighted-average cost of marginal capital, the analyst's judgment is required again and again. The costs of debt and equity and our marginal capital structure all are needed to calculate a WACC. We must try to estimate what investors expect from owning a share of our company, what lenders will require, and how we are expected to raise our capital. While we have several approaches that will help the analyst make these estimates, each must be used thoughtfully. Furthermore, as conditions in the world and domestic economies change, the capital markets react, and investors' expectations change—sometimes quite rapidly. When these changes occur, the firm itself may change: new projects may be announced, and old projects succeed or fail. Once again, investors' and lenders expectations will change, and so will their required returns. The analyst must not only estimate elusive figures, but must do so at the same time that figures are changing. Skill and judgment take the financial analyst's job beyond the mechanical and the routine, making it a continual challenge.

SELECTED REFERENCES

For more on estimating and using the weighted-average cost of capital, see references in Chapter 7 and:

Ehrhardt, Michael C. *The Search for Value: Measuring the Company's Cost of Capital.* Boston, Mass.: Harvard Business School Press, 1994.

Shapiro, Alan C. *Modern Corporate Finance.* 2nd. ed. New York: Macmillan, 1994, chap. 12.

For more on the weighted-average cost of capital in an international context, see:

Cooper, Ian, and Evi Kaplanis. "Home Bias in Equity Portfolios and the Cost of Capital For Multinational Firms." *Journal of Applied Corporate Finance*, Fall 1995, pp. 95-102.

Madura, Jeff. *International Financial Management.* 2nd ed. St. Paul, Minn.: West Publishing Co., 1989, chap. 16.

Shapiro, Alan C. *Multinational Financial Management.* Needham Heights, Mass.: Allyn & Bacon, 1989, chap. 18.

Stulz, Rene. "Globalization of Capital Markets and the Cost of Capital: The Case of Nestle." *Journal of Applied Corporate Finance*, Fall 1995, pp. 30-38.

STUDY QUESTIONS

1. Bakelite Company, located in rural Ohio, is a commercial bakery specializing in biscuit-making. Recent substantial declines in grain prices have resulted in significant raw material savings. Because prices do not need to be cut—Bakelite is already at the low-priced end of the market—its cash reserves have built up well beyond historical levels. This wealth of cash spurs management, with the support of the board, to consider some capital investments it has long deferred. The various division heads are asked to propose capital investments to Carl Borg, vice president of finance. Mr. Borg has the job of evaluating the projects and making recommendations to the board. Because it has been years since Bakelite made any really significant investments, Mr. Borg is concerned about choosing the right ones. To get some advice about making these decisions, he calls an old college friend, Jane Wilson, now a finance professor at a nearby university. Professor Wilson says that, because Mr. Borg already has cash flow forecasts from the divisions, the only thing left is to discount the flows at the relevant cost of capital.

   Mr. Borg is well aware that the company's bonds were rated B when they were issued several years earlier. The coupon rate was 17.3 percent. At present, the bonds are all held by two insurance companies, so they do not trade. The current yield on newly issued B-rated bonds is 14.5 percent.

   Bakelite is too small a company to be followed by investment services such as *Value Line*. It pays a $3 dividend, and its current market price in the over-the-counter market is $25. However, a regional investment banker has just published a brief report on the company. It includes a beta of 1.32, and the analyst's estimates for Bakelite's nominal long-term growth of 4.9 percent, a figure with which management agrees. At present, U.S. Treasury seven-year bonds are yielding 8.9 percent, and 90-day Treasury bills yield 6.5 percent. Historically, the stock market has yielded about 8.5 percent above Treasury bills and 6 percent above longer-term bonds. Bakelite's balance sheet is as follows:

BAKELITE CORPORATION
(in millions)

Assets		Liabilities and Equity	
Cash	$0.2	Accounts payable	$0.8
Marketable securities	2.3	Taxes payable	0.3
Accounts receivable	1.1	Total current liabilities	1.1
Total current assets	3.6	Long-term debt	1.3
Net property, plant,		Common stock	0.5
and equipment	1.2	Retained earnings	1.9
Total assets	$4.8	Total equity	2.4
		Total liabilities and equity	$4.8

Mr. Borg believes that Bakelite's current capital structure represents the mix the company will continue to use. Its taxes are 34 percent. What is Bakelite's weighted-average cost of capital?

2. The Select Company is in the process of developing a discount rate to evaluate capital projects that have been proposed for the following year. The company, with net income of $504,000 in 1996, has been growing steadily, with both sales and earnings increasing at about 10 percent per year. The firm's return on equity has also been fairly constant at about 12 percent per year. Without any change in the company's strategy, these trends are expected to continue into the future. At the end of 1996, the Select Company had an A bond rating. Debt on the balance sheet had been issued at an average rate of 10 percent. Long-term A-rated bonds are currently being sold at 10.4 percent. Select's stock is selling for $8.60, 300,000 shares are outstanding, and the company consistently pays out 24 percent of earnings in dividends. Because of its steady growth and performance, Select's beta is estimated at 0.98.

Based on the following data, compute the company's marginal weighted-average cost of capital, using:

a. The dividend discount model, where $g = (1 - \text{Payout})(\text{ROE})$.

b. The capital asset pricing model (six-month Treasury bills are selling for approximately 8.5 percent; U.S. Treasury seven-year bonds are selling for 10.1 percent; the expected market return is 16 percent).

SELECT COMPANY
FINANCIAL INFORMATION

	1995	1996	1997 (projected)
Profit after tax (34% tax rate)	$458,182	$504,000	$554,400
Earnings per share	1.52	1.68	1.85
End-of-year market price/share	7.40	8.60	6.90
Current assets	2,255,665	2,383,661	2,729,354
Net long-term assets	4,793,289	5,305,569	5,799,876
Total assets	$7,048,954	$7,689,230	$8,529,230
Current liabilities	$1,174,826	$1,227,692	$1,421,538
Long-term debt	2,055,945	2,261,538	2,487,692
Common stock ($5 par value)	1,500,000	1,500,000	1,500,000
Retained earnings	2,318,185	2,700,000	3,120,000
Total long-term debt and equity	5,874.128	6,461,538	7,107,692
Total liabilities and equity	$7,048,954	$7,689,230	$8,529,230

Leveraged Acquisitions

everaged acquisitions in the United States in the 1980s came to be called leveraged buyouts. Leveraged acquisitions, or leveraged buyouts, are acquisitions in which the form of the financing has the potential of significantly affecting the value of the company being bought. These highly leveraged acquisitions might be made by a management group buying its publicly held company and making it private, often in conjunction with an investment partnership, or made by an individual or company, in which case the target firm would be held, or dismantled and sold.

In general, those making these acquisitions used substantial amounts of debt to acquire a company, with the expectation of repaying the debt from the acquired company's future cash flows or from the proceeds of selling assets the acquired company owned. In the earliest part of the highly leveraged takeover binge in the United States, attractive candidates had several or all of the following characteristics:

1. Stable, predictable cash flows.
2. Little, if any, debt.
3. Assets that could be stripped from the company and sold.
4. Good quality management.

Later, as attractive candidates disappeared, many companies were acquired that met few or none of these characteristics. Many of these companies are the ones that, in the 1990s, have had considerable difficulty repaying the debt that was used to acquire them.

It is important for the manager to understand highly leveraged transactions for three reasons. First, these transactions created some of the problems that were evident in the early 1990s in the United States. Second, the analysis of these transactions is somewhat different from the basic cash flow analysis discussed in the preceding chapters. Third, "highly leveraged" is a matter of semantics: the acceptance of higher amounts of debt financing varies by country and industry and over time within a country or industry. The good manager will understand the difference between high and excessive leverage and will not underutilize leverage in the future in an overreaction to the difficulties faced by some companies acquired during periods of market excess.[1]

This appendix discusses the changes in an analysis that must occur when evaluating a highly leveraged transaction. For this discussion, we will return to an example that was used in Chapter 5, the acquisition of Tract Co. Let's evaluate the acquisition, but this time let's use significant amounts of leverage.

Lifelike Cabinet Co. management agreed to pay the full value, $5.7 million, for Tract Co. Management approached its bank about financing part of the purchase. Its bankers agreed to provide $3.7 million in debt, 65 percent of the capital needed for the acquisition. With timely principal repayments, debt/total capital would drop to 20 percent by the end of 2001. Would the value of the acquisition change if significant amounts of debt were used in its acquisition?

To determine this value, we must forecast the cash flows for the Tract acquisition, including the debt-related flows. Except for the debt-related cash flows, these cash flows are similar to those we forecast in Chapter 5 and are shown in Exhibit 7B-1. The debt repayment schedule is shown in Exhibit 7B-2. To value the leveraged acquisition, we discount the residual cash flows (cash flows to owners) by their required return on equity.

The required return on equity is more difficult to determine in a highly leveraged transaction than in a transaction where the proportion of debt used does not change over time. This is because the debt/total capital ratio changes each year. Because leverage changes each year, the owners' required return on equity also changes each year. In the case of the Tract acquisition, leverage changes until the end of 2001 when the company reaches its target capital structure of 20 percent debt/total capital.

To determine the change in the owners' required return on equity each year, we can use the capital asset pricing model described in Chapter 6 and the following hypothetical relationship:

Leveraged beta = 1 + [Unleveraged beta × (Debt/Equity) × (1 - Tax rate)]

The beta for a company such as Tract, with no debt, is estimated to be 1.05. With a risk-free rate of 5.6 percent and a market premium of 7.8 percent, the required return on equity for Tract with no debt would be 13.8 percent. The required return on equity at various debt/equity ratios would be as shown in Exhibit 7B-3. Given its leverage, Tract's required return on equity would be over 20 percent in 1997. By 2001, however, the required return on equity would be just 14.7 percent. Because Lifelike Cabinet Co. management expects to maintain a debt/total capital ratio of 20 percent (12.7 percent debt/equity ratio) into the

---

[1]   Some of the difficulties can be traced to over-leveraging companies that were not good candidates for high leverage. Other difficulties can be traced to the fact that the euphoric 1980s had not prepared many managers for the unexpectedly deep and protracted recession that followed.

EXHIBIT 7B-1 Tract's Debt Repayment and Interest Payment Schedules

Payment Schedule	1997	1998	1999	2000	2001	2002
Permanent Debt						
Beginning of year	$1,140.0	$1,140.0	$1,140.0	$1,140.0	$1,140.0	$1,140.0
Payment	(228.0)	(228.0)	(228.0)	(228.0)	(228.0)	(228.0)
New principal inflows	228.0	228.0	228.0	228.0	228.0	228.0
End of year	1,140.0	1,140.0	1,140.0	1,140.0	1,140.0	1,140.0
Interest	$ 125.4	$ 125.4	$ 125.4	$ 125.4	$ 125.4	$ 125.4
Temporary Debt						
Beginning of year	$2,565.0	$2,153.1	$1,539.0	$1,026.0	$ 622.3	—
Payment	(694.0)	(694.0)	(694.0)	(694.0)	(694.0)	—
New principal inflows	—	—	—	—	—	—
End of year	2,153.1	1,695.0	1,188.5	622.3	—	—
Interest	$ 282.2	$ 236.8	$ 186.6	$ 130.7	$ 68.8	—
Total Principal and Interest						
Principal—beg. of year	$3,705.0	$3,293.0	$2,836.0	$2,328.5	$1,765.3	$1,140.0
Principal payments	(639.9)	(685.2)	(735.5)	(791.3)	(853.2)	(228.0)
Principal inflows	228.0	228.0	228.0	228.0	228.0	228.0
Principal—end of year	$3,293.1	$2,836.0	$2,328.5	$1,765.3	$1,140.0	$1,140.0
Interest—temporary debt	$ 282.2	$ 236.8	$ 186.6	$ 130.7	$ 68.8	—
Interest—perm. debt	125.4	125.4	125.4	125.4	125.4	125.4
Total interest	$ 407.6	$ 362.2	$ 312.0	$ 256.1	$ 194.2	$ 125.4

Note: 60 percent of the purchase price is financed by debt at 11 percent interest. The principal is repaid in five years; 20 percent of the debt remains outstanding after 2001.

EXHIBIT 7B-2   Tract's Income Statement and Residual Cash Flow Forecasts (in thousands)

	1997	1998	1999	2000	2001	2002
Sales	$10,300.0	$10,300.0	$10,300.0	$10,300.0	$10,300.0	$10,300.0
Operating expenses	(9,476.0)	(9,476.0)	(9,476.0)	(9,476.0)	(9,476.0)	(9,476.0)
Depreciation	(50.0)	(50.0)	(50.0)	(50.0)	(50.0)	(50.0)
Earnings before interest and taxes	774.0	774.0	774.0	774.0	774.0	774.0
Interest	(407.6)	(362.2)	(312.0)	(256.1)	(194.2)	(125.4)
Income before taxes	366.4	411.8	462.0	517.9	579.8	648.6
Taxes	(124.6)	(140.0)	(157.1)	(176.1)	(197.1)	(220.5)
Income after taxes	241.8	271.8	304.9	341.8	382.7	428.1
Depreciation	50.0	50.0	50.0	50.0	50.0	50.0
Change in PPE	(50.0)	(50.0)	(50.0)	(50.0)	(50.0)	(50.0)
Principal inflows	3,933.0	228.0	228.0	228.0	228.0	228.0
Principal payments	(639.9)	(685.2)	(735.5)	(791.3)	(853.2)	(228.0)
Residual cash flow—no synergies	$ 3,535.0	$ (185.4)	$ (202.5)	$ (221.5)	$ (242.5)	$ 428.1
Synergies	$ 265.0	$ 265.0	$ 265.0	$ 265.0	$ 265.0	$ 265.0
Total annual residual cash flow	$ 3,800.0	$ 79.6	$ 62.5	$ 43.5	$ 22.5	$ 693.1
Terminal value*						$ 4,714.8
Total residual cash flow with synergies	$ 3,800.0	$ 79.6	$ 62.5	$ 43.5	$ 22.5	$ 5,407.9

* The terminal value was calculated using the perpetuity method, a discount rate of 14.7 percent, and no future growth.

EXHIBIT 7B-3 Tract's Required Return on Equity With a Changing Capital Structure

	1997	1998	1999	2000	2001	2002
Debt/Total capital	56.0%	47.0%	38.0%	29.0%	20.0%	20.0%
Debt/Equity	127.3%	88.7%	61.3%	40.8%	25.0%	25.0%
Leveraged beta	1.88	1.61	1.42	1.28	1.17	1.17
Required return on equity	20.3%	18.2%	16.7%	15.6%	14.7%	14.7%

* To calculate the re-leveraged beta, use the following formula:

Re-leveraged beta = 1 + [Unleveraged beta × (Debt/Equity) × (1 - Tax rate)]

Assuming: Unleveraged beta = 1.05
   Tax rate = 34.00 percent
   Risk-free rate = 5.60 percent
   Market premium = 7.80 percent

future, the required return on equity in 2001 can be used from then onward. This rate is used to determine the value of the perpetuity, the terminal value, in 2001.

The value of Tract, if the acquisition is highly leveraged, is $5.66 million. The price paid for the acquisition was $5.7 million. So where is the value? The value is in the hands of the shareholders. If the acquisition is financed with 65 percent debt, there will be 35,000 shares. The value per share is $161.71; however, if the acquisition were financed only with equity, there would be 100,000 shares. Their value per share would be $57.00 per share. This is the same impact from debt financing that we saw in Chapter 7. The added value is attributable to the tax impact of interest deductions. Clearly, using leverage in the acquisition of Tract is worth considering.

In this evaluation of a leveraged transaction, we used very high leverage. However, it is not excessive if the company can service its debt (pay its interest and principal payments). In Exhibit 7B-2 you could see that Tract could cover its principal payments in each period. Using the cash flow forecasts and doing some simple interest coverage ratios, we can determine that Tract is able to cover its interest payments, and appears to have considerable flexibility in case of an economic or business downturn. This is shown in Exhibit 7B-4. Indeed, Tract, a stable cash flow business, could easily take on high degrees of leverage, leverage that could be used in the acquisition. The limits on such leverage depend on the supply of willing lenders and the buyer's appetite for risk.[2]

....

[2]   We have not included study questions at the end of this appendix. The analytical techniques used are like those used in Chapter 5.

EXHIBIT 7B-4   Tract Co. Interest Coverage Ratios

	1997	1998	1999	2000	2001	2002
Earnings before interest and taxes	$774.0	$774.0	$774.0	$774.0	$774.0	$774.0
Interest	$407.6	$362.2	$312.0	$256.1	$194.2	$125.4
Interest coverage ratio	190%	214%	248%	302%	399%	617%

CONCLUSION

The analysis of leveraged transactions shows the attraction of using considerable debt in the financing of acquisitions. Unfortunately, some of those who made such acquisitions in the 1980s failed to evaluate fully the highly leveraged company's ability to service its debt, particularly in an economic downturn. Leverage is not the problem; the problem is that the analyst must evaluate both the potential return and the risks.

REFERENCES

For more on leveraged buyouts, see:

Brealey, Richard A., and Stewart C. Myers. *Principles of Corporate Finance.* 5th ed. New York: McGraw Hill, 1996, chap. 33.

Brigham, Eugene F., and Louis C. Gapenski. *Financial Management.* Fort Worth, TX: Dryden, 1994, chap. 24.

Clark, John J., John T. Gerlach, and Gerard Olson. *Restructuring Corporate America.* Fort Worth, TX: Dryden, 1996.

Donaldson, Gordon. "Corporate Restructuring in the 1980s—and Its Import for the 1990s." *Journal of Applied Corporate Finance,* Winter 1994, pp. 55-69.

Ferenbach, C. "Leveraged Buyouts: A New Capital Market Evolution." *Midland Corporate Finance Journal,* Winter 1983, pp. 56-62.

Fridson, Martin S. "What Went Wrong with the Highly Leveraged Deals?" *Journal of Applied Corporate Finance,* Fall 1991, pp. 57-67.

Pinches, George E. *Financial Management.* New York: Harper Collins, 1994, chap. 26.

Rock, Milton, Robert H. Rock. *Corporate Restructuring.* New York: McGraw Hill, 1990.

Ross, Stephen A., Randolph W. Westerfield, and Jeffrey F. Jaffe. *Corporate Finance.* 4th ed. Homewood, Ill.: Richard D. Irwin, 1996, chap. 17.

Shapiro, Alan C. *Modern Corporate Finance.* 2nd ed. New York: Macmillan, 1994, chap. 30.

Financial Modeling

It has long been recognized that forecasting performance—whether it is estimating the effect of marketing plans, predicting the cost savings from introducing new production methods, or forecasting future cash needs—is an art rather than a science. Although sophisticated statistical and mathematical techniques have been developed to aid in forecasting, these procedures have only assisted managers in considering the impacts on the company of various scenarios for the future.

One technique that helps managers deal with uncertainty is financial modeling. Modeling consists of determining the factors that affect the results in a situation and defining the relationships between those factors in mathematical terms. Because the results of such models are typically stated in financial terms, the technique has come to be known as financial modeling. If properly used, the modeling process can provide insights that will assist managers in making informed decisions.

I. INTRODUCTION TO MODELING

Modeling is a means for managers to examine the effects of the uncertainty of forecasts through sensitivity analysis. This analysis is also called "what-if" analysis. Using this approach, managers develop forecasts and then change the values of the information used in estimating the future results. Managers can then determine what the results would be if the values for the factors were to differ from those originally projected. By evaluating the sensitivity of the results to these changes, managers can examine the riskiness or uncertainty of the projections. In addition, managers are able to determine what factors may have the greatest impact on the results and, therefore, warrant the greatest scrutiny if the plans are implemented.

Despite the managerial value of this approach, it has typically been used to evaluate only plans or projects that would have a significant impact on the company. The primary reason for restricting its use has been the cost of developing the projections and recalculations needed for sensitivity analysis. Before the development of computers, the practicality of sensitivity analysis was very limited. In recent years, using the computer to perform the calculations for sensitivity analysis has been greatly facilitated by the development of computer languages designed to simplify the creation of models. The languages are user friendly; that is, managers can use them without the assistance of computer programmers. They allow the manager to do what he or she does best—think—and the computer to do what it does best—calculate. Using computer assisted forecasting, the manager can concentrate on understanding and describing the relationships among the important, but uncertain, factors.

Originally, these languages were developed to run on mainframe systems. Now, many modeling programs have been created for use on microcomputers: microcomputers have achieved memories once contained only in large computers. The best known of these programs are called electronic spreadsheets because of their similarity to the spreadsheets used in manual projections. Appendix B provides an introduction to one of the most popular spreadsheet programs, Excel©. In addition, the mainframe modeling languages have been adapted to the microcomputer environment. The combination of these spreadsheet and modeling programs has made computer-based modeling available for all levels of management, and for everyday decision making.

II. THE MODELING PROCESS

Regardless of the type of modeling approach used, either a spreadsheet or modeling language, the general process of developing a model is similar. The procedure for creating a model can be summarized in the following six steps.

1. Determine the Objectives

Before starting to create the model, it is important to understand the purpose of the model: what information the model is expected to provide. This understanding will let the manager know what details the model should include. Without knowing what the model should accomplish before the development process commences, the manager has no way to know whether the model is effective. Although this step may seem obvious, many modeling projects start with managers deciding to build a model before considering the model's purpose. However, unless the manager has a specific use in mind, and constructs the model to fit that use, the model is very unlikely to be a useful managerial tool.

2. Specify the Important Factors

After determining the model's purpose, the manager can then determine which factors must be included. The number of factors and detail of the data depend on the model's structure and purpose. For example, if the objective is to provide information about required inventory levels, the model will require detailed forecasts about such things as expected orders, delivery times, production capacities, and throughput times. On the other hand, a financial statement forecast might require information about general income, expense, and balance sheet accounts.

The time over which the forecast will be used also affects the level of detail required for the model. Monthly cash account projections for the next year require more detail than an annual cash account projection in a five-year model.

The general approach the manager should take is to match the detail of the input with the required detail of the output. If the objectives of the model are to provide detailed results, it should include as many important factors, stated as specifically and in as much detail, as possible. If the objectives are broad and general, the data needed are also more general and less detailed.

3. Define the Relationships

After determining the relevant information to include in the model, the next step is to define the relationships between the important factors. These relationships are stated in mathematical terms. For example, if maintenance expense for a particular machine is expected to be $100 for each 500 hours of operation, the relationship would be expressed as

$$\text{Maintenance expense} \;=\; \$100 \times (\text{Operating hours}/500)^1$$

In determining the relationships, most managers start with history. For instance, if the cost of goods sold for a company has been 85 percent of sales revenue, this would be a good basis for forecasting future cost of goods sold. This forecast is a simple one and will suffice, unless the relationship is expected to differ from its historical pattern. In addition to this exception, the manager may be forecasting relationships with which there is no past experience. When this is true, the manager must rely on expectations to describe the relationship. Fortunately, any relationship in a model can be changed, and the new forecast can be evaluated as often as the manager chooses or as conditions change.

4. Construct the Model

After the relationships among the relevant factors are defined, these relationships, in the form of mathematical expressions, are combined to form the model. The specific procedures for combining these relationships will depend on the modeling system being used. (See Appendix B for instructions on entering model statements using Excel©). Different systems require the model to be

------

[1] The procedures for naming the variables and the mathematical operations used to specify the relationships are different in each modeling system.

constructed in different ways. Some systems require no particular order, while other systems are more procedural in nature and require that the statements be placed in a specific order.

Managers often undertake the model-construction step as the first rather than the fourth step in the modeling process. This mistake often results in a less usable or an unusable model. Thus, having a plan and understanding the various relationships facilitates the final construction.

5. Validate the Model

Once the model is constructed, it is critical to ensure that it is working correctly by verifying the accuracy of the output. Unusual results are an immediate clue that a mistake may have been made. While unusual results are an obvious clue to a potential mistake, the only reliable way to ensure that the model is providing reliable results is to verify its accuracy manually: a process that is much easier with simple models. For more complicated models, it is useful to separate the model into simpler pieces and validate each piece. This approach simplifies the building and testing of the model.

6. Document the Model

Unfortunately, most modelers stop once the model has been constructed and tested. The problem with ending at this stage is that few models are self-explanatory, and although an explanation of the model and the nature of the relationships is not critical when the manager uses the model immediately, problems can occur when others use it or when the manager returns to it later. For this reason, it is important to document the variables and relationships used, the critical assumptions, and other relevant factors. The usefulness of the model is greatly increased if other managers can understand and use it. If it is only to be used occasionally, a well-documented model will save the manager time each time it is used.

The documentation process begins with the construction of the model itself. The interpretation of the model can be increased by using variable names whenever possible. SALES IN YEAR 1 or SALES1 is more understandable than B3. Most spreadsheet programs allow the assigning of names to ranges or blocks of variables, and the inclusion of comments. The use of these features provides a type of self-documentation for the model.

III. SENSITIVITY ANALYSIS

The process of planning, constructing, and testing a model is a time-consuming task. If the manager has no intention of evaluating any of the relationships included in a model, then the use of a computer-based modeling system may not be required. However, since the relationships between variables are rarely known with certainty, the ability to change the relationships and observe the results is an important managerial tool. It is in this process of sensitivity analysis that computer-based modeling excels.

Sensitivity analysis is often called "what-if" analysis because it allows the manager to ask the question, "What if the nature of a relationship or the value of a factor were to change?" Because the computer can quickly recompute the model forecasts following a change in any of the variables, it is a simple task for the manager to vary any of the relationships. The computer reduces recalculation time to less than seconds, and in some cases performs almost instantaneously.

Sensitivity analysis has its dangers, however. Because it is so easy to make changes in the variables, one can become overwhelmed with numbers. When calculations are done by hand, managers make only a few changes in relationships, those that are believed to be realistic and possible. Although computer modeling systems have removed the time constraint, they should not be used to replace managerial deliberation. Changing factors over unrealistic ranges may result in more data than the manager can assimilate and use. Instead of providing too much data, the modeling approach should lead to better managerial analysis and decision making.

The crucial skill is determining which variables to analyze. The manager should be seeking insights to and understanding of the problem, not simply a vast array of numbers. Although the critical factors will differ from situation to situation, a few general comments can be made.

1. Most models are based on a few key assumptions. Sensitivity analysis should be performed on these factors to determine how sensitive the results are to changes in these key assumptions.
2. The manager should examine with special care the effects of changes in relationships that were based on changes from historical results or were forecasted for areas where the company had no previous experience. An efficient means of doing this is through an iterative approach: the manager changes the value for one variable for each iteration, or time, the model is run. The more uncertainty surrounding any relationship, the greater the need for analysis of the relationship.

In addition to "what-if" sensitivity analysis, accomplished by changing the value of one or more relationships, some modeling systems are designed to allow the manager to perform optimization or goal-seeking analysis. It is possible to do the analysis through a trial-and-error process of changing the value of one variable and observing the effect on the goal or target variable. This process is repeated until the target is reached. Although a laborious process, this approach can provide useful results.

Another approach to sensitivity analysis is to develop various sets of relationships based on different scenarios. The manager determines possible future events or combinations of events and runs the model, using the appropriate relationships for each of these scenarios. For example, in modeling a new product introduction, the manager might develop scenarios for possible competitive reactions, different economic environments, and alternative marketing strategies.

Some modeling systems also allow the manager to use probability distributions instead of a specific relationship between variables. To use this approach, the manager includes a range of values for each factor and a probability distribution for the values in the range. The model then randomly selects one value from the range, calculates the results of the model using that value, selects another value, and recalculates the results. This approach, known as simulation, provides the manager with a distribution of outcomes instead of a specific estimate of the results.[2]

Simulation provides useful information about the range of possible results. Unlike goal seeking, however, if simulation capabilities are not available on the modeling system, it is difficult to duplicate the process through successive recalculations of the model.

IV. SUMMARY

The purpose of modeling is to provide the manager with useful information for decision making. The advantage of using modeling is that the manager can directly examine the results of various decisions or the impact of various factors before having to implement the decision. Modeling helps the manager understand the risks of the alternatives and provides useful information for monitoring critical variables.

With the development of microcomputers and modeling systems that run on these systems, the power of modeling is now available to all managers. The proper use of financial models provides better information for managerial decision making.

---

[2] For a description of the process, see David B. Hertz, "Risk Analysis in Capital Investment," *Harvard Business Review*, September-October 1979, pp. 169-181.

Using Excel©

A s discussed in Appendix A, computer-based financial modeling has revolutionized the use of computers for business applications. Many different modeling programs are available for both large and microcomputers. The programs vary in price, ease of use, and level of sophistication.

A popular approach to financial modeling on microcomputers uses electronic spreadsheets. These programs simulate the familiar spreadsheet format used in accounting. Their popularity comes from the ease with which managers can make changes in the spreadsheet. This, along with their flexibility, facilitates their use in sensitivity analysis.

One of the most popular spreadsheet programs is Excel©. This program follows the current trend in software development by including several different capabilities into one integrated package. In addition to a well-developed spreadsheet program, Excel© also includes a graphics program and data management system. The advantage of this integrated approach is that it allows the user to shift easily from one type of data analysis to another. Most of these spreadsheet programs also are a part of a package that includes word processing and presentation preparation programs. These packages of programs, or suites, when coupled with computers with sufficient internal memory, allow the user to switch between programs freely and to move data, pictures, and text from one program to another.

This appendix provides an introduction to the spreadsheet and graphics capabilities of Excel©. We choose Excel© because of its widespread use among business professionals. It should be understood that this appendix is not an endorsement for Excel©. It is a guide to one standard spreadsheet program. Other programs, such as Lotus 1-2-3©, could have been used to demonstrate the process.

The approach used by Excel© is similar to that taken by most popular spreadsheet programs available for use on personal computers in a Windows-like environment. The following instructions are designed to provide only the bare essentials necessary to begin the program. For a description of capabilities other than those we have described, refer to the Excel© User's Manual. This appendix is not intended as a replacement for the manual.

I. THE COMPUTER

The computer is the device that is used to store and process data. The computer consists of several pieces: a monitor, a central processing unit, disk drives, a keyboard, and a mouse. The **monitor** resembles the screen on a television and is used to view what you are doing. The box to which the monitor is attached is the **central processing unit** (CPU), where the commands of the program are executed. The **disk drives** are the slots where you insert your **diskettes**. Diskettes contain data or the programs that provide instructions for the CPU. Diskettes are inserted into disk drives every time you want to use data or a program not contained in the internal memory or **hard disk**, the permanent storage for a large number of files contained in the CPU. You can think of a diskette as a file folder in an ordinary office. Generally the diskettes are made of plastic, and need to be handled with some care. The disk can also be a compact disk to be read in a laser disk reader, now available with many computers. The compact disk holds much more information than a diskette. The hard drive can be thought of as a file cabinet filled with files. The hard disk enhances the speed, memory, and capabilities of your CPU. Finally, the **keyboard** and the **mouse** are the tools by which you communicate with your computer. A keyboard is like the keyboard of a typewriter with an added numeric keypad and directional arrow keys. The mouse is a device that allows you to move an arrow, or cursor, around the screen and to execute instructions in certain kinds of programs and on certain kinds of computers. Keyboards and mice vary in style and capabilities, so you must become familiar with the one attached to your computer. Exhibit B-1 is a diagram of a typical desktop computer.

Instead of a desktop computer, you may be using a **laptop** or **notebook** computer, one in which the CPU, monitor, and keyboard are integrated in one piece. Even the smallest notebook computers are composed of the same pieces as a desktop computer. Only the configuration and the size is different.

II. GETTING STARTED

1. Hard Disk Drive Without Windows

1. Turn on your computer.
2. The C > prompt will appear. The letter in the prompt corresponds to the letter assigned to the hard disk drive. It is usually "C."
3. Type **CD\EXCEL**, and press [ENTER]. This command tells the computer to go to the directory that contains the program or instructions for using Excel©.[1] The directory containing Excel© on your computer may be called something other than Excel©. If so, type **CD** and the name of

---

[1] All entries to be typed are boldface and underlined. If they involve letters, the letters are capitalized. Brackets [ ] indicate a key on the keyboard to press.

EXHIBIT B-1 The Typical Desktop Computer

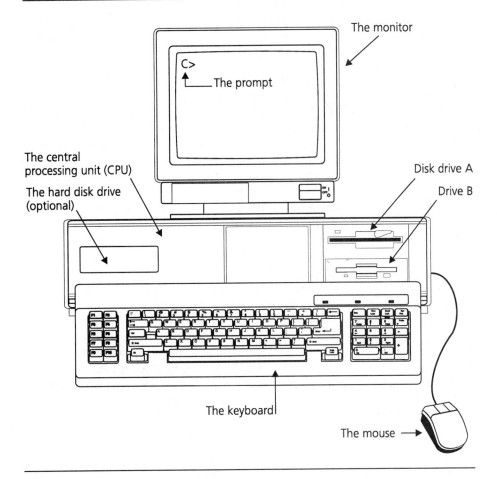

the directory containing the Excel© program files. Note: Some computers have been programmed to show a menu after the initial loading routine. If such a menu appears, select Excel. If Excel does not appear, exit
to DOS and type **CD\EXCEL**.

4. Do not turn off the computer while you are using the Excel© program.
   Exit the program before turning off the computer.

2. Hard Disk Drive With Windows

1. Turn on your computer.
2. After the Windows main desktop appears find the icon (picture) that
   represents the Excel© program, point to it with the mouse, and double-

click with the left mouse button, or press [Enter].[2] The icon representing the Excel program usually looks like a three-dimensional letter X.[3]

3. Excel© will be automatically loaded.
4. Do not turn off the computer while you are using the Excel© program. Exit the program before turning off the computer. Follow the manufacturer's instructions for turning off the computer.

After Excel© has been loaded, the Access Command Menu shown in Exhibit B-2 will appear. The words on this row indicate the functions available. As you point and click on one of the words, a drop-down menu containing the subcommands will appear. One drop-down menu is shown in Exhibit B-3. For more information about any of the functions, or for instructions on how to do any of the activities, use the *Help* command, the command at the end of the row.[4] Help will guide you through any of the activities.[5] Note, different versions of Excel© will have variations of the command and subcommand lines. You must become familiar with the version installed on your computer.

Below the Access Command Menu line are a number of icons or pictures which represent frequently repeated tasks. The whole row is called a **toolbar**. You may bypass the Access Command Menu line by using the mouse to point the cursor arrow at the icon representing the task you want accomplished and clicking on it with the left mouse button. You may customize this icon line and/or add other toolbars having specialized uses.[6]

After the program is loaded, you will have a spreadsheet with up to 256 columns (labeled by letters or combinations of letters) and 16,384 rows (labeled by numbers). Each position on the spreadsheet is identified by a column letter and row number—for instance, A1 or B45. When a new spreadsheet is loaded, the cursor will be located in cell A1. The spreadsheet on the screen will be Rows 1 through 20 and Columns A through H. To see other parts of the spreadsheet, you must move the cursor, or use the [Tab] or [Page Up] and [Page Down] keys.

EXHIBIT B-2   Top of Excel© Screen with Cell Contents Line

File	Edit	View	Insert	Format	Tools	Data	Window	Help

---

[2]   There are a number or ways that your computer might access Excel.
[3]   If your computer is using Excel© Version 7.0, you will access the Excel program via the choice of a file. Consult your manual if this version is installed on your computer.
[4]   Bold italics indicate a command or subcommand in Excel. To execute the command, point with the mouse and click on the command with the left mouse button.
[5]   For Lotus 1-2-3© users, the Excel program allows you to use the same keystrokes as used in Lotus, and it will provide a step-by-step tutorial on the Excel procedure.
[6]   There are a number of icon lines or task bars. You may choose the ones that you want to have readily available using the *Toolbars* subcommand under the *View* command.

EXHIBIT B-3   Excel© File Drop-Down Menu[7]

File	
<u>N</u>ew <u>O</u>pen <u>C</u>lose	
<u>S</u>ave Save <u>A</u>s Save <u>W</u>orkspace	
<u>F</u>ind File Summary <u>I</u>nfo	
Page Set<u>u</u>p Print Pre<u>v</u>iew <u>P</u>rint	

III. CREATING A SPREADSHEET MODEL

To learn to use Excel©, the best approach is to create a model. Assume you are the financial analyst for Quickstudy Co., and you want to create and study a forecast of the company's income statement for the next year. Before you start, you will need a few basics about moving around the spreadsheet. First point to and click on the *File* command, followed by the *New* subcommand.[8] Using the mouse, move the cursor to where you want to make your first entry in the spreadsheet.

1. Moving the Cursor

The cursor is always in position A1 when a new worksheet is started. The position of the cursor determines where entries are made on the worksheet. The position of the cursor is indicated in the upper-left corner of the screen above the worksheet on what is called the cell contents line, the line that shows what was typed or entered into the cell.

The cursor can be moved in six ways:

1. **The Mouse.** The mouse is a small, hand-manipulated roller ball that moves the cursor smoothly around the screen. The ball may be on the

----

[7]   Throughout this appendix we describe Excel© commands and subcommands that may vary somewhat from version to version. For instance, Excel© 7.0 adds three subcommands in the File command.

[8]   Throughout this appendix, we will note commands and subcommands using bold italics, underlined boldface to indicate what should be typed, and brackets to indicate keys to press or click.

top or the bottom of the mouse, and the mouse may be stationary or may move. The cursor is normally shown as an arrow on your screen. If an hourglass appears, it is your indication to wait as the program executes a task. To execute an action once the mouse has moved the cursor to the correct spot, click with the left mouse button. The cell will now appear highlighted. To highlight an area, point the cursor at one corner of the area you wish to format, click the left mouse button, and, keeping it depressed, move the cursor to the other corner of the area and then release the button.[9] The highlighted area is outlined.

2. **Arrow Keys.** The four arrow keys located on the numeric or cursor control keypads are used to move the cursor when no mouse is available.[10] Pressing on one of the arrow keys moves the cursor one cell in the direction the arrow is pointing. To increase the speed of movement while using arrow keys, just depress and hold down the key. To highlight an area, using the appropriate arrow key, move your cursor to the beginning of the area to be highlighted. Depress [Shift] and the appropriate arrow key until the cursor moves to the end of the area. The area will be highlighted. Once you have highlighted the area you want, release both keys. The area will remain highlighted.

3. **End Key.** Pressing the [End] key followed by one of the arrow keys will move the cursor to the next blank cell if the cursor is on an entry, or onto the next entry if the cursor is on an empty cell.

4. **Pg Up, Pg Dn**, and **Tab Keys.** Pressing either the [Pg Up] or [Pg Dn] key will move up or down one page at a time. Pressing the [Tab] key will move the worksheet one column to the right or left. To access the left tab key, depress the [Shift] key while pressing the [Tab] key. To move one page to the left or right, use either the [Pg Up] or [Pg Dn] key in conjunction with the [Control] key. You may also use the page up and down functions by pointing the mouse to the double arrow up or down to the right side of the spreadsheet, and clicking with the left mouse button.

5. **Go To** Command. Pressing the [F5] key invokes the *Go To* command. When you press this key, a box, called a dialog box, will appear.[11] You may type in the coordinates of the position you would like the cursor to be and then click on [OK]. The cursor will move to the entered position. You may also click on *Edit*, and in the dialog box that appears, enter the cell to which you wish to go.

6. **Home** and **End Keys.** Pressing the [Home] key will move the cursor to column A. By pressing the [Home] and [Control] keys together, the

---

[9]   You may also change the column width in the *Format* command.
[10]   You may also move the spreadsheet up or down one line at a time by pointing the cursor at the single arrows on the right side of the spreadsheet, and depressing the left mouse button.
[11]   A dialog box is a box that appears when executing a command or subcommand. In the box you are queried for information to perform the command.

cursor will return to cell A1. Pressing the [End] and [Control] keys together will move the cursor to the end of the spreadsheet area.

2. Entering Words and Numbers

Now that you have familiarized yourself with the movement of the cursor, you can begin to enter words and numbers. As you make an entry, it appears on the screen on the entry line above the worksheet. The column width is 10 characters, so longer entries will show only the first 10 characters when entered on the worksheet. To widen or narrow the column, click on the *Format* command, *Column* subcommand, and either type in the width you want or use the autofit or best-fit function. This will automatically make the cell as wide as what it contains. To do this for a range of cells, highlight the area before formatting it.

There are three types of entries: labels, values, and relationships. The easiest way to learn to use each of these is to create a model. Using the following information, we will create a simple income statement for Quickstudy, Inc.

- Sales will be $100,000.
- Cost of goods will be 65 percent of sales.
- Selling, general, and administrative expenses will be 15 percent of sales.
- Interest expense will be $5,000.
- Tax rate will be 34 percent.

To create an income statement using Excel©, you will need to label the items (for instance, sales), enter values (for instance, $100,000), and enter relationships (for instance, -0.65 × Sales, for cost of goods sold).

Label. A label can be a combination of letters, symbols, and numbers. All labels are shown starting at the left of the column, or left justified. If you want the label centered or right justified, use the icon on the toolbar that shows the text justification. For our example, make sure the cursor is on cell A1, and type **Sales**. After you have typed any entry in a cell, you must press [ENTER] to signal that you have completed the entry.

After the word SALES has been typed and entered, move the cursor to cell A2 and type **Cost Of Goods Sold** and press [ENTER]. Enter the rest of the labels in cells A3, A4, and A5.

Value. Values are entered in a similar way. For our example, after all the income statement labels are entered, move the cursor to cell B1, type in the value of the sales, **100000,** and press [ENTER]. Values are fixed or constant numbers and are entered with decimals but without currency signs or commas. We will discuss how to create spreadsheets in currency and other formats later. If the number is negative, type a minus sign (-) before entering the number.

Relationship. In our income statement example, cost of goods sold is expressed as a relationship. A relationship is a formula or mathematical relationship relating one item to another. In our example, cost of goods sold is related to sales. Remember that every formula entered in Excel© must be preceded by an equal sign and an operator such as an addition (+) or subtraction (-) sign. Because cost of goods sold is a cost, we will enter the relationship in B2 as =-.65*B1, or =-B1*.65, followed by [ENTER]. Note the multiplication sign is a star (*). At the top of the screen beside the cell address B2, you will see the formula that you typed. In the cell itself, you will not see the formula. Instead, you will see the result of multiplying the value in B1 by negative 0.65, or -65000, as shown in Exhibit B-4.

In addition to typing in the formula, you can use the cursor to indicate the cell address being used in the formula. For instance, move the cursor to B2 again. This time, type in the equal and minus signs and then move the cursor to cell B1, click, and type *.65. Press [Enter] to indicate that you are finished. At the top of the screen you will see the same formula you previously entered by typing =-B1*.65. You may use the cursor to point out the appropriate cell after each operator in a formula.

One very useful command is the sum command, also shown as Σ on the toolbar. This command sums all the highlighted numbers. If the numbers you want to include are not highlighted when you have clicked on Σ, use the cursor to highlight the area you want summed, then press [Enter]. In Exhibit B-4 we added the gross income; selling, general, and administrative expenses; and interest expense to get the profit before taxes. To do this we used the sum command to calculate the income before taxes and the net profit. Note, costs must be entered as negative numbers for the summation command to be successfully used.

For more complex formulas, you must indicate how the formula is to be executed. For instance, suppose the we had the following situation:

Position	Contains the Value
A6	10
A7	2
A8	5

EXHIBIT B-4   Excel© Spreadsheet for Quickstudy Income Statement

Sales	100,000
Cost of goods sold	-65000
Gross income	35000
Selling, general, and administrative	-15000
Interest expense	-5000
Income before taxes	15000
Taxes	-5100
Net income	9900

If you entered the expression $= + A6 + A7*A8$ into a cell, the result will be 20. Excel© first multiplies A7 times A8, and then adds the result to A6 (2 * 5 = 10 then 10 + 10 = 20). If you wanted to add 10 + 2 and then multiply the result by 5, you needed to enter it as $= + (A6 + A7)*A8$.

When you have entered all the remaining data for the income statement, you may decide that you want to add underlining to indicate totals, for instance, under cost of goods sold and before the net income total. Excel© will allow you to underline any cell by having your cursor on the cell, then pointing to the underline icon (a "**U**" on the toolbar) and clicking on it. You may underline more than one cell by highlighting the range and then pressing the underline icon. You may also change to double underlining using the *Format* command.

3. Adding Rows or Columns

To add a row or column, go to the *Insert* command and select *Rows* or *Columns*, depending upon which you want to add. You should have your cursor below where you want the row added, or to the right of where you want the column added. You may add several columns or rows by highlighting the area where you want them inserted before executing the command.

After you have added the rows and the underlines, your spreadsheet should appear in cells A1 to B11 and look like that shown in Exhibit B-4. Computer notations, also called the **spreadsheet background**, should look like Exhibit B-5. The background can be seen only by moving the cursor to the appropriate cell address and viewing the cell contents at the top of the screen.

4. Mistakes and Typographical Errors

Before [ENTER] is pressed, errors may be corrected using the [Del] or [Backspace] keys. The [Del] key deletes the character at the current entry posi-

EXHIBIT B-5   Excel© Spreadsheet Background to Quickstudy Income Statement

ROWS	COLUMNS	
	A	B
1	Sales	100000
2	Cost of goods sold	=-0.65*C3
3	Gross income	=+C3+C4
4	Selling, general, and administrative	=-0.15*C3
5	Interest expense	-5000
6	Income before taxes	=SUM(C5:C7)
7	Taxes	=-0.34*C8
8	Net income	=SUM(C8:C9)

tion. Pressing the [Backspace] key erases the character to the left of the current entry position. Use the arrow keys to move your cursor in position to make the correction.

After [ENTER] has been pressed, there are three methods of making changes. First, you can position the cursor at the cell you want to change and retype the entry. This overrides the previous entry. Second, you can point your cursor at the cell you want changed, click, then move your cursor to the entry line shown at the top of the spreadsheet. Click, change the entry, and press [Enter] when you are done. Third, you can use the [F2] key to enter the edit function. You can then add, delete, or change any section of the entry in the command line. New commands are automatically inserted without deleting any of the previous characters. When you are finished, remember to complete the entry by pressing [ENTER].

If you mistakenly delete something, Excel© allows you to undo the last operation, whether it is deleting the contents of a cell, range, or other operation. To undo the last operation, press the undo arrows on the toolbar, the arrows with curved lines. The *Undo* arrow points to the left, the *Redo* arrow points to the right.

5. Getting Help

The Excel© program will provide help on demand. Press the *Help* command or the help icon, an arrow and question mark on the same icon. Once you have the help menu, you may either look at the *Contents*, or you may choose the *Index* or *Search For Help On* command. Once you have made this choice, you will see a blank line. Type in the key word for which you want help, and Excel© will move you to that portion of the index. Highlight the entry for which you want more information, click, and a dialog box containing an explanation will appear. You may also use the [F1] key to obtain help at any time.

6. Saving Your Spreadsheet

To save your spreadsheet, click on the *File* command and *Save As* subcommand. You will see a dialog box. In the box you will need to enter two things, the file name and the directory to which you want it saved. The file name is the name you want to give your file. It is wise to give files recognizable names. There are two directories into which you can save your file. You can save it to the hard disk or to a diskette.

1. **Hard drive.** To save the file to the hard, or internal, disk drive, designate the "C" drive in the dialog box. This is the drive that is usually shown in the dialog box. You can also choose to save the file to a specific directory on the designated drive. You must tell the computer which directory you want, for instance, Excel. You may also designate a subdirectory to which you want the file saved, for instance, "myfiles." Directories and subdirectories must have been named and created before they are used

the first time. Directories and subdirectories can be created from File Manager in Windows or the file management section on your computer's main menu. The combination of the drive, directory, subdirectory, and file name create what is called the path. The path for Quickstudy might look something like C:\MSWORKS\Excel\myfiles\quick. Consult the instructions for your computer for creating directories and subdirectories. After you have entered the drive, directory, and file name, click on [OK].

2. **Save to a diskette.** Make sure you have a formatted disk of the appropriate size for your computer. If you are not using a formatted disk, Excel© will query if you want the disk formatted when you try to save. The disk must be formatted before a file can be saved. To save the file:

   a. insert the formatted disk in the external disk drive, usually designated as "A,"[12]

   b. change the drive to which you want the file saved to "A" in the dialog box,

   c. enter a name for your file in the appropriate box, and

   d. click on [OK].

Once you have saved your file the first time, the name for your file will be shown at the top of the spreadsheet. You can use the quicksave icon on the toolbar, which looks like a computer disk, to save your file once you have chosen its name and saved it the first time.

7. Printing the Spreadsheet

Now that you have completed the income statement and saved it, you may wish to print a copy. To print the Quickstudy income statement model, follow these steps:

1. Make sure the printer is turned on and set for online.

2. Using the cursor, point to the upper-left position of the block of your spreadsheet, A1. Depress the left mouse button and highlight the area to be printed, A1 to B9.

3. Click on the *File* command, *Print* subcommand, and choose *Print*. Use the mouse to move the cursor in the dialog box. You do not need to select and enter choices for all the boxes shown. Once all the data are entered, click on [OK] to begin the printing. You may preview what will be printed before it is sent to the printer by clicking on *Print Preview* in the *File* command.

Most printers used with microcomputers print 80 columns across a page. Therefore, if you have a model with a large number of columns, one part of the

---

[12] In most computers the external disk drive is designated as "A." It may, however, be designated by a different letter in your computer.

model will be printed on the first page and the rest on subsequent pages. The same continuation procedure is followed for models with more than 56 rows.

You may change how the model is printed in two ways. First, if the model has many columns, you may choose to print the model sideways on the paper. To do this choose the *File* command, *Page Setup* subcommand, and, on the *Page* section, choose *Landscape*. If you wish to print in the normal way, choose *Portrait*. Once this is done, choose the *Print* subcommand and then *Print to Fit*.

Once you have chosen how to print, you must choose what to print. You many print the whole spreadsheet by choosing *Whole Spreadsheet* in the "Print What" section of the *Print* dialog box, or you may highlight the area you want to print and then choose *Selection*.

8. Ending a Session

After you have completed a model and printed it, you may want to exit from Excel©. To do this, click on *File, Close, File, Exit*. Follow the manufacturer's instructions for turning off your computer. Do not turn off the computer until the disk drive light is off.

IV. MORE COMPLEX MODELS

In the preceding section, you learned how to enter a simple income statement for one year. The same principles can be applied to creating more complex income statements or other financial models. In this section we will demonstrate how to use Excel© for financial forecasting and planning. In order to do this, let's go back to the income statement spreadsheet model already developed. First, load the Excel© worksheet program as described in the GETTING STARTED section. Click on *File* and *Open*. You will see a dialog box. Enter or click on the drive where your file is located, "C" for the hard drive, "A" for the external drive. If your drive has a number of directories, they will be listed. Choose the one where your file is located by highlighting the selection and clicking on [OK]. Once you have designated the drive, directory, and/or subdirectory where your file is located, you will see a menu of the files contained in that directory or subdirectory. Highlight your file by clicking on it with your mouse, and click on [OK]. You may also use the *Open File* icon, which looks like an open file folder.

1. Creating a New Worksheet

If you have been working on one model and wish to start a different one, you can do this in two ways. If you want to add a new page to the spreadsheet file you are using, click on *Sheet 2* at the bottom of your screen. If you want to start a whole new file, click on *File, New*. A new spreadsheet file will appear. You will have to give it a new name. You may also open a new worksheet by clicking on the icon that looks like a piece of blank paper on the toolbar. When a new spreadsheet file is opened, the file you were working on does not disappear. Instead, it is "underneath" the new file. To access it, click on *Window*. At the bottom of the drop-down menu is a list of the open files. Click on the one you want to use.

2. Copy Command

In order to use Excel© for financial modeling, you will want to use the *Copy* command. The *Copy* command enables you to copy or duplicate relationships, values, or labels across many columns or down many rows. The relationship, value, or label that you wish to copy is called the **source position**, and the location into which you wish to copy it is the **target position**. The source position can be replicated into another position:

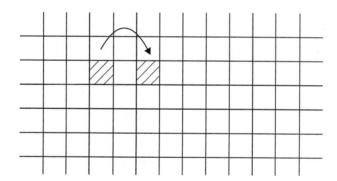

into a range of positions across a row:

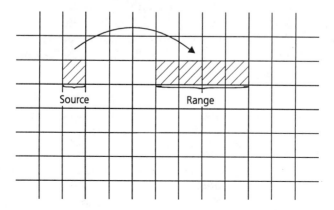

or into a range of positions down a column:

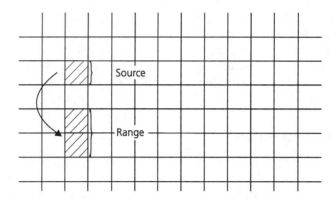

It is also possible to copy a range of source positions into a range of target positions:

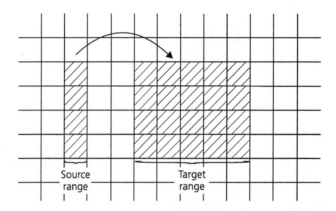

The *Copy* command facilitates quickly expanding a model across a number of columns or rows once the basic relationships in the source range are established. Obviously, it would be possible to expand the model by laboriously retyping all of the relationships for each Excel©. However, the *Copy* command makes this very easy.

Copying One Position. The simplest thing to copy is the contents of a single cell. To see how easy it is to copy the cell's contents, copy the contents of cell A1, the word "Sales" on your spreadsheet, to cell A15.

1. Highlight the source cell, the cell you want to copy, by pointing to it with the cursor and clicking on it with the left mouse button. Once it is highlighted, click on *Edit, Copy*. You may also use the shortcut by clicking on the toolbar icon that shows two pieces of paper.

2. Move the cursor to the target, the cell you want the source copied onto, and highlight it. Click on *Edit, Paste*. You may use the toolbar shortcut that looks like a clipboard and a piece of paper.

For practice, try this with your model. Let's move the word "Sales" to cell A15. To do this, move your cursor to cell A1 and highlight it. Then click on *Edit, Copy*, move the cursor to cell A15, click on it and click on *Edit, Paste*. "Sales" now will appear in cells A15 and A1.

Copying a Range of Positions. To copy a range of positions to another range, move the cursor to the beginning of the range and click and highlight the range you wish to move. Once the range is highlighted, move the cursor to the first cell of the target range and click on it. Click on *Edit, Paste*. The range will be copied. You may also use the toolbar icons for copy and paste.

For practice, try this with your model. To copy all the labels, move the cursor to cell A1 and highlight the range A1 to A9. Click on *Edit, Copy* or the appropriate icon. Next, move your cursor to the first cell, A11, of the target range, A11 to A20, and click. Click on *Edit, Paste* or the appropriate icon. The labels will appear in cells A1 to A9 and in cells A11 to A20.

Copying Relationships. Although copying labels demonstrates the usefulness of the *Copy* command, it does not demonstrate the ability of this command to deal with changing relationships. For example, suppose you want a Quickstudy Co. income statement for the next five years. If you expect Quickstudy sales to increase by 10 percent from the first to second years, move your cursor to cell C1 and type =+1.1*B1. This is the expression that indicates that the sales in the second year, cell C1, will increase by 10 percent from those in the first year, cell B1.

If you expect sales to increase 10 percent per year for each of the next three years, you could type into each cell the sales increase formula, or you could use the *Copy* command. To accomplish this with Excel©, follow the procedures detailed above. However, there is a shortcut. By placing the cursor in the bottom right-hand corner of the source cell, you will see a small black cross or plus sign. To copy the relationship, just drag the cross through the target cells.

Once again, let's demonstrate this with our example. First, type into cell C1 **=+1.1*B1**, to indicate that sales in the second year will grow by 10 percent over those in the first. Now you will see 110000 in cell C1. This is a relationship. To copy this relationship for three more years, position your cursor at the bottom right-hand corner of cell C1 until the black cross appears. Depressing the left mouse button, drag the cursor to cell F1 and release the button. The sales of 100000, 110000, 121000, 133100, and 146410 will appear. To copy the relationships in cells B2-B9 into cells C2-F9, highlight B2-B9. Position your cursor until the black cross appears at the bottom of cell C9. Drag the cross across to cell F9. Now you will have the original income statement and statements for four more years, as shown in Exhibit B-6.

EXHIBIT B-6   Quickstudy Income Statements

ROWS	A	B	C	D	E	F
			COLUMNS			
1	Sales	100000	110000	121000	133100	146410
2	Cost of goods sold	-65000	-71500	-78650	-86515	-95167
3	Gross income	35000	38500	42350	46585	51243
4	Selling, general, and administrative	-15000	-16500	-18150	-19965	-21962
5	Interest expense	-5000	-4999	-4998	-4997	-4996
6	Income before taxes	15000	17001	19202	21623	24285
7	Taxes	-5100	-5780	-6529	-7352	-8257
8	Net income	9900	11221	12673	14271	16028

Changing Relationships. Once you have the original income statement and forecasts for four additional years, they can be changed easily. For instance, you might want to see what would happen to Quickstudy Co. if cost of goods sold changed from 65 to 70 percent of sales. To do this, move your cursor to cell B2 and either retype the formula to read **=-.7*B1** or correct the formula in the cell contents line. Press [Enter] when you are through. This will change the cost of goods sold in cell B2. Use the *Copy* command to change the entries in cells C2 through F2.

In defining relationships, cell positions are often used. For example, in the income statement you created, the entry in cell B5 is =-.15*B1. Excel© interprets this to mean that the value for B5 is calculated by multiplying the value four rows above by -.15. If this relationship were copied into the C column, it would appear as =-.15*C1. Therefore, in calculating the value for C5, Excel© would look for a value four rows above in the same column, which would now be position C1. This is known as a relative relationship, and it is the nature of most relationships in a model.

Absolute relationships are those where a specific value is accessed regardless of where it may appear in the model. For example, if you wish the model to use the specific value in B1, the relationship in B5 would be written as **=-.15*$B$1**. The $ signs indicate an absolute row and column address. You may indicate an absolute relationship by typing in the dollar signs or pressing F4 after the cell address. When a fixed position is copied, the specified position does not change. For example, if **=-.15*$B$1** were to be copied to C5, the relationship would remain **=-.15*$B$1**. If you only want one portion of the address to remain fixed, put the dollar sign before it.

V. CREATING DATA TABLES

One of the features of using Excel©, or any other spreadsheet program, is the ability to change the value of a variable easily and determine the impact on the results. This process is known as "what-if" or sensitivity analysis. Typically, the user changes the value of a specific variable, such as the selling price, and then observes the effect this change has on another variable, such as net income.

It is easy to change the value of a variable and have the computer recompute the model. Often the user would like to change the value, using a range of several possibilities. This could be done by changing the values one at a time and then manually writing down the results. Rather than using this labor-intensive process, it is possible to have Excel© automatically make changes in the values and record the results in a data table. A **data table** is also called a sensitivity analysis table.

A data table consists of three parts: the input, the output, and the formula that relates the two. The input is the variable we want to have changed. The output is the value that results when the input is changed. The formula is the relationship between the two.

For example, suppose we wanted to evaluate the effect that changing the sales levels would have on the profitability of Quickstudy. The relationship between sales and net income is defined in the income statement. Exhibits B-4 and B-5 showed the numbers and background for Quickstudy's income statement. To determine the effect of changing Quickstudy's sales revenue in the first year from $100,000 to as low as $40,000 and as high as $200,000, we could enter each value into the spreadsheet and record the net income that results. However, we can create a data table that will give us the outcomes directly.

1. Enter the range of possible sales—for instance, 40000, 60000, 80000, 100000, 120000, and 140000, etc., into cells where you want the output. For Quickstudy, place them in cells A13 to A21, remembering not to type the dollar signs or commas.
2. Type the formula for the relationship, in this case net income, from the source cell A9 [=sum(c8:c9)], into the cell to the right and above the range of values, in this case cell B12. The Quickstudy data table is a column-oriented table since the income statement calculations are in a column. If your data is row oriented, put the input values in a row and type the formula into the cell below and to the left of the first value.
3. Click on *Data, Table*. A dialog box will appear asking you to indicate the input cell. In our case the input is sales, thus the cell is B1. Since net income is at the bottom of the income statement column, put B1 into the *Column Input Cell* box.
4. Click on [OK].

Exhibit B-7 shows the results of creating the data table. For Quickstudy it shows that even if sales are as low as $40,000, it will still have a positive net income of $1,980.

Once the data table is created, you can expand the range by adding additional rows of sales figures, or determine the impact on more than one value by putting additional formulas to the right and above the sales figures, for instance in cell C12. You can use this function to determine the impact of changes in more than one variable on the output variable.[13]

VI. CHANGING THE WORKSHEET

In the previous sections, you learned the basics of using Excel©. However, there are a number of modeling commands that will allow you to alter the display or change the model you have entered without retyping it.

---

[13] To learn more about creating this table, see the *Help* menu in Excel© or the accompanying manual.

EXHIBIT B-7 Sensitivity of Quickstudy's Income to Sales Changes

	A	B
	Sales	Net Income
11		
12		9900
13	40000	1980
14	60000	4620
15	80000	7260
16	100000	9900
17	120000	12540
18	140000	15180
19	160000	17820
20	180000	20460
21	200000	23100

Input Cell:
=SUM(C8:C9)

1. Changing the Column Width

You may change the column width for the entire model, for a range of columns, or for a single column. To change the column width for the entire model, click *Format, Column, Standard Width.* Into the dialog box that appears, type a new column width, then click on [OK]. To change the width for a single column or group of columns, place your cursor on the column or highlight the columns you wish to change, click *Format, Column, Width,* and enter the width you want. If you want the column to accommodate a wide entry or entries, click on *Format, Column, Autofit Selection.* This will make the column fit the maximum size of the selections you have outlined.

2. Changing the Numerical Format

When you entered the income statement for Quickstudy, you noted that the number was shown as 100000. The format used for displaying numbers can be changed for the entire worksheet, for a range of columns or rows, or for a single position. If you want the numbers to be shown as dollars, you do not enter the number with the dollar sign and commas into the cell, instead you format it after it is entered. To do this, first indicate how you want the cell or range of cells formatted by clicking on *Edit, Format,* and choosing the *Number* page in the dialog box. Second, when you are presented with a number of categories of formats such as *Number, Accounting, Percentage, Currency,* and *Text,* click on the one you want and choose the format code from the list shown at the right. The format code allows you to customize the format even further. Once you have chosen the *Category* and *Format Code,* click on [OK]. You will find the most frequently used formats as icons on the tool bar. They are a dollar sign, $, to indicate currency; % to indicate percentage; and a comma, , , to indicate the currency format without the dollar sign. If you want to change the number of decimal places, use the two buttons to the right of the format icons. Exhibit B-8 shows the formatted statement for Quickstudy.

To change the display format for the entire worksheet, click on *Format, Style.* You will see a dialog box. Click on *Number* and then *Modify.* You will be given a list of choices. Choose the one you would like to have used for all the numerical entries on your spreadsheet. Click on [OK] two times to have your choice take effect.

To change the format for a specific position or a range of positions, highlight the cell or cells you would like to format, then click on *Format, Cell,* choose *Number,* and select the style you want from the menu followed by [OK]. If any of these operations result in number signs (###) appearing in the cell or cells, your column is not wide enough to accommodate the style you have chosen. Reformat the width of the column.

You may also wish to change the currency in which your spreadsheet is denominated. The default currency is dollars. To change the entire spreadsheet, you must go to the Windows Control Panel, or the relevant location for your computer, and make the changes in the appropriate section. In the Windows Control Panel it would be in the Regional Settings area.

3. Inserting or Deleting a Row or Column

Earlier in this appendix, we discussed how to add a row to a spreadsheet. To delete a row or column, or several rows or columns, highlight what you want deleted, click *Edit, Delete,* and select *Entire Row* or *Entire Column,* finishing by clicking on [OK].

4. Blanking a Position or Range

If you have a position or a range with entries that you would like to change to blanks, this can be done by highlighting what you want to be blank and press-

---

EXHIBIT B-8   Quickstudy Income Statement Reformatted For Currency

Sales	$ 100,000
Cost of goods sold	(65,000)
Gross income	35,000
Selling, general, and administrative	(15,000)
Interest expense	(5,000)
Income before taxes	15,000
Taxes	(5,100)
Net income	$ 9,900

ing the [DEL] key on the keyboard, or *Edit, Clear, All*. Again, caution in using this command is warranted, because the contents are lost once the range is erased unless the *Undo* function is operational.

5. Keeping Titles on Your Monitor

When the cursor is moved to the right beyond the first 12 columns, the contents of Column A will disappear, then those in Column B, and so on. A similar thing happens when you go below Row 24. Often the leftmost columns and/or topmost rows contain labels or values you would like to be able to see wherever you are on your spreadsheet. You can freeze the column headings or the row labels by highlighting the row below the column headings or the column to the right of the row labels and clicking on *Window, Freeze Panes*. To reverse the process, click on *Window, Unfreeze Panes*.

6. Built-In Functions

Some mathematical relationships are used so frequently by spreadsheet users that they have been built into Microsoft Excel©. The simple way to access the functions is to click on the function wizard, the icon that shows f_x on the toolbar. There are a number of categories of functions available such as *Financial, Statistical, Date And Time*, and *Math And Trig*. Once you click on a category you will see a menu of the available functions. Once you have chosen a function, a dialog box will appear. Fill in the data requested. There is a *Help* function within the dialog box to help you. You may also type into a cell the formula for the function you want to perform.

A wide variety of preprogrammed functions are available using the function wizard. For instance, within the financial category are present value, future value, payments, and internal rate of return, as well as depreciation methods such as double declining balance, sum of the years' digits, and straight line. Consult the help function or your Excel© manual when you are ready to use this special feature.

VII. USING GRAPHICS

The graphics facility of Excel© allows you to present data that are attractive and easily understood. The Graphics section of Excel© displays data that have been entered into or generated by the worksheet. You must specify the data to be displayed and how they are to be displayed, then Excel© does the rest. Follow these steps to create your chart.

1. To begin, highlight the data you want graphed. You should include any titles that you want to appear in the chart.

2. Once you have the data outlined, click on *Insert, Chart*. You may choose to put the chart either on the spreadsheet page containing your data or on its own separate page.
3. If you choose to put it on the same page, a small icon looking like a bar chart will appear instead of the arrow of your cursor. Point to the upper left-hand corner of where you wish the chart to appear and highlight the area where you want the chart. If you choose a separate page, it is not necessary to highlight an area.
4. A dialog box will appear. The *Range* box contains the data range you previously chose. If it does not, type in the appropriate range, or highlight the range, and click *Next*.
5. You will see a screen with a variety of chart types. Choose the one you want to use for your data by clicking on it, then click *Next*.
6. On the next screen are more detailed versions of the chart type you chose. Choose the one you want by clicking on it, then click *Next*.
7. A box appears with a sample of your chart and the source of the data used in creating it. Adapt the criteria if the chart does not meet your needs, then click *Next*.
8. The next dialog box that appears allows you to customize your chart. You may enter titles and indicate whether you want a legend to appear that identifies each line when there is more than one set of input data. Enter the titles you want and click *Next*.
9. Throughout the operation, a sample graph in the dialog box will show the final graph as it will appear. Once you are satisfied with the chart, click *Finish*.

You may also access the *Chart* function using the icon that looks like a bar chart on the toolbar if you want your chart on the same page as the spreadsheet.

To illustrate how to use graphics, we will create a graph of Quickstudy's sales for five years using the data from the Quickstudy Co. income statements you created in the previous sections. To create the chart:

1. Highlight cells B3 to G3.
2. Click on the chart wizard icon.
3. Using the mouse, click on cell A24 and highlight the area to cell E37, to indicate the range in which you want your chart to appear.
4. In the next two boxes, choose the simple line chart.
5. The next dialog box will show your graph. It should show that the data is in rows, and the source of the labels. In this case the *Axis Label* should show 0 row, since our data axis is not labeled, and the *Legend*, column 1, will show the placement of the word Sales.
6. In the final dialog box, enter Quickstudy Sales for the title, Year for the X-axis, and Sales for the Y-axis. The titles will now appear on your sample graph. In addition to adding titles in this dialog box, you will be

asked, "Add A Legend?" Since we are only graphing sales, there is no need for a legend, so click *No*.

7. Once you are satisfied with your chart, click *Finish*.

The Quickstudy chart that results is shown in Exhibit B-9.

Exhibit B-9 only graphs Quickstudy's sales. Thus, it is not very instructive. You may include up to six different data ranges to be graphed. To add more ranges to your chart, point your cursor at the box containing the graph and double-click to highlight it. Once it is highlighted, click on the sales line and small boxes that appear along the line. Click *Insert, New Data*, and enter the new data range into the dialog box that appears, followed by clicking [OK]. You may also highlight the data range using your mouse. The new data will appear on the chart. You may also use more than one set of data in creating your original chart. Exhibit B-10 shows a chart with sales, cost of goods sold, and net income.

You will note that once the chart has been highlighted using double-click on the left mouse button, many other things may be added or changed using the *Insert* command.

VIII. OTHER MODELING SYSTEMS

Now that we have created a spreadsheet and a graph, you can see the power of using a spreadsheet modeling system like Excel©. While Excel© is a powerful and popular spreadsheet program, many other similar programs are available such as Lotus 1-2-3© and QuatroPro©. In addition to spreadsheet pro-

EXHIBIT B-9   Quickstudy Co. Sales

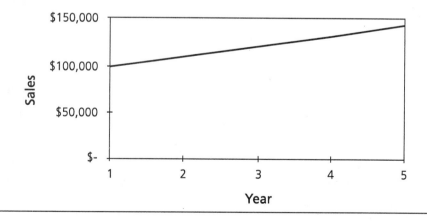

EXHIBIT B-10　Quickstudy Co. Sales, Cost of Goods Sold, and Net Income

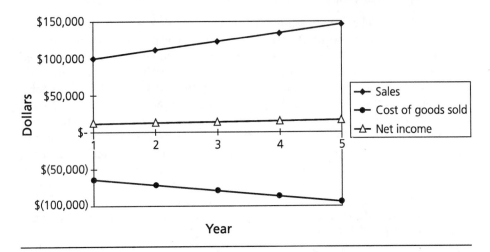

grams, there are programs that allow the user to specify relationships between variables, using English language-like statements.[14] A detailed review of all of these programs is beyond the scope of this book. However, a wide variety of different types of modeling programs are available.[15] These programs are an effective managerial tool, and the analyst should become familiar with one of the widely used programs.

[14]　Rather than requiring specific cell references, as with the spreadsheet programs, these programs generate the matrix of cells based on the model relationships.
[15]　In addition to a wide variety of spreadsheet programs, there are spreadsheet add-ons. These are programs to be used in conjunction with the spreadsheet to perform such things as more detailed risk analysis or to create a neural network.

Solutions to Study Questions

This appendix consists of two parts. The first section has detailed solutions to the study questions at the end of each chapter. The second section explains the entries that could be used in creating Excel models for solving the study questions.

C-1 MANUAL SOLUTIONS TO STUDY QUESTIONS

CHAPTER 1

1a. To calculate the ratios, use the formulas in the chapter and the data provided in the problem. To determine the sustainable growth rate, both the return on equity and the earnings retained must be computed.

Step 1. The return on equity for 1994 is net income divided by the total equity ($26.5/$178.8 = 0.148, or 14.8 percent).

Step 2. To determine earnings retained, subtract the dividends from the net income and divide the result by net income. Make sure that the amounts are all totals for the company or per-share amounts.

The following table provides the results of these calculations for 1992-96. As you can see, the company's sustainable growth rate has declined over the 5-year period.

	EASY CHAIR CO. FINANCIAL RATIOS				
	1992	1993	1994	1995	1996
Return on sales	6.7%	5.9%	5.4%	5.0%	4.8%
Sales/assets	146.7	155.6	144.6	158.5	163.7
Return on assets	9.9	9.2	7.9	7.9	7.8
Assets/equity	158.5	163.3	188.3	179.6	168.6
Return on equity	15.6	14.9	14.8	14.2	13.2
Earnings/share	$1.26	$1.34	$1.45	$1.54	$1.58
Dividend payout ratio	31.8%	29.8%	27.6%	32.5%	31.6%
Retention rate	68.2	70.2	72.4	67.5	68.4
Sustainable growth rate	10.7	10.5	10.7	9.5	9.0

1b. To compare *EASY* to the industry, the simplest approach is to subtract the company's ratios from those of the industry. The result is shown in the table that follows.

EASY CHAIR CO.
DIFFERENCE BETWEEN HOME FURNISHINGS INDUSTRY AND *EASY*

	1993	1994	1995	1996
Return on equity	-0.84%	-0.51%	-1.34%	-1.90%
Retention rate	-1.80%	1.40%	-3.50%	-2.60%
Sustainable growth rate	-0.83%	-0.17%	-1.53%	-1.73%

EASY's return on equity and sustainable growth rate have been below the industry average. In 1996, the difference widened.

2. Because there have been changes in the *EASY* Chair Co. ratios over the past five years, the next thing the analyst should examine is the income statement. To do this, first do a percentage of sales analysis by dividing each income statement item by the sales and then calculate the change in each item from year to year. The results of these two analyses are shown in the following tables.

EASY CHAIR COMPANY
PERCENTAGE OF SALES—INCOME STATEMENTS
(in millions)

	1993	1994	1995	1996
Net sales	100.0%	100.0%	100.0%	100.0%
Cost of sales	-69.0	-72.3	-71.9	-72.7
Gross profit	31.0	27.7	28.1	27.3
Selling, general, and administrative expense	-20.4	-18.8	-19.3	-18.8
Income from operations	10.6	8.9	8.8	8.5
Interest expense	-0.5	-0.8	-1.4	-1.2
Other income	0.5	0.6	0.6	0.4
Income before taxes	10.6	8.7	8.0	7.7
Taxes	-4.8	-3.2	-3.0	-2.9
Net income	5.8%	5.5%	5.0%	4.8%

EASY CHAIR COMPANY
PERCENTAGE CHANGES—INCOME STATEMENTS
(in millions)

	1994	1995	1996
Net sales	15.9%	13.6%	7.1%
Cost of sales	21.5	13.0	8.2
Gross profit	3.5	15.4	4.2
Selling, general, and administrative expense	6.9	17.0	4.4
Income from operations	(3.1)	12.0	3.7
Interest expense	110.5	90.0	-5.3
Other income	28.6	14.8	(19.4)
Income before taxes	(6.5)	4.8	3.6
Taxes	(23.6)	6.5	4.8
Net income	7.7%	3.8%	2.9%

As you can see from these analyses, *EASY's* gross profit margin has been declining, and interest costs have risen. The negative impact on the net income has been offset somewhat by a decline in selling, general, and administrative expenses. The item changes from year to year reveal that the decrease in gross margin was the worst in 1994. However, this decrease has slowed in 1996, perhaps suggesting some improvement. These changes should be real concerns for the management of *EASY* Chair Co.

3. To forecast financial statements for *EASY* Chair Co. based on Ms. Hampton's target ratios, the following process is used.
   a. To calculate dividends of $0.78 per share, multiply the market price of $15.00 by the dividend yield of 5.2 percent.
   b. Since the dividend payout ratio is 45 percent, divide it into the dividend to calculate the net income of $1.73 per share, or a total net income of $31,200.
   c. With net income of 5.1 percent of sales, return on assets (net income/assets) of 9.4 percent, and a return on equity of 13.7 percent, the equity, sales, and assets amounts can be determined by dividing the net income by the relevant ratio.
   d. Once the sales are determined, the accounts receivable can be calculated. To do so, divide the sales of $611,765 by 365 and multiply by the days in accounts receivable. The payables is cost of sales divided by 365 times the payables payment period.

e. Inventory is calculated by dividing cost of sales by the inventory turnover of 733 percent.
f. Debt is 27.3 percent of equity.
g. Current liabilities are total assets minus debt and equity.
h. Current assets are 573.2 percent of current liabilities.
i. Cash is current assets minus inventory and accounts receivable.
j. Other current liabilities are current liabilities minus accounts payable.
k. Interest is gross profit less taxes.

The statements that result from this analysis follow.

EASY CHAIR COMPANY
FINANCIAL STATEMENTS
(in millions)

Income Statement	Revised
Sales	$ 611,765
Cost of sales	(442,918)
Gross profit	168,847
Selling, general, and administrative expense	(115,623)
Gross profit	53,224
Interest	(5,951)
Earnings before taxes	47,273
Taxes	(16,073)
Net income	$ 31,200

Balance Sheet	
Cash	$ 15,988
Accounts receivable	155,036
Inventory	60,425
Total current assets	231,449
Net property, plant, and equipment	100,465
Total assets	$ 331,914
Accounts payable	$ 25,240
Other current liabilities	16,765
Total current liabilities	42,005
Long-term debt	62,172
Total liabilities	104,177
Owners' equity	227,737
Total liabilities and owners' equity	$ 331,914
Dividends per share	$0.78

---

4. To determine Peterson's position relative to the industry, estimate the ratios using the formulas described in the chapter. The result is shown below.

PETERSON'S CHEMICALS
FINANCIAL RATIOS RELATIVE TO INDUSTRY

	Industry	1995	1996
Current ratio	150.0%	163.7%	112.9%
Acid-test ratio	90.0%	108.0%	72.8%
Receivables collection period	65 days	111.2	106.7
Payables payment period	60 days	139.8	154.4
Debt/equity	110.0%	75.0%	78.8%
Return on assets	7.0%	-9.5%	-14.3%
Return on equity	19.0%	-28.8%	-77.0%

From the analysis of the ratios, Peterson's is apparently not in a favorable position relative to its industry on any dimension except its debt ratios—current, acid-test, and debt/equity.

5. To revise the statements, recalculate the sales, cost of goods sold, accounts payable and receivable, and debt as described in the problem. The only challenge is the debt. To estimate the debt, determine the 1996 equity account (the 1995 equity account balance added to the revised 1996 earnings). From this, deduct the new equity balance, accounts payable, and other liabilities from the total assets for 1996. The difference between the two is the debt.

The revised 1996 statements are as follows.

PETERSON'S CHEMICALS
REVISED FINANCIAL STATEMENTS
(in millions)

Income Statement	Original	Revised
Sales	$ 1,478	$ 1,434
Cost of goods sold	(1,182)	(1,076)
Gross profit	296	358
Selling and administrative expenses	(443)	(443)
Operating profit	(147)	(85)
Interest expense	(27)	(27)
Net income	$ (174)	$ (112)

(continued)

PETERSON'S CHEMICALS
REVISED FINANCIAL STATEMENTS *(cont.)*

Balance Sheet	Original	Revised
Cash and equivalent	$ 120	$ 120
Accounts receivable, net	432	306
Inventory	324	324
Other current assets	37	37
Total current assets	913	787
Plant, property, and equipment	300	300
Total assets	$1,213	$1,087

	Original	Revised
Accounts payable	$ 500	$ 202
Other current liabilities	309	309
Total current liabilities	809	511
Long-term debt	178	288
Total liabilities	987	799
Owners' equity	226	288
Total liabilities and owners' equity	$1,213	$1,087

The ratios, calculated in the usual way, follow:

PETERSON'S CHEMICALS
FINANCIAL RATIOS RELATIVE TO INDUSTRY

Ratios	Industry	1995	1996	Revised
Current ratio	150%	164%	113%	154%
Acid-test ratio	90%	108%	73%	91%
Receivables collection period (days)	65 days	111	107	78
Payables payment period (days)	60 days	140	154	69
Debt/equity	110%	75%	79%	100%
Return on assets	7%	-10%	-14%	-10%
Return on equity	19%	-29%	-77%	-39%

If Peterson management had implemented the changes in 1996, Peterson's would still have lost money, but the ratios would have been significantly improved.

CHAPTER 2

1. To create the financial statements for Honda, follow these steps.

Step 1. Sales. Increase the 1990 U.S. sales by 25 percent and the sales in Japan by 5 percent. To do this for Japan, multiply the 1990 sales by 1 plus the rate of growth. However, because the U.S. sales reported in 1990 are in yen:

a. translate the 1990 U.S. sales into dollars by dividing by the exchange rate of ¥154:$1.00,

b. multiply the U.S. dollar sales by 1 plus the rate of growth (25 percent) to determine the estimated 1991 sales in the United States,

c. convert the 1991 sales in the United States in dollars to yen by multiplying the U.S. sales in dollars by the estimated yen/dollar exchange rate of ¥140:$1.00.

d. The total sales figure for Honda in 1991 is the sum of the yen-translated U.S. sales and the sales in Japan.

Step 2. Cost of Sales. Cost of sales is expected to be 75 percent of total U.S. and Japanese sales, in yen terms. Operating costs grow at a simple rate of 10 percent, and research stays at ¥200.

Using this information, the following income statement is created.

HONDA MOTOR COMPANY
1990-1991 INCOME STATEMENT
(in billions of yen)

	1990	1991
Net sales		
Japan	¥ 1,300.0	¥ 1,365.0
United States	2,200.0	2,500.0
Total sales	3,500.0	3,865.0
Cost of goods sold	(2,625.0)	(2,898.8)
Research and development	(200.0)	(200.0)
Gross profit	675.0	766.2
Operating expenses	(500.0)	(550.0)
Operating profit	175.0	216.2
Taxes	(70.0)	(86.5)
Net profit	¥ 105.0	¥ 129.7

Step 3. Balance Sheet. To estimate the 1991 balance sheet, the following steps must be taken:

a. Calculate the average daily sales:

$$\text{Average daily sales} = \text{Total sales}/365$$
$$= ¥3865/365$$
$$= ¥10.58 \text{ million}$$

b. Multiply the average daily sales by the collection period of 45 days to obtain the value of the accounts receivable.
c. Inventory is 1/6 of cost of sales.
d. Cash is 10 percent of sales.
e. Payables are 60 days × (Cost of sales/365).
f. Retained earnings are the sum of the 1990 retained earnings and the 1991 profit after taxes.
g. The short-term debt is the "plug" or balancing figure for the balance sheet. The total liabilities and equity, with no change in short-term debt, are ¥2,831.2 million, and the assets are ¥2,846.1 million. Thus, the new short-term debt will be ¥14.9 million.

The balance sheet is shown in the exhibit that follows.

HONDA MOTOR COMPANY
1990-1991 BALANCE SHEET
(in billions of yen)

Assets	1990	1991
Cash	¥ 250.0	¥ 386.5
Accounts receivable	400.0	476.5
Inventory	475.0	483.1
Total current assets	1,125.0	1,346.1
Net property, plant, and equipment	1,500.0	1,500.0
Total assets	¥2,625.0	¥2,846.1
Liabilities and Equity		
Accounts payable	¥ 400.0	¥ 476.5
Other short-term debt	350.0	350.0
Total current liabilities	750.0	826.5
Long-term debt	1,050.0	1,050.0
Common stock	75.0	75.0
Retained earnings	750.0	879.7
Total equity	825.0	954.7
Subtotal	2,625.0	2,831.2
New short-term financing	—	14.9
Total liabilities and equity	¥2,625.0	¥2,846.1

Step 4. Net Working Capital. To determine the change in net working capital, first subtract the current liabilities from the current assets in 1990 and 1991. The change of ¥145 billion is divided by the 1990 net working capital of ¥375 to determine the change of 38.7 percent.

Step 5. Current Ratio and Working Capital.

Current ratio   =   Current assets/Current liabilities

For 1990, the current ratio is:

Current ratio   =   ¥1,125/¥750
=   1.50, or 150 percent

The current ratios and net working capital changes are as follows:

HONDA MOTOR COMPANY
CURRENT RATIOS AND CHANGES IN WORKING CAPITAL
(currency in billions of yen)

Working Capital

Net working capital	375	520
Change in net working capital	N.A.	39%
Current ratio	150%	163%

---

2. To revise your balance sheet, use the assumptions detailed in the problem and follow the steps described in the solution to Study Question 1. The revised statement is as follows:

HONDA MOTOR COMPANY
REVISED BALANCE SHEET
(currency in billions of yen)

Assets	1990	Revised 1991
Cash	¥ 250.0	¥ 270.6
Accounts receivable	400.0	635.3
Inventory	475.0	483.1
Total current assets	1,125.0	1,389.0
Net property, plant and equipment	1,500.0	1,500.0
Total assets	¥ 2,625.0	¥ 2,889.0
Liabilities and Equity		
Accounts payable	¥ 400.0	¥ 357.4
Other short-term debt	350.0	350.0
Total current liabilities	750.0	707.4
Long-term debt	1,050.0	1,050.0
Common stock	75.0	75.0
Retained earnings	750.0	879.8
Total equity	825.0	954.8
Subtotal	2,625.0	2,712.2
New short-term financing	—	176.8
Total liabilities and equity	¥ 2,625.0	¥ 2,889.0

The current ratios and net working capital changes are as follows:

HONDA MOTOR COMPANY
CURRENT RATIOS AND CHANGES IN WORKING CAPITAL
(currency in billions of yen)

Net working capital	¥375	¥682
Change in net working capital	N.A.	82%
Current ratio	150%	196%

As you can see from your analysis, the changes that occur if Honda Motor Company extends its collection period (relaxes its credit terms) and pays its suppliers more quickly include a greater need for financing. This need results from the increase in accounts receivable. While the changes in accounts receivable and payables ought to have a net negative impact on the working capital and the current ratio, they do not in this case: the decrease in cash and increase in financing from short-term sources offset the increase.

Thus, the impact on Honda of these changes appears to be neutral. If Honda management decided not to reduce its cash position, and if it financed the changes from long-term sources of capital, the change would not be neutral.

This analysis reveals Honda's financial strength. Its current ratio exceeds the average for the industry. If payables lengthened and receivables were to be collected more slowly in economic downturns, Honda could easily endure the changes. This should concern Honda's competitors.

3. With a change in the dollar:yen exchange rate, the following statements would result.

HONDA MOTOR COMPANY
REVISED FINANCIAL STATEMENTS—¥85:$1.00
(currency in billions of yen)

Income Statements	1990	1991
Net sales		
Japan	¥ 1,300.0	¥ 1,365.0
United States	2,200.0	1,517.9
Total sales	3,500.0	2,882.9
Cost of goods sold	(2,625.0)	(2,162.1)
Research and development	(200.0)	(200.0)
Gross profit	675.0	520.8
Operating expenses	(500.0)	(550.0)
Operating profit	175.0	(29.2)
Taxes	(70.0)	11.6
Net profit	¥ 105.0	¥ (17.6)

Balance Sheets	1990	1991
Assets		
Cash	¥ 250.0	¥ 201.8
Accounts receivable	400.0	355.4
Inventory	475.0	360.4
Total current assets	1,125.0	917.6
Net property, plant, and equipment	1,500.0	1,500.0
Total assets	¥ 2,625.0	¥ 2,417.6
Liabilities and Equity		
Accounts payable	¥ 400.0	¥ 266.6
Other short-term debt	350.0	350.0
Total current liabilities	750.0	616.6
Long-term debt	1,050.0	1,050.0
Common stock	75.0	75.0
Retained earnings	750.0	732.4
Total equity	825.0	807.4
Subtotal	2,625.0	2,474.0
New short-term financing	—	(56.4)
Total liabilities and equity	¥ 2,625.0	¥ 2,417.6

Working Capital

Net working capital	¥375	¥301
Change in net working capital	N.A.	-20%
Current ratio	150%	149%

Honda would be hurt by the change and might raise its U.S. prices, thus making G.M. products more price competitive.

4. To create pro forma financial statements for Top C. Company (statements that are adapted for changes in assumptions), a number of steps are needed:

Step 1. To create the changes that Mr. Duncan suggests are possible:
a. Multiply the current sales by 1.2 to obtain Mr. Duncan's estimate of sales.
b. Multiply sales per day by 45 [($10,320/360) × 45] to calculate accounts receivable.
c. Divide Mr. Duncan's estimate of inventory turnover (600 percent) into cost of goods sold.
d. Multiply the revised sales by 2 percent for the bad debt expense, 0.2 × $1,320.
e. All else remains the same.

Step 2. To create the changes Ms. Fisher suggests:
a. Multiply current sales by 10 percent.
b. Multiply revised sales by 5 percent to calculate bad debt expense.
c. Maintain operating expenses at $3,000.
d. Multiply revised sales by 15 percent to estimate cash.

e. Take 30 days of average sales for accounts receivable.
f. For inventory, use 1/3 of cost of sales.

The current and revised financial statements are as follows:

TOP C. COMPANY
CURRENT AND REVISED FINANCIAL STATEMENTS AND RATIOS
(dollars in millions)

Income Statements	Historic	Duncan	Fisher
Sales	$ 8,600.0	$10,320.0	$ 9,460.0
Bad debt	(430.0)	(206.4)	(473.0)
Net sales	8,170.0	10,113.6	8,987.0
Cost of goods sold	(3,500.0)	(4,128.0)	(3,784.0)
Gross profit	4,670.0	5,985.6	5,203.0
Operating expense	(3,000.0)	(3,600.0)	(3,000.0)
Operating income	1,670.0	2,385.6	2,203.0
Taxes	(668.0)	(954.2)	(881.2)
Net profit	$ 1,002.0	$ 1,431.4	$ 1,321.8

Balance Sheets

Assets			
Cash	$ 1,200.0	$ 2,064.0	$ 1,419.0
Accounts receivable	850.0	1,272.3	777.5
Inventory	800.0	688.0	1,261.3
Total current assets	2,850.0	4,024.3	3,457.8
Net property, plant, and equipment	4,000.0	4,000.0	4,000.0
Total assets	$ 6,850.0	$ 8,024.3	$ 7,457.8

Liabilities and Equity			
Accounts payable	$ 1,400.0	$ 1,289.3	$ 1,181.9
Short-term debt	1,500.0	1,500.0	1,500.0
Total current liabilities	2,900.0	2,789.3	2,681.9
Long-term debt	550.0	550.0	550.0
Common stock	420.0	420.0	420.0
Retained earnings	2,980.0	4,411.4	4,301.8
Total equity	3,400.0	4,831.4	4,721.8
Subtotal	6,850.0	8,170.7	7,953.7
New financing needed	0	(146.4)	(495.9)
Total liabilities and equity	$ 6,850.0	$ 8,024.3	$ 7,457.8
Net short-term debt	$ 1,500.0	$ 1,353.6	$ 1,004.1

Ratios

Net working capital	$(50.0)	$1,381.4	$1,271.8
Current ratio	98%	152%	158%

Step 3. After reviewing the financial statements that you have created, you can see that either of the analysts' plans results in greater profits for the company than does the current approach. Under both plans, the current ratio is improved from its marginal position, net working capital is positive, and there is no new capital needed. In spite of the positive results, however, the forecasts raise issues:

a. Mr. Duncan's plan of relaxing credit policy would actually result in a 20 percent increase in sales. This increase is substantial, and it would not be accompanied by significantly increased bad debts.
b. Ms. Fisher's concerns regarding Mr. Duncan's forecasts seem warranted. Her forecasts contain increased bad debts and a smaller increase in sales because of the recession. She also includes an increase in inventories to service the new sales. However, she does not increase the company's liquid cash reserves as did Mr. Duncan.

The question of which plan to follow depends largely on your view of the impact of the widespread recession on the company's markets. At the time, a recession appeared to be affecting Asian and European countries. However, the time might have been right for the company to lure new customers to its products with increased credit availability.

5. To forecast a monthly cash budget for Mary's Ski Chalet for 1997, first create 12 columns headed by the months of the year beginning with January. Then determine the cash receipts and disbursements.

Step 1. Cash receipts are determined as follows:

a. Cash is received from cash sales and collections from accounts receivable. Credit sales—75 percent of sales—are collected 30 days after the sale is made. Sales forecasts and beginning accounts receivable are provided in the problem.
b. Cash collections are the total of cash sales—25 percent of sales—plus the collections from accounts receivable.

Step 2. Disbursements are determined as follows:

a. Purchases are cost of goods sold (75 percent of sales) plus 6 percent of sales (a total of 81 percent of sales), and are paid for 30 days after the goods are ordered. The accounts payable account at the end of the month is the beginning accounts payable less the accounts payable payments plus the purchases.

b. The disbursements are the payments of accounts payable plus the selling, general, and administrative expenses of 19 percent of sales and lease and interest expenses of $2,000 per month ($24,000 for the year).

Step 3. Net receipts are the receipts less the disbursements.

Step 4. The cash balance is the beginning cash account plus the net receipts.

The forecasts for Mary's Ski Chalet are shown in the following table. As you can see, although Mary's Ski Chalet will have negative receipts for most months until August, the beginning cash balance of $65 plus the receipts in January will provide sufficient cash to operate through the difficult spring and summer months.

MARY'S SKI CHALET
CASH RECEIPTS AND ACCOUNTS RECEIVABLE ACCOUNT
(in thousands)

	Jan.	Feb.	Mar.	Apr.	May	June	July	Aug.	Sept.	Oct.	Nov.	Dec.
Sales	$210.0	$175.0	$160.0	$140.0	$50.0	$30.0	$30.0	$75.0	$90.0	$125.0	$165.0	$230.0
Cost of goods sold	$157.5	$131.3	$120.0	$105.0	$37.5	$22.5	$22.5	$56.3	$67.5	$93.8	$123.8	$172.5
Accounts Receivable Schedule												
Beginning accts. receivable	$184.0	$157.5	$131.3	$120.0	$105.0	$37.5	$22.5	$22.5	$56.3	$67.5	$93.8	$123.8
Credit sales	157.5	131.3	120.0	105.0	37.5	22.5	22.5	56.3	67.5	93.8	123.8	172.5
Collections on accts. receivable	184.0	157.5	131.3	120.0	105.0	37.5	22.5	22.5	56.3	67.5	93.8	123.8
Ending accts. receivable	$157.5	$131.3	$120.0	$105.0	$37.5	$22.5	$22.5	$56.3	$67.5	$93.8	$123.8	$172.5
Accounts Payable Schedule												
Beginning accts. payable	$173.0	$170.1	$141.8	$129.6	$113.4	$40.5	$24.3	$24.3	$60.8	$72.9	$101.3	$133.7
Purchases	170.1	141.8	129.6	113.4	40.5	24.3	24.3	60.8	72.9	101.3	133.7	186.3
Payments on accts. payable	173.0	170.1	141.8	129.6	113.4	40.5	24.3	24.3	60.8	72.9	101.3	133.7
Ending accts. payable	$170.1	$141.8	$129.6	$113.4	$40.5	$24.3	$24.3	$60.8	$72.9	$101.3	$133.7	$186.3
Receipts												
Cash sales	$52.5	$43.8	$40.0	$35.0	$12.5	$7.5	$7.5	$18.8	$22.5	$31.3	$41.3	$57.5
Collections on accts. receivable	184.0	157.5	131.3	120.0	105.0	37.5	22.5	22.5	56.3	67.5	93.8	123.8
Total receipts	$236.5	$201.3	$171.3	$155.0	$117.5	$45.0	$30.0	$41.3	$78.8	$98.8	$135.1	$181.3
Disbursements												
Payments on accounts payable	$173.0	$170.1	$141.8	$129.6	$113.4	$40.5	$24.3	$24.3	$60.8	$72.9	$101.3	$133.7
Selling, general, and administrative expenses	39.9	33.3	30.4	26.6	9.5	5.7	5.7	14.3	17.1	23.8	31.4	43.7
Lease and interest expenses	2.0	2.0	2.0	2.0	2.0	2.0	2.0	2.0	2.0	2.0	2.0	2.0
Total disbursements	$214.9	$205.4	$174.2	$158.2	$124.9	$48.2	$32.0	$40.6	$79.9	$98.7	$134.7	$179.4
Cash Account												
Beginning cash	$65.0	$86.6	$82.5	$79.6	$76.4	$69.0	$65.8	$63.8	$64.5	$63.4	$63.5	$63.9
Receipts less disbursements	21.6	(4.1)	(2.9)	(3.2)	(7.4)	(3.2)	(2.0)	0.7	(1.1)	0.1	0.4	1.9
Ending cash	$86.6	$82.5	$79.6	$76.4	$69.0	$65.8	$63.8	$64.5	$63.4	$63.5	$63.9	$65.8

6. Once the cash balance has been determined, the income statement and balance sheet are simple.

Step 1. Income Statement.
a. The sales are the sum of the monthly sales for the year.
b. Cost of goods sold is 81 percent of sales.
c. Selling, general, and administrative expenses are 19 percent of the total sales.
d. Interest and lease expenses are $24,000.
e. Depreciation is $12,000.

The income statement for 1997 follows.

MARY'S SKI CHALET
1997 INCOME STATEMENT
(in thousands)

Sales	$ 1,480.0
Cost of goods sold	(1,110.0)
Gross income	370.0
Selling and general expenses	(281.2)
Depreciation	(12.0)
Lease and interest expenses	(24.0)
Net income	$ 52.8

Step 2. Balance Sheet.
a. The cash, accounts receivable, and accounts payable accounts are those for the ending balances from the cash budget.
b. Inventory is the beginning inventory account given in the problem, plus the purchases, less cost of goods sold.
c. Property, plant, and equipment is the account at the beginning of the year, less the depreciation of $12,000.
d. Equity is the beginning equity plus the net income for the year.

The balance sheets for 1996 and 1997 follow.

**MARY'S SKI CHALET
BALANCE SHEETS**
(in thousands)

Assets	1996	1997
Cash	$ 65.0	$ 65.8
Accounts receivable	184.0	172.5
Inventory	50.0	138.8
Current assets	299.0	377.1
Net property, plant, and equipment	345.0	333.0
Total assets	$644.0	$710.1
Liabilities and Equity		
Accounts payable	$173.0	$186.3
Current liabilities	173.0	186.3
Equity	471.0	523.8
Total liabilities and equity	$644.0	$710.1

7. To make forecasts for Aries Corporation you must use the information in the problem and information from the 1995 and 1996 actual financial statements. The first step is to do a percentage of sales analysis of the 1995 and 1996 financial statements. This analysis is shown next to the "Actual" columns on the statements that follow. Once the analysis is done, the forecasts can be made. These forecasts are made like those in preceding problems.

ARIES CORPORATION
PROJECTED FINANCIAL STATEMENTS

	HISTORIC						FORECAST		
Income Statements	1995	Percent	1996	Percent	1997	1998	1999	2000	2001
Sales	$ 221.0	100.0%	$ 266.0	100.0%	$ 320.1	$ 352.2	$ 390.9	$ 437.8	$ 494.7
Cost of goods sold	(145.0)	-65.6	(166.0)	-62.4	(167.8)	(177.5)	(197.1)	(220.7)	(249.2)
Gross profit	76.0	34.4	100.0	37.6	152.3	174.7	193.8	217.1	245.5
Operating expenses	(38.0)	-17.2	(35.0)	-13.2	(42.1)	(46.3)	(51.4)	(57.6)	(65.3)
Operating profit	38.0	17.2	65.0	24.4	110.2	128.4	142.4	159.5	180.2
Taxes	(19.0)	-50.0	(33.0)	-50.8	(55.9)	(65.2)	(54.1)	(60.6)	(68.5)
Net profit	$ 19.0	8.6%	$ 32.0	12.0%	$ 54.3	$ 63.2	$88.3	$ 98.9	$ 111.7
Sales growth				20.3%	20.3%	10.0%	11.0%	12.0%	13.0%
Balance Sheets									
Assets									
Cash	$ 22.0		$ 37.0		$ 44.5	$ 49.0	$ 54.4	$ 60.9	$ 68.8
Accounts receivable	49.0		31.0		37.3	41.0	45.6	51.0	57.7
Inventory	47.0		45.0		21.0	25.4	32.8	36.8	41.6
Total current assets	118.0		113.0		102.8	115.4	132.8	148.7	168.1
Fixed assets	70.0		122.0		265.0	291.0	323.0	403.0	513.0
Total assets	$ 188.0		$ 235.0		$ 367.8	$ 406.4	$ 455.8	$ 551.7	$ 681.1
Liabilities and Equity									
Accounts payable	$ 19.0		$ 34.0		$ 27.6	$ 29.2	$ 32.4	$ 36.3	$ 41.0
Total current liabilities	19.0		34.0		27.6	29.2	32.4	36.3	41.0
Equity	169.0		201.0		255.3	318.4	406.8	505.7	617.4
Subtotal	188.0		235.0		282.9	347.6	439.2	542.0	658.4
New notes payable	—		—		84.9	58.8	16.6	9.7	22.7
Total liabilities and equity	$ 188.0		$ 235.0		$ 367.8	$ 406.4	$ 455.8	$ 551.7	$ 681.1

CHAPTER 3

1. Forecasting the 1997 financial statements for Chateau Royale requires several steps:

Step 1. Income Statement.
a. Sales for 1997 are 160 percent of 1996 sales.
b. Cost of goods sold is 75 percent of 1997 sales.
c. Operating expenses are 110 percent of 1996 operating expenses.
d. Depreciation is $8,000.
e. Operating income is sales minus cost of goods sold, operating expenses, and depreciation.
f. Taxes are 34 percent of operating income.
g. Net income after taxes is operating income minus taxes.

The resulting income statements follow.

CHATEAU ROYALE INTERNATIONAL
1996-97 INCOME STATEMENTS
(in millions)

	1996	1997
Sales	$ 375,000	$ 600,000
Cost of goods sold	(276,150)	(450,000)
Gross profit	98,850	150,000
Operating expenses	(75,000)	(82,500)
Depreciation	(5,100)	(8,000)
Operating profit	18,750	59,500
Taxes	(7,500)	(20,230)
Net profit	$ 11,250	$ 39,270

Step 2. Balance Sheet.
a. Long-term debt and common stock remain unchanged from 1996.
b. Property, plant, and equipment assets are the 1996 account less the 1997 depreciation of $8,000.
c. Retained earnings are the prior year's retained earnings plus net profit from 1997.
d. Accounts receivable are 45/365 times 1997 sales, and inventory is one-third of cost of goods sold.
e. Accounts payable are 30/365 times 1997 cost of goods sold. We use cost of goods sold since no information about purchases is given.
f. Cash is 20 percent of 1997 sales.
g. Since we do not know what Chateau Royale management expects to do with short-term debt, we enter a zero.

h. Forecasted assets will not balance with liabilities and equity. The best way to balance the assets and liabilities is to put in a balancing account called "net financing needed."

The balance sheets for Chateau Royale follow.

CHATEAU ROYALE INTERNATIONAL
1996-97 BALANCE SHEETS
(in millions)

Assets	1996	1997
Cash	$ 75,000	$ 120,000
Accounts receivable	46,233	73,973
Inventory	93,750	150,000
Current assets	214,983	343,973
Net property, plant, and equipment	115,000	107,000
Total assets	$ 329,983	$ 450,973

Liabilities and Equity	1996	1997
Accounts payable	$ 23,116	$ 36,986
Short-term debt	51,867	—
Current liabilities	74,983	36,986
Long-term debt	125,000	125,000
Common stock	100,000	100,000
Retained earnings	30,000	69,270
Subtotal	329,983	331,256
Net financing needed (excess cash)	—	119,717
Total liabilities and owners' equity	$ 329,983	$ 450,973

Step 3. The net working capital is current assets minus current liabilities. To calculate the current ratio divide the two accounts. The net working capital and current ratios for 1996 and 1997 follow.

CHATEAU ROYALE INTERNATIONAL
WORKING CAPITAL RATIOS

Ratios	1996	1997
Current ratio	287%	930%
Net working capital change	N.A.	$166,986

2. Only these assumptions for Chateau Royale International change for 1997:
   a. Cash/sales is reduced to 15 percent.

b. Days of cost of goods sold in payables is increased to 45 days.
c. Inventory turnover is increased to 400 percent.

The following statements reflect these changes.

CHATEAU ROYALE INTERNATIONAL
1996-97 REVISED FINANCIAL STATEMENTS
(in millions)

Income Statements	1996	1997
Sales	$ 375,000	$ 600,000
Cost of goods sold	(276,150)	(450,000)
Gross profit	98,850	150,000
Operating expenses	(75,000)	(82,500)
Depreciation	(5,100)	(8,000)
Operating profit	18,750	59,500
Taxes	(7,500)	(20,230)
Net profit	$ 11,250	$ 39,270

Balance Sheets
(as of December 31)

	1996	1997
Assets		
Cash	$ 75,000	$ 90,000
Accounts receivable	46,233	73,973
Inventory	93,750	112,500
Current assets	214,983	276,473
Net property, plant, and equipment	115,000	107,000
Total assets	$ 329,983	$ 383,473
Liabilities and Equity		
Accounts payable	$ 23,116	$ 55,479
Short-term debt	51,867	—
Current liabilities	74,983	55,479
Long-term debt	125,000	125,000
Common stock	100,000	100,000
Retained earnings	30,000	69,270
Subtotal	329,983	349,749
New financing needed (excess cash)	—	33,724
Total liabilities and owners' equity	$ 329,983	$ 383,473

Ratios

	1996	1997
Current ratio	287%	498%
Net working capital change	N.Ap.	$80,993

As a result of the lower cash balance and quicker inventory turnover, the current ratio is above the industry average of 320 percent. Chateau Royale management must take into consideration that the increase in the payables period may result in higher supplier costs, such as interest on unpaid balances, or may result in increased prices. Management should also consider whether lower cash and inventory could result in insufficient inventory to service customers or insufficient cash to transact business.

3. The process used in forecasting the statement revisions according to Mr. Dine and Mr. Triano is similar to the process used in solving Study Questions 1 and 2. The assumptions are those provided in the problem and are used to create the following financial statements:

KURZ CORP.
FINANCIAL STATEMENTS
(Canadian dollars in thousands)

Income Statements	Original	Triano	Dine
Sales	CD$505,000	CD$757,500	CD$505,000
Bad debt	(5,000)	(15,150)	0
Net sales	500,000	742,350	505,000
Cost of goods sold	(375,000)	(568,125)	(378,750)
Gross profit	125,000	174,225	126,250
Operating expenses	(90,900)	(90,900)	(90,900)
Operating profit	34,100	83,325	35,350
Taxes	(11,935)	(29,164)	(12,373)
Net profit	CD$ 22,165	CD$ 54,161	CD$ 22,977

Balance Sheets	Original	Triano	Dine
Assets			
Cash	CD$ 90,000	CD$148,470	CD$ 75,750
Accounts receivable	61,644	124,521	41,507
Inventory	62,500	108,214	101,000
Current assets	214,144	381,205	218,257
Net property, plant, and equipment	130,000	130,000	130,000
Total assets	CD$344,144	CD$511,205	CD$348,257
Liabilities and Equity			
Accounts payable	CD$ 30,822	CD$ 46,280	CD$ 30,853
Short-term debt	86,322	—	0
Current liabilities	117,144	46,280	30,853
Long-term debt	110,000	110,000	110,000
Common stock	75,000	75,000	75,000
Retained earnings	42,000	96,161	64,978
Subtotal	344,144	327,441	280,831
New financing needed (excess cash)	—	183,764	67,426
Total liabilities and owners' equity	CD$344,144	CD$511,205	CD$348,257

Ratios	Base	Triano	Dine
Current assets	CD$214,144	CD$381,205	CD$218,257
Current liabilities	117,144	46,280	30,853
Net working capital	CD$ 97,000	CD$334,925	CD$187,404
Current ratio	183%	824%	707%

Based on these statements, Ms. Brittain should implement Mr. Triano's plan. Despite the higher cost, this plan results in a higher net profit and higher asset growth. However, this policy also results in having to borrow more short-term money and thus increases the risk of financial distress if sales decline substantially.

4. The steps followed in making the forecast for THE CRESCENT are similar to those followed in the previous problems. The only special considerations that this problem presents are as follows:
   a. Some of the payments are made in Philippine pesos and some in dollars.
   b. The dollar/Philippine peso exchange rate is expected to change as early as February, and that exchange rate change must be built into the forecasts.
   c. Some of the goods ordered require a funded letter of credit before delivery. Thus, some of the expenses are incurred well before the goods arrive. For instance, the letter of credit for the cement purchases must be opened one month prior to delivery. Thus, the first payment for cement is for the letter of credit in January.

The full forecasts are in the following table. These forecasts show that Mr. Dizon will need to have a credit line with United Coconut, and will be rapidly paid down as revenues are received. Mr. Lucas should ask the United Coconut Planters' Bank for a revolving line of credit of at least P10,732,000. This is the total needed by July, before the expenses begin to decline and the revenues begin to offset the costs of building materials for THE CRESCENT. Mr. Dizon will not need the credit line after September 1998.

THE CRESCENT
MONTHLY CASH FLOW FORECASTS
(in millions of Philippine pesos)

	Jan.	Feb.	March	April	May	June	July
Receipts							
Cash receipts	4,500				9,000		
Cash Disbursements							
Cement	3,402						
Granite tiles			3,645		3,645		3,645
Window frames					5,000		
Elevators			120	120	120	120	120
Generator		600					
Bathroom fixtures					2,000		
Salaries and benefits	375	375	375	375	375	375	375
Overhead	10	10	10	10	10	10	10
Total disbursements	3,787	985	4,150	505	11,150	505	4,150
Cash Balance							
Beginning cash	1,000	1,713	728	(3,422)	(3,927)	(6,077)	(6,582)
Net cash flow	713	(985)	(4,150)	(505)	(2,150)	(505)	(4,150)
Cumulative net cash flow	1,713	728	(3,422)	(3,927)	(6,077)	(6,582)	(10,732)

THE CRESCENT (cont.)

	Aug.	Sept.	Oct.	Nov.	Dec.	Jan.	Feb.	March
Receipts								
Cash receipts	9,000		9,000		9,000			4,500
Cash Disbursements								
Cement								
Granite tiles								
Window frames	120	120	120	120	120			
Elevators								
Generator								
Bathroom fixtures		585						
Salaries and benefits	375	375	375	375	375			
Overhead	10	10	10	10	10			
Total disbursements	505	1,090	505	505	505			
Cash Balance								
Beginning cash	(10,732)	(2,237)	(3,327)	5,168	4,663	13,158	13,158	13,158
Net cash flow	8,495	(1,090)	8,495	(505)	8,495	—		4,500
Cumulative net cash flow	(2,237)	(3,327)	5,168	4,663	13,158	13,158	13,158	17,658

CHAPTER 4

1.

Step 1. The first thing the analyst must do to determine whether Metalwerk's management should develop a new assembly line is to forecast the residual cash flows for the project. These cash flows are straightforward. If the pattern in the chapter is followed, only two tricky things must be considered—depreciation and calculating the payback period.

a. To calculate the double-declining-balance depreciation, take the balance left to be depreciated and calculate double the straight-line depreciation. For instance, in the first year, the machinery is valued at DM 1,400,000. Straight-line depreciation would be DM 1,400,000 divided by 20, the number of years remaining in the equipment life. The double-declining-balance depreciation is twice the DM 70,000 of straight-line depreciation, or DM 140,000. The table calculating the depreciation follows the residual cash flow forecast.

b. The depreciation for any year is either the double-declining-balance amount or the straight-line value if the latter is larger. Straight-line depreciation is larger in the 12th year. The depreciation for years 11-20 is the straight-line value that depreciates the equipment in the remaining 8 years, or DM 48,815 per year.

Step 2. To determine the payback, subtract the annual residual cash flow from the initial cost of DM 1,400,000. In the fourth year, the remainder to be covered is DM 338,500, while the residual cash flow is DM 530,750, which means that the equipment will be fully covered by the residual cash flow in an additional 0.64 years (DM 338,500/DM 530,750). Because the payback is less than the four years the management requires, the project should be accepted. However, to analyze this project fully, management should estimate the net present value using an appropriate discount rate.

The full forecasts and calculations for payback and depreciation are shown in the following table.

METALWERKS
ANALYSIS OF NEW ASSEMBLY LINE—RESIDUAL CASH FLOWS
(in thousands of deutsch marks)

PERIOD

	0	1	2	3	4	5	6	7	8	9
Income Statement Changes										
Sales		1,625	1,625	1,625	1,625	1,625	1,625	1,625	1,625	1,625
Cost of goods sold		(601)	(601)	(601)	(601)	(601)	(601)	(601)	(601)	(601)
Gross profit		1,024	1,024	1,024	1,024	1,024	1,024	1,024	1,024	1,024
Repairs and utilities		(13)	(13)	(13)	(13)	(13)	(13)	(13)	(13)	(13)
Salaries and benefits		(480)	(480)	(480)	(480)	(480)	(480)	(480)	(480)	(480)
Depreciation		(140)	(126)	(113)	(102)	(92)	(83)	(74)	(67)	(60)
Profit before taxes		391	405	418	429	439	448	457	464	471
Taxes		(133)	(138)	(142)	(146)	(149)	(152)	(155)	(158)	(160)
Net profit		258	267	276	283	290	296	302	306	311
Noncash Charges										
Depreciation		140	126	113	102	92	83	74	67	60
Balance Sheet Changes										
New equipment	(1,400)									
Residual net cash flow	(1,400)	398	393	389	385	382	379	376	373	371
Payback										
Unrecovered investment value	1,400	1,002	609	220	(165)					
Partial year calculation				57.1%						
Payback (years)	2.57									
Benefit/cost ratio	4.76									

Depreciation Schedule		1	2	3	4	5	6	7	8	9
Value yet undepreciated		1,400	1,260	1,134	1,021	919	827	744	670	603
Straight-line rate		5%								
Depreciation		140	126	113	102	92	83	74	67	60
Straight-line for remaining life		70	66	63	60	57	55	53	52	50
Depreciation		140	126	113	102	92	83	74	67	60

METALWERKS (cont.)
PERIOD

	10	11	12	13	14	15	16	17	18	19	20
	1,625	1,625	1,625	1,625	1,625	1,625	1,625	1,625	1,625	1,625	1,625
	(601)	(601)	(601)	(601)	(601)	(601)	(601)	(601)	(601)	(601)	(601)
	1,024	1,024	1,024	1,024	1,024	1,024	1,024	1,024	1,024	1,024	1,024
	(13)	(13)	(13)	(13)	(13)	(13)	(13)	(13)	(13)	(13)	(13)
	(480)	(480)	(480)	(480)	(480)	(480)	(480)	(480)	(480)	(480)	(480)
	(54)	(49)	(49)	(49)	(49)	(49)	(49)	(49)	(49)	(49)	(48)
	477	482	482	482	482	482	482	482	482	482	483
	(162)	(164)	(164)	(164)	(164)	(164)	(164)	(164)	(164)	(164)	(164)
	315	318	318	318	318	318	318	318	318	318	319
	54	49	49	49	49	49	49	49	49	49	48
	369	367	367	367	367	367	367	367	367	367	367

	10	11	12	13	14	15	16	17	18	19	20
	542	488	439	391	342	293	244	195	146	97	48
	54	49	44	39	34	29	24	20	15	10	24
	49	49	49	49	49	49	49	49	49	49	49
	54	49	49	49	49	49	49	49	49	49	48

2. The single biggest difficulty in making these forecasts is dealing with the depreciation associated with the two investments. Cash flows show that depreciation is important in this case since the largest portion of the net present value is directly related to the high depreciation allowances. Given the magnitude of the net present value, management of Sun Co. should pursue this investment. The forecasted residual cash flows are as follows:

SUN COMPANY
RESIDUAL CASH FLOW ANALYSIS
(in thousands of lira)

			PERIOD			
	0	1	2	3	4	5
Income Statement Changes						
Sales		120.0	138.0	158.7	182.5	209.9
Operating expenses		(46.8)				
Depreciation—initial investment		(30.0)	(44.0)	(42.0)	(42.0)	(42.0)
Depreciation— additional investment		—	—	(15.6)	(19.2)	(25.2)
Profit before taxes		43.2	94.0	101.1	121.3	142.7
Taxes (@ 34%)		(14.7)	(32.0)	(34.4)	(41.2)	(48.5)
Net profit		28.5	62.0	66.7	80.1	94.2
Noncash Charges						
Depreciation		30.0	44.0	57.6	61.2	67.2
Capital Investments						
Property, plant, and equipment	(200.0)		(60.0)			
Residual net cash flow	(200.0)	58.5	46.0	124.3	141.3	161.4
Net present value (at 10%)	181.3					

3. In general, the solution to this problem follows that of the previous problems in this chapter. Project 1 is the most straightforward of the two. The cash flows are forecasted on the basis of data in the problem and are shown in the following project evaluation. The depreciation schedule requires that the larger of the double-declining-balance or straight-line methods be used on the undepreciated balance. The schedule to calculate the depreciation follows the residual cash flow forecasts.

   Three things may be a problem in making the forecasts: market research expenses have already been spent and, thus, are irrelevant to this project's value; production training is an expense at the beginning of the project life; and tax credit of $68,000 is expected to offset income received by Cloud Frame from other parts of its business. For the tax credit, if Cloud Frame had no other business, the tax credit could be carried forward; if no income were ever earned, the tax credit would be useless.

   The net present value, benefit/cost ratio, and payback are calculated as demonstrated in the chapter. For Project 2, the same pattern is followed.

   Based on the three measures of attractiveness, Project 1 is dominant, and management should choose to expand the existing production facilities.

CLOUD FRAME COMPANY
ANALYSIS OF TWO PROJECTS
(in thousands of libras)

Project 1

Income statement changes	0	1	2	3	4	5	6	7	8	9	10
Sales		500.0	500.0	500.0	500.0	500.0	500.0	500.0	500.0	500.0	500.0
Cost of goods sold		(245.0)	(245.0)	(245.0)	(245.0)	(245.0)	(245.0)	(245.0)	(245.0)	(245.0)	(245.0)
Gross income		255.0	255.0	255.0	255.0	255.0	255.0	255.0	255.0	255.0	255.0
Advertising		(50.0)	(50.0)	(50.0)	(50.0)	(50.0)	(50.0)	(50.0)	(50.0)	(50.0)	(50.0)
Depreciation		(160.0)	(128.0)	(102.4)	(81.9)	(65.5)	(52.4)	(52.4)	(52.4)	(52.4)	(52.4)
Operating income		45.0	77.0	102.6	123.1	139.5	152.6	152.6	152.6	152.6	152.6
Taxes		(15.3)	(26.2)	(34.9)	(41.8)	(47.4)	(51.9)	(51.9)	(51.9)	(51.9)	(51.9)
Net income		29.7	50.8	67.7	81.3	92.1	100.7	100.7	100.7	100.7	100.7
Noncash charges											
Depreciation		160.0	128.0	102.4	81.9	65.5	52.4	52.4	52.4	52.4	52.4
Capital changes:											
New machinery	(800.0)					(59.5)					
Residual cash flow	(800.0)	189.7	178.8	170.1	163.2	157.6	153.1	153.1	153.1	153.1	153.1
Payback											
Payback period in years	4.62										
Investment to recover	800.0	610.3	431.5	261.4	98.1						
Benefit-cost ratio	203.1				62.3%						
Net present value	217.84										

Depreciation schedule		1	2	3	4	5	6	7	8	9	10
Double-declining-balance		160.0	128.0	102.4	81.9	65.5	52.4	41.9	33.6	26.8	21.5
Straight-line depreciation		80.0	71.1	64.0	58.5	54.6	52.4	52.4	52.4	52.4	52.4
Remaining balance		640.0	512.0	409.6	327.7	262.1	209.7	157.3	104.9	52.4	—
Depreciation to be taken		160.0	128.0	102.4	81.9	65.5	52.4	52.4	52.4	52.4	52.4

CLOUD FRAME COMPANY (cont.)

Project 2

	0	1	2	3	4	5	6	7	8	9	10
Income statement changes											
Sales		350.0	385.0	423.5	465.9	535.7	616.1	708.5	779.3	857.3	943.0
Cost of goods sold		(175.0)	(192.5)	(211.7)	(232.9)	(267.9)	(308.0)	(354.2)	(389.6)	(428.7)	(471.5)
Gross income		175.0	192.5	211.8	233.0	267.8	308.1	354.3	389.7	428.6	471.5
Advertising		(87.5)	(96.3)	(105.9)	(100.0)	(100.0)	(100.0)	(100.0)	(100.0)	(100.0)	(100.0)
Production training	(200.0)										
Depreciation		(120.0)	(96.0)	(76.8)	(61.4)	(49.2)	(39.3)	(39.3)	(39.3)	(39.3)	(39.3)
Operating income	(200.0)	(32.5)	0.2	29.1	71.6	118.6	168.8	215.0	250.4	289.3	332.2
Taxes	68.0	11.1	(0.1)	(9.9)	(24.3)	(40.3)	(57.4)	(73.1)	(85.1)	(98.3)	(112.9)
Net income	(132.0)	(21.4)	0.1	19.2	47.3	78.3	111.4	141.9	165.3	191.0	219.3
Noncash charges											
Depreciation		120.0	96.0	76.8	61.4	49.2	39.3	39.3	39.3	39.3	39.3
Capital changes											
New machinery	(600.0)	(591)	(494)	(398)	(290)	(162)	(12)				
Residual cash flow	(732.0)	141.4	96.1	96.0	108.7	127.5	150.7	181.2	204.6	230.3	258.6
Payback											
Payback period in years	6.3										
Investment to recover	(732)										
Benefit-cost ratio	217.9							6.36%			
Net present value	172.45										
Depreciation schedule											
Double-declining-balance		120.0	96.0	76.8	61.4	49.2	39.3	31.5	25.2	20.1	16.1
Straight-line depreciation		60.0	53.3	48.0	43.9	41.0	39.3	39.3	39.3	39.3	39.3
Remaining balance		480.0	384.0	307.2	245.8	196.6	157.3	118.0	78.6	39.3	—
Depreciation to be taken		120.0	96.0	76.8	61.4	49.2	39.3	39.3	39.3	39.3	39.3

CHAPTER 5

1. The maximum price that Magnus' management should be willing to pay to acquire Carr is the value of Carr plus the value of the synergies that result from the merger. To determine this total, first determine the value of Magnus, of Carr, and of the combined companies. Because the problem states that there will be no growth, the value of each of the entities can be estimated using the shortcut perpetuity:

$$\text{Value} = \frac{\text{Residual net cash flow}}{(\text{Required return on equity - Growth in residual cash flow})}$$

Step 1. Use the formula above to calculate the value of Magnus, $355,556 [$40,000/(0.1125 - 0.0].

Step 2. The value per share is $7.11, the value of Magnus divided by the number of shares ($355,556/50,000).

Step 3. The value of Carr and the combined companies are calculated in the same way.

Step 4. The value of the synergies is $164,444, the value of the combined companies less the values of Carr and Magnus.

Step 5. The maximum price that Magnus' management should offer for Carr Co. is the value of the synergies, $164,444, plus the value of Carr, $355,556. This is a total of $520,000, or $10.40 per share price.

These values are shown in the following table.

	Magnus Corp.	Carr Co.	Combined Companies
Profit after taxes	$48,000	$30,000	$92,000
Residual net cash flow/year	60,000	40,000	120,000
Required return on equity	12.50%	11.25%	12.00%
Value	$480,000	$355,556	$1,000,000
Number of shares	N.A.	50,000	N.A.
Value per share	N.A.	$7.11	N.A.
Equity book value	N.A.	595,000	N.A.
Book value per share	N.A.	$5.95	N.A.

Step 6. The minimum price that Carr should accept from Magnus' management for the sale of Carr is the value of Carr in the marketplace, i.e., its share price. Carr management should target a price equal to the value of Carr, however, because this value is higher than the current stock price. The current stock market equity value is $300,000 ($6/share with 50,000 shares). The value from the perpetuity shortcut valuation is $355,556, $7.11 per share, or $1.11 per share higher. Book value, often considered the floor value, is lower than the current market valuation and thus should play no role in determining the minimum acceptable price. While the minimum price is the current stock market value, Carr management should price the sale at the value of the company and bargain for Carr's shareholders to gain some of the $164,444 in synergies. Thus, the final price of this acquisition should be above $355,556, and between $7.11 per share and $10.40 per share.

2. To estimate the price Smyth should offer for Robinson Research, the first step is to estimate the value of each of the entities—Smyth, Robinson, and the combined companies. The simple approach is to use the shortcut perpetuity method of valuation, as we did in Study Question 1. The only problem in dealing with this analysis is the net residual cash flow/year for the combined companies. That cash flow is management's estimate of the cash flow that would have been earned had they been merged. Since the estimate is for the prior year, the CD $10.12 is grown at 8 percent, the real rate of growth plus the estimate for inflation. The total residual cash flow is $10.92.

   Using this data, the following table shows the values of each of the three companies.

SMYTH ACQUISITION OF ROBINSON LABS
(in millions of Canadian dollars)

	Smyth Instrument Co.	Robinson Research Lab	Combined Companies
Net residual cash flow/year	CD $6.45	CD $2.20	CD $10.12
Expected real growth in residual cash flow	4.0%	4.0%	4.0%
Expected nominal growth in residual cash flow	8.0%	8.0%	8.0%
Required return on equity (nominal)	16.2%	14.5%	15.5%
Value of company	CD $78.66	CD $33.85	CD $145.73

Once the value of each of the companies has been found, use the following formula to estimate the maximum price that Smyth could pay and still maintain value for its shareholders.

$$\text{Maximum value of merger to Smyth} = \text{Value of combined companies - Value of Smyth}$$

$$= \text{CD \$145.9 - CD \$78.66}$$

$$= \text{CD \$67.24}$$

Robinson Research Lab management should accept a price no lower than its current value of CD $33.85 million. Any price above that will result in value being created for the Robinson shareholders. The difference between the combined values of Smyth and Robinson operating separately of CD $112.51 (CD $78.66 + CD $33.85) and the value of the combined companies of CD $145.6 is CD $33.09. This is the value of the synergies. Smyth management can pay up to the value of Robinson plus the value of the synergies before it risks losing value for its shareholders.

3. To determine the value of Action, and the price for which the company should be sold, first forecast the 1997 residual net cash flow:

   1. Forecast the 1997 sales at a growth of 5 percent from 1996 sales of $250 million. Sales from 1997 to 2003 grow at 5 percent per year, sales after 2003 grow at 3 percent.
   2. Cost of sales and selling, general, and administrative expenses are 75 percent and 10 percent of sales, respectively, and are deducted from sales.
   3. Depreciation of $7 million is deducted from sales.
   4. To calculate the profit before taxes, deduct all expenses except taxes from sales. Taxes are 34 percent of the profit before taxes.
   5. Once net income has been estimated, add back the noncash expense (depreciation) and deduct the $7 million spent on additions to working capital and property, plant, and equipment.
   6. Because the rate of growth slows after 2003, the perpetuity shortcut can be used to estimate the value of Action from then on. Because the cash flows in this level-growth world will be different from those when the company was growing more rapidly, however, first estimate the 2004 residual cash flow (a "steady-state" cash flow) and then estimate the terminal value from then on.
   7. The terminal value is the 2004 cash flow divided by the required return on equity of 11.2 percent, less the permanent growth rate of 3 percent. The resulting terminal value is $381.7 [$31.3/(0.112 - 0.03)].

The forecasted residual cash flows are as follows:

ACTION CORPORATION
RESIDUAL CASH FLOWS 1996-2004
(in millions)

Income Statement Changes	1996	1997	1998	1999	2000	2001	2002	2003	2004
Sales growth	N.A.	5%	5%	5%	5%	5%	5%	5%	3%
Sales	$ 250.0	$ 262.5	$ 275.6	$ 289.4	$ 303.9	$ 319.1	$ 335.1	$ 351.9	$ 362.5
Cost of sales	(187.5)	(196.9)	(206.7)	(217.1)	(227.9)	(239.3)	(251.3)	(263.9)	(271.9)
Gross profit	62.5	65.6	68.9	72.3	76.0	79.8	83.8	88.0	90.6
Selling, general & admin.	(25.0)	(26.3)	(27.6)	(28.9)	(30.4)	(31.9)	(33.5)	(35.2)	(36.3)
Depreciation	(7.0)	(7.0)	(7.0)	(7.0)	(7.0)	(7.0)	(7.0)	(7.0)	(7.0)
Profit before taxes	30.5	32.3	34.3	36.4	38.6	40.9	43.3	45.8	47.3
Taxes	(10.4)	(11.0)	(11.7)	(12.4)	(13.1)	(13.9)	(14.7)	(15.6)	(16.1)
Profit after taxes	$ 20.1	$ 21.3	$ 22.6	$ 24.0	$ 25.5	$ 27.0	$ 28.6	$ 30.2	$ 31.2
Noncash Charges									
Depreciation	7.0	7.0	7.0	7.0	7.0	7.0	7.0	7.0	7.0
Balance Sheet Changes									
PP&E and working capital changes	(7.0)	(7.0)	(7.0)	(7.0)	(7.0)	(7.0)	(7.0)	(7.0)	(7.0)
Annual residual cash flow	20.1	21.3	22.6	24.0	25.5	27.0	28.6	30.2	31.2
Terminal value	0	0	0	0	0	0	0	0	380.5
Net residual cash flow	$ 20.1	$ 21.3	$ 22.6	$ 24.0	$ 25.5	$ 27.0	$ 28.6	$ 30.2	$ 411.7

Present value = $293.03

CHAPTER 6

1. The following data are provided in the case:

• Dividend	$3.00
• Market price	$25.00
• Beta	1.32
• Long-term growth	4.9%
• 7-year Treasury bond yield	8.9%
• 90-day Treasury bill yield	6.5%
• Market risk premium above:	
• Treasury bonds	6.0%
• Treasury bills	8.5%

To determine the cost of equity, two methods can be used.

Method 1. Dividend-Discount Model.

Required return on equity = (Dividend/Market price) + Dividend growth

The dividend yield, the dividend divided by the market price, is 12.0 percent ($3.00/$25.00). To the dividend yield, add management's estimated growth rate of 4.9 percent, for a total required return on equity of 16.9 percent.

Method 2. Capital Asset Pricing Model.

Required return on equity = Risk-free rate + Beta × (Market risk premium)

Using the 7-year Treasury bond rate as the nominal risk-free rate of 8.9 percent and the matching market risk premium of 6.0 percent yields a required return on equity of 16.8 percent [8.9 percent + 1.32 × (6.0 percent)]. This required return on equity is very close to that estimated by the dividend-discount model. Because an equity is a long-term instrument, the short-term Treasury bill rate and its matching premium are not appropriate to use.

2. Using the following data and the pattern used in the answer to Study Question 1, the dividend-discount model required return on equity for Kelly Services is 12.5 percent [($3.00/$36.00) + 4.2 percent].

Growth rate	4.2%
U.S. Treasury bill yield	3.8%
U.S. Treasury bond yield	6.3%
Beta	0.95
Dividend	$3.00
Market price	$36.00

To use the capital asset pricing model, the market expected return first must be estimated. The problem says that the market return is expected to be 8.9 percent above the yield on U.S. Treasury bills. Thus, the market return is estimated at 12.7 percent. Using this, the U.S. Treasury bond return of 6.3 percent as the risk-free rate of return, and a beta of 0.95, the required return on equity is 12.4 percent [6.3 percent + 0.95 × (12.7 percent - 6.3 percent)]. Note, adding the U.S. Treasury bill rate to the premium to create a market estimate does not mean that the Treasury bill rate is being used as the risk-free rate of return.

CHAPTER 7

1. In order to determine the EPS-EBIT break-even table,

Step 1. Calculate the earnings per share at two different levels of earnings before interest and taxes. The most logical choices for the two EBIT levels are Zumar's current revenues and the revenues when the store is expanded, $100 million and $120 million, respectively.

Step 2. Calculate the profit after taxes. To do this, you must account for $2.8 million in interest expense on existing debt ($40 million at 7 percent), and the costs of new financing. The cost of debt financing is 10 percent, and the cost of equity financing is dilution, or the increase in the number of shares from 2.0 million to 2.75 million. The following table provides the EBIT and EPS under the two financing schemes for two levels of revenue.

ZUMAR, INC.
EARNINGS WITH EXISTING AND EXPECTED REVENUES
(in millions, except per share)

	Debt Financing		Equity Financing	
	Old Revenues	*New Revenues*	*Old Revenues*	*New Revenues*
Revenues	$100.0	$120.0	$100.0	$120.0
Earnings before interest and taxes	13.0	15.6	13.0	15.6
Interest:				
Old	(2.8)	(2.8)	(2.8)	(2.8)
New	(1.5)	(1.5)	0.0	0.0
Profit before taxes	8.7	11.3	10.2	12.8
Taxes	(3.0)	(3.8)	(3.5)	(4.4)
Profit after taxes	$ 5.7	$ 7.5	$ 6.7	$ 8.4
Number of shares	2.00	2.00	2.75	2.75
Earnings per share	$2.85	$3.75	$2.44	$3.06

Step 3. To determine the equivalency point, the following data are used:

Debt (millions):	
Old	$40.0
New	$15.0
Interest rate:	
Old	7.0%
New	10.0%
Number of shares (millions):	
Debt financing	2.00
Equity financing	2.75

The formula for the EBIT break-even or equivalency point with no preferred dividends is:

$$\text{EBIT Break-even} = \frac{(2.0 \times \$2.8) - (2.75 \times \$2.8) - (2.75 \times \$1.5)}{2.0 - 2.75} \times \frac{P}{(1 - t)}$$

$$= \$8.3$$

Graphically, the result is shown below. Note, the two lines do not intersect since the crossover point is $8.3 million outside the chart's range.

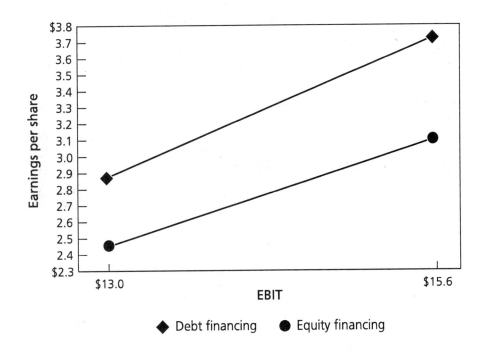

Debt financing   Equity financing

If Zumar expects to earn more than $8.3 million in earnings before interest and taxes, the debt alternative results in a higher EPS for the shareholders.

2. To determine the dividend coverage, the dividends per share to be paid by Zumar are divided into the earnings per share for each alternative method of financing, as follows.

ZUMAR, INC.
DIVIDEND COVERAGE WITH EXISTING AND EXPECTED REVENUES
(in millions)

	Debt Financing		Equity Financing	
	Old Revenues	New Revenues	Old Revenues	New Revenues
Revenues	$100.0	$120.0	$100.0	$120.0
Earnings before interest and taxes	13.0	15.6	13.0	15.6
Interest:				
Old	(2.8)	(2.8)	(2.8)	(2.8)
New	(1.5)	(1.5)	0.0	0.0
Profit before taxes	8.7	11.3	10.2	12.8
Taxes	(3.0)	(3.8)	(3.5)	(4.4)
Profit after taxes	$ 5.7	$ 7.5	$6.7	$ 8.4
Number of shares	2.00	2.00	2.75	2.75
Earnings per share	$2.85	$3.75	$2.44	$3.05
Dividends per share	$0.75	$0.75	$0.75	$0.75
Dividend coverage	380%	500%	325%	407%

Regardless of the financing method used, Zumar has sufficient earnings to cover dividend payments generously.

3. Using the dividend-discount model and this data:

Dividends =	$0.75
Dividend growth =	5.00%
Required return on equity:	
Debt alternative =	15.40%
Equity alternative =	16.90%

the value of the company under the two financing alternatives is:

$$\text{Debt alternative value per share} = \frac{\text{Dividends}}{\text{Required return on equity with debt financing} - \text{Dividend growth}}$$

$$= \frac{\$0.75}{0.154 - 0.05}$$

$$= \$7.21$$

$$\text{Equity alternative value per share} = \frac{\text{Dividends}}{\text{Required return on equity with equity financing} - \text{Dividend growth}}$$

$$= \frac{\$0.75}{0.169 - 0.05}$$

$$= \$6.30$$

The value per share when debt is used to finance the expansion is higher than if equity were used. Thus, Zumar should finance with debt.

APPENDIX 7A

1.

Step 1. This problem is an extension of Study Question 1, Chapter 6. In this problem Bakelite Co. has debt financing the company. Thus, it is the weighted-averaged cost of capital that must be determined. In Chapter 6, you first determined the required return on equity using the following steps. The following data are provided in the problem:

Dividend	$3.00
Market price	$25.00
Beta	1.32
Long-term growth	4.9%
7-year Treasury bond yield	8.9
90-day Treasury bill yield	6.5
Market risk premium above:	
Treasury bonds	6.0
Treasury bills	8.5%

To determine the cost of equity, several methods can be used.

Method 1. Dividend-Discount Model.

$$\begin{aligned}
\text{Required return on equity} &= (\text{Dividend}/\text{Market price}) + \text{Dividend growth} \\
&= (\$3.00/\$25.00) + .049 \\
&= .169 \text{ or } 16.9 \text{ percent}
\end{aligned}$$

Method 2. Capital Asset Pricing Model.

Required return on equity = Risk-free rate + Beta × (Risk premium)

Using the 7-year Treasury bond rate of 8.9 percent as the nominal risk-free rate and the matching market risk premium of 6.0 percent results in a required return on equity of 16.8 percent (8.9% + 1.32 × (6.0%). This is a required return on equity that is very close to that estimated by the dividend-discount model. Since an equity is a long-term instrument, the short-term Treasury bill rate and its matching premium are not appropriate to use.

Step 2. The next step is to determine the cost of debt for Bakelite. The marginal cost of debt is best estimated from the current yield-to-maturity on newly issued B-rated bonds of 14.5 percent. The coupon of 17.3 percent on the company's bonds reflect their cost of borrowing in an economic environment where rates were higher. The cost of this debt to the company is partially offset by the tax deductibility of the interest expense on the debt. With a tax rate of 34 percent the after-tax cost of debt is 9.57 percent [14.5 percent × (1 - 0.34)].

Step 3. Finally, the required return on equity and the company's after-tax cost of debt should be weighted by the proportions in which management expects to raise capital. Since management expects to raise capital in the same proportions as they have in the past, the debt/total capital proportion on the balance sheet must be calculated. The debt/total capital ratio is currently 35 percent:
a. Since debt is $1.3 and equity is $2.4, total capital is

$$
\begin{aligned}
\text{Total capital} \;&=\; \text{Debt + Equity} \\
&=\; \$1.3 + \$2.4 \\
&=\; \$3.7
\end{aligned}
$$

b. As a proportion of the capital structure:

$$
\begin{aligned}
\text{Debt/Total capital} \;&=\; \frac{\$1.3}{\$3.7} \\
&=\; 0.35 \text{ or } 35\% \\[6pt]
\text{Equity/Total capital} \;&=\; \frac{\$2.4}{\$3.7} \\
&=\; 0.65 \text{ or } 65\%
\end{aligned}
$$

Step 4. Weighting the debt cost and required return on equity by their proportions, the weighted-average cost of Bakelite's capital is 14.27 percent.

Source	Cost	Proportion	Weighting
Debt	9.57%	35%	3.35%
Equity	16.80	65	10.92
Weighted average			14.27%

2.

Step 1. The dividend-discount model required return on equity is:

$$
\begin{aligned}
\text{Required return on equity} \ &= \ (\text{Dividend}/\text{Market price}) + \text{Dividend growth} \\
&= \ (\$0.44/\$8.60) + 0.092 \\
&= \ 0.051 + 0.092 \\
&= \ 0.143 \text{ or } 14.3\%
\end{aligned}
$$

Where:

a. the dividend yield (dividend/market price) is 5.1 percent with a market price of $8.60 and a dividend that is 24 percent of earnings per share, or $0.44 ($1.85 × 0.24). Note, the next year's earnings of $1.85 should be used, not the past earnings in calculating the dividend expected.

b. the growth rate is 9.12 percent when calculated using:

$$
\begin{aligned}
\text{Growth rate} \ &= \ (1 - \text{Payout}) \times \text{ROE} \\
&= \ (1 - 0.24) \times 0.12 \\
&= \ 0.0912 \text{ or } 9.12\%
\end{aligned}
$$

Step 2. The capital asset pricing model required return on equity is

$$\text{Required return on equity} \ = \ \text{Risk-free rate} + \text{Beta} \times (\text{Risk premium})$$

Given the data in the problem, the result is

$$
\begin{aligned}
\text{Required return on equity} \ &= \ 10.1\% + 0.98 \times (16.0\% - 10.1\%) \\
&= \ 10.1\% + 5.78\% \\
&= \ 15.9\%
\end{aligned}
$$

Step 3. For the weights in 1996, debt is $2.26 million, equity is $4.2 million, and total capital is $6.46 million. Thus, debt is 35 percent of total capital, and equity is 65 percent. In 1997 the weights are the same.

Step 4. Using the same process as in Study Question 1, the weighted-average cost of capital using the dividend-discount model is 12.9 percent [(35% × 10.4%) + (65% × 14.3%)]; using the capital asset pricing model it is 13.98 percent [(35% × 10.4%) + (65% × 15.9%)]. While the outcomes using both models are not too different, the analyst should reexamine the assumptions that underlie both models and attempt to reconcile them.

This section shows examples of solutions to chapter study questions using Excel© and is provided to allow the user of this financial planning tool to practice. Please note that these are examples, and your solution may be entered into different cells, rows, or include other titles. The solutions portrayed in this appendix vary to demonstrate the possible styles that you may use. In general, titles were not modeled, so that the model would begin in cell A1.

For each of the models, the entries for the rows and columns are stated.[1] The solutions are preceded by a title that is not a part of the model. This is merely to serve as a guide to the study question.

CHAPTER 1

1a.

EASY CHAIR CO.
FINANCIAL RATIOS

	1992	1993	1994	1995	1996	Rows
	1992	1993	1994	1995	1996	1
Sales	341.7	420.0	486.8	553.2	592.3	2
Net income	23	24.7	26.5	27.5	28.3	3
Dividends per share	0.4	0.4	0.4	0.5	0.5	4
Number of shares						5
(in thousands)	18.3	18.4	18.3	17.9	17.9	6
Total assets	233	269.9	336.6	349	361.9	7
Total equity	147.0	165.3	178.8	194.3	214.6	8
Ratios	1992	=+B9+1	=+C9+1	=+D9+1	=+E9+1	9
Return on sales	=+B3/B2	=+C3/C2	=+D3/D2	=+E3/E2	=+F3/F2	10
Sales/assets	=+B2/B7	=+C2/C7	=+D2/D7	=+E2/E7	=+F2/F7	11
Return on assets	=+B11*B10	=+C11*C10	=+D11*D10	=+E11*E10	=+F11*F10	12
Assets/equity	=+B7/B8	=+C7/C8	=+D7/D8	=+E7/E8	=+F7/F8	13
Return on equity	=+B12*B13	=+C12*C13	=+D12*D13	=+E12*E13	=+F12*F13	14
Earnings/share	=+B3/B6	=+C3/C6	=+D3/D6	=+E3/E6	=+F3/F6	15
Dividend payout ratio	=+B4/B15	=+C4/C15	=+D4/D15	=+E4/E15	=+F4/F15	16
Retention rate	=1-B16	=1-C16	=1-D16	=1-E16	=1-F16	17
Sustainable growth rate	=+B14*B17	=+C14*C17	=+D14*D17	=+E14*E17	=+F14*F17	18
Net income growth	NAp.	=(C2-B2)/B2	=(D2-C2)/C2	=(E2-D2)/D2	=(F2-E2)/E2	19
A	B	C	D	E	F	

Columns

---

[1]   The results of these models may differ slightly from the manual solutions to the study questions because of differences in rounding.

1b.

Note, this solution follows the solution for Question 1a on the spreadsheet.

***EASY* CHAIR CO.**
DIFFERENCE BETWEEN HOME FURNISHINGS INDUSTRY AND *EASY*

					Rows
Industry	=+C1	=+D1	=+E1	=+F1	20
Return on equity	0.1574	0.1531	0.1554	0.1512	21
Retention rate	=72/100	=71/100	=71/100	=71/100	22
Sustainable growth rate	=11.33/100	=10.87/100	=11.03/100	=10.73/100	23
Differences	1993	1994	1995	1996	24
Return on equity	=+C14-C21	=+D14-D21	=+E14-E21	=+F14-F21	25
Retention rate	=+C17-C22	=+D17-D22	=+E17-E22	=+F17-F22	26
Sustainable growth rate	=+C18-C23	=+D18-D23	=+E18-E23	=+F18-F23	27
A B		C	D	E	F

Columns

2. Note, this solution follows the solution for Question 1b on the spreadsheet.

EASY CHAIR COMPANY
PERCENTAGE OF SALES—INCOME STATEMENTS

A	B	C	D	E	F	Rows
Income Statement		=+C1	=+D1	=+E1	=+F1	28
Net sales		420	486.8	553.2	592.3	29
Cost of sales		-289.8	-352.1	-397.8	-430.4	30
Gross profit		130.2	134.7	155.4	161.9	31
Selling, general, and						32
administrative expense		-85.5	-91.4	-106.9	-111.6	33
Income from operations		44.7	43.3	48.5	50.3	34
Interest expense		-1.9	-4.0	-7.6	-7.2	35
Other income		2.1	2.7	3.1	2.5	36
Income before taxes		44.9	42.0	44.0	45.6	37
Taxes		-20.3	-15.5	-16.5	-17.3	38
Net income		24.6	26.5	27.5	28.3	39
Component Percent		=+C1	=+D1	=+E1	=+F1	40
Net sales		=+C29/$C$29	=+D29/$D$29	=+E29/$E$29	=+F29/$F$29	41
Cost of sales		=+C30/$C$29	=+D30/$D$29	=+E30/$E$29	=+F30/$F$29	42
Gross profit		=+C31/$C$29	=+D31/$D$29	=+E31/$E$29	=+F31/$F$29	43
Selling, general, and		=+C32/$C$29	=+D32/$D$29	=+E32/$E$29	=+F32/$F$29	44
administrative expense		=+C33/$C$29	=+D33/$D$29	=+E33/$E$29	=+F33/$F$29	45
Income from operations		=+C34/$C$29	=+D34/$D$29	=+E34/$E$29	=+F34/$F$29	46
Interest expense		=+C35/$C$29	=+D35/$D$29	=+E35/$E$29	=+F35/$F$29	47
Other income		=+C36/$C$29	=+D36/$D$29	=+E36/$E$29	=+F36/$F$29	48
Income before taxes		=+C37/$C$29	=+D37/$D$29	=+E37/$E$29	=+F37/$F$29	49
A	B	C	D	E	F	

Columns

EASY CHAIR COMPANY (cont.)

A	B	C	D	E	F	Rows
Taxes		=+C38/$C$29	=+D38/$D$29	=+E38/$E$29	=+F38/$F$29	50
Net income		=+C39/$C$29	=+D39/$D$29	=+E39/$E$29	=+F39/$F$29	51
Percentage						52
Changes			=+D1	=+E1	=+F1	53
Net sales			=+(D29-C29)/C29	=+(E29-D29)/D29	=+(F29-E29)/E29	54
Cost of sales			=+(D30-C30)/C30	=+(E30-D30)/D30	=+(F30-E30)/E30	55
Gross profit			=+(D31-C31)/C31	=+(E31-D31)/D31	=+(F31-E31)/E31	56
Selling, general, and administrative expense						57
Income from operations			=+(D33-C33)/C33	=+(E33-D33)/D33	=+(F33-E33)/E33	58
Interest expense			=+(D34-C34)/C34	=+(E34-D34)/D34	=+(F34-E34)/E34	59
Other income			=+(D35-C35)/C35	=+(E35-D35)/D35	=+(F35-E35)/E35	60
Income before taxes			=+(D36-C36)/C36	=+(E36-D36)/D36	=+(F36-E36)/E36	61
Taxes			=+(D37-C37)/C37	=+(E37-D37)/D37	=+(F37-E37)/E37	62
Net income			=+(D38-C38)/C38	=+(E38-D38)/D38	=+(F38-E38)/E38	63
A	B	C	D	E	F	

Columns

3. Note, this solution follows the solution for Study Question 2 on the spreadsheet.

EASY CHAIR COMPANY
FINANCIAL STATEMENTS

A	B	C	Rows
Income Statement		Revised	64
Sales		=+C74/0.051	65
Cost of sales		=+C67-C65	66
Gross profit		=+C65*0.276	67
Selling, general,			68
and administrative expense		=-C67+C70	69
Operating profit		=+C65*0.087	70
Interest		=+C72-C70	71
Earnings before taxes		=+C74/0.66	72
Taxes		=-C72*0.34	73
Net income		=+(C89/0.45)*18000	74
Balance Sheet			75
Cash		=+C79-C77-C78	76
Accounts receivable		=+(C65/365)*92.5	77
Inventory		=-C66/7.33	78
Total current assets		=+C84*5.51	79
Net property, plant, and equipment		=+C81-C79	80
Total assets		=+C74/0.094	81
Accounts payable		=-(C66/365)*20.8	82
Other current liabilities		=+C84-C82	83
Total current liabilities		=+C81-C85-C87	84
Long-term debt		=+C87*0.273	85
Total liabilities		=SUM(C84:C85)	86
Owners' equity		=+C74/0.137	87
Total liabilities and owners' equity		=+C81	88
Dividends		=15*0.052	89

Columns

4.

PETERSON'S CHEMICALS
FINANCIAL RATIOS RELATIVE TO INDUSTRY

Industry Average columns (E, F) headed 1995 / 1996. Peterson's columns (B, C). RATIOS section: Peterson's spans columns C (1995) and D (1996).

A	B	C	D	E	F	Rows
Income Statement	1995	1996		1995	1996	1
						2
Sales	1435	1478		1	1	3
Cost of goods sold	-1076	-1182		-.67	-.68	4
Gross profit	359	296		.33	.32	5
Selling and admin. expenses	-445	-443		-.27	-.26	6
Operating profit	-86	-147		.06	.06	7
Interest expense	-29	-27		-.01	-.02	8
Net income	-115	-174		.05	.04	9
Balance Sheet	1994	1995		1994	1995	10
Cash and equiv.	76	120	Accounts payable	412	500	11
Accounts receivable, net	437	432	Other current	98	309	12
Inventory	284	324	Total current	510	=SUM(F11:F12)	13
Other current assets	38	37	Long-term debt	300	178	14
Total current assets	835	913	Total liabilities	810	=SUM(F13:F14)	15
Plant, property, and equipment	375	300	Owners' equity	400	226	16
Total assets	1210	1213	Total liabilities and owners' equity	1210	=SUM(F15:F16)	17
						18
RATIOS	Industry	Peterson's 1995	1996			19
Current ratio	1.5	=+B15/E13	=+C15/F13			20
Acid-test ratio	0.9	=+(B15-B13)/E13	=+(C15-C13)/F13			21
Receivables collection period	65 days	=+B12/(C3/365)	=+C12/(D3/365)			22
Payables payment period	60 days	=+E11/(-C4/365)	=+F11/(-D4/365)			23
Debt/equity	1.1	=+E14/E16	=+F14/F16			24
Return on assets	0.07	=+C9/B17	=+D9/C17			25
Return on equity	0.19	=+C9/E16	=+D9/F16			26
A	B	C	D	E	F	

Columns

5a. This solution follows Question 4 on the spreadsheet.

PETERSON'S CHEMICALS
REVISED FINANCIAL STATEMENTS AND FINANCIAL RATIOS

Rows	A	B	C	D	E	F
	Income Statement	Original	Revised			
28	Sales	1478	=+B28*0.97			
29	Cost of goods sold	-1182	=+B29*0.91			
30	Gross profit	296	=SUM(C28:C29)			
31						
32	Selling and admin. expenses	-443	=+B32			
33	Operating profit	-147	=SUM(C30:C32)			
34	Interest expense	-27	=+B34			
35	Net income	-174	=SUM(C33:C34)			
36	**Balance Sheet**	Original	Revised		Original	Revised
37	Cash and equiv.	120	=+B37	Accounts payable	500	=+(-B29/365)*62
38	Accounts receivable, net	432	=+(C28/365)*78	Other current	309	=+E38
39	Inventory	324	=+B39	Total current	=SUM(E37:E38)	=SUM(F37:F38)
40	Other current assets	37	=+B40	Long-term debt	178	=+F42
41	Total current assets	913	=SUM(C37:C40)	Total liabilities	=SUM(E39:E40)	=SUM(F39:F40)
42	Plant, property, and equipment	300	=+B42	Owners' equity	226	=+(E42-B35)+C35
43	Total assets	1213	=SUM(C41:C42)	Total liabilities and owners' equity	=SUM(E41:E42)	=SUM(F41:F42)

Columns

PETERSON'S CHEMICALS (cont.)

A	B	C	D	E	Rows
RATIOS	Peterson's Industry	1995	1996	Revised	44
Current ratio	1.5	1.63725490196078	1.12855377008653	=+C41/F39	45
Acid-test ratio	0.9	1.08039215686275	0.728059332509271	=(C41-C39)/F39	46
Receivables collection period	65 days	111.15331010453	106.684709066306	=+C38/((C28/365)	47
					48
Payables payment period	60 days	139.758364312268	154.399323181049	=+F37/(-C29/365)	49
Debt/equity	1.1	0.75	0.787610619469027	=+F40/F42	50
Return on assets	0.07	-0.0950413223140496	-0.143446001648805	=+C35/C43	51
Return on equity	0.19	-0.2875	-0.769911504424779	=+C35/F42	52
A	B	C	D	E	

Columns

CHAPTER 2

1.

HONDA MOTOR COMPANY
FINANCIAL STATEMENTS AND RATIOS

	1990	1991	Rows
	1990	1991	1
Net sales			2
Japan	1300	=+B3*1.05	3
United States	2200	=+(B4/154)*(1.25*140)	4
Total sales	=SUM(B3:B4)	=SUM(C3:C4)	5
Cost of goods sold	-2625	=+C5*-0.75	6
Research and development	-200	=+B7	7
Gross profit	=SUM(B5:B7)	=SUM(C5:C7)	8
Operating expenses	-500	=+B9*1.1	9
Operating profit	=SUM(B8:B9)	=SUM(C8:C9)	10
Taxes	-70	=+C10*-0.4	11
Net profit	=SUM(B10:B11)	=SUM(C10:C11)	12
	=+B1	=+C1	13
Cash	250	=+C5*0.1	14
Accounts receivable	400	=+(C5/365)*45	15
Inventory	475	=+C6/-6	16
Total current assets	=SUM(B14:B16)	=SUM(C14:C16)	17
Net property, plant, and equipment	1500	1500	18
Total assets	=SUM(B17:B18)	=SUM(C17:C18)	19
Accounts payable	400	=+(-C6/365)*60	20
Other short-term debt	350	350	21
Total current liabilities	=SUM(B20:B21)	=SUM(C20:C21)	22
Long-term debt	1050	1050	23
Common stock	75	75	24
Retained earnings	750	=+B25+C12	25
Total equity	=SUM(B24:B25)	=SUM(C24:C25)	26
Subtotal	=+B26+B23+B22	=+C26+C23+C22	27
New short-term financing	=+B19-B27	=+C19-C27	28
Total liabilities and equity	=+B27+B28	=+C27+C28	29
Net working capital	=+B17-B22	=+C17-C22	30
Change in net working capital	N.Ap.	=+(C30-B30)/B30	31
Current ratio	=+B17/B22	=+C17/C22	32
A	**B**	**C**	

Columns

2.

HONDA MOTOR COMPANY
REVISED FINANCIAL STATEMENTS

			Rows
	1990	1991 - Revised	1
Net sales			2
Japan	1300	=+B3*1.05	3
United States	2200	=+(B4/154)*(1.25*140)	4
Total sales	=SUM(B3:B4)	=SUM(C3:C4)	5
Cost of goods sold	-2625	=+C5*-0.75	6
Research and development	-200	=+B7	7
Gross profit	=SUM(B5:B7)	=SUM(C5:C7)	8
Operating expenses	-500	=+B9*1.1	9
Operating profit	=SUM(B8:B9)	=SUM(C8:C9)	10
Taxes	-70	=+C10*-0.4	11
Net profit	=SUM(B10:B11)	=SUM(C10:C11)	12
Assets	=+B1	=+C1	13
Cash	250	=+C5*0.07	14
Accounts receivable	400	=+(C5/365)*60	15
Inventory	475	=+C6/-6	16
Total current assets	=SUM(B14:B16)	=SUM(C14:C16)	17
Net property, plant, and equipment	1500	1500	18
Total assets	=SUM(B17:B18)	=SUM(C17:C18)	19
Liabilities and Equity			20
Accounts payable	400	=+(-C6/365)*45	21
Other short-term debt	350	350	22
Total current liabilities	=SUM(B20:B21)	=SUM(C20:C21)	23
Long-term debt	1050	1050	24
Common stock	75	75	25
Retained earnings	750	=+B25+C12	26
Total equity	=SUM(B24:B25)	=SUM(C24:C25)	27
Subtotal	=+B26+B23+B22	=+C26+C23+C22	28
New short-term financing	=+B19-B27	=+C19-C27	29
Total liabilities and equity	=+B27+B28	=+C27+C28	30
Net working capital	=+B17-B22	=+C17-C22	31
Change in net working capital	N.Ap.	=+(C30-B30)/B30	32
Current ratio	=+B17/B22	=+C17/C22	33
A	B	C	
	Columns		

3.

HONDA MOTOR COMPANY
REVISED FINANCIAL STATEMENTS - ¥85:$1.00

	1990	1991	Rows
			1
Net sales			2
Japan	1300	=+B3*1.05	3
United States	2200	=+(B4/154)*(1.25*85)	4
Total sales	=SUM(B3:B4)	=SUM(C3:C4)	5
Cost of goods sold	-2625	=+C5*-0.75	6
Research and development	-200	=+B7	7
Gross profit	=SUM(B5:B7)	=SUM(C5:C7)	8
Operating expenses	-500	=+B9*1.1	9
Operating profit	=SUM(B8:B9)	=SUM(C8:C9)	10
Taxes	-70	=+C10*-0.4	11
Net profit	=SUM(B10:B11)	=SUM(C10:C11)	12
Assets	=+B1	=+C1	13
Cash	250	=+C5*0.07	14
Accounts receivable	400	=+(C5/365)*45	15
Inventory	475	=+C6/-6	16
Total current assets	=SUM(B14:B16)	=SUM(C14:C16)	17
Net property, plant, and equipment	1500	1500	18
Total assets	=SUM(B17:B18)	=SUM(C17:C18)	19
Liabilities and Equity			20
Accounts payable	400	=+(-C6/365)*45	21
Other short-term debt	350	350	22
Total current liabilities	=SUM(B20:B21)	=SUM(C20:C21)	23
Long-term debt	1050	1050	24
Common stock	75	75	25
Retained earnings	750	=+B25+C12	26
Total equity	=SUM(B24:B25)	=SUM(C24:C25)	27
Subtotal	=+B26+B23+B22	=+C26+C23+C22	28
New short-term financing	=+B19-B27	=+C19-C27	29
Total liabilities and equity	=+B27+B28	=+C27+C28	30
Net working capital	=+B17-B22	=+C17-C22	31
Change in net working capital	N.Ap.	=+(C30-B30)/B30	32
Current ratio	=+B17/B22	=+C17/C22	33
A	**B**	**C**	

Columns

4.

TOP C. COMPANY
CURRENT AND REVISED FINANCIAL STATEMENTS AND RATIOS

	B	C	D	Rows
Income Statements	Historic	Duncan	Fisher	1
Sales	8600	=+B2*1.2	=+B2*1.1	2
Bad debt	-430	=+C2*-0.02	=+D2*-0.05	3
Net sales	=SUM(B2:B3)	=SUM(C2:C3)	=SUM(D2:D3)	4
Cost of goods sold	-3500	=+C2*-0.4	=+D2*-0.4	5
Gross profit	=SUM(B4:B5)	=SUM(C4:C5)	=SUM(D4:D5)	6
Operating expense	-3000	=+B7*1.2	=+B7	7
Operating income	=SUM(B6:B7)	=SUM(C6:C7)	=SUM(D6:D7)	8
Taxes	-668	=+C8*-0.4	=+D8*-0.4	9
Net profit	=SUM(B8:B9)	=SUM(C8:C9)	=SUM(D8:D9)	10
Balance Sheets	Historic	Duncan	Fisher	11
Cash	1200	=+C2*0.2	=+D2*0.15	12
Accounts receivable	850	=+(C2/365)*45	=+(D2/365)*30	13
Inventory	800	=+C5/-6	=+D5/-3	14
Total current assets	=SUM(B12:B14)	=SUM(C12:C14)	=SUM(D12:D14)	15
Net property, plant, and equipment	4000	4000	4000	16
Total assets	=SUM(B15:B16)	=SUM(C15:C16)	=SUM(D15:D16)	17
Accounts payable	1400	=+(C5/365)*114	=+(-D5/365)*114	18
Other short-term debt	1500	1500	1500	19
Total current liabilities	=SUM(B18:B19)	=SUM(C18:C19)	=SUM(D18:D19)	20
Long-term debt	550	550	550	21
Common stock	420	420	420	22
Retained earnings	2980	=+B23+C10	=+B23+D10	23
Total equity	=+B23+B22	=+C23+C22	=+D23+D22	24
Subtotal	=+B24+B21+B20	=+C24+C21+C20	=+D24+D21+D20	25
New financing needed	=+B17-B25	=+C17-C25	=+D17-D25	26
Total liabilities and equity	=+B25+B26	=+C25+C26	=+D25+D26	27
Net short-term debt	=+B19+B26	=+C19+C26	=+D19+D26	28
Net working capital	=+B15-B20-B26	=+C15-C20-C26	=+D15-D20-D26	29
Current ratio	=+B15/(B20+B26)	=+C15/(C20+C26)	=+D15/((D20+D26)	30
A	**B**	**C**	**D**	

Columns

5.

MARY'S SKI CHALET
CASH RECEIPTS AND ACCOUNTS RECEIVABLE ACCOUNT
(in thousands)

Rows	A	B	C	D	E	F	G
1		JAN.	FEB.	MARCH	APRIL	MAY	JUNE
2	Sales	210	175	160	140	50	30
3	Cost of goods sold	=+B2*0.75	=+C2*0.75	=+D2*0.75	=+E2*0.75	=+F2*0.75	=+G2*0.75
4	*Accounts Receivable Schedule*						
5	Beginning accounts receivable	184	=+B8	=+C8	=+D8	=+E8	=+F8
6	Credit sales	=0.75*B2	=0.75*C2	=0.75*D2	=0.75*E2	=0.75*F2	=0.75*G2
7	Collections on accounts receivable	=+B5	=+C5	=+D5	=+E5	=+F5	=+G5
8	Ending accounts receivable	=+B5+B6-B7	=+C5+C6-C7	=+D5+D6-D7	=+E5+E6-E7	=+F5+F6-F7	=+G5+G6-G7
9	*Receipts*						
10	Cash sales	=+B2*0.25	=+C2*0.25	=+D2*0.25	=+E2*0.25	=+F2*0.25	=+G2*0.25
11	Collections on accounts receivable	=+B7	=+C7	=+D7	=+E7	=+F7	=+G7
12	Total receipts	=SUM(B10:B11)	=SUM(C10:C11)	=SUM(D10:D11)	=SUM(E10:E11)	=SUM(F10:F11)	=SUM(G10:G11)
13	*Accounts Payable Schedule*						
14	Beginning accounts payable	173	=+B17	=+C17	=+D17	=+E17	=+F17
15	Purchases	=+B3+(B2*0.06)	=+C3+(C2*0.06)	=+D3+(D2*0.06)	=+E3+(E2*0.06)	=+F3+(F2*0.06)	=+G3+(G2*0.06)
16	Payments on accounts payable	=+B14	=+C14	=+D14	=+E14	=+F14	=+G14
17	Ending accounts payable	=+B14+B15-B16	=+C14+C15-C16	=+D14+D15-D16	=+E14+E15-E16	=+F14+F15-F16	=+G14+G15-G16
18	*Disbursements*						
19	Payments on accounts payable	=+B16	=+C16	=+D16	=+E16	=+F16	=+G16
20	Selling, general, and administrative expense	=+B2*0.19	=+C2*0.19	=+D2*0.19	=+E2*0.19	=+F2*0.19	=+G2*0.19
21	Lease and interest expenses	=24/12	=24/12	=24/12	=24/12	=24/12	=24/12
22	Total disbursements	=SUM(B19:B21)	=SUM(C19:C21)	=SUM(D19:D21)	=SUM(E19:E21)	=SUM(F19:F21)	=SUM(G19:G21)
23	*Cash Account*						
24	Beginning cash	65	=+B26	=+C26	=+D26	=+E26	=+F26
25	Receipts less disbursements	=+B12-B22	=+C12-C22	=+D12-D22	=+E12-E22	=+F12-F22	=+G12-G22
26	Ending cash	=B24+B25	=C24+C25	=D24+D25	=E24+E25	=F24+F25	=G24+G25

Columns

MARY'S SKI CHALET (cont.)

Rows	H (JULY)	I (AUG.)	J (SEPT.)	K (OCT.)	L (NOV.)	M (DEC.)	N (TOTAL)
1	JULY	AUG.	SEPT.	OCT.	NOV.	DEC.	TOTAL
2	30	75	90	125	165	230	=SUM(B2:M2)
3	=+H2*0.75	=+I2*0.75	=+J2*0.75	=+K2*0.75	=+L2*0.75	=+M2*0.75	=SUM(B3:M3)
4							
5	=+G8	=+H8	=+I8	=+J8	=+K8	=+L8	
6	=0.75*H2	=0.75*I2	=0.75*J2	=0.75*K2	=0.75*L2	=0.75*M2	
7	=+H5	=+I5	=+J5	=+K5	=+L5	=+M5	
8	=+H5+H6-H7	=+I5+I6-I7	=+J5+J6-J7	=+K5+K6-K7	=+L5+L6-L7	=+M5+M6-M7	
9							
10	=+H2*0.25	=+I2*0.25	=+J2*0.25	=+K2*0.25	=+L2*0.25	=+M2*0.25	
11	=+H7	=+I7	=+J7	=+K7	=+L7	=+M7	
12	=SUM(H10:H11)	=SUM(I10:I11)	=SUM(J10:J11)	=SUM(K10:K11)	=SUM(L10:L11)	=SUM(M10:M11)	
13							
14	=+G17	=+H17	=+I17	=+J17	=+K17	=+L17	
15	=+H3+(H2*0.06)	=+I3+(I2*0.06)	=+J3+(J2*0.06)	=+K3+(K2*0.06)	=+L3+(L2*0.06)	=+M3+(M2*0.06)	
16	=+H14	=+I14	=+J14	=+K14	=+L14	=+M14	
17	=+H14+H15-H16	=+I14+I15-I16	=+J14+J15-J16	=+K14+K15-K16	=+L14+L15-L16	=+M14+M15-M16	
18							
19	=+H16	=+I16	=+J16	=+K16	=+L16	=+M16	
20	=+H2*0.19	=+I2*0.19	=+J2*0.19	=+K2*0.19	=+L2*0.19	=+M2*0.19	
21							
22	=24/12	=24/12	=24/12	=24/12	=24/12	=24/12	
23	=SUM(H19:H21)	=SUM(I19:I21)	=SUM(J19:J21)	=SUM(K19:K21)	=SUM(L19:L21)	=SUM(M19:M21)	
24	=+G26	=+H26	=+I26	=+J26	=+K26	=+L26	
25	=+H12-H22	=+I12-I22	=+J12-J22	=+K12-K22	=+L12-L22	=+M12-M22	
26	=H24+H25	=I24+I25	=J24+J25	=K24+K25	=L24+L25	=M24+M25	

Columns: H   I   J   K   L   M   N

6. Note, this spreadsheet follows that for Study Question 5.

MARY'S SKI CHALET
1997 INCOME STATEMENT AND BALANCE SHEETS
(in thousands)

A	B	C	Rows
Sales	=+N2		27
Cost of goods sold	=-N3		28
Gross income	=B27+B28		29
Selling and general expenses	=-0.19*B27		30
Depreciation	-12		31
Lease and interest expenses	-24		32
Net income	=SUM(B29:B32)		33
Assets	1996	1997	34
Cash	=B24	=M26	35
Accounts receivable	184	=+M8	36
Inventory	50	=+B37+N3-N3+(0.06*N2)	37
Current assets	=SUM(B35:B37)	=SUM(C35:C37)	38
Net property, plant, and equipment	345	=B39+B31	39
Total assets	=B39+B38	=C39+C38	40
Liabilities and Equity			41
Accounts payable	173	=+M17	42
Current liabilities	=B41	=C41	43
Equity	471	=B43+B33	44
Total liabilities and equity	=B43+B42	=C43+C42	45

Columns

7.

ARIES CORPORATION
PROJECTED FINANCIAL STATEMENTS

	A	B	C	D	E	Rows
		1995	Percentage	=+B1+1	Percentage	1
Income Statements						
Sales		221	=+B2/$B$2	266	=+D2/$D$2	2
Cost of goods sold		-145	=+B3/$B$2	-166	=+D3/$D$2	3
Gross profit		=SUM(B2:B3)	=+B4/$B$2	=SUM(D2:D3)	=+D4/$D$2	4
Operating expenses		-38	=+B5/$B$2	-35	=+D5/$D$2	5
Operating profit		=SUM(B4:B5)	=+B6/$B$2	=SUM(D4:D5)	=+D6/$D$2	6
Taxes		-19	=+B7/B6	-33	=+D7/D6	7
Net profit		=SUM(B6:B7)	=+B8/$B$2	=SUM(D6:D7)	=+D8/$D$2	8
Sales growth				=(D2-B2)/B2		9
Balance Sheets						10
Assets						11
Cash		22		37		12
Accounts receivable		49		31		13
Inventory		47		45		14
Total current assets		=SUM(B12:B14)		=SUM(D12:D14)		15
Fixed assets		70		122		16
Total assets		=SUM(B15:B16)		=SUM(D15:D16)		17
Liabilities and Equity						18
Accounts payable		19		34		19
Total current liabilities		=SUM(B19:B19)		=SUM(D19:D19)		20
Equity		169		201		21
Subtotal		=SUM(B20:B21)		=SUM(D20:D21)		22
New notes payable		=+B17-B22		=+D17-D22		23
Total liabilities and equity		=+B22+B23		=+D22+D23		24
	A	B	C	D	E	25
			Columns			

ARIES CORPORATION (cont.)

Rows	F	G	H	I	J
1	=+D1+1	=+F1+1	=+G1+1	=+H1+1	=+I1+1
2					
3	=+D2*(1+D9)	=+F2*(1.1)	=+G2*(1.11)	=+H2*(1.12)	=+I2*(1.13)
4	=+F4-F2	=+G4-G2	=+H4-H2	=+I4-I2	=+J4-J2
5	=(E4+0.1)*F2	=+($E$4+0.12)*G2	=+($E$4+0.12)*H2	=+($E$4+0.12)*I2	=+($E$4+0.12)*J2
6	=+F2*$E$5	=+G2*$E$5	=+H2*$E$5	=+I2*$E$5	=+J2*$E$5
7	=SUM(F4:F5)	=SUM(G4:G5)	=SUM(H4:H5)	=SUM(I4:I5)	=SUM(J4:J5)
8	=+E7*F6	=+G6*E7	=+H6*-0.38	=+I6*-0.38	=+J6*-0.38
9	=SUM(F6:F7)	=SUM(G6:G7)	=SUM(H6:H7)	=SUM(I6:I7)	=SUM(J6:J7)
10	=+(F2-D2)/D2	=+(G2-F2)/F2	=+(H2-G2)/G2	=+(I2-H2)/H2	=+(J2-I2)/I2
11					
12					
13	=+F2*$E$26	=+G2*$E$26	=+H2*$E$26	=+I2*$E$26	=+J2*$E$26
14	=(F2/365)*$E$27	=(G2/365)*$E$27	=(H2/365)*$E$27	=(I2/365)*$E$27	=(J2/365)*$E$27
15	=-F3/8	=-G3/7	=-H3/6	=-I3/6	=-J3/6
16	=SUM(F12:F14)	=SUM(G12:G14)	=SUM(H12:H14)	=SUM(I12:I14)	=SUM(J12:J14)
17	265	291	323	403	513
18	=SUM(F15:F16)	=SUM(G15:G16)	=SUM(H15:H16)	=SUM(I15:I16)	=SUM(J15:J16)
19					
20	=-(F3/365)*60	=-(G3/365)*60	=-(H3/365)*60	=-(I3/365)*60	=-(J3/365)*60
21	=SUM(F19:F19)	=SUM(G19:G19)	=SUM(H19:H19)	=SUM(I19:I19)	=SUM(J19:J19)
22	=+D21+F8	=+F21+G8	=+G21+H8	=+H21+I8	=+I21+J8
23	=SUM(F20:F21)	=SUM(G20:G21)	=SUM(H20:H21)	=SUM(I20:I21)	=SUM(J20:J21)
24	=+F17-F22	=+G17-G22	=+H17-H22	=+I17-I22	=+J17-J22
25	=+F22+F23	=+G22+G23	=+H22+H23	=+I22+I23	=+J22+J23

Columns

CHAPTER 3

1.

CHATEAU ROYALE INTERNATIONAL
1996-97 FINANCIAL STATEMENTS AND RATIOS

A	B	C	Rows
Sales	375000	=+B1*1.6	1
Cost of goods sold	-276150	=+C1*-0.75	2
Gross profit	=SUM(B1:B2)	=SUM(C1:C2)	3
Operating expenses	-75000	=+B4*1.1	4
Depreciation	-5100	-8000	5
Operating profit	=SUM(B3:B5)	=SUM(C3:C5)	6
Taxes	-7500	=-0.34*C6	7
Net profit	=SUM(B6:B7)	=SUM(C6:C7)	8
Cash	75000	=0.2*C1	9
Accounts receivable	46233	=+(C1/365)*45	10
Inventory	93750	=+C2/-3	11
Current assets	=SUM(B9:B11)	=SUM(C9:C11)	12
Net property, plant, and equipment	115000	=+B13-8000	13
Total assets	=SUM(B12:B13)	=SUM(C12:C13)	14
Accounts payable	23116	=-(C2/365)*30	15
Short-term debt	51867	0	16
Current liabilities	=SUM(B15:B16)	=SUM(C15:C16)	17
Long-term debt	125000	=+B18	18
Common stock	100000	=+B19	19
Retained earnings	30000	=+B20+C8	20
Subtotal	=SUM(B17:B20)	=SUM(C17:C20)	21
New financing needed (excess cash)	=+B14-B21	=+C14-C21	22
Total liabilities and owners' equity	=SUM(B21:B22)	=SUM(C21:C22)	23
Current ratio	=+B12/B17	=+C12/C17	24
Net working capital change		=+(C12-C17)-(B12-B17)	25

Columns

2.

CHATEAU ROYALE INTERNATIONAL
1996-97 REVISED FINANCIAL STATEMENTS

A	B	C	Rows
Sales	375000	=+B1*1.6	1
Cost of goods sold	-276150	=+C1*-0.75	2
Gross profit	=SUM(B1:B2)	=SUM(C1:C2)	3
Operating expenses	-75000	=+B4*1.1	4
Depreciation	-5100	-8000	5
Operating profit	=SUM(B3:B5)	=SUM(C3:C5)	6
Taxes	-7500	=-0.34*C6	7
Net profit	=SUM(B6:B7)	=SUM(C6:C7)	8
Cash	75000	=0.15*C1	9
Accounts receivable	46233	=+(C1/365)*45	10
Inventory	93750	=+C2/-4	11
Current assets	=SUM(B9:B11)	=SUM(C9:C11)	12
Net property, plant, and equipment	115000	=+B13-8000	13
Total assets	=SUM(B12:B13)	=SUM(C12:C13)	14
Accounts payable	23116	=-(C2/365)*45	15
Short-term debt	51867	0	16
Current liabilities	=SUM(B15:B16)	=SUM(C15:C16)	17
Long-term debt	125000	=+B18	18
Common stock	100000	=+B19	19
Retained earnings	30000	=+B20+C8	20
Subtotal	=SUM(B17:B20)	=SUM(C17:C20)	21
New financing needed (excess cash)	=+B14-B21	33724	22
Total liabilities and owners' equity	=SUM(B21:B22)	=SUM(C21:C22)	23
Current ratio	=+B12/B17	=+C12/C17	24
Net working capital change	N.Ap.	=+(C12-C17)-(B12-B17)	25

Columns

3.

KURZ CORP.
FINANCIAL STATEMENTS

A	B	C	D	Rows
Sales	505000	=+B1*1.5	B1	1
Bad debt	-5000	=+C1*-0.02	0	2
Net sales	=SUM(B1:B2)	=SUM(C1:C2)	=SUM(D1:D2)	3
Cost of goods sold	-375000	=+C1*-0.75	=+D1*-0.75	4
Gross profit	=SUM(B3:B4)	=SUM(C3:C4)	=SUM(D3:D4)	5
Operating expenses	-90900	+B6	+B6	6
Operating profit	=SUM(B5:B6)	=SUM(C5:C6)	=SUM(D5:D6)	7
Taxes	=+B7*-0.35	=+C7*-0.35	=+D7*-0.35	8
Net profit	=SUM(B7:B8)	=SUM(C7:C8)	=SUM(D7:D8)	9
Cash	90000	=+C3*0.2	=+D3*0.15	10
Accounts receivable	61644	=+(C1/365)*60	=+(D1/365)*30	11
Inventory	62500	=+C17	=+D1/5	12
Current assets	=SUM(B10:B12)	=SUM(C10:C12)	=SUM(D10:D12)	13
Net property, plant, and equipment	130000	=B14	=+C14	14
Total assets	=SUM(B13:B14)	=SUM(C13:C14)	=SUM(D13:D14)	15
Accounts payable	30822	=+(C1/365)*22.3	=+(D1/365)*22.3	16
Short-term debt	86322	0	0	17
Current liabilities	=SUM(B16:B17)	=SUM(C16:C17)	=SUM(D16:D17)	18
Long-term debt	110000	=+B19	=+C19	19
Common stock	75000	=+B20	=+C20	20
Retained earnings	42000	=+B21+C9	=+B21+D9	21
Subtotal	=SUM(B18:B21)	=SUM(C18:C21)	=SUM(D18:D21)	22
New financing needed (excess cash)	=+B15-B22	=+C15-C22	=+D15-D22	23
Total liabilities and owners' equity	=SUM(B22:B23)	=SUM(C22:C23)	=SUM(D22:D23)	24
Current assets	=+B13	=+C13	=+D13	25
Current liabilities	=+B18	=+C18	=+D18	26
Net working capital	=+B25-B26	=+C25-C26	=+D25-D26	27
Current ratio	=+B25/B26	=+C25/C26	=+D25/D26	28

Columns

4.

THE CRESCENT
CASH FLOWS
(currency in millions of Philippine pesos)

A	B	C	D	E	Rows
	January	February	March	April	1
Cash receipts	4500				2
Cash Disbursements					3
Cement	=33750*0.0036*28		=33750*0.0036*30		4
Granite tiles					5
Window frames		=10*2*30	=40*0.1*30	=40*0.1*30	6
Elevators					7
Generator					8
Bathroom fixtures					9
Salaries and benefits	=200*1.875	=200*1.875	=200*1.875	=200*1.875	10
Overhead	10	10	10	10	11
Total disbursements	=SUM(B4:B11)	=SUM(C4:C11)	=SUM(D4:D11)	=SUM(E4:E11)	12
Cash Balance					13
Beginning cash	1000	=B16	=C16	=D16	14
Net cash flow	=B2-B12	=C2-C12	=D2-D12	=E2-E12	15
Cumulative net cash flow	=B14+B15	=C14+C15	=D14+D15	=E14+E15	16
A	B	C	D	E	

Columns

THE CRESCENT (cont.)

Rows	May	June	July	August	September	October
1	9000			9000		9000
2						
3	=33750*0.0036*30		=33750*0.0036*30			
4	5000					
5	=40*0.1*30	=40*0.1*30	=40*0.1*30	=40*0.1*30	=40*0.1*30	=40*0.1*30
6						
7	2000					
8				=130*30*0.15		
9	=200*1.875	=200*1.875	=200*1.875	=200*1.875	=200*1.875	=200*1.875
10	10	10	10	10	10	10
11	=SUM(F4:F11)	=SUM(G4:G11)	=SUM(H4:H11)	=SUM(I4:I11)	=SUM(J4:J11)	=SUM(K4:K11)
12						
13	=E16	=F16	=G16	=H16	=I16	=J16
14	=F2-F12	=G2-G12	=H2-H12	=I2-I12	=J2-J12	=K2-K12
15	=F14+F15	=G14+G15	=H14+H15	=I14+I15	=J14+J15	=K14+K15
16						
Columns	F	G	H	I	J	K

THE CRESCENT (cont.)

Rows	November	December	January	February	March
1		9000			4500
2					
3					
4	=40*0.1*30	=40*0.1*30			
5					
6					
7					
8					
9	=200*1.875	=200*1.875			
10	10	10			
11	=SUM(L4:L11)	=SUM(M4:M11)			
12					
13					
14	=K16	=L16	=M16	=N16	=O16
15	=L2-L12	=M2-M12	=N2-N12	=O2-O12	=P2-P12
16	=L14+L15	=M14+M15	=N14+N15	=O14+O15	=P14+P15
	L	M	N	O	P

Columns

CHAPTER 4

1.

METALWERKS
ANALYSIS OF NEW ASSEMBLY LINE—RESIDUAL CASH FLOWS

Rows	A	B	C	D	E
1		0	=+B1+1	=+C1+1	=+D1+1
2	**Income Statement Changes**				
3	Sales		1625	1625	1625
4	Cost of goods sold		=-0.37*C3	=-0.37*D3	=-0.37*E3
5	Gross profit		=SUM(C3:C4)	=SUM(D3:D4)	=SUM(E3:E4)
6	Repairs and utilities		=-260/20	=-260/20	=-260/20
7	Salaries and benefits		-480	-480	-480
8	Depreciation		=-C28	=-D28	=-E28
9	Profit before taxes		=SUM(C5:C8)	=SUM(D5:D8)	=SUM(E5:E8)
10	Taxes		=-0.34*C9	=-0.34*D9	=-0.34*E9
11	Net profit		=SUM(C9:C10)	=SUM(D9:D10)	=SUM(E9:E10)
12	**Noncash Charges**				
13	Depreciation		=-C8	=-D8	=-E8
14	**Balance Sheet Changes**				
15	New equipment	-1400			
16	Residual net cash flow	=+B11+B13+B15	=+C11+C13+C15	=+D11+D13+D15	=+E11+E13+E15
17	**Payback**				
18	Unrecovered investment value	=-B16	=+B18-C16	=+C18-D16	=+D18-E16
19	Partial year calculation			=+D18/E16	
20	Payback (years)	=1+D19			
21	**Benefit/cost ratio**				
22	Benefit/cost ratio	=SUM(C16:W16)/-B16			
23					
24	**Depreciation Schedule**		0	=+C24+1	=+D24+1
25	Value yet undepreciated		1400	=+C25-C29	=+D25-D29
26	Straight-line rate		=1/20		
27	Depreciation		=+C25*($C$26*2)	=+D25*($C$26*2)	=+E25*($C$26*2)
28	Straight-line for remaining life		=+C25/(20)	=+D25/(20-D24)	=+E25/(20-E24)
29	Depreciation		=IF(C28>C27,C28,C27)	=IF(D28>D27,D28,D27)	=IF(E28>E27,E28,E27)

Columns

METALWERKS (cont.)

Rows	F	G	H	I	J
1	=+E1+1	=+F1+1	=+G1+1	=+H1+1	=+I1+1
2					
3	1625	1625	1625	1625	1625
4	=-0.37*F3	=-0.37*G3	=-0.37*H3	=-0.37*I3	=-0.37*J3
5	=SUM(F3:F4)	=SUM(G3:G4)	=SUM(H3:H4)	=SUM(I3:I4)	=SUM(J3:J4)
6	=-260/20	=-260/20	=-260/20	=-260/20	=-260/20
7	-480	-480	-480	-480	-480
8	=-F27	=-G27	=-H27	=-I27	=-J27
9	=SUM(F5:F8)	=SUM(G5:G8)	=SUM(H5:H8)	=SUM(I5:I8)	=SUM(J5:J8)
10	=-0.34*F9	=-0.34*G9	=-0.34*H9	=-0.34*I9	=-0.34*J9
11	=SUM(F9)	=SUM(G9)	=SUM(H9)	=SUM(I9)	=SUM(J9)
12					
13	=-F8	=-G8	=-H8	=-I8	=-J8
14					
15					
16	=+F11+F13+F15	=+G11+G13+G15	=+H11+H13+H15	=+I11+I13+I15	=+J11+J13+J15
17					
18	=+E18-F16	=+F18-G16	=+G18-H16	=+H18-I16	=+I18-J16
19					
20					
21					
22					
23					
24	=+E24+1	=+F24+1	=+G24+1	=+H24+1	=+I24+1
25	=+E25-E29	=+F25-F29	=+G25-G29	=+H25-H29	=+I25-I29
26					
27	=+F25*($C$26*2)	=+G25*($C$26*2)	=+H25*($C$26*2)	=+I25*($C$26*2)	=+J25*($C$26*2)
28	=+F25/(20-F24)	=+G25/(20-F24)	=+H25/(20-G24)	=+I25/(20-H24)	=+J25/(20-I24)
29	=IF(F28>F27,F28,F27)	=IF(G28>G27,G28,G27)	=IF(H28>H27,H28,H27)	=IF(I28>I27,I28,I27)	=IF(J28>J27,J28,J27)

Columns

METALWERKS (cont.)

Rows	K	L	M	N	O	P
1	=+J1+1	=+K1+1	=+L1+1	=+M1+1	=+N1+1	=+O1+1
2	1625	1625	1625	1625	1625	1625
3	=-0.37*K3	=-0.37*L3	=-0.37*M3	=-0.37*N3	=-0.37*O3	=-0.37*P3
4	=SUM(K3:K4)	=SUM(L3:L4)	=SUM(M3:M4)	=SUM(N3:N4)	=SUM(O3:O4)	=SUM(P3:P4)
5	-260/20	-260/20	-260/20	-260/20	-260/20	-260/20
6	-480	-480	-480	-480	-480	-480
7	=-K27	=-L27	=-M27	=-N27	=-O27	=-P27
8	=SUM(K5:K8)	=SUM(L5:L8)	=SUM(M5:M8)	=SUM(N5:N8)	=SUM(O5:O8)	=SUM(P5:P8)
9	=-0.34*K9	=-0.34*L9	=-0.34*M9	=-0.34*N9	=-0.34*O9	=-0.34*P9
10	=SUM(K9)	=SUM(L9)	=SUM(M9)	=SUM(N9)	=SUM(O9)	=SUM(P9)
11						
12						
13	=-K8	=-L8	=-M8	=-N8	=-O8	=-P8
14						
15						
16	=+K11+K13+K15	=+L11+L13+L15	=+M11+M13+M15	=+N11+N13+N15	=+O11+O13+O15	=+P11+P13+P15
17						
18						
19						
20						
21						
22						
23						
24	=+J24+1	=+K24+1	=+L24+1	=+M24+1	=+N24+1	=+O24+1
25	=+J25-J29	=+K25-K29	=+L25-L29	=+M25-M29	=+N25-N29	=+O25-O29
26						
27	=+K25*($C$26*2)	=+L25*($C$26*2)	=+M25*($C$26*2)	=+N25*($C$26*2)	=+O25*($C$26*2)	=+P25*($C$26*2)
28	=+K25/(20-K24)	=+L25/(20-L24)	=+M25/(20-M24)	=+N25/(20-N24)	=+O25/(20-O24)	=+P25/(20-P24)
29	=IF(K28>K27,K28,K27)	=IF(L28>L27,L28,L27)	=IF(M28>M27,M28,M27)	=+M29	=+M29	=+M29

Columns

METALWERKS (cont.)

Rows	Q	R	S	T	U	V
1	=+P1+1	=+Q1+1	=+R1+1	=+S1+1	=+T1+1	=+U1+1
2	1625	1625	1625	1625	1625	1625
3	=-0.37*Q3	=-0.37*R3	=-0.37*S3	=-0.37*T3	=-0.37*U3	=-0.37*V3
4	=SUM(Q3:Q4)	=SUM(R3:R4)	=SUM(S3:S4)	=SUM(T3:T4)	=SUM(U3:U4)	=SUM(V3:V4)
5	=-260/20	=-260/20	=-260/20	=-260/20	=-260/20	=-260/20
6	-480	-480	-480	-480	-480	-480
7	=-Q27	=-R27	=-S27	=-T27	=-U27	=-V27
8	=SUM(Q5:Q8)	=SUM(R5:R8)	=SUM(S5:S8)	=SUM(T5:T8)	=SUM(U5:U8)	=SUM(V5:V8)
9	=-0.34*Q9	=-0.34*R9	=-0.34*S9	=-0.34*T9	=-0.34*U9	=-0.34*V9
10	=SUM(Q9)	=SUM(R9)	=SUM(S9)	=SUM(T9)	=SUM(U9)	=SUM(V9)
11						
12						
13	=-Q8	=-R8	=-S8	=-T8	=-U8	=-V8
14						
15	=+Q11+Q13	=+R11+R13	=+S11+S13	=+T11+T13	=+U11+U13	=+V11+V13
16						
17						
18						
19						
20						
21						
22						
23						
24	=+P24+1	=+Q24+1	=+R24+1	=+S24+1	=+T24+1	=+U24+1
25	=+Q25-Q29	=+R25-R29	=+S25-S29	=+T25-T29	=+U25-U29	=+U25-U29
26						
27	=+Q25*($C$26*2)	=+R25*($C$26*2)	=+S25*($C$26*2)	=+T25*($C$26*2)	=+U25*($C$26*2)	=+V25*($C$26*2)
28	=+Q25/(20-Q24)	=+R25/(20-R24)	=+S25/(20-S24)	=+T25/(20-T24)	=+U25/(20-U24)	=+V25/(20-V24)
29	=+M29	=+M29	=+M29	=+M29	=+M29	=+V25
Columns	Q	R	S	T	U	V

2.

SUN COMPANY
RESIDUAL CASH FLOW ANALYSIS
(in thousands of lira)

		PERIOD	
		0	=+B2+1
Income Statement Changes			
Sales			120
Operating expenses			=-0.39*C4
Depreciation—initial investment			=+$B$14*0.15
Depreciation—additional investment			0
Profit before taxes			=SUM(C4:C7)
Taxes (@ 34%)			=-0.34*C8
Net profit			=SUM(C8:C9)
Noncash Charges			
Depreciation			=-C6-C7
Capital Investments			
Property, plant, and equipment		-200	
Residual net cash flow		=SUM(B10:B14)	=SUM(C10:C14)
Net present value (at 10%) =		=NPV(0.1,C15:G15)+B15	
	A	B	C

Columns

SUN COMPANY (cont.)

				Rows
				1
=+C2+1	=+D2+1	=+E2+1	=+F2+1	2
				3
=+C4*1.15	=+D4*1.15	=+E4*1.15	=+F4*1.15	4
				5
=+$B$14*0.21	+$B$14*0.21	=+$B$14*0.21	=+$B$14*0.21	6
0	=+$D$14*0.26	=+$D$14*0.32	=+$D$14*0.32	7
=SUM(D4:D7)	=SUM(E4:E7)	=SUM(F4:F7)	=SUM(G4:G7)	8
=-0.34*D8	=-0.34*E8	=-0.34*F8	=-0.34*G8	9
=SUM(D8:D9)	=SUM(E8:E9)	=SUM(F8:F9)	=SUM(G8:G9)	10
				11
=-D6-D7	=-E6-E7	=-F6-F7	=-G6-G7	12
				13
-60				14
=SUM(D10:D14)	=SUM(E10:E14)	=SUM(F10:F14)	=SUM(G10:G14)	15
				16
D	E	F	G	

Columns

3.

CLOUD FRAME COMPANY
ANALYSIS OF TWO PROJECTS
(libras in thousands)

Rows	A	B	C	D	E
1	Project 1				
2	Income Statement Changes	0	=+B2+1	=+C2+1	=+D2+1
3	Sales		500	500	500
4	Cost of goods sold		=-0.49*C3	=-0.49*D3	=-0.49*E3
5	Gross income		=SUM(C3:C4)	=SUM(D3:D4)	=SUM(E3:E4)
6	Advertising		-50	-50	-50
7	Depreciation		=-C26	=-D26	=-E26
8	Income before taxes		=SUM(C5:C7)	=SUM(D5:D7)	=SUM(E5:E7)
9	Taxes		=-0.34*C8	=-0.34*D8	=-0.34*E8
10	Net income		=SUM(C8:C9)	=SUM(D8:D9)	=SUM(E8:E9)
11	Noncash Charges				
12	Depreciation		=-C7	=-D7	=-E7
13	Balance Sheet Changes				
14	New equipment	-800			
15	Residual net cash flow	=SUM(B10:B14)	=SUM(C10:C14)	=SUM(D10:D14)	=SUM(E10:E14)
16	Payback				
17	Unrecovered investment value		=-B15-C15	=+C17-D15	=+D17-E15
18	Partial year calculation		=4+G18		
19	Payback (years)		=SUM(C15:L15)/-B15		
20	Benefit/cost ratio				
21	Benefit/cost ratio				
22	Depreciation Schedule		1	=+C22+1	=+D22+1
23	Value yet undepreciated		800	=+C23-C26	=+D23-D26
24	Double-declining-balance		=DDB(800,0,10,C2)	=DDB(800,0,10,D2)	=DDB(800,0,10,E2)
25	Straight-line for remaining life		=+C23/(10)	=+D23/(10-C22)	=+E23/(10-D22)
26	Depreciation to be taken		=IF(C25>C24,C25,C24)	=IF(D25>D24,D25,D24)	=IF(E25>E24,E25,E24)
	A	B	C	D	E

Columns

CLOUD FRAME COMPANY (cont.)

Rows	F	G	H	I
1	=+E2+1	=+F2+1	=+G2+1	=+H2+1
2	500	500	500	500
3	=-0.49*F3	=-0.49*G3	=-0.49*H3	=-0.49*I3
4	=SUM(F3:F4)	=SUM(G3:G4)	=SUM(H3:H4)	=SUM(I3:I4)
5	-50	-50	-50	-50
6	=-F26	=-G26	=-H26	=-I26
7	=SUM(F5:F7)	=SUM(G5:G7)	=SUM(H5:H7)	=SUM(I5:I7)
8	=-0.34*F8	=-0.34*G8	=-0.34*H8	=-0.34*I8
9	=SUM(F8:F9)	=SUM(G8:G9)	=SUM(H8:H9)	=SUM(I8:I9)
10				
11	=-F7	=-G7	=-H7	=-I7
12				
13				
14	=SUM(F10:F14)	=SUM(G10:G14)	=SUM(H10:H14)	=SUM(I10:I14)
15				
16				
17	=+E17-F15	=+F17-G15		
18		=-G17/G15		
19				
20				
21				
22	=+E22+1	=+F22+1	=+G22+1	=+H22+1
23	=+E23-E26	=+F23-F26	=+G23-G26	=H23-H26
24	=DDB(800,0,10,F2)	=DDB(800,0,10,G2)	=DDB(800,0,10,H2)	=DDB(800,0,10,I2)
25	=+F23/(10-E22)	=+G23/(10-F22)	=+H23/(10-G22)	=I23/(10-H22)
26	=IF(F25>F24,F25,F24)	=IF(G25>G24,G25,G24)	=IF(H25>H24,H25,H24)	=IF(I25>I24,I25,I24)

Columns

CLOUD FRAME COMPANY (cont.)

Rows	J	K	L
1	=+I2+1	=+J2+1	=+K2+1
2	500	500	500
3	=-0.49*J3	=-0.49*K3	=-0.49*L3
4	=SUM(J3:J4)	=SUM(K3:K4)	=SUM(L3:L4)
5	-50	-50	-50
6	=-J26	=-K26	=-L26
7	=SUM(J5:J7)	=SUM(K5:K7)	=SUM(L5:L7)
8	=-0.34*J8	=-0.34*K8	=-0.34*L8
9	=SUM(J8:J9)	=SUM(K8:K9)	=SUM(L8:L9)
10			
11	=-J7	=-K7	=-L7
12			
13			
14	=SUM(J10:J14)	=SUM(K10:K14)	=SUM(L10:L14)
15			
16			
17			
18			
19			
20			
21	=+I22+1	=+J22+1	=+K22+1
22	=+I23-I26	=+J23-J26	=+K23-K26
23	=DDB(800,0,10,J2)	=DDB(800,0,10,K2)	=DDB(800,0,10,L2)
24	=+J23/(10-J22)	=+K23/(10-K22)	=+L23/(10-L22)
25	=IF(J25>J24,J25,J24)	=IF(K25>K24,K25,K24)	=IF(L25>L24,L25,L24)
26			

Columns

CLOUD FRAME COMPANY (cont.)

Rows	A	B	C	D	E	F
28	**Project 2**					
29	**Income Statement Changes**	0	=+B29+1	=+C29+1	=+D29+1	=+E29+1
30	Sales		350	=+C30*1.1	=+D30*1.1	=+E30*1.1
31	Cost of goods sold		=+C30*-0.5	=+D30*-0.5	=+E30*-0.5	=+F30*-0.5
32	Gross income		=SUM(C29:C31)	=SUM(D29:D31)	=SUM(E29:E31)	=SUM(F29:F31)
33	Advertising		=+C30*-0.25	=+D30*-0.25	=+E30*-0.25	=+F30*-0.25
34	Production training	-200				
35	Depreciation		=+$B$42*0.2	=+$B$42*0.32	=+$B$42*0.1921	=+$B$42*0.1152
36	Income before taxes	=SUM(B32:B35)	=SUM(C32:C35)	=SUM(D32:D35)	=SUM(E32:E35)	=SUM(F32:F35)
37	Taxes	=+B36*-0.34	=+C36*-0.34	=+D36*-0.34	=+E36*-0.34	=+F36*-0.34
38	Net income	=SUM(B36:B37)	=SUM(C36:C37)	=SUM(D36:D37)	=SUM(E36:E37)	=SUM(F36:F37)
39	**Noncash Charges**					
40	Depreciation		=-C35	=-D35	=-E35	=-F35
41	**Balance Sheet Changes**					
42	New equipment	-600				
43	Residual net cash flow	=SUM(B38:B42)	=SUM(C38:C42)	=SUM(D38:D42)	=SUM(E38:E42)	=SUM(F38:F42)
44	**Payback**					
45	Unrecovered investment value		=-B42-C43	=+C45-D43	=+D45-E43	=+E45-F43
46	Partial year calculation					
47	Payback (years)	=5+H46				
48	**Benefit/cost ratio**					
49	Benefit/cost ratio	=SUM(C43:L43)/-B42				

Columns

CLOUD FRAME COMPANY (cont.)

Rows	G	H	I	J	K	L
28						
29	=+F29+1	=+G29+1	=+H29+1	=+I29+1	=+J29+1	=+K29+1
30	=+F30*1.15	=+G30*1.15	=+H30*1.15	=+I30*1.1	=+J30*1.1	=+K30*1.1
31	=+G30*-0.5	=+H30*-0.5	=+I30*-0.5	=+J30*-0.5	=+K30*-0.5	=+L30*-0.5
32	=SUM(G29:G31)	=SUM(H29:H31)	=SUM(I29:I31)	=SUM(J29:J31)	=SUM(K29:K31)	=SUM(L29:L31)
33	=+G30*-0.25	=+H30*-0.25	=+I30*-0.25	=+J30*-0.25	=+K30*-0.25	=+L30*-0.25
34						
35	=+$B$42*0.1152	=+$B$42*0.0576	0	0	0	0
36	=SUM(G32:G35)	=SUM(H32:H35)	=SUM(I32:I35)	=SUM(J32:J35)	=SUM(K32:K35)	=SUM(L32:L35)
37	=+G36*-0.34	=+H36*-0.34	=+I36*-0.34	=+J36*-0.34	=+K36*-0.34	=+L36*-0.34
38	=SUM(G36:G37)	=SUM(H36:H37)	=SUM(I36:I37)	=SUM(J36:J37)	=SUM(K36:K37)	=SUM(L36:L37)
39						
40	=-G35	=-H35	=-I35	=-J35	=-K35	=-L35
41						
42						
43	=SUM(G38:G42)	=SUM(H38:H42)	=SUM(I38:I42)	=SUM(J38:J42)	=SUM(K38:K42)	=SUM(L38:L42)
44						
45	=+F45-G43	=+G45-H43				
46		=+G45/H43				
47						
48						
49						

Columns

CHAPTER 5

1.

VALUE OF MAGNUS, CARR, AND COMBINED COMPANIES

	Magnus Corp.	Carr Co.	Combined Companies	Rows
				1
Profit after taxes	48000	30000	92000	2
Residual net cash flow/year	60000	40000	120000	3
Required return on equity	0.125	0.1125	0.12	4
Value	=+B3/B4	=+C3/C4	=+D3/D4	5
Number of shares	N.Ap.	50000	N.Ap.	6
Value per share	N.Ap.	=+C5/C6	N.Ap.	7
Equity book value	N.Ap.	595000	N.Ap.	8
Book value per share	N.Ap.	=+C8/C6	N.Ap.	9
A	B	C	D	

Columns

2.

VALUE OF SMYTH, ROBINSON, AND COMBINED COMPANIES

	Smyth Instrument Co.	Robinson Research Lab	Combined Companies	Rows
				1
Net residual cash flow/year	6.45	2.2	=10.12*1.08	2
Expected real growth in residual cash flow	0.04	0.04	0.04	3
Expected nominal growth in residual cash flow	=+B3+0.04	=+C3+0.04	=+D3+0.04	4
Required return on equity (nominal)	0.162	0.145	0.155	5
Value of company	=+B2/(B5-B4)	=+C2/(C5-C4)	=+D2/(D5-D4)	6
A	B	C	D	

Columns

3.

ACTION CORPORATION
RESIDUAL CASH FLOWS 1996-2004

	A	B	C	D	E	Rows
		1996	=+B1+1	=+C1+1	=+D1+1	1
Sales growth		N.Ap.	0.05	0.05	0.05	2
Sales		250	=+B3*(1+C2)	=+C3*(1+D2)	=+D3*(1+E2)	3
Cost of sales		=-0.75*B3	=-0.75*C3	=-0.75*D3	=-0.75*E3	4
Gross profit		=SUM(B3:B4)	=SUM(C3:C4)	=SUM(D3:D4)	=SUM(E3:E4)	5
S,G&A		=-0.1*B3	=-0.1*C3	=-0.1*D3	=-0.1*E3	6
Depreciation		-7	-7	-7	-7	7
Profit before taxes		=SUM(B5:B7)	=SUM(C5:C7)	=SUM(D5:D7)	=SUM(E5:E7)	8
Taxes		=-0.34*B8	=-0.34*C8	=-0.34*D8	=-0.34*E8	9
Profit after taxes		=SUM(B8:B9)	=SUM(C8:C9)	=SUM(D8:D9)	=SUM(E8:E9)	10
Depreciation		=-B7	=-C7	=-D7	=-E7	11
Changes in debt principal		0	0	0	0	12
PP&E and						13
working capital changes		-7	-7	-7	-7	14
Annual residual cash flow		=SUM(B10:B14)	=SUM(C10:C14)	=SUM(D10:D14)	=SUM(E10:E14)	15
Terminal value		0	0	0	0	16
Net residual cash flow		=SUM(B15:B16)	=SUM(C15:C16)	=SUM(D15:D16)	=SUM(E15:E16)	17
Present value =		=NPV(0.112,C17:J17)				18
						19
	A	B	C	D	E	

Columns

ACTION CORP. *(cont.)*

Rows	F	G	H	I	J
1	=+E1+1	=+F1+1	=+G1+1	=+H1+1	=+I1+1
2	0.05	0.05	0.05	0.05	0.03
3	=+E3*(1+F2)	=+F3*(1+G2)	=+G3*(1+H2)	=+H3*(1+I2)	=+I3*(1+J2)
4	=-0.75*F3	=-0.75*G3	=-0.75*H3	=-0.75*I3	=-0.75*J3
5	=SUM(F3:F4)	=SUM(G3:G4)	=SUM(H3:H4)	=SUM(I3:I4)	=SUM(J3:J4)
6	=-0.1*F3	=-0.1*G3	=-0.1*H3	=-0.1*I3	=-0.1*J3
7	-7	-7	-7	-7	-7
8	=SUM(F5:F7)	=SUM(G5:G7)	=SUM(H5:H7)	=SUM(I5:I7)	=SUM(J5:J7)
9	=-0.34*F8	=-0.34*G8	=-0.34*H8	=-0.34*I8	=-0.34*J8
10	=SUM(F8:F9)	=SUM(G8:G9)	=SUM(H8:H9)	=SUM(I8:I9)	=SUM(J8:J9)
11	=-F7	=-G7	=-H7	=-I7	=-J7
12	0	0	0	0	0
13					
14	-7	-7	-7	-7	-7
15	=SUM(F10:F14)	=SUM(G10:G14)	=SUM(H10:H14)	=SUM(I10:I14)	=SUM(J10:J14)
16	0	0	0	0	=+J15/(0.112-J2)
17	=SUM(F15:F16)	=SUM(G15:G16)	=SUM(H15:H16)	=SUM(I15:I16)	=SUM(J15:J16)
18					
19					

Columns

CHAPTER 6

Not appropriate for Excel© modeling.

CHAPTER 7

1.

ZUMAR, INC.
EARNINGS WITH EXISTING AND EXPECTED REVENUES

	A	B	C	D	E	Rows
		Debt Financing	New	Equity Financing	New	1
		Old Revenues	Revenues	Old Revenues	Revenues	2
						3
Revenues		100	120	100	120	4
Earnings before interest and taxes		=0.13*B4	=0.13*C4	=0.13*D4	=0.13*E4	5
Interest:						6
Old		-2.8	-2.8	-2.8	-2.8	7
New		=-0.1*15	=-0.1*15	0	0	8
Profit before taxes		=B5+B7+B8	=C5+C7+C8	=D5+D7+D8	=E5+E7+E8	9
Taxes		=-0.34*B9	=-0.34*C9	=-0.34*D9	=-0.34*E9	10
Profit after taxes		=B9+B10	=C9+C10	=D9+D10	=E9+E10	11
Number of shares		2	2	2.75	2.75	12
Earnings per share		=B11/B12	=C11/C12	=D11/D12	=E11/E12	13
	A	B	C	D	E	

Columns

2.

ZUMAR, INC.
DIVIDEND COVERAGE WITH EXISTING AND EXPECTED REVENUES

	A	B	C	D	E	Rows
						1
		Debt Financing	New	Equity Financing	New	2
		Old Revenues	Revenues	Old Revenues	Revenues	3
Revenues		100	120	100	120	4
Earnings before interest and taxes		=0.13*B4	=0.13*C4	=0.13*D4	=0.13*E4	5
Old		-2.8	-2.8	-2.8	-2.8	6
New		=-0.1*15	=-0.1*15	0	0	7
Profit before taxes		=B5+B6+B7	=C5+C6+C7	=D5+D6+D7	=E5+E6+E7	8
Taxes		=-0.34*B8	=-0.34*C8	=-0.34*D8	=-0.34*E8	9
Profit after taxes		=B8+B9	=C8+C9	=D8+D9	=E8+E9	10
Number of shares		2	2	2.75	2.75	11
Earnings per share		=B10/B11	=C10/C11	=D10/D11	=E10/E11	12
Dividends per share		0.75	0.75	0.75	0.75	13
Dividend coverage		=B12/B13	=C12/C13	=D12/D13	=E12/E13	14

Columns

3. Not suitable for modeling.

Chapter 7—Appendix A

Study questions are not suitable for modeling.

I N D E X